The Development of the Social Self

The Development of the Social Self

Edited by
Mark Bennett and Fabio Sani

Psychology Press
Taylor & Francis Group
HOVE AND NEW YORK

First published 2004
by Psychology Press

27 Church Road, Hove, East Sussex BN3 2FA

Simultaneously published in the USA and Canada
by Psychology Press
29 West 35th Street, New York, NY 10001

Psychology Press is a member of the Taylor & Francis Group

Copyright © 2004 Psychology Press

Typeset in Times by
RefineCatch Limited, Bungay, Suffolk
Printed and bound in Great Britain by
Biddles Ltd, King's Lynn

British Library Cataloguing in Publication Data
A catalogue record for this book is available
from the British Library

Library of Congress Cataloging-in-Publication Data

ISBN 1-841-69294-8

TO OUR BELOVED SONS,
NICHOLAS AND LEONARDO

Contents

List of tables   xi
List of figures   xii
List of contributors   xiii

1 **Introduction: Children and social identity**   1
   MARK BENNETT AND FABIO SANI

   Social and developmental perspectives on the self-concept 2
   On the benefits of a closer association between social and
     developmental psychology 4
   The social identity approach 6
   Organisation of the book 17
   References 22

PART I
Basic issues

2 **The development of a sense of "we": The emergence and**
   implications of children's collective identity   29
   DIANE N. RUBLE, JEANNETTE ALVAREZ, MEREDITH BACHMAN,
   JESSICA CAMERON, ANDREW FULIGNI, CYNTHIA GARCIA COLL,
   AND EUN RHEE

   The nature of social identity 30
   When and how do children understand and identify with social
     categories? 33
   Developmental changes in the significance of collective
     identity 42
   Consequences of developmental changes in collective
     identity 51
   Summary and conclusions 63
   References 64

3 **Developmental aspects of social identity**   77
  FABIO SANI AND MARK BENNETT

  Children's conception of social identities 78
  The flexibility of children's understanding of in-group
      identity 85
  The emergence of social identity 91
  General summary and conclusions 95
  References 97

PART II
Identities

4 **Gender as a social category: Intergroup processes and**
  gender-role development   103
  KIMBERLY K. POWLISHTA

  Intergroup processes 104
  The development of gender categories 107
  Exaggeration of between-sex differences and within-sex
      similarities 108
  Own-sex favouritism 112
  The impact of social context on the salience of gender 113
  Individual and group differences in gender-based intergroup
      processes 115
  How is gender different from other social categories? 122
  Conclusions and implications for improving cross-sex
      relations 125
  References 126

5 **The gender wars: A self-categorisation theory perspective on**
  the development of gender identity   135
  BARBARA DAVID, DIANE GRACE, AND MICHELLE K. RYAN

  The developmental sequence 136
  Theories of gender development 139
  Matching the theories and the evidence 140
  The self as a process 141
  Self-categorisation, the dominant theories, and gender
      development 145
  Summary and suggestions 150
  References 152

6   **The development of national identity and social identity processes: Do social identity theory and self-categorisation theory provide useful heuristic frameworks for developmental research?**   159

MARTYN BARRETT, EVANTHIA LYONS, AND ARANTZA DEL VALLE

The principal phenomena that characterise the development of national identity 160
The relevance of SIT and SCT to the study of national identity development 161
The application of SIT and SCT to the development of national identity 164
Evaluation of the predictions 165
So do SIT and SCT provide useful heuristic frameworks for developmental research? 182
References 185

7   **Ethnic identity and social context**   189

MAYKEL VERKUYTEN

From social cognition to situation 190
Intergroup theories 192
Perceived discrimination 195
Cultural orientations 199
Ethnic self-esteem and context 201
Ethnic self-categorisation 202
Ethnic self-categorisation and behaviour 203
Conclusion 207
References 210

PART III
Applications

8   **Social identity processes and children's ethnic prejudice**   219

DREW NESDALE

Explanations of children's prejudice 220
Social identity theory and ethnic prejudice 225
Social identity development theory of children's ethnic prejudice 226
Conclusions 238
References 240

9   **The development and self-regulation of intergroup attitudes
     in children**   247

ADAM RUTLAND

*Children's intergroup attitudes and cognitive-developmental
     theory 247*
*Recent research on children's national intergroup
     attitudes 249*
Social identity theory 251
Self-regulation and children's intergroup attitudes 252
Implicit measures of children's intergroup attitudes 254
Dissociation between implicit and explicit measures 255
The Implicit Association Test 257
*Public self-focus and children's ethnic intergroup
     attitudes 258*
Conclusion 260
References 261

10   **Reducing stepfamily conflict: The importance of inclusive
      social identity**   267

BRENDA S. BANKER, SAMUEL L. GAERTNER, JOHN F. DOVIDIO,
MISSY HOULETTE, KELLY M. JOHNSON, AND BLAKE M. RIEK

*The role of social categorisation and intergroup
     relations 269*
Reducing intergroup bias and conflict 271
Stepfamily marriages 276
Conclusions 283
References 285

**PART IV
Epilogue**

11   **The development of social identity: What develops?**   291

DOMINIC ABRAMS

The chapters 291
Conclusions 305
References 307

12   Towards a developmental social psychology of the social self   313
KEVIN DURKIN

The family as the first group 314
Developmental changes and continuities 315
Competition between developmental and social processes 317
Language 319
Age as a social identity 320
Social identities are diverse – and may develop differently 321
Can we create better social selves? 322
Social selves through the lifespan 323
Conclusions 324
References 325

Author index   327

Subject index   335

Tables

6.1   Evaluations of the national in-group versus various national
      out-groups   167
6.2   Affect expressed towards the national in-group versus
      various national out-groups   169
6.3   Evaluation of each individual national group and either the
      importance of national identity or degree of national
      identification   171
6.4   Positive distinctiveness of the national in-group and either
      the importance on national identity or degree of national
      identification   172
6.5   Affect expressed towards each individual national group
      and either the importance of national identity or degree of
      national identification   173
6.6   Affective distinctiveness of the national in-group and either
      the importance of national identity or degree of national
      identification   174
6.7   Perceived variability of each individual national group and
      either the importance of national identity or degree of
      national identification   179
6.8   Importance of national identity, degree of national
      identification, and perceived variability of the national
      in-group   180

Figures

10.1 Longitudinal analysis: Contact and conflict   281
10.2 Longitudinal analysis: Contact and one family   282
10.3 Longitudinal analysis: One family and conflict   282

Contributors

Dominic Abrams, Department of Psychology, University of Kent, Canterbury, Kent CT2 7NP, UK

Jeannette Alvarez, Department of Psychology, New York University, 6 Washington Place, 419, New York, NY 10003, USA

Meredith Bachman, Department of Psychology, New York University, 6 Washington Place, 7th Floor, New York, NY 10003, USA

Brenda S. Banker, Department of Psychology, University of Delaware, Newark, DE 19716, USA

Martyn Barrett, Department of Psychology, University of Surrey, Guildford GU2 7XH, UK

Mark Bennett, Department of Psychology, University of Dundee, Dundee DD1 4HN, Scotland, UK

Jessica Cameron, Department of Psychology, New York University, 6 Washington Place, 4th Floor, New York, NY 10003, USA

Barbara David, School of Psychology, The Australian National University, Canberra ACT 0200 Australia

Arantza del Valle, Departament de Psicologia, Universitat de Girona, Placa Sant Domenech, 9, 17071 Girona, Spain

John F. Dovidio, Department of Psychology, Colgate University, Hamilton, NY 13346, USA

Kevin Durkin, School of Psychology, University of Western Australia, Crawley, Western Australia 6009

Andrew J. Fuligni, Center for Culture and Health, UCLA Neuropsychiatric Institute, 760 Westwood Plaza, Box 62, Los Angeles, CA 90024-1759, USA

Cynthia Garcia Coll, Education Department, Brown University, P.O. Box 1938, Providence, RI 02912, USA

Samuel L. Gaertner, Department of Psychology, University of Delaware, Newark, DE 19716, USA

Diane Grace, School of Psychology, Australian National University, Canberra ACT 0200, Australia

Missy Houlette, Department of Psychology, University of Delaware, Newark, DE 19716, USA

Kelly M. Johnson, Department of Psychology, University of Delaware, Newark, DE 19716, USA

Evanthia Lyons, Department of Psychology, University of Surrey, Guildford GU2 7XH, UK

Drew Nesdale, School of Applied Psychology, Gold Coast Campus, Griffith University, PMB 50, Queensland 9726, Australia

Kimberly K. Powlishta, Department of Psychology, Saint Louis University, 3511 Laclede Avenue, St. Louis, MO 63103-2010, USA

Eun Rhee, Department of Psychology, University of Delaware, Newark, DE 19716, USA

Blake M. Riek, Department of Psychology, University of Delaware, Newark, DE 19716, USA

Diane N. Ruble, Department of Psychology, New York University, 6 Washington Place, 751, New York, NY 10003, USA

Adam Rutland, Department of Psychology, University of Kent at Canterbury, Canterbury, Kent CT2 7NP, UK

Michelle K. Ryan, School of Psychology, Australian National University, Canberra ACT 0200, Australia

Fabio Sani, Department of Psychology, University of Dundee, Dundee DD1 4HN, Scotland, UK

Maykel Verkuyten, Department of Social Sciences, Utrecht University, PO Box 80140, 3508 TC Utrecht, The Netherlands

1 Introduction: Children and social identity

Mark Bennett and Fabio Sani

The developing self has been a source of intermittent interest to psychologists ever since the early pioneering contributions of Baldwin (1895), Cooley (1902), James (1890), and Mead (1934). Though much research has been directed at the development of that aspect of the self-concept referred to as the *personal* self (the self defined by idiosyncratic features, such as personality traits), the aim of this book is to consider the development of the *social* self, that is, the self defined by one's membership of social groups – for example, gender, age, ethnicity, nationality, religion, and subcultural groups. Broadly, our project is undertaken within the framework afforded by the social identity approach (Tajfel, 1972, 1978; Tajfel & Turner, 1979; Turner, 1975, 1982), a social-cognitive perspective that sees the self-concept as the outcome of a self-categorisation process. At its heart is an acknowledgement of the interdependence of self and social context. The chapters of this volume address the development of a range of phenomena that fall within the purview of the social identity perspective – for example, social categorisation, self-conception, social comparison, and prejudice.

One of the central insights of the social identity approach is that groups can become part of the self-concept. This contention contrasts starkly with developmental psychologists' almost exclusive treatment of groups as external to the self, as merely an *influence* upon the self. Within the social identity approach, the self is taken to comprise *both* personal and social identity, and neither is seen as in any sense more fundamental or authentic than the other. Theoretically, treating groups as constitutive of the self is important in that it becomes possible to specify relations between self-conceptions and many aspects of social behaviour; moreover, it is to recognise that our social identity is associated with actions and cognitions that are discontinuous with those that arise from personal identity.

In this chapter we note the case for a developmental approach to the study of social identity. Briefly, we also consider the complementarity of social psychological and developmental approaches to the self. Following this we provide an introduction to the theoretical position underpinning this volume, that is, the social identity approach. Finally, we outline the content of the book's chapters.

SOCIAL AND DEVELOPMENTAL PERSPECTIVES ON THE SELF-CONCEPT

A major impetus for this volume has been the recognition, on the one hand, that social psychologists have neglected the *development* of self, and on the other, that developmentalists have focused largely upon the *personal* self. That is, most research on the development of the self-concept has been conducted by developmentalists and has addressed children's conceptions of themselves in terms of idiosyncratic attributes, such as personality traits, abilities, and preferences. (See, for example, Harter, 1998, 1999, for comprehensive reviews.) Little attention has been directed at the development of the social self. Nonetheless, it is clear that children are de facto members of many social groups; they are also members of groups that they themselves create. In our view, it is important to understand when and how social categories become constitutive of the self, such that children subjectively identify with them. As Ruble et al. (Chapter 2) put it, we need to understand children's developing sense of "we". In addition to its importance at the level of description, the developmental study of the social self is important insofar as it is clear that, among adults, social identities mobilise specific forms of group-related action and perception, such as cooperation with and attraction to in-group members (e.g., see Hogg & Abrams, 1988). As we see it, a key aim in the longer term is to understand the ontogenesis of the relation between social self-conceptions and social action. More generally, the focus upon children's developing social identities seems a significant enterprise given that one's social identity "creates and defines the individual's place in society" (Tajfel & Turner, 1979, pp. 40–41).

To address the development of the social self, we believe, necessitates reference to both social and developmental psychology. However, a backward glance at self research in developmental and social psychology reveals a striking degree of disciplinary insularity. A cursory inspection of papers in the two disciplines shows that, apart from standard genuflections towards founding figures, such as Baldwin, Cooley, James, and Mead, references are largely nonoverlapping. This is perhaps surprising given clear parallels in terms of the sorts of topics that have been studied. For example, both developmental and social psychologists have examined self-esteem, self-efficacy, and, most conspicuously of all, self-representations. And both have adopted broadly cognitive views of the self, reflecting a commitment, whether implicit or explicit, to Mead's (1934) fundamental insight that "Self-consciousness, rather than affective experience [. . .], provides the core and primary structure of the self, which is thus essentially a cognitive rather than an emotional phenomenon" (p. 173).

Despite obvious disciplinary similarities at the level of substantive inter-ests, there have nonetheless been considerable differences in terms of theor-etical orientation and methods. For example, considering the two fields' study of self-representations, quite contrasting traditions are apparent. Within social psychology, cognitive approaches to the self have been highly influential at least since Markus' (1977) introduction of the concept of *self-schemas*, that is, knowledge structures pertaining to the self. (See also Higgins, 1987; Kihlstrom & Cantor, 1984.) Among developmentalists, too, the self has been conceived in cognitive terms and a considerable amount of attention has been given to self-representations (Harter, 1999). However, the developmental study of the self has been embedded in an entirely different tradition: that of cognitive-developmental theory – specifically, Piagetian and neo-Piagetian theory (e.g., Case, 1992; Fischer, 1980). Here, a guiding assumption has been that general conceptual development plays a central role in determining the emergence, form, and increasing differentiation of self-conceptions. That is, researchers have sought to account for age-related structural growth in self-conceptions in terms of cognitive ontogenesis.

A further difference is that social psychologists, unlike most developmentalists, have asked questions about process-related issues. For example, what are the motivations underlying particular social identities (e.g., Brewer, 1999; Deaux, Reid, Mizrahi, & Cotting, 1999), and how do social identities guide particular types of action (e.g., Reicher, 1984)? Developmental psychologists, however, have more typically sought to describe the changing *contents* of children's self-conceptions (e.g., Damon & Hart, 1988; Keller, Ford & Meacham, 1978).

A further and key difference is that within social psychology, particularly under the influence of social identity theory, social self-conceptions (i.e., social identities) have been studied insofar as they are hypothesised to be consequential with respect to a broad range of inter- and intragroup phenomena. That is, social identity theorists have examined the relationship between self-conception and many forms of social behaviour, such as cooperation, conformity, crowd behaviour, group polarisation, and so on. Developmentally oriented work, however, has typically sought to describe developing self-conceptions as an end in themselves, or as outcomes of particular socialisation experiences (although for exceptions, see for example Abrams, Rutland, Cameron, & Marques, 2003; Bigler, Jones, & Lobliner, 1997; Harter, 1998, 1999).

A more general difference between the developmental and social psychological study of the self is in the sheer range of topics studied: Unsurprisingly, perhaps, given the greater prominence of the self-concept in social psychology, many more topics have been studied here than within developmental psychology. Thus, broadly speaking, developmental psychologists have been concerned primarily (though not exclusively) with the initial emergence of the self-concept (Brooks-Gunn & Lewis, 1979; Rochat, 2001), the development of, and social influences upon, self-representations (Harter, 1999), and self-esteem (Harter, 1987). Social psychologists, however, have addressed a prodigious range of self-related topics, including self-affirmation (Steele, 1988), self-awareness (Fenigstein, Scheier, & Buss, 1975), self-complexity (Linville, 1985), self-discrepancy (Higgins, 1987), self-enhancement (Wills, 1981), self-handicapping (Jones & Berglas, 1978), self-evaluation maintenance (Tesser, 1988), self-monitoring (Snyder, 1974) self-representations (Markus, 1977) self-presentation (Schlenker, 1980), self-verification (Swann & Read, 1981), and so on. Nonetheless, there are signs that the developmental study of the self is poised to become an increasingly significant focus of research (as reflected, for example, in major symposia at international conferences and recent research-based volumes, e.g., Brandstädter & Lerner, 1999; Demetriou & Kazi, 2001; Harter, 1999; Moore & Lemmon, 2001).

ON THE BENEFITS OF A CLOSER ASSOCIATION
BETWEEN SOCIAL AND DEVELOPMENTAL PSYCHOLOGY

Such differences as we have thus far identified to some extent reflect differences in the disciplines' orientations. Social psychologists are interested in processes of social influence, conceived in its broadest sense (see Allport, 1968; McGarty & Haslam, 1997). Developmentalists, however, focus primarily on change over time. These differences in orientation suggest possible benefits of closer association between the two disciplines, something noted by many before us (e.g., Brehm, Kassin, & Gibbons, 1981; Durkin, 1995; Eckes & Trautner, 2000; Flavell & Ross, 1981; Masters & Yarkin-Levin, 1984). Initially, let us turn to possible contributions of developmental psychology to social psychology.

Typically, social psychology has not dealt well with the issue of change, either generally or in the specific field of the study of self. Nor has it been much interested in the particular *contents* of self-representations. However, it seems reasonable to suggest that important changes in the content of the self-concept occur over the life-course, and that these may have significant implications for many aspects of psychological functioning. As Eckes and Trautner (2000) have commented, "transitions such as reaching puberty, becoming a parent, or retiring can be conceptualised as sensitive periods systematically influencing an individual's self-construal" (p. 7). Thus, an appreciation of the particular contents of self-representations and how they change is likely to be central to an understanding of self-functioning during the various phases of adulthood. Clearly, developmental psychology offers much in terms of the analysis and measurement of change (e.g., Brandstädter & Lerner, 1999; Lerner, 1998) and may represent a valuable resource to self theorists working within social psychology.

In addition to highlighting the need to look at development during adulthood, there is a need too to understand early origins of self-processes. "It is elementary yet widely overlooked by social psychologists that the phenomena they study do not arise out of nowhere, forming miraculously just before their subjects come to university" (Durkin, 1995, p. 3). That is, we need to acknowledge the developmental histories associated with social processes, specifying origins and developmental trajectories. Moreover, the possible antecedents of aspects of adult functioning in childhood experiences could profitably be addressed. In the absence of an appreciation of these sorts of distal causes, as Durkin comments, social psychology "risks becoming a science of proximal effects" (p. 6).

Recently, Pomerantz and Newman (2000) have argued forcefully that "attention to developmental psychology would enrich research programs within social psychology by providing new perspectives on the issues with which the field grapples" (p. 301). For example, they suggest that the study of developmental origins can provide insights into individual differences. They also discuss how young children's initial reactions to classes of social stimuli may provide a window onto what become basic and automatic responses in adulthood. At a methodological level they note that replication on samples of children (invariably more representative than samples based on undergraduate populations; Sears, 1986) provides evidence for the robustness of effects. Thus, developmental research can provide a powerful source of theory confirmation. And in the *absence* of confirmatory evidence (i.e., where children's behaviour is found to differ from that of adults), we must question the assumption of a theory's universality; the challenge to understand developmental origins and change then becomes pressing.

Turning to the benefit to developmental psychology of a closer acquaintance with social psychology, we suggest that a fundamental gain will be a better understanding of cognitive and behavioural variability over social contexts – a theme that emerges in many of the chapters of this volume. A key feature of much social psychological theorising (and particularly self-categorisation theory) is the attempt to specify relationships between contextual variables and intra-individual variability in social behaviour and cognition, including, of course, self-related phenomena. A central goal, then, is to account for the fact that individuals' behaviour and cognition covaries with social contexts. Generally speaking, at the intra-individual level, developmental psychologists have not accorded context an essential role[1]: In looking primarily at change over time, change over contexts has frequently been overlooked. Where contextual variation *has* been examined, this has often been in an ad hoc empirical way, rather than in a more principled and theorised way, as is typical in social psychology generally, and within the social identity approach particularly.

In seeking to understand the development of the self, it is apparent that social and developmental psychology each provide important insights. Social psychologists, while neglecting processes of change over time, give attention to social processes within given contexts; developmentalists, however, focus upon change over time, often disregarding changes over contexts. Thus, an

---

1 This is patently not true at the inter-individual level, where context has been accorded a foundational role in development, especially from a Vygotskian perspective.

approach that integrates the strengths of the two disciplines may be fertile indeed. However, as Eckes and Trautner (2000) have argued, an integrative approach "must not confine itself to simply adding to the first perspective what the second has to offer and vice versa. Quite the contrary. At the intersection of developmental and social psychology many issues will emerge that pose new kinds of challenges for theorizing and research" (p. 12). In particular, a social-developmental perspective should aspire to explore the possible ways in which context varies with age, since the impact of contexts upon self-processes is likely to be importantly mediated by cognitive-developmental factors. Following Eckes and Trautner, then, we suggest that the social-developmental study of the self must recognise that the self is subject to both social and developmental processes, and that these processes are likely to be reciprocally influential.

Our discussion thus far implies an ambitious programme of work on the development of the social self. This book represents an attempt to make a start on this project, bringing together some of the best current work in this new area of inquiry. In seeking to explore children's social selves, we take the view that the social identity approach represents a valuable theoretical resource. It is a theoretical perspective that has had a colossal impact on the social-psychological literature; if there is a more promising theoretical basis for the investigation of the developing social self, we are unaware of it. For our developmental readership, to whom the social identity approach may be relatively unfamiliar, we now provide a brief statement of the origins and major features of the two main theories that comprise the social identity approach.

THE SOCIAL IDENTITY APPROACH

During the late 1960s and early 1970s, both the theoretical and the methodological foundations of social psychology were shaken by a wave of criticism coming from social psychologists themselves (Gergen, 1973; McGuire, 1973; Ring, 1967). A pervasive sense of dissatisfaction rapidly spread throughout the community, causing what has been characterised as a "crisis of confidence" (Elms, 1975). It was in this climate that a fast-growing group of European social psychologists – led by Henri Tajfel in Britain and Serge Moscovici in France – attempted to create a "new look" social psychology. The declared aim of this group of scholars was to revalue and emphasise the "social" dimension of human behaviour (Doise, 1982; Jaspars, 1980; Tajfel, 1984) by creating an anti-individualistic and anti-reductionistic social psychology.

As far as the specific field of group processes was concerned, the anti-reductionistic stance was represented by what we now know as the "social identity approach" (Hogg & Abrams, 1988), which developed throughout the 1970s and the 1980s. This approach now comprises two main theories, *social identity theory* and latterly *self-categorisation theory*.

Social identity theory

The initial focus of the social identity approach was the study of intergroup behaviour (Billig, 1976; Tajfel, 1970; Tajfel, Flament, Billig, & Bundy, 1971), which resulted in the creation of a formally stated theory that became known as social identity theory, or SIT for short (Tajfel & Turner, 1986). The explicit objective of SIT was that of generating a truly social-psychological perspective on intergroup relations, as opposed to the dominant individualistic outlook. The metatheoretical distinction between individualistic theories and social psychological theories of group processes and intergroup relations is clearly summarised in the following statement:

> Many of the 'individual' theories start from general descriptions of psychological processes which are assumed to operate in individuals in a way which is independent of the effects of social interaction and social context. The social context and interaction are assumed to affect these processes, but only in the sense that society provides a variety of settings in which the 'basic' individual laws of motivation or cognition are uniformly displayed. In contrast, 'social psychological' theories [. . .] stress the need to take into account the fact that group behaviour – and even more so intergroup behaviour – is displayed in situations in which we are not dealing with random collections of individuals who somehow come to act in unison because they all happen to be in a similar psychological state.
>
> (Tajfel, 1981, p. 403)

In order to appreciate the empirical base from which the theory emerged, it is necessary to discuss some of the experiments conducted by Tajfel and his colleagues during the early 1970s.

The "minimal groups experiments"

The impetus for the development of SIT was the need to explain unexpected results emerging from some experiments conducted by Tajfel and his colleagues at Bristol University in the early 1970s. Tajfel was interested in intergroup discrimination, and was intrigued by the fact that various studies had cast doubts on Sherif's (1967) assumption that realistic intergroup competition is the necessary condition for conflict and ethnocentrism. For example, Ferguson and Kelley (1964) had found that even in the absence of competition, people tend to evaluate the performance of the in-group more favourably than that of the out-group. Other authors (Rabbie & Horwitz, 1969; Rabbie & Wilkens, 1971) had established that the simple anticipation of future interaction between groups may determine negative bias in the participants' evaluation of the out-group.

In the light of such findings, Tajfel decided to investigate the minimal necessary condition for intergroup discrimination. In order to do so, he set up a series of experiments reproducing a situation in which both the characteristics of the two groups and the nature of their relation were minimal, in the sense that they lacked all the common characteristics of real contexts. That situation was supposed to constitute a "no discrimination" baseline to which other variables could be cumulatively added in order to investigate the necessary preconditions for the emerging of discriminative and ethnocentric behaviour. One of these experiments turned out to be crucial, and was successfully replicated several times and by different authors.

In this experiment, 14- to 16-year-old boys were assigned to one of two groups, ostensibly on the basis of their preferences for paintings by either Klee or Kandinsky. In fact, assignment was random. Subsequently, each participant was placed in a separate cubicle, and was told to which group – either "Klee" or "Kandinsky" group – he belonged. Participants had no contact with other in-group members, nor with the out-group. They were then requested to allocate points representing money to various participants in the experiment, using specially prepared decision matrices. Each matrix allowed allocation of money to two recipients. The recipients were anonymous, but their group affiliation was revealed: one was an in-group member and the other an out-group member. However, the participants were told that giving money to the in-group members would not contribute to what they themselves would receive.

The structure of the matrices was such that it was possible to assess the strategies adopted by the participants for the allocation of points. The strategies were: (a) maximising the total number of points for the two recipients irrespective of their group membership; (b) maximising the number of points for in-group members; (c) maximising the difference in favour of the in-group members in the number of points allocated; (d) distributing an equal number of points to the members of the in-group and those of the out-group.

Because of the "minimal" nature of the intergroup context, Tajfel and his colleagues were expecting not to find any discrimination between groups; indeed, this situation had been conceived as a baseline against which the impact of further variables could be judged. However, the results came as a surprise in that the participants showed a clear tendency to discriminate against the out-group by assigning more money to in-group members. Most interestingly, their concern was not with maximising the absolute profit of the in-group, but with maximising the *difference* between the profit of the in-group and that of the out-group in favour of the in-group. Thus, rather than adopting a simple economic strategy ("Let's get as much as we can"), they adopted a strategy that ensured superiority over the out-group ("Let's make sure that *we* do better than *them*"). In other words, mere categorisation in terms of in-group/out-group proved to be connected with the emergence of discrimination.

These results were initially explained in terms of "norms" prevalent in some societies (Tajfel et al., 1971). However, Tajfel and colleagues soon rejected this explanation: It was seen as uninteresting in the sense that it was not genuinely heuristic, since whatever the result of the experiment, an explanation in terms of norms could be invoked. Therefore the central question was still unanswered: Why does discrimination follow from categorisation? Is discrimination a straightforward consequence of the process of social categorisation, or is there a more articulated story to be revealed? SIT sought to answer this question.

The core features of social identity theory

The theory elaborated by Tajfel is underpinned by three basic and interconnected concepts: social identity, social categorisation, and social comparison. Social identity – which self-categorisation theory eventually distinguished from personal identity (Turner & Reynolds, 2001) – is defined as "that part of an individual's self-concept which derives from his knowledge of his membership of a social group (or groups) together with the value and emotional significance attached to that membership" (Tajfel, 1981, p. 255). The identification of the self with a social group, and therefore the acquisition of a social identity, goes hand-in-hand with the process of social categorisation.

Social categorisation refers to the cognitive segmentation of the social environment into different social categories. This operation both systematises the social world and provides a system of orientation for the self, by creating and defining the individual's place in society. In other words, an individual in a given social situation could not identify him/herself with a certain social group without psychologically structuring the context in terms of relatively discrete social categories. The tendency to segment the social environment into distinct social units is partly made possible by the peculiar characteristics of the process of categorisation. In turn, categorisation of stimuli – either natural or social – leads to the cognitive accentuation both of differences between stimuli belonging to different categories and of similarities between stimuli belonging to the same category (Doise, 1978; Eiser & Stroebe, 1972; Tajfel & Wilkes, 1963).

Social comparison refers to the tendency to evaluate the categories constituting the context by comparing them on relevant dimensions. This process contributes fundamentally to an understanding of the social world and the in-group within it. As Tajfel has argued, "the characteristics of one's group as a whole (such as its status, its richness or poverty, its skin colour or its ability to reach its aims) achieve most of their significance in relation to perceived differences from other groups and the value connotations of these differences" (1981, p. 258).

Obviously, the way the in-group is evaluated has important implications for an individual's social identity. In other words, one's own social identity may be positive or negative depending on the evaluations of those groups that form one's social identity. This notion leads to the central hypothesis of SIT: If it is assumed that individuals strive for a positive self-concept in order to maintain or enhance their self-esteem, "the in-group must be perceived as positively different or distinct from the relevant out-groups" (Tajfel & Turner, 1986, p. 16). Thus, SIT hypothesises that in every intergroup context people are driven both to gain a positive image and to make the context as unambiguous and meaningful as possible; they try to satisfy both needs by means of a positive differentiation of the in-group from the out-group on those dimensions which are relevant for the comparison.

It is through this hypothesis that the results of the minimal group experiments can be explained. Since the context created by the researchers was deliberately vague and ill-defined, subjects looked for some sort of meaning and structure by using the only categorisation available, that is, the one based on the distinction between Klee and Kandinsky supporters. The categorisation process makes the two groups cognitively central and clearly distinct from each other. A positive identity is then achieved through a social comparison based on the only available dimension of comparison, that is, the distribution of money.

However, in the real world the achievement and maintenance of a positive social identity is a much more complex matter. Rather than being populated by such groups as Klee and Kandinsky supporters, the social world comprises groups and categories that stand in status relations with one another, and are often in competition for resources, prestige, and power. This means that, while members of more powerful groups normally have a positive social identity, subordinate groups may confer negative social identity upon their members, especially if the values of the dominant groups are accepted. As a consequence, SIT hypothesises that powerful groups try to maintain their positive identity by maintaining the status quo, while subordinate groups may either accept the superiority of the more powerful group, which may be associated with out-group favouritism (Reynolds, Turner, & Haslam, 2000), or use a variety of strategies in order to improve their social identity.

The strategy chosen usually depends on individuals' system of belief. Tajfel makes a distinction between two main systems of belief, namely "social mobility" and "social change". The system of beliefs in social mobility holds that boundaries between social groups are flexible and permeable, and that individuals can move from one group to another through talent and effort. Those individuals who subscribe to this system of belief usually try to achieve a positive identity by means of an individualistic strategy defined as "individual mobility", consisting of leaving their group in order to enter a higher-status group. On the other hand, social change beliefs make the supposition that group boundaries are impermeable and that it is therefore impossible to leave one's group. In this case social identity may be improved through the use of one of two general strategies, depending on the perception of the degree of legitimacy of the status quo: Where the status quo is seen as essentially legitimate, subordinate groups may employ some form of "social creativity" aimed at re-evaluating the group ("We may not be as smart as them, but we're better in the sense of being nicer and more honest"). On the other hand, where the status quo is perceived as illegitimate, subordinate groups may tend to choose the strategy of "social competition", in which real attempts are made to change the relative positions of the in-group and the out-group on key dimensions (e.g., in industrial settings, in union-based action).

Self-categorisation theory

A recognised weakness of SIT, rather ironically perhaps, was that it had little to say about the cognitive aspects of social identity salience. Moreover, the focus of SIT was *inter*group processes; *intra*group processes, for the most part, were ignored. Self-categorisation theory (SCT), pioneered by John Turner and colleagues (Oakes, Haslam, & Turner, 1994; Turner et al. 1987), sought to address these weaknesses.

SCT shares with SIT the crucial postulate that in many circumstances individuals define themselves in terms of their group membership, and in turn a group-defined perception of the self produces specific psychological effects that affect social behaviour. However, the theory differs from SIT in that it has a greater explanatory scope, as it is not limited to issues of social structure and intergroup relations.

As a general social psychological theory of group phenomena, SCT was explicitly created in order to deal with the individual–group dilemma, which, according to Turner, is to be conceptualised in terms of the following questions: "How does a collection of individuals become a social and psychological group? How do they come to perceive and define themselves and act as a single unit, feeling, thinking and self-aware as a collective entity?" (Turner, Hogg, Oakes, Reicher, & Wetherell, 1987, p. 1). The dominant theories of the 1960s reduced the group to little more than a complex system of interpersonal relations based upon the interdependence and attraction among the group's members. The concept of "group" was seen as virtually superfluous since it was considered to be descriptively useful but unnecessary at an explanatory level. However, SCT emphasises that a collection of people will act as a group as long as they feel that they belong to the same whole, that is, to the same social category. This conviction is principally based on the result of the experiments on "minimal groups" discussed earlier.

According to Turner and his colleagues (Turner et al., 1987), group formation precedes – rather than follows – most of the interpersonal phenomena that characterise our daily life. To be more specific, group formation is seen as "an adaptive social psychological process that makes social cohesion, cooperation and influence possible" (Turner et al., 1987, p. 40). This way of conceiving the group makes it possible for the concept of "group" itself to become essential from both an empirical and a theoretical point of view.

The key aspects of SCT, which we will consider shortly, can be described in terms of three fundamental aspects of group functioning: (a) the antecedents of the psychological group; (b) the basic process underlying the psychological group; and (c) the consequences of the psychological group. First, however, it is necessary to mention the main assumptions underpinning the theory.

Central assumptions of self-categorisation theory

The central, even defining, assumption is that in any circumstance the way in which an individual experiences him/herself depends on the specific self-conception that is "activated". In turn, a self-conception derives from a self-categorisation, which consists of the cognitive grouping of the self as identical to some class of stimuli in contrast to some other class of stimuli. SCT then assumes that any specific self-categorisation is part of a hierarchical system of classification. Self-categorisations form at different levels of inclusiveness. For instance, a given self-category (e.g., "social science student") is more inclusive than another (e.g., "sociology student"), where the former can contain the latter, but the latter cannot contain the former.

A further important assumption is that although the number of levels of abstraction is potentially infinite, each self-category can be seen – for the sake of theoretical clarity – as pertaining to one of three main levels of abstraction. The superordinate level is that of the self as a human being, by means of which the self is grouped as similar to all human beings, and as different from all other species in nature. When one is identified in a given situation with the human race, one is said to behave according to *human identity*. The intermediate level concerns the self as member of a social group; at this level the self is grouped as similar to the other members of the in-group and as different from the members of the out-groups. Categories like "biologist", "French", "liberal", "Juventus supporter", "Greenpeace activist", and so on belong to this level of abstraction. When self-conception in a specific circumstance is shaped by the categorisation as a member of a social group, one is seen as behaving and self-perceiving according to one's *social identity*. Finally, there is the subordinate level of abstraction, which is that of the self as an individual person. In this case the person perceives him/herself as unique and idiosyncratic, that is, as different and distinct from anybody else. When prominent characteristics are related to one's specific and particular features (e.g., kindness, intelligence, etc.), one is seen as behaving according to *personal identity*.

This hierarchical system of self-categories is equivalent to all systems of natural categories as described by Rosch (1978). However, in opposition to Rosch's point of view on natural categories, SCT does not propose that some self-categories are more central, or somehow more important, than others. There is not a way of categorising, and therefore experiencing, the self, that can be said to be deeper or more authentic than other ways. Thus, when we act on the base of our social identity, and therefore structure the context of action in terms of "we" versus "them", we are not experiencing the self in a way that is less valuable than when we act according to our personal identity. Turner, Oakes, Haslam, and McGarty (1994) explain:

> when we think of and perceive ourselves as "we" and "us" (social identity) as opposed to "I" and "me" (personal identity), this is ordinary and

normal self-experience in which the self is defined in terms of *others who exist outside the individual person doing the experiencing* and therefore cannot be reduced to personal identity. At certain times the self is defined and experienced as identical, equivalent, or similar to a social class of people in contrast to some other class. The self can be defined and experienced *subjectively* as a social collectivity".

(pp. 454–455) [italics in the original]

Antecedents of the psychological group

As we mentioned earlier, SCT hypothesises that "psychological group formation takes place to the degree that two or more people come to perceive and define themselves in terms of some shared in-group–out-group categorisation" (Turner et al., 1987, p. 51). This hypothesis implies that the group with which a collection of people identify in a given situation can be determined either by the characteristics of a much greater number of people than those present in that situation, or by the features exclusively shared by those present. In Hogg's (1987) words, "five individuals in a room have just as much become a group in that situation if they are behaving in terms of a large-scale category membership they share (such as race, sex, or religion) as if in terms of an emergent group whose norms and defining features are unique to that specific collection of five people (a friendship group, an experimental decision-making group, etc.)" (p. 103). This principle is important because it represents a "rupture" with traditional social psychology of group processes, in the sense that it obviates the usual distinction between small groups and large-scale social categories as far as the central psychological mechanisms bounding people together are concerned. Indeed, this principle takes it that face-to-face interaction is unnecessary for group formation.

Once it is established that the existence of a shared self-categorisation is a necessary condition for a collection of people to feel that they are a group, the question arises of how it is that within a particular context certain self-categories become salient while other potential self-categories remain in the background. In dealing with this problem, SCT borrows from the theory of Bruner (1957) on the activation of categories in the perceptual field. For SCT the salience of a particular self-category is determined by an interaction between "accessibility" and "fit." Accessibility refers to the tendency to use those categories that are meaningful in terms of past experience and current expectations, goals, needs, and values. Oakes, Haslam, and Turner (1994) also use the term "perceiver readiness", which clearly indicates that certain categories are more readily used because of their relevance, usefulness, and centrality, and because they are likely to be confirmed by the evidence of reality.

Fit refers to the degree of correspondence between the categories selected and the stimulus reality to be represented by the categories. Fit has two aspects: "comparative fit" and "normative fit" (Oakes, 1987; Oakes, Turner, & Haslam, 1991). Comparative fit is defined by the *principle of metacontrast*, according to which "any collection of individuals in a given setting is more likely to categorise themselves as a group (become a psychological group) to the degree that the subjectively perceived differences between them are less than the differences perceived between them and other people (psychologically) present in the setting (i.e., as the ratio of intergroup to intragroup differences increases)" (Turner et al., 1987, pp. 51–52).

Normative fit refers to the fact that the objective differences between groups must also match the expected stereotypical features of the groups themselves. For example, to categorise a set of people as Liberals as opposed to Conservatives, they must not only differ from Conservatives in their attitudes and behaviour more than from one another, but they must also be different on particular content dimensions of comparison that are typically seen as differentiating the two categories. This means that the categorisation in terms of Liberals versus Conservatives would probably take place promptly in a situation in which, for instance, the Liberals were arguing in favour of abortion, while the Conservatives were arguing against it.

The main implication of the fit hypothesis is that self-categories become salient as a result of an intergroup comparison, and that they therefore vary as a function of the frame of reference. They can vary in different forms. First of all they vary in level of inclusiveness. A person can categorise him/herself either as Sicilian, or Italian, or European, usually depending on the extension of the context. Self-categories also vary in meaning, in order to reflect the content of the diagnostic intergroup differences in a given situation. For example, Haslam, Oakes, Turner, and McGarty (1995) found that Australians perceive themselves as sportsmanlike, straightforward, and happy-go-lucky when judged on their own, but when judged in the context of Americans they see themselves as even more sportsmanlike, less happy-go-lucky, but also pleasure-loving. Finally, self-categories vary in internal structure, that is, in terms of the relative prototypicality of their members. In other words, categories are not defined by a fixed prototype: The relative prototypicality of a member of a category changes according to the context.

The variability and fluidity of self-categories is a core feature of SCT. In fact, it underlines the functionality of the self-categories. As stressed by Turner et al. (1994):

> the concept of self as a separate mental structure does not seem necessary, because we can assume that any and all cognitive resources – long-term knowledge, implicit theories, cultural beliefs, social representations, and so forth – are recruited, used, and deployed when necessary to create the needed self-category. Rather than a distinction between the activated self and the stored, inactive self, it is possible to think of the self *as the product of the cognitive system at work, as a functional property of the cognitive system as a whole*" (p. 459) [italics in the original].

Thus, fluidity and variability of self-categories reflect "functionality" and "adaptation". Self-categories are created and made salient in order to facilitate behaviour that is appropriate to the situation.

The basic process of the psychological group

When a collection of people share the same social identity, that is, when they categorise themselves as members of the same social group, a core process called *depersonalisation* takes place. The notion of depersonalisation refers to the fact that when a collective self-identification is salient, "individuals tend to define and see themselves less as differing individual people and more as the interchangeable representatives of some shared social category membership" (Turner et al., 1994, p. 455).

Depersonalisation is facilitated by the already-mentioned "accentuation effect", by means of which, when the context is divided into discrete categories, there is a tendency to exaggerate intragroup similarities and inter-group differences. This promotes among members of the same group a sense of being similar (identical, equivalent, interchangeable), and leads to self-perception in terms of "we" and "us" instead of "I" and "me". This mechanism also generates a perception of out-group members in terms of "they" and "them". For example, when a psychologist categorises herself as a "psychologist" in contrast to, say, sociologists, she will accentuate perceptually her similarities to other psychologists – reducing at the same time her specific personal differences from other psychologists – and will magnify her stereotypical differences from sociologists.

To be depersonalised does not imply the emergence of some sort of primitive or inferior form of identity, but a change in the level of abstraction of the self-category. There is a shift from personal identity to social identity, which is cognitively and behaviourally functional in terms of adaptation of the self to the social context of action. Indeed, in many circumstances (for example, involving intergroup competition) it is more adaptive to perceive ourselves as interchangeable members of a category rather than as unique individuals. That perception and cognition are at the service of the self and its needs, goals, and values, is hardly surprising. As Oakes, Haslam and Turner note, "perception that was not relative to self would be pointless, futile, unimaginable and meaningless. It would not be human. [. . .] It is hard to imagine how and why any biological (or other) system would evolve a capacity for perception unaffected by the functions, aims, properties and location of the perceiver" (1994, p. 205).

The consequences of depersonalisation

Depersonalisation is seen by SCT as the basis of all those processes that typically take place within a group context. Processes such as attraction, cohesion, ethnocentrism, cooperation, influence, polarisation, crowd behaviour, and so on can be seen as resulting from depersonalisation, via the assumption that salient self-categories tend to be positively evaluated, and that the self and others are positively evaluated to the degree that they are perceived as prototypical of the self-category.

Consider, for instance, mutual attraction. Depersonalisation increases the mutually perceived prototypicality of in-group members on the stereotypical dimensions that characterise the in-group category. As a result, since the in-group category is positively valued, the mutual attraction between members of the in-group will increase. Ethnocentrism, that is, attraction to one's group as a whole, is explained in a similar fashion: It is the consequence of the perceived prototypicality of the in-group in comparison with relevant out-groups on relevant dimensions. With regard to social cooperation, this is seen as resulting from the fact that the perception of similarity between oneself and in-group members, induced by depersonalisation, leads to a perceived commonality of interests, which in turn increases the level of intragroup cooperation.

According to SCT, crucial social phenomena such as social influence and conformity can also be interpreted as being determined by depersonalisation (Turner et al., 1987). The process leading from depersonalisation to conformity via social influence has been named "referent informational influence" and comprises three distinct phases. (1) A collection of people sharing the same social identity – who are therefore depersonalised – tend to agree, or at least expect to agree, with each other, as far as their judgment of, and reactions to, certain stimuli are concerned. (2) This state of affairs leads the group members either to learn the existing stereotypic norms of the group, or to create some common norms *tout court*. Since the norms of a social group are generally rather flexible and multifaceted, there is usually a subgroup or an individual that best expresses and embodies those norms. This subgroup, or individual, can be considered as prototypical, and as such is seen as the most appropriate referent for information about valid and correct norms. (3) Once the norms are known, group members assign these norms to themselves along with other stereotypical characteristics of the category, and in so doing they conform to the normative behaviour of the group.

In conclusion, this way of explaining group phenomena reflects SCT's contention that the sense of being a group is not a consequence of interdependence and attraction but instead *precedes* such group phenomena. As such, it seems fair to judge that SCT fulfils its aim of reinstating the "group" as a central psychological and theoretical tool in the explanation of collective phenomena. (For a fuller account of the social identity approach, see

Haslam, 2001; for recent extensions and modifications to the "classic" position presented here, see Turner & Onorato, 1999.)

ORGANISATION OF THE BOOK

Briefly stated, the first two substantive chapters of this volume address basic and general issues in the study of children's social identities. Following this, several chapters each examine a particular social identity: gender, nationality, and ethnicity. Next, applications of the social identity perspective to phenomena contingent upon identity are considered. Finally, commentaries on the book's chapters are provided. Although the basic structure is to some extent artificial, in the sense, for example, that all the chapters at some level address both identities and applications, it is a structure that draws attention to the distinction between self-conceptions and phenomena that are contingent upon self-conceptions. Looking to the future, we believe that one of the major contributions of developmentally oriented research inspired by the social identity perspective will be the articulation of the relationship between developing self-conceptions and many diverse forms of social action. However, coming back to the present, we turn to a more detailed account of the chapter contents.

In any relatively new field of inquiry, such as the focus of the present volume, it is vital not to lose sight of the relevance of previous research. Such research, though perhaps not *directly* pertinent to new issues, may nonetheless provide important insights or may offer a basis for the generation of new hypotheses. On the other hand, conducting work in relatively uncharted territory poses fundamental challenges of conceptualisation. The volume's first substantive chapter tackles these twin demands admirably. Diane Ruble, Jeannette Alvarez, Meredith Bachman, Jessica Cameron, Andrew Fuligni, Cynthia Garcia Coll, and Eun Rhee provide a broadly based discussion that serves to contextualise many of the issues arising in later chapters. They provide a valuable review of the available research on children's understanding of and identification with social categories, particulary gender, race, and ethnicity. Ruble et al. go on to make the case that social identity must be understood as a complex, multidimensional construct. Specifically, four dimensions are addressed: salience, centrality, knowledge, and evaluation. Attention is given to developmental evidence pertaining to each of these dimensions, and the case is made showing a pressing need to explore these key components of identity further. Finally, Ruble et al. consider the consequences of developmental changes in collective identity, for example, with respect to in-group biases, self-esteem, information-search, and personal choices.

Fabio Sani and Mark Bennett, in the following chapter, address three main themes bearing upon the development of social identity. First of all, they outline their work on children's conceptions of the normative features of social groups, arguing that up until mid-childhood, children's focus is upon the dispositional and behavioural features defining a social identity. Only at mid to late childhood do they start to consider the role of socially shared beliefs associated with many identities. Next, they make the case that not only are there developmental variations in conceptions of social groups, but there are also contextual variations. That is, drawing upon SCT they argue that children's conceptions of particular groups vary as a function of the context in which they consider particular groups. Evidence is provided suggesting that flexibility in conceptions of groups increases with age. Finally, Sani and Bennett raise questions about the extent to which previous research relying on verbal self-descriptions has provided insights into the internalisation of social identities. Using two separate methods, they provide evidence suggesting that the internalisation of social identities may not be established until at least the age of 7 years.

The chapters that follow each address a particular type of identity. The first two consider perhaps the most fundamental of social identities, namely gender. In looking at research on aspects of gender identity, Kimberly Powlishta notes extensive evidence for the sorts of generic intergroup processes predicted by the social identity approach. For example, from an early age, children show strong preferences for members of their own gender, and accentuate within-group similarities and between-group differences (although interestingly, these findings seem to be more pronounced in girls than boys). On the basis of such findings, Powlishta argues that,

> Children may view their own sex as superior in order to achieve a positive social identity, which in turn should motivate them to adopt gender-typed characteristics and prefer same-sex playmates. The resulting gender-segregated play exposes boys and girls to different socialization contexts, potentially creating or amplifying sex differences. The generic tendency to exaggerate between-group differences and within-group similarities may contribute to gender stereotypes, further encouraging boys and girls to adopt different behaviors and roles.

Thus generic intergroup processes, she suggests, play an important role in gender-role development.

The following chapter, by Barbara David, Diane Grace, and Michelle Ryan, also looks at gender identity, but where Powlishta's focus is largely on social identity theory, David et al. consider self-categorisation theory. As such, they see the self in process rather than structural terms and argue that "gender is one aspect of the flexible, changing, context-dependent self process. What it means to a child to be a girl or a boy will change with context, as it does for adults, but the changes will be more dramatic due to developmental growth in cognitive skills and knowledge . . .". Drawing upon both SCT and cognitive developmental considerations, they make the novel case that early gender identity is no more than an aspect of personal identity; only later does it become a social identity, properly conceived. More generally, in arguing for SCT, they make the case that the adoption of a more fluid conceptualisation of self addresses some of the shortcomings of classic approaches to gender development.

Martyn Barrett, Evanthia Lyons, and Arantza del Valle consider the social identity approach in the context of national identity. They outline eight key predictions made by SIT and SCT and examine how far the predictions are upheld by their own extensive, multinational studies of national identity development. In contrast to the research reported by Powlishta on gender identity, Barrett et al. find inconsistent support for the predictions. Indeed, the only finding to emerge consistently in all national groups (though only on one of their measures) was preference for the national in-group, which appears from 6 years of age. The striking feature of their data is the extent to which different patterns of findings emerge in different national contexts. Thus, in seeking to make a judgment about the value of the social identity approach in a developmental context, Barrett et al. argue that, taken at face value, the approach might be seen as falling short. However, drawing upon Turner's more recent writings (e.g., Turner & Onorato, 1999), they propose that

> the extent to which particular identity phenomena are exhibited may actually be a product of a much more complex interaction between, for example, the strength of subjective identification with the in-group, the individual's beliefs about the nature of the group boundaries (for example, whether they are legitimate or illegitimate) and about the status of the different groups within that system (for example, whether the ingroup is high or low status, and whether this status is secure or insecure), and the individual's own personal motivations, values, needs and expectancies in relationship to these beliefs.

From this, Barrett et al. make two important observations. One is that future research may need to examine complex *patterns* of findings rather than *correlations* between pairs of variables. However, their more trenchant observation is that, to the extent that some cognitive or motivational variable might always be appealed to, post hoc, to "save" the theory, recent formulations of SCT, being invulnerable to refutation, might arguably be viewed as a degenerating research programme.

Maykel Verkuyten draws upon SIT and SCT to examine ethnic identity in children. Looking at majority-group Dutch children and Moroccan, Surinamese, and Turkish immigrant children in the Netherlands, he demonstrates that not only are there important differences between the majority group and the minorities, but there are also differences between ethnic minority groups. In addition, there are important identity-related individual differences within ethnic groups (e.g., in collectivism and in experiences with discrimination). Verkuyten argues that "Ethnic identity does not only depend on cognitive

structures and processes but is also determined by social beliefs and context
. . . . . . status differences, cultural values and situational conditions play an
important role in children's ethnic self-understanding". Although SCT is
seen as an important theoretical resource, Verkuyten comments critically that
its emphasis is on "the processes of category use in context, and not on how
self-understandings are conceptually organized and change in structure with
age". To this extent, interestingly, Verkuyten's position is somewhat different
from that of David et al., in that he asserts the need to acknowledge cross-
situationally stable features of the self, and developmental changes in those
features.

The chapters just described each consider a particular type of identity and
look at phenomena predicted by the social identity approach. In contrast, the
chapters that follow take a particular phenomenon and ask how a social
identity approach could cast light on it. Thus, Drew Nesdale considers ethnic
prejudice in children and begins by arguing that traditional approaches
(e.g., cognitive and socialisation-based accounts) are inadequate to account
for the considerable body of evidence on this matter. Instead, he proposes an
identity-based model of the development of children's prejudice. Nesdale's
social identity development theory (SIDT) draws both upon social identity
theory and self-categorisation theory and takes it that children's early intergroup biases are expressions of in-group preference rather than out-group
hostility (i.e., liking the in-group more than out-groups, but not actively
disliking out-groups). The appearance of subsequent prejudice is seen as
resulting from the incorporation of negative out-group attitudes as part of an
in-group identity. He states that, "Importantly, SIDT emphasises the critical
significance of social identity processes in the development of children's
ethnic attitudes and, in so doing, facilitates a long overdue shift away from
the prevailing emphasis in much social developmental research on the predominance of cognitive processes". Much evidence is provided that lends
support to this position.

Similarly, Adam Rutland's chapter argues against traditional accounts of
prejudice suggesting that it is an inevitable consequence of young children's
cognitive limitations. Rutland begins by noting previous research that has
been taken to support cognitive-developmental accounts of prejudice (e.g.,
Aboud, 1988), particularly that which shows a "peaking" of prejudicial
attitudes at around 7 years of age, with a decline thereafter. In a series of
experiments, he explores the possibility that this developmental progression
instead reflects an increasing capacity, with age, to regulate the expression of
prejudice in a socially appropriate way. Consistent with his hypothesis, he
shows that when in a state of heightened self-consciousness, 6- to 8-year-old
children reveal no evidence of prejudicial attitudes (though they did so in a
standard condition). However, perhaps the most novel aspect of Rutland's
research is the employment of implicit measures of prejudice, that is,
response latency measures (widely used on adults), which tap aspects of cognition that are relatively automatic. Using such techniques, older children's

out-group attitudes were found to be significantly more negative than was the case when they were directly questioned about their attitudes. According to Rutland, children can thus be seen as social tacticians who strategically express their intergroup attitudes through a process of effortful on-line construction in context. Rutland's findings are valuable both because they raise difficult questions for theoretical accounts that explain prejudice in cognitive-developmental terms, and because they demonstrate the value and tractability of response latency techniques in developmental work.

In a relatively unusual application of the social identity approach, Brenda Banker, Sam Gaertner, John Dovidio, Missy Houlette, Kelly Johnson, and Blake Riek consider the stepfamily as a key intergroup context in many children's lives. They note that bringing together two separate family groups into a single structure is a complex and problematic matter. In seeking to understand the difficulties that so often arise in this context, and the factors associated with positive outcomes for stepfamilies, Banker et al. appeal to the *common in-group identity model*. This model emerged out of the social identity approach and "proposes that factors that induce members of two groups to conceive of themselves as members of a common, more inclusive in-group, reduce intergroup conflict by enabling cognitive and motivational processes that contribute to pro-in-group favouring biases to be redirected to include former out-group members". Consistent with the model, two studies of stepchildren's perceptions and experiences provide strong evidence that seeing the stepfamily as a single entity is a significant causal link in the achievement of harmony within stepfamilies. Moreover, insofar as the findings point to a factor ("conditions of contact") that contributes importantly to the perception of a single family unit, the practical implications of this work are considerable.

In the two closing chapters, Dominic Abrams and Kevin Durkin each reflect on some of the key issues arising out of this volume. Abrams addresses three main themes and considers these with respect to each chapter. First, he notes that most chapters in the book address the cognitive and motivational elements of self-categorisation and social identity. Abrams questions whether there are other aspects of children's group memberships that need to be examined. In particular, he sees a need for further research that tackles "the processes by which intergroup relationships are defined, sustained, and given continued meaning for children". Second, he remarks that chapters typically focus either on the role of social context or cognitive development, and asserts that our understanding would be enhanced by directing greater attention to the fact that identities presuppose *shared* meanings that in turn depend on social interaction between people. Finally, Abrams comments that research on the development of social identity should be expanded to embrace some of the key controversies that feature in the adult literature – for example, the impact of different motivational elements of identity, and the relationship between communication and social identity.

Durkin considers several major themes, reminding us first that for the dependent infant, social groups are a "raw necessity". The family, as the fundamental social group, provides experiences that will foster children's earliest feelings and cognitions about groups. It is also in the context of family interactions that children will be guided towards socially significant identities, such as gender and ethnicity. The diverse range of social identities that children are afforded, suggests Durkin, may militate against the establishment of a broad overarching developmental framework in that "the development of any one [identity] is multidetermined and intersects with other powerful social processes" so that identities may develop differently. In considering the forces that shape social identity, Durkin goes so far as to note the need to acknowledge *competition* between developmental and social processes, something that further complicates our understanding in this domain. Moreover, he asserts the necessity to give greater prominence to the role of language in the development of social identities. In addition to addressing formative processes, Durkin also notes that identities have consequences, in terms of opportunity, social status, well-being, and so on, and more needs to be understood about such consequences in childhood. In the final part of his chapter, Durkin observes that little is known about changing social identities across the lifespan: "The overwhelming expectation we can derive from the present volume is that we will need to draw on both developmental and social psychological perspectives if we are to investigate adequately the longer-term construction and maintenance of social selves".

REFERENCES

Aboud, F. E. (1988). *Children and prejudice*. Oxford: Blackwell.

Abrams, D., Rutland, A., Cameron, L., & Marques, J. M. (2003). The development of subjective group dynamics: When in-group bias gets specific. *British Journal of Developmental Psychology, 21*, 155–176.

Allport, G. W. (1968). The historical background of modern social psychology. In G. Lindzey & E. Aronson (Eds.), *The handbook of social psychology, Vol. 1* (2nd ed.). Reading, MA: Addison-Wesley.

Baldwin, J. M. (1895). *Mental development of the child and the race: Methods and processes*. New York: Macmillan.

Bigler, R. S., Jones, L. C., & Lobliner, D. B. (1997). Social categorization and the formation of intergroup attitudes in children. *Child Development, 68*, 530–543.

Billig, M. (1976). *Social psychology and intergroup relations*. London: Academic Press.

Brandstädter, J., & Lerner, R. M. (Eds.) (1999). *Action and self-development*. Thousand Oaks, CA: SAGE Publications.

Brehm, S. S., Kassin, S. M., & Gibbons, F. X. (Eds.) (1981). *Developmental social psychology: Theory and research*. New York: Oxford University Press.

Brewer, M. B. (1999). The psychology of prejudice: Ingroup love or outgroup hate? *Journal of Social Issues, 55*, 429–444.

Brooks-Gunn, J., & Lewis, M. (1979). *Social cognition and the acquisition of self*. New York: Plenum Press.

Bruner, J. S. (1957). On perceptual readiness. *Psychological Review, 64*, 123–152.

Case, R. (1992). *The mind's staircase.* Hillsdale, NJ: Lawrence Erlbaum Associates, Inc.

Cooley, C. H. (1902). *Human nature and social order.* New York: Charles Scribner's Sons.

Damon, W., & Hart, D. (1988). *Self-understanding in childhood and adolescence.* New York: Cambridge University Press.

Deaux, K., Reid, A., Mizrahi, K., & Cotting, D. (1999). Connecting the person to the social: The functions of social identification. In T. R. Tyler, R. M. Kramer, & O. P. John (Eds.), *The psychology of the social self.* Mahwah, NJ: Lawrence Erlbaum Associates, Inc.

Demetriou, A., & Kazi, S. (2001). *Self-image and cognitive development: Structure functions and development of self-evaluation and self-representation in adolescence.* London: Routledge.

Doise, W. (1978). *Individuals and groups: Explanations in social psychology.* Cambridge: Cambridge University Press.

Doise, W. (1982). Report on the European Association of Experimental Social Psychology. *European Journal of Social Psychology, 12,* 105–111.

Durkin, K. (1995). *Developmental social psychology: From infancy to old age.* Oxford: Blackwell.

Eckes, T., & Trautner, H. M. (Eds.) (2000). *The developmental social psychology of gender.* Mahwah, NJ: Lawrence Erlbaum Associates, Inc.

Eiser, J. R., & Stroebe, W. (1972). *Categorization and social judgment: European Monographs in Social Psychology, no. 3.* London: Academic Press.

Elms, A. C. (1975). The crisis of confidence in social psychology. *American Psychologist, 30,* 967–976.

Fenigstein, A., Scheier, M. F., & Buss, A. A. (1975). Public and private self consciousness: Assessment and theory. *Journal of Consulting and Clinical Psychology, 43,* 522–527.

Ferguson, C. K., & Kelley, H. H. (1964). Significant factors in over-evaluation of own groups' products. *Journal of Abnormal and Social Psychology, 69,* 223–228.

Fischer, K. W. (1980). A theory of cognitive development: The control and construction of hierarchies of social skills. *Psychological Review, 87,* 477–531.

Flavell, J. H., & Ross, L. (1981). *Social cognitive development.* Cambridge: Cambridge University Press.

Gergen, K. J. (1973). Social psychology and history. *Journal of Personality and Social Psychology, 26,* 309–320.

Harter, S. (1987). The determinants and mediational role of global self worth in children. In N. Eisenberg (Ed.), *Contemporary issues in developmental psychology* (pp. 219–242). New York: John Wiley & Sons.

Harter, S. (1998). The development of self-representations. In W. Damon (Series Ed.) & N. Eisenberg (Vol. Ed.), *Handbook of child psychology: Vol. 3. Social, emotional, and personality development* (5th ed., pp. 553–617). New York: John Wiley & Sons.

Harter, S. (1999). *The construction of the self: A developmental perspective.* New York: Guilford Press.

Haslam, S. A., Oakes, P. J., Turner, J. C., & McGarty, C. (1995). Social categorization and group homogeneity: Changes in the perceived applicability of stereotype content as a function of comparative context and trait favourableness. *British Journal of Social Psychology, 34,* 139–160.

Haslam, S. A. (2001). *Psychology in organizations: The social identity approach.* London: Sage.

Higgins, E. T. (1987). Self-discrepancy: A theory relating self and affect. *Psychological Review*, *94*, 319–340.

Hogg, M. A. (1987). Social identity and group cohesiveness. In J. C. Turner, M. A. Hogg, P. J. Oakes, S. D. Reicher, & M. S. Wetherell (1987), *Rediscovering the social group: A self-categorization theory*. Oxford: Blackwell.

Hogg, M. A., & Abrams, D. (1988). *Social identifications: A social psychology of intergroup relations and group processes*. London: Routledge.

James, W. (1890). *Principles of psychology*. Chicago: Encyclopaedia Britannica.

Jaspars, J. M. F. (1980). The coming of age of social psychology in Europe. *European Journal of Social Psychology*, *10*, 421–429.

Jones, E. E., & Berglas, S. (1978). Control of attributions about the self through self-handicapping strategies: The appeal of alcohol and the role of under achievement. *Personality and Social Psychology Bulletin*, *4*, 200–206.

Keller, A., Ford, L., & Meacham, J. (1978). Dimensions of self-concept in preschool children. *Developmental Psychology*, *14*, 483–489.

Kihlstrom, J. F., & Cantor, N. (1984). Mental representations of the self. In L. Berkowitz (Ed.), *Advances in experimental social psychology, Vol. 17* (pp. 2–40). New York: Academic Press.

Lerner, R. M. (1998). Theories of human development: Contemporary perspectives. In R. M. Lerner (Ed.), *Handbook of child development Vol. 1* (pp. 1–24). New York: Wiley.

Lewis, M., & Brookes-Gunn, J. (1979). *Social cognition and the acquisition of the self*. New York: Plenum Press.

Linville, P. W. (1985). Self-complexity and affective extremity: Don't put all your eggs in one cognitive basket. *Social Cognition*, *3*, 94–120.

Markus, H. (1977). Self-schemata and processing information about the self. *Journal of Personality and Social Psychology*, *35*, 63–78.

Masters, J. C., & Yarkin-Levin, K. (Ed.) (1984). *Boundary areas in social and developmental psychology*. New York: Academic Press.

McGarty, C., & Haslam, S. A. (1997). Introduction and a short history of social psychology. In C. McGarty & S. A. Haslam (Eds.), *The message of social psychology*. Oxford: Blackwell.

McGuire, W. (1973). The yin and yang of progress in social psychology: Seven koan. *Journal of Personality and Social Psychology*, *26*, 446–456.

Mead, G. H. (1934). *Mind, self, and society from the standpoint of a social behaviourist*. Chicago: University of Chicago Press.

Moore, C., & Lemmon, K. (Eds.) (2001). *The self in time*. Mahwah, NJ: Lawrence Erlbaum Associates, Inc.

Oakes, P. J. (1987). The salience of social categories. In J. C. Turner, M. A. Hogg, P. J. Oakes, S. D. Reicher, & M. S. Wetherell (Eds.), *Rediscovering the social group: A self-categorization theory*. Oxford: Blackwell.

Oakes, P. J., Haslam, A., & Turner, J. C. (1994). *Stereotyping and social reality*. Oxford: Blackwell.

Oakes, P. J., Turner, J. C., & Haslam, S. A. (1991). Perceiving people as group members: The role of fit in the salience of social categorizations. *British Journal of Social Psychology*, *30*, 124–144.

Pomerantz, E. M., & Newman, L. S. (2000). Looking in on the children: Using developmental psychology as a tool for hypothesis testing and model building in social psychology. *Personality and Social Psychology Review*, *4*, 300–316.

Rabbie, J. M., & Horwitz, M. (1969). Arousal of ingroup–outgroup bias by a chance win or loss. *Journal of Personality and Social Psychology, 13*, 269–277.

Rabbie, J. M., & Wilkens, G. (1971). Ingroup competition and its effect on intragroup relations. *European Journal of Social Psychology, 1*, 215–234.

Reicher, S. D. (1984). Social influence and the crowd: Attitudinal and behavioural effects of deindividuation in conditions of high and low group salience. *British Journal of Social Psychology, 23*, 341–350.

Reynolds, K. J., Turner, J. C., & Haslam, S. A. (2000). When are we better than them and they worse than us? A closer look at social discrimination in positive and negative domains. *Journal of Personality and Social Psychology, 78*, 64–80.

Ring, K. (1967). Experimental social psychology: Some sober questions about some frivolous values. *Journal of Experimental Social Psychology, 3*, 113–123.

Rochat, P. (2001). Origins of self-concept. In G. Bremner & A. Fogel (Eds.), *Blackwell handbook of infant development* (pp. 191–212). Oxford: Blackwell.

Rosch, E. (1978). Principles of categorization. In E. Roschand & B. B. Lloyd (Eds.), *Cognition and categorization*. Hillsdale, NJ: Lawrence Erlbaum Associates, Inc.

Schlenker, B. (1980). *Impression management: The self-concept, social identity, and interpersonal relations*. Monterey, CA: Brooks/Cole.

Sears, D. O. (1986). College sophomores in the laboratory: Influences of a narrow databasee on social psychology's view of human nature. *Journal of Personality and Social Psychology, 51*, 515–530.

Sherif, M. (1967). *Group conflict and co-operation: Their social psychology*. London: Routledge & Kegan Paul.

Snyder, M. (1974). Individual differences in self-control of expressive behaviour. *Dissertation Abstracts International, 33*, 4533A–4534A.

Steele, C. M. (1988). The psychology of self-affirmation: Sustaining the integrity of the self. In L. Berkowitz (Ed.), *Advances in experimental social psychology, Vol. 21* (pp. 261–302). San Diego, CA: Academic Press.

Swann, W. B., & Read, S. J. (1981). Self-verification processes: How we sustain our self-conceptions. *Journal of Experimental Social Psychology, 17*, 351–370.

Tajfel, H. (1970). Experiments in intergroup discrimination. *Scientific American, 223*, 96–102.

Tajfel, H. (1972). Social categorization. In S. Moscovici (Ed.), *Introduction a la psychologie sociale, Vol. 1*. Paris: Larouse.

Tajfel, H. (1978). *Differentiation between social groups: Studies in the social psychology of intergroup relations*. London: Academic Press.

Tajfel, H. (1981). *Human groups and social categories*. Cambridge: Cambridge University Press.

Tajfel, H. (1984). Intergroup relations, social myths and social justice in psychology. In H. Tajfel (Ed.), *The social dimension, Vol. 2*. Cambridge: Cambridge University Press.

Tajfel, H., Flament, C., Billig, M. G., & Bundy, R. F. (1971). Social categorization and intergroup behaviour. *European Journal of Social Psychology, 1*, 149–177.

Tajfel, H., & Turner, J. C. (1979). An integrative theory of intergroup conflict. In W. G. Austin & S. Worchel (Eds.), *The social psychology of intergroup relations*. Monterey, CA: Brooks/Cole.

Tajfel, H., & Turner, J. C. (1986). The social identity theory of intergroup behaviour. In S. Worchel & W. G. Austin (Eds.), *Psychology of intergroup relations* (2nd ed.). Chicago: Nelson-Hall.

Tajfel, H., & Wilkes, A. L. (1963). Classification and quantitative judgement. *British Journal of Psychology*, *54*, 101–114.

Tesser, A. (1988). Toward a self-evaluation maintenance model of social behaviour. In L. Berkowitz (Ed.), *Advances in experimental social psychology, Vol. 21* (pp. 181–227). New York: Academic Press.

Turner, J. C. (1975). Social comparisons and social identity: Some prospects for intergroup behaviour. *European Journal of Social Psychology*, *5*, 149–178.

Turner, J. C. (1982). Towards a cognitive redefinition of the social group. In H. Tajfel (Ed.), *Social identity and intergroup relations*. Cambridge: Cambridge University Press.

Turner, J. C., Hogg, M. A., Oakes, P. J., Reicher, S. D., & Wetherell, M. S. (1987). *Rediscovering the social group: A self-categorization theory*. Oxford: Blackwell.

Turner, J. C., Oakes, P. J., Haslam, S. A., & McGarty, C. A. (1994). Self and collective: Cognition and social context. *Personality and Social Psychology Bulletin*, *20*, 454–463.

Turner, J. C., & Onorato, R. S. (1999). Social identity, personality, and the self-concept: A self-categorization perspective. In T. R. Tylor, R. M. Kramer, & O. P. John (Eds.), *The psychology of the social self* (pp. 11–46). Mahwah, NJ & London: Lawrence Erlbaum Associates, Inc.

Turner, J. C., & Reynolds, K. J. (2001). The social identity perspective in intergroup relations: Theories, themes, and controversies. In R. Brown & S. Gaertner (Eds.), *Blackwell handbook of social psychology: Intergroup processes* (pp. 133–152). Oxford: Blackwell.

Wills, T. A. (1981). Downward comparison principles in social psychology. *Psychological Bulletin*, *90*, 245–271.

Part I
Basic issues

2 The development of a sense of "we": The emergence and implications of children's collective identity

Diane N. Ruble, Jeannette Alvarez,
Meredith Bachman, Jessica Cameron,
Andrew Fuligni, Cynthia Garcia Coll,
and Eun Rhee

The emergence of the self is one of the most fundamental developmental tasks faced by the young child (see Durkin, 1995; Kohlberg, 1969; Lewis, 1990). Self-concept development begins in early childhood and continues through adolescence and adulthood. This self-concept consists of both a personal self (a sense of self as different from the other) and a social self (a sense of self as connected to the other) (see Brewer & Gardner, 1996). This latter social self consists of not only the selves present when interacting with family and friends, but also with the selves that are a product of the child's membership in particular social groups.

In understanding the development of the self, two primary perspectives have dominated: (1) assessing the structure and content of the personal self-concept at different developmental periods (e.g., Damon & Hart, 1988; Harter, 1983; Livesley & Bromley, 1973) and (2) examining the role of significant others, specifically parents, on the development of the self (e.g., Bowlby, 1980; Cooley, 1902; Higgins, 1991; Mead, 1934). Clearly absent from these approaches is the development of the self that is constructed on the basis of one's membership in particular social categories (e.g., gender, ethnicity/race). Indeed, in Harter's (1998) chapter on the self in the *Handbook of child psychology*, the only mention of social identity is a brief note of the relation between ethnicity and self-esteem.

This is not to say that psychologists have not assessed the development of specific social categories, primarily gender and race, in children. In particular, there has been a focus on the developmental stages necessary for the achievement of gender and racial constancy: identification of the gender/race of self and other, the stability of gender and race over time, and the immutable nature of gender and race (e.g., Aboud & Skerry, 1983, Rhee, Ruble, Awarcz, Stangor, & Jones, 2003b; Ruble & Martin, 1998). This approach has been based on cognitive-developmental theories proposing that understanding the immutability of one's social identities motivates children to learn the relevant norms and act in accordance with them (Kohlberg, 1966). But this perspective is limited to a focus on knowledge and awareness of social categories or labelling oneself as a member of one. What is missing is an account of real identification – a sense of belonging with a particular social group. Hence, this perspective does not address such questions as whether a particular social identity is evaluated positively or negatively, whether it is salient and central to the self-concept, how it influences important developmental outcomes, such as self-esteem and academic engagement, or how it changes as a function of context.

The goal of this chapter is to examine the development and consequences of children's understanding of and identification with social categories. First, we begin with a brief description of previous approaches to social identity in adults and adolescents to provide a theoretical background. Second, we introduce some of the developmental research on the self and highlight why social identification is integral to an understanding of changes in children's self-knowledge. Third, we discuss the current literature on children's developing understanding of social categories and their membership of them. Fourth, we present social-psychological perspectives on the multidimensionality of social identity and review relevant developmental research. Finally, we outline the importance of taking this social psychological approach in understanding the link between social identity, the self-concept, and various developmental outcomes.

THE NATURE OF SOCIAL IDENTITY

Theoretical distinctions

Although the nature and consequences of identification with social groups has not been a focus of much developmental research, such questions have been extensively explored by social psychologists. An individual's social identities have been defined in different ways, but all definitions refer to certain key elements. First, they refer to aspects of the self-concept that are defined in terms of or in relation to other people and groups (e.g., a daughter; a girl) (Ashmore, Jussim, Wilder, & Heppen, 2001). Second, they are socially constructed and interpersonally significant categories (Thoits & Virshup, 1997). Third, certain values and emotional significance are attached to these role or category memberships (Tajfel, 1978).

A detailed discussion of this literature is beyond the scope of this chapter (see Ashmore et al., 2001; Deaux & Martin, 2001, for reviews), but certain constructs are of particular interest for a developmental analysis. One is a distinction within social identity between self as fulfilling a role (e.g., teacher) and self as a member of a collective group (e.g., Asian-American) (Thoits & Virshup, 1997). Although both types of social identity are relevant to childhood, collective identity provides a connection to the long-standing interest in the development of categorisation in the cognitive-development literature (e.g., Gelman & Markman, 1986) as well as representing influential processes during early socialisation (e.g., becoming a girl). Thus, in the present chapter, consistent with this volume's aims, we focus on the development of children's social identities as members of social categories: i.e., collective identity, or what Thoits and Virshup (1997) have labelled the "we".

Collective identities are viewed as serving a number of different motives and having significant personal and interpersonal consequences (see Hewstone, Rubin, & Willis, 2002; and Brewer & Brown, 1998, for reviews). A few of these include feelings of inclusion and a need for differentiation, both of which can be satisfied through identification with optimally distinct groups (Brewer, 1991) and a reduction of uncertainty through social comparison processes and by belonging to groups that provide clear norms (Hogg, 2000). Perhaps most influential in the literature is social identity theory (Tajfel & Turner, 1979), which proposes that individuals strive for positive self-concept, and that identification with and comparison across groups are in the service of this goal. According to Turner (1982), once the self is perceived in terms of group membership the stereotypes that apply to the group such as status, prestige, emotional experiences, goals, norms, and traits will all influence self-perception. The nature of such categorisation and comparison processes are likely to change dramatically between the early and middle elementary school years (Lutz & Ruble, 1995; Ruble & Frey, 1991). Moreover, the mere act of categorising individuals into social groups changes the nature of interpersonal perceptions and behaviours (Tajfel, 1978). For example, there is an increased perception of between-group differences and within-group similarity and increased in-group favouritism. Such "minimal group" changes occur even if the social categories are completely arbitrary (e.g., wearing different coloured teeshirts) (Bigler, Jones, & Lobliner, 1997). For not so minimal social categorisation (i.e., membership in real social groups), consequences can be more critical. In the present chapter, we focus on the development and consequences of collective identity for gender, ethnicity, and race.

Previous approaches to identity development

Social psychologists have also been interested in some developmental aspects of social identification, particularly the process by which adolescents and adults become committed to a particular identity. According to Erikson's (1963) theory of ego identity formation, the development of one's identity arises out of the identity crisis that takes place during the adolescent years. To deal with this fundamental psychosocial crisis, one must engage in a period of exploration of different identities and roles, eventually emerging to commit to specific occupational, political, and ideological identities (Marcia, 1988).

Perhaps the most concerted attempt to take a developmental approach to collective identity has taken place within the study of ethnic identity development during adolescence. For example, Cross's model of nigrescence

(1978), which was based upon the emergence of race-consciousness among black college students during the American civil rights period, included a stage-like progression that began with a period in which one's ethnic identity was never explored ("pre-encounter"). This period was then interrupted by an "encounter", which represented an awakening of the significance of one's race in the social world, followed by an "immersion" stage, which involved extensive exploration of one's race and culture. The ultimate end-point of immersion was internalisation, which was a fuller understanding and acceptance of one's racial and cultural identity.

Similarly, Phinney (1989) outlined a three-stage Eriksonian-type progression that began with an unexamined ethnic identity, followed by an ethnic identity search and exploration, which eventually culminated in an achieved ethnic identity. Though very similar to Cross's model, Phinney's model did not include an encounter event that stimulated an exploration or immersion phase, primarily because Phinney developed a model with several different ethnic groups in mind.

Although both models implied a developmental progression through stages, they have been examined mostly from an individual-differences perspective. That is, adolescents or young adults have been categorised according to their stage or status, and subsequently compared in terms of personality traits and well-being (Phinney, 1990). Rarely have the stages of ethnic identity development been examined within the same individuals over time in order to test whether there is indeed a typical ordering of stages. Although some evidence exists to suggest that older adolescents are more likely to reach "higher" levels of identity development than younger adolescents, it is unclear as to the order at which these youths progressed through the hypothesised stages (Phinney & Chavira, 1992).

The extent to which an encounter is necessary for ethnic or racial identity development is also unclear. Such a possibility has been acknowledged recently by Cross and Fhagen-Smith (2001), who suggest that the majority of African-American children do develop some type of black identity as a result of their socialisation experiences inside and outside of the family, implying that an encounter phase may not be essential. Moreover, both Cross and Phinney have recently suggested that the final stages of their original models are not developmental end states, and that individuals may "revisit" earlier stages and continue to explore the meaning of their ethnic and racial identity throughout the lifespan (Cross & Fhagen-Smith, 2001; Phinney, 1996). It will be interesting in future research to examine how collective context (e.g., the quality of interracial relationships, or being of majority or minority status) relates to the emergence or re-emergence of these stages.

WHEN AND HOW DO CHILDREN UNDERSTAND AND IDENTIFY WITH SOCIAL CATEGORIES?

The fact that previous research on the development of social identification has focused primarily on adolescence and adulthood, rather than childhood, is surprising in two ways. First, the developmental literature clearly demonstrates that social categories, particularly gender and race, are salient and meaningful categories for young children (see, e.g., Aboud, 1988; Ruble & Martin, 1998). Second, the acquisition of self as distinct from others, yet connected to others, is a primary goal of social development (Ruble & Goodnow, 1998). Thus, from infancy until adolescence, individuals are formulating a sense of identity based both on their characteristics, abilities, and preferences (psychological self) and on their social identification with parents, peers, and social groups (social self).

Yet the personal self, rather than the social self, has been the primary emphasis of developmental researchers. Of particular interest have been the developmental changes in the self-concept that occur between early childhood and middle childhood. Prior to the age of 7–8 years, children's self-descriptions typically refer to external characteristics and social relationships (e.g., "I am a boy, my name is Jason. I live with my father and mother in a big house", Harter, 1998, p. 47). By the age of 8 years, children's self-descriptions consist of statements that refer more to stable trait-like characteristics (Livesley & Bromley, 1973; Newman & Ruble, 1988) and evaluative statements that involve comparisons with others (Ruble & Frey, 1991). Although children's self-descriptions clearly suggest a developmental progression from the concrete to the psychological, experimental research suggests that young children can use psychological terms with reference to self and others (e.g., Bretherton, McNew, & Beeghly-Smith, 1981; Wellman, 1990) and show an understanding of global evaluative personal characteristics, such as good or mean (Eder, 1990; Ruble & Dweck, 1995). Nevertheless, it is not until middle childhood that persons, including the self, are viewed as having a more general, stable, organising structure that directs behaviours (Rholes, Newman, & Ruble, 1990). Moreover, children's sense of the stability and predictability of people is no longer conceived primarily through global evaluations (good or bad person), but also through recognition of individual differences in dispositional characteristics (Alvarez, Ruble, & Bolger, 2001).

These changes in self and other perceptions during early to middle childhood should have important implications for both children's understanding of social categories and their identification with them. First, social categories, particularly gender and race, should no longer be seen as referring to overt physical characteristics (e.g., long hair, dark skin), but should now begin to take on deeper meanings. Second, group membership becomes a comparative process, whereby information about social categories received from the social environment can be used to imbue social categories with evaluative meaning (see J. A. Cameron, Alvarez, Ruble, & Fuligni, 2001). Hence, collective identities may become quite significant to children's self-concept, at least by middle childhood, particularly in an environment where a social category membership is salient (e.g., only black child in a class) or where a social category is made central (e.g., parents teaching their child about what it means to be Mexican).

A recent ethnographic study conducted by Connolly (1998) supports our claim that social identity development must be examined in young children. Finding fault with the lack of social scientific research that was focused on young children's conceptualisations of their social worlds, Connolly spent a year observing and conducting unstructured interviews with 5- and 6-year-old children in an English multi-ethnic, inner-city primary school. Based on this research, Connolly argues that many young children play an active role in negotiating their identities through drawing upon discourses on race, class, gender, and age. Connolly's work is admittedly ethnographic and provides a description of just one specific community. However, transcripts from his studies highlight the manner in which very young children often do spontaneously discuss race, gender, and other social groupings in a sophisticated manner. This leads Connolly to question the appropriateness of making assumptions about children's cognitive ability or their level of awareness on matters of race, gender, or sexuality simply by their age. To us, this work signals the need for a comprehensive exploration of social identity formation in young children employing developmental psychological methods.

In short, ignoring collective identity development in younger children may be a serious omission. Middle childhood (ages 7–10) would seem to be a key period in which to examine the incorporation of social category memberships into the emerging self-concept. It is during this period that children's sense of self becomes more complex as they are exposed to a new social environment outside of the family. As such this is one of the most important social transitions for development (see Ruble, 1994; Ruble & Seidman, 1996). At school, children must learn the specific roles, rules, and expectations associated with peer and teacher relations (e.g., Akiba, Garcia Coll, & Magnuson, 2001; Higgins & Parsons, 1983). It is through these interactions with peers and teachers that children develop new social roles (e.g., student) and collective identities (e.g., Asian), revise current social identities beyond that of the family, adopt or contest the prevalent social valences associated with each category, and integrate all of these identities into a coherent self-concept.

Despite the relative lack of attention to social or collective identity in reviews on the development of self, several sets of literature provide information about certain aspects of children's understanding of and identification with social categories. In this section, we review those literatures and attempt to integrate them around the question of the developmental course of children's sense of "we".

The development of social category knowledge and identification

The major social categories relevant to young children are those that involve clear physical differences – sex and race – suggesting perhaps that children's early understanding of social categories begins with an awareness of physical differences and similarities. Although one might surmise that age would also be a salient social identity, it has not attracted research interest. There is an extensive body of literature examining infants' and young children's understanding of categorical sex and a comparable literature on slightly older children's understanding of categorical race. These findings are reviewed with respect to three basic levels of children's developing understanding— awareness, identification, and constancy – integrating findings of studies of sex and of race when possible.

Awareness

The term "awareness" is often used very generally to refer to any behaviour suggesting a response on the basis of sex or race, such as preferences and attitudes (e.g., Brand, Ruiz, & Padilla, 1974; Newman, Liss, & Sherman, 1983). In this section, we use the term much more specifically to refer only to children's ability to distinguish the sexes or races or to label them correctly, regardless of whether they view themselves correctly as a member of one or prefer one or the other.

Until recently, studies of awareness have examined children's ability to point to or sort photographs in response to social category labels or to generate the correct label. Studies of gender categories (see Ruble & Martin, 1998, for a review) have shown that many children begin to label the sexes shortly after their second birthdays, at least half can do so by 2½ years of age, and virtually all can sort photographs on the basis of sex by 3 years of age (Leinbach & Fagot, 1986; Thompson, 1975; Weinraub, Clemens, Sockloff, Ethridge, Gracely, & Myers, 1984). Interestingly, the ability to label adult males and females occurs somewhat earlier than the ability to label children (Leinbach & Fagot, 1986). Children's ability to label the races seems to occur a bit later, after 3 years of age (Katz & Kofkin, 1997), but awareness of ethnicity and racial categories seems to develop rapidly after 4 years of age (Aboud & Amato, 2001).

Recent studies using habituation techniques have suggested, however, that infants are capable of discriminating social categories at some level by 12 months of age (Leinbach & Fagot, 1993) and perhaps even younger. For example, in one study, after viewing repeated instances of faces of a single sex or race, the face of an unseen sex or race category was found to elicit more looking in 6-month-olds than a novel but same sex or race face (Katz & Kofkin, 1997). Interestingly, these researchers found that African-American infants were more sensitive to racial cues than were European-American infants. Such findings suggest that social category awareness may emerge before preschool age, but it is important at this point to be cautious. Not all studies find such awareness of race so young (e.g., Fagan & Singer, 1979), and the level of social category understanding required for perceptual discrimination of faces may be quite minimal.

Identification

When can children verbally label themselves accurately in terms of social categories? The findings suggest that children can label their own sex and place a picture of themselves with other same-sex children by approximately 24–36 months of age, but there is considerable variability across children and studies and this ability does not necessarily show a parallel to the ability to label others (Ruble & Martin, 1998). For example, one recent study found that the majority of children at 30 months of age were able to identify themselves using gender labels but were unable to do so for others (Katz & Kofkin, 1997). Research with infants has not yet tackled directly the question of how early young children show even implicit understanding of their own category membership. It is known that children develop a concept of themselves as a distinct physical entity by 18 months of age and that this achievement precedes other self-related developments, such as the use of self-referential terms (Stipek, Gralinski, & Kopp, 1990). Moreover, some research suggests that infants' knowledge of attributes associated with gender categories increases substantially during the second year of life (see Martin, Ruble, & Szkrybalo, 2002).

Studies of children's racial or ethnic labelling and identification have not typically looked at very young children. Some studies suggest that children's abilities to self-identify using racial labels emerges soon after the awareness of categorical sex, between the ages of 4 and 5 (Ramsey, 1991; Rhee & Ruble, 1997). In one recent study examining the emergence of sex and racial identification in the same children, Katz and Kofkin (1997) reported that by 3 years of age, most (77%) of the Euro-American children accurately self-labelled based on race, but only 32% of the African-American children did so. The authors argue that this difference is not a cognitive one, because the African-American children performed equally well on gender labelling and had no difficulty performing a racial sorting task that did not require the use of a verbal label. Instead, they suggest that race labels may produce more conflict in African-American children.

Most studies have examined children's ability to discriminate between children with black and white skin in both self- and other-identification, but some studies of ethnic identification have shown similar effects. For example, Vaughan (1963) reported that Maori and Pakeha children could classify themselves correctly by age 4 years. There appears to be considerable variability across studies, however, as to when ethnic identity is learnt, perhaps because ethnic awareness may require an understanding of relatively complex features such as customs and beliefs (Aboud, 1984; Bernal & Knight, 1997). Taken together, these various findings suggest that the ability to label oneself in terms of race or ethnicity may emerge between 3 and 5 years of age, but other factors determine whether or not children do accurately self-identify at this age. Moreover, it is not clear whether, at this age, such identification means anything more than empty labels (e.g., "I'm Mexican because my mother said so"; Bernal & Knight, 1993, p. 35).

Constancy

Kohlberg (1966) argued that when children learn that a social category is not changeable, they have achieved a new level of understanding. According to his cognitive-developmental model, children's comprehension of social category membership changes in accordance with cognitive development, specifically the acquisition of conservation. He proposed three stages leading to children's comprehension of the immutability of sex category membership: (1) accurate *identification* of category membership for oneself and others; (2) *stability* of category membership over time; and (3) *consistency* of category membership across superficial transformations in appearance or context. According to Kohlberg, the development of this understanding was highly significant, because once children understood the unchanging nature of being a boy or a girl, mastery motives propel them to seek out information about what is appropriate for their sex and to behave in accordance with the conclusions that they draw (Stangor & Ruble, 1987). Similar motivational processes would seem to apply to racial constancy, and a few researchers have examined this hypothesis (e.g., Bernal, Knight, Garza, Ocampo, & Cota, 1990; Ocampo, Bernal, & Knight, 1993; Semaj, 1980).

The literature generally suggests that gender constancy develops in three stages (identity, stability, and consistency) between 3 and 7 years of age. There is some controversy about the exact developmental time course, however, due largely to methodological issues. For example, the attainment of gender constancy can vary depending on whether children are provided only with a forced-choice measure (e.g., requiring only a yes or no response) or are additionally asked to explain their choices (Ruble & Martin, 1998). Although many 3- to 4-year-old children give mostly correct responses to forced-choice questions about whether, for example, a boy would still be a boy if he had long hair or wore a dress, it is not until 6–7 years of age that most children can explain their responses in a way that indicates true constancy understanding (Szkrybalo & Ruble, 1999).

Relatively few studies have examined the development of racial or ethnic constancy. The findings have suggested that this kind of constancy develops later than gender constancy, sometime between 7 and 9 years of age in white children (Aboud & Ruble, 1987; Ocampo et al., 1993). The exact developmental trajectory varies considerably, depending on whether race or ethnicity is being examined and depending on the race or ethnicity of the children

participating in the study (Bernal et al., 1990; Semaj, 1980). The later development of race or ethnicity constancy may be because it is less salient than
gender in the young child's environment (Aboud, 1988), but it may also be
due to measurement issues such as the use of perceptual transformation
measures (e.g., Aboud & Skerry, 1983), which may be more difficult than
verbal measures.

One recent study, conducted in a racially heterogeneous community, used
comparable measures for gender and racial constancy and found similar
developmental patterns for the two types of constancy (Rhee & Ruble, 1997).
Children's understanding of gender and racial constancy developed in the
same stage progression (identity, stability, consistency). In addition, both
gender and racial constancy developed significantly with age and were correlated with each other. Furthermore, when children were asked to explain their
responses, similar responses were found for the two types of constancy:
operational reasoning (e.g., "that's the way God made him and he cannot
change") for constant responses, and norm reasoning (e.g., "only girls have
long hair") for nonconstant responses. Moreover, for European-American
children, understanding gender and racial constancy increased with age in a
parallel fashion. That is, in contrast to previous findings that racial constancy
developed considerably later than gender constancy, most 7-year-olds showed
constancy understanding for both social identities (83% for gender and 73%
for race). For African-American and Asian-American children, however, the
proportion of children who understood constancy was much lower for race
than for sex. For these groups, gender constancy understanding increased
with age in parallel with the European-American children, but only one in
four of the Asian-American children and one in three of the African-
American children showed racial constancy understanding by age 7.

Interpreting the pattern of developmental findings

According to social-cognitive theories, changes in children's understanding
of social categories mirrors changes in children's cognitive development (see,
e.g., Aboud, 1988; Kohlberg, 1969). For example, in the Rhee and Ruble
(1997) study, parallel findings in gender and racial constancy provide
supportive evidence for the role of cognition. In other words, when children
understand the Piagetian principle of conservation, such that classes of
categories, even social categories, are indicative of specific seemingly inherent, immutable properties of objects and persons, children understand the
permanence of social category membership.

As argued by Katz (1983), however, children's social cognitive processes
cannot be understood without considering both social and cognitive factors
(see also Bigler, 1995). Although cognitive factors can explain some of the
changes in social category understanding, social context factors can often
provide better explanations for some of the findings. First, gender identification occurs prior to racial identification for both the self and others, possibly

because children are constantly exposed to distinctions between boys and girls in appearance and in behaviour from the moment they are born (Bem, 1981,1983; Katz & Kofkin, 1997).

Second, several studies report differences in majority and minority children's social category understanding. Specifically, African-American children have been found to be (1) more aware of race, (2) less accurate in racial identification than European-American children, and (3) achieve racial constancy later than European-American children and achieve gender constancy prior to racial constancy (similar results were found for Asian-American children). A social context account would seem to be implicated in these findings, given that cognitive understanding of constancy was demonstrated for gender. For European-American children, racial identification is simple, as they comprise the majority group, not only in numbers but also in the sense of representing the norm and the group in power. Within this context, African-American children may need to be more flexible about race (Harrison, Wilson, Pine, Chan, & Buriel, 1990; Katz & Kofkin, 1997) as they face the challenge of identifying with both their own racial and ethnic group and the larger European-American society (see Alejandro-Wright, 1985; Cross, 1985).

A final, possible social-motivational explanation is that minority children's awareness of the social status of their respective groups leads them to either disidentify with their group or to perceive race as changeable. Thus, consistent with the verbal labelling findings described above (Katz & Kofkin, 1997), and consistent with previous suggestions in the literature (e.g., Spencer, 1984), racial minority children may know their group membership but choose not to view themselves as inevitably linked to their group because they sense that it is devalued relative to the majority group. Although this hypothesis has not been tested directly, there are some supportive findings. For example, in one study, kindergarten and second-grade children were shown drawings of a white, Hispanic, and black child and asked a preference question, "which one would you like to be?" (Newman et al., 1983). The findings showed that whereas most European-American children (especially at second grade) selected their own group, the black and Hispanic children tended not to select their own ethnicity, possibly suggesting that they were aware of the lower status of their own group. To examine these alternative possible social-motivational explanations, further future research should assess children's understanding of status differences more directly. In addition, future studies (like those of Verkuyten, Chapter 7) should examine minority children in different contexts, ones likely to vary in the extent to which they make children feel valued, such as multicultural versus regular classrooms, or homogeneous settings (where they are the majority) versus heterogeneous settings (where they are in the minority). More generally, such differences across groups raises a question about the meaning of social identities to children of different ages and backgrounds, a topic we turn to next.

Developmental changes in the meaning of a sense of "we"

What exactly does it mean when children say they are or are not a member of a particular social group? At the earliest levels, it seems mostly to be based on physical correlates of gender and race. In other words, children label themselves and others as being a member of a social category by noticing, for example, that girls have long hair and wear dresses (Ruble & Martin, 1998). Similarly, Spencer (1985) notes that young children use racial terms before they understand their functional character. That is, young children become aware of skin colour before they begin to understand that it will place them in a particular racial group (Semaj, 1985). For instance, when young children refer to their brown skin, it is probably not connected to being socially labelled in our society as African-American (Spencer, 1988), nor to refer to a racial or ethnic group of individuals (Holmes, 1995).

Once children understand constancy, however, their social category understanding should become more sophisticated, as they realise that changes in physical appearance do not lead to changes in social category membership. That is, children's comprehension of social categories changes from one based on superficial, physical characteristics to one based on socially constructed intrinsic properties. Nevertheless, even once children understand constancy, it is still not clear to what extent such identities reflect a sense of connection to other members of the group, including heritage, family, country, class, and so on. Relatively little research has tried to trace the development changes in the meaning and significance of social category labels.

In a large study of ethnic identity in children from many different backgrounds, Quintana (1998) characterised children's understanding of ethnicity and race in terms of four developmental levels. At the first level, which emerges between the ages of 3 and 6 years, racial/ethnic differences are primarily seen as physical, so that racial status is perceived as changeable (i.e., not constant). So, for example, if someone's skin gets dark because they have a tan, young children conclude that the person's race has changed. At the second level, which develops between the ages of 6 and 10, racial/ethnic differences are viewed in terms of concrete cultural practices, such as food preferences, language, and activities. To illustrate, in our ongoing study of Russian, Dominican, and Chinese immigrant second and fourth graders, being Chinese for one second grader meant "You just talk Chinese, not English, and not Spanish" and being Dominican for one second grader meant "You were born in the Dominican Republic".

Between the ages of 10 and 14, children recognise the broader implications of racial/ethnic differences, such as the link to social class and allocation of resources. In other words, it is at this third level of identity that children clearly are aware of the social status differences between racial/ethnic groups, and the stereotypes and evaluations associated with these groups. Furthermore, children at this age often begin to identify more closely with their racial/ethnic group and want to associate more with members of this group. Thus, this is the age when children often segregate themselves into same-race/ ethnicity friendship groups. It is not until adolescence, however, that a clearer sense of belonging to a group is forged. Thus, it is at this fourth level of identification that pride in racial/ethnic heritage becomes expressed.

In short, Quintana's analysis, taken together with previous findings, suggests that before the age of approximately 10 years, social categorisation and identification is based on external characteristics, such as possessing certain physical characteristics or engaging in particular activities. After this age, a more sophisticated understanding of social categories develops as these categories are viewed as meaningful constructs both in society and for themselves. In other words, social categories are now internal social constructs rather than simply external descriptions of what a person looks like or does.

Others do not advocate this developmental account, whereby children under the age of 10 years simply view social categories as externally fixed constructs. Specifically, Hirschfeld (1995) argues that young children are not simply relying on perceptual cues when they make distinctions based on racial categories. Whereas perceptually based theories predict that young children's reasoning is based on surface cues rather than abstract, non-obvious criteria, Hirschfeld argues that young children have biologically grounded adult-like theories of race. According to Hirschfeld, adults "appeal to the notion that race emerges from a material but non-obvious, and typically unspecifiable essence, part of each individual's underlying nature derived from group membership" (p. 217). He argues that children also have a complex essentialised theory of race that is based on a domain-specific disposition to view the world in terms of discrete human kinds. In support of his contention, Hirschfeld demonstrated that 3-year-old children expect race (but not other characteristics such as body build) to be derived from family background and that by 4 years of age children believe that race is fixed by birth, biologically mediated, and immutable.

This, along with other similar findings by Hirschfeld, seems to contradict both the racial constancy findings and Quintana's stage model. (See, too, Sani & Bennett, Chapter 3.) These disparate findings need not be contradictory, however. It is possible that children at young ages are aware of the biological nature of race in the sense of being sensitive to the hereditary component of certain physical characteristics (e.g., dark skin). Yet they may still not understand the relation between the biology of physical characteristics of race and the immutability of the social categories of race and gender. In other words, even though these studies ask questions that are similar on some levels, they may in actuality be addressing different issues (i.e., biology, stability, and meaning). Thus, future research should try to incorporate different measures in order to assess children's complete understanding of racial categories.

DEVELOPMENTAL CHANGES IN THE SIGNIFICANCE OF COLLECTIVE IDENTITY

Awareness and knowledge of one's own and others' category memberships is a somewhat limited view of the development of collective identity. Social psychologists have increasingly come to the understanding that simply knowing that an individual is a member of a social group is not enough to predict the consequences that will stem from their membership. For example, according to Tajfel and Turner's social identity theory (1979, 1986), a person must internalise an identity and incorporate the identity into their self-concept before group membership will have personal consequences. Unfortunately, models of social identity development have overlooked the need to include such additional aspects of identifying with a social category. Highlighting this oversight, Parke and Buriel's (1998) critique of early ethnicity models states, "ethnicity was equated with culture as if all members of an ethnic group were equally involved with the ethnic culture" (p. 495). In this section, we argue that to assess the link between collective identity and specific developmental outcomes, collective identity, even in childhood, must be viewed as a multidimensional construct.

Collective identity and its multidimensionality

Previous research with adolescents and adults has examined in considerable depth the various dimensions of social identification (e.g., Luhtanen & Crocker, 1992; Phinney, 1990) and have found that many consequences of collective identity are mediated by the meaning a person derives from group membership. For example, Sellers, Rowley, Chavous, Shelton, and Smith (1997) developed the Multidimensional Model of Racial Identity (MMRI) of African-American racial identity that reflects the multifaceted nature of social identities. Specifically, four dimensions of racial identity are evaluated: salience (the extent to which individuals' race is a relevant part of their self-concept at a particular moment in time), centrality (the extent to which individuals normatively define themselves with regard to race), ideology (the individuals' beliefs, opinions, and attitudes with regard to the way that the members of their race should act), and regard (the individuals' affective and evaluative judgment of their race).

Each of these components of identity has unique characteristics that relate differentially to specific outcomes. For example, Rowley, Sellers, Chavous, and Smith (1998) found that personal regard for African-Americans predicted self-esteem only for African-American college students who reported that race was central to their self-concept. Similarly regarding gender, J. E. Cameron and Lalonde (2001) found that in-group ties, centrality, and in-group affect were empirically distinct components of gender identity that were differentially related to gender-related beliefs and behaviours. For example, women with higher perceptions of in-group ties and greater gender centrality demonstrated more egalitarian views than women with lower perceptions of in-group ties and less gender centrality.

We propose that developmental researchers interested in social identities must investigate how young children think about and understand their social group memberships in a complex and comprehensive manner, reflective of the important findings derived from the social-psychological literature. In the following section, we highlight some of the important social identity dimensions (salience, centrality, knowledge, and evaluation), which we believe clarify the link between collective identity and the overall self-concept and subsequent developmental outcomes.

Salience

Social category salience, or the concept that individuals may be more "ready" to perceive and process information relevant to elaborated or interconnected categories, has been prominent in the cognitive schema literature (e.g., Bem, 1981; Martin & Halverson, 1981; Ruble & Stangor, 1986; Signorella, Bigler, & Liben, 1993). Several different methods have been used to assess social category salience in children. Reaction-time measures, which look at the speed with which persons respond to social category information, have found individual differences in the salience of gender and race (Carter & Levy, 1988; Levy, 2000; Levy & Carter, 1989). Specifically, as early as preschool, social category salience predicts differences in memory and stereotyping of gender and race. In addition, researchers have used a "who said what" method, developed by Taylor, Fiske, Etcoff, and Ruderman (1978), as an unobtrusive measure of spontaneous categorisation. Studies using this procedure have shown that children as young as 5 years of age spontaneously assimilate information to social categories, and that salience effects assessed in this way do not change between 5 and 11 years of age (Bennett & Sani, 2001; Bennett & Sani, 2003; Bennett, Sani, Hopkins, Agostini, & Malucchi, 2000). In these studies, salience effects were only found for social categories that have clear perceptual cues (race and sex); for more conceptual social categories (e.g., English vs. Scottish), no salience effect was found.

The primary means for assessing social category salience in children, however, has been through the use of sorting tasks. When shown pictures of people who can be classified along several social dimensions, children prefer to sort by race and sex (e.g., Bigler & Liben, 1993; Ramsey, 1991; Ramsey & Myers, 1990). Some studies find children using sex over race in the sorting of photographs (e.g., Bigler & Liben, 1993), whereas other studies find children using race over sex (e.g., Ramsey, 1991; Yee & Brown, 1988). The differential salience of these social categories is often the result of differences in methodology (Brown, 1995). To illustrate, Davey (1983) found that children use race when asked to sort the pictures that go together, but use sex when asked to show which children play together. In addition, Ramsey and Myers (1990) found that children used sex when sorting on the basis of similarity but used race when sorting on the basis of dissimilarity.

Relative salience also depends on context and developmental level. Previous research suggests that social identity salience varies as a function of context, such as being the only child of a particular race or sex in a group (e.g., McGuire, McGuire, Child, & Fujioka, 1978; Verkuyten, Chapter 7). Similarly, when the context emphasises social categories, such as when gender is used as a basis for classroom organisation (e.g., having boys and girls line up separately to go out for recess), children may become predisposed to process information in terms of gender (Bigler, 1995). Moreover, the wider cultural or structural context may make certain social identities chronically salient for some groups of children but not for others. For instance, Holmes (1995) found that when children were describing their self-portraits, all of the African-American children emphasised their skin colour, whereas European-American children were less likely to do so. She suggests that for the African-American children, skin colour is not simply an overt characteristic but rather is basic to self and group identity and is highlighted by being in a context dominated by European-American persons and culture.

In terms of the influence of development on the relative salience of gender and race, some research suggests that sorting by race increases between 4–7 years of age, presumably in response to increasing awareness of racial categories (Aboud, 1988; Davey, 1983). As other social information (e.g., race, facial expressions) becomes more informative in social judgments, sex salience decreases (e.g., Serbin & Sprafkin, 1986; Yee & Brown, 1992). The attainment of constancy may also influence salience. In one study, sex-related salience was higher for children at more advanced levels of gender constancy (Coker, 1984). In a recent study, the role of age and racial constancy in the salience of both sex and race was assessed in 5- to 10-year-old African-American, Asian-American, and European-American children (Rhee et al., 2003b). When children were asked to sort photographs on the basis of similarity, race was used more than sex at all age levels. When children were asked to select the photograph that was the most like them, however, they overwhelmingly selected on the basis of sex, but constant children selected on the basis of race about half of the time

In short, several lines of research suggest that sex- and race-based social categories may be salient to children at a young age. Sorting measures suggest that race may be somewhat more salient than sex; but, as suggested by social identity theorists, relative salience of a particular social category may depend heavily on context (Sani & Bennett, 2001). Finally, studies examining the development of salience show mixed findings, and the variability in age-related trends across studies and measures suggests that more theoretically based developmental analyses are needed. For example, some evidence suggests that sex and race may become more salient as a function of increasing knowledge about the constancy of these social categories.

How do these findings regarding the salience of social categories relate to the salience of these categories for the self-concept? Research on the development of both the self-concept and person perception has found that social identities are not frequently mentioned spontaneously about the self or others (e.g., Damon & Hart, 1988; Livesley & Bromley, 1973; Ramsey, 1991). One might predict, however, that collective identity, particularly race and ethnicity, would be quite salient in the self-concept of some children, specifically children of colour and children of recent immigrants. Research by some of the present authors (Akiba, DiMartino, & Rodriguez, 2001a; Akiba & Garcia Coll, in press: Akiba et al., 2001b; Alvarez, Cameron, Garfinkle, Ruble, & Fuligni, 2001) assessed salience using measures of accessibility: whether or not sex and racial identity was listed among the first few attributes when children were asked to describe themselves. In these studies, children older than 7–8 years focused heavily on personality characteristics, but not on race/ethnicity and gender, consistent with prior research on developmental changes in self-perceptions (e.g., Newman & Ruble, 1988). However, some ethnic differences were found. Specifically, the Alvarez et al. study of second- to fourth-grade Dominican and Chinese children of immigrants found that even though most children rarely spontaneously mentioned sex, race/ethnicity, or age, Chinese children were more likely to refer to ethnicity, especially as they got older. Akiba and Garcia Coll found that 6- to 12-year-old children of colour were more likely to mention race, ethnicity, or language than were European-American children, but this difference did not change with age, nor was it salient enough to replace the other common sources of identity, such as activity preferences.

These data suggest that there are wide individual and group differences in how salient various social categories are to the self-concept. Several factors might be influential. For example, variation in homogeneity of school populations might make race or ethnicity more or less salient. In addition, self-presentational concerns taken together with the conflictual nature of race and ethnic identities might make it difficult for a child to mention such identities spontaneously. One might suspect that immigrant children would be especially hesitant because of parental directives to blend in as much as possible. Thus, it will be important in future research to consider alternative means of assessing social identity salience. In particular, measures that avoid the sensitivity of mentioning race while at the same time allowing comparisons to multiple identities may be necessary to more fully understand the developmental course of social identity salience. Furthermore, future research must examine the moderating influence of context to assess how individual and group differences influence collective identity salience.

Centrality

A number of investigators have identified the personal importance, strength, or centrality of identification with a social category as a critical component of social identity (Luhtanen & Crocker, 1992; Sellers, Smith, Shelton, Rowley,

& Chavous, 1998). Centrality refers, in part, to the importance of a particular social identity in relation to other aspects of identity, and in part, to the frequency and preference for engaging in group-related activities and sense of attachment to group members (Phinney, 1992). It may also be represented in terms of a hierarchy, such that features assuming a superordinate position are more inclusive, presumably more important, and having great implications for action (Ashmore & Ogilvie, 1992; Ogilvie & Ashmore, 1991). Centrality differs from salience in that salience usually refers to a particular moment or situation, whereas centrality refers to the extent to which individuals define themselves in terms of a particular identity across situations (see Sellers et al., 1998). Nonetheless they are related, in that a particular identity is likely to be salient in more situations for individuals for whom that identity is a central part of their self-concept. In addition, if features of the environment make a particular identity salient, it is likely to become a more central identity in that context.

The centrality of identity has not been directly addressed in studies of either the development of social category knowledge or self-concept. It seems possible, however, that centrality is a key aspect of social identity constancy and possibly the primary consequence of the attainment of constancy (see Semaj, 1980). That is, at the point that children learn that gender or race is an unchanging part of their self-concept, these social categories become central aspects of their self-concept (Lutz & Ruble, 1995). Based on the developmental trends in constancy described above, one might predict that gender would become particularly central between 5–8 years of age, with race following shortly after. An alternative developmental account, based on social learning theory, argues that socialisation pressures to behave in accordance with category norms is gradually internalised such that basic self-regulatory processes maintain normative behaviour (Bussey & Bandura, 1999). Based on this account, one might predict that a particular social identity assumes greater centrality as self-regulatory processes assume behavioural control, presumably at about the same age as constancy, or perhaps a bit earlier (Bussey & Bandura, 1992). Thus, differences in socialisation could also account for individual or group differences in centrality.

It is difficult to measure self-perceptions of centrality in young children, and thus these hypotheses have not been directly tested. However, the studies on children of immigrants by the present authors, mentioned earlier, have attempted to assess social identity centrality in various ways during middle childhood. In the Alvarez et al. (2001) study, Dominican and Chinese children in the second–fourth grades were presented with seven social identities on index cards in the following order: age, gender, basic ethnicity, daughter/son, best ethnic descriptor, student, and American. Basic ethnicity referred to the nationality of the child's family (Dominican or Chinese). Best ethnic descriptor was determined by presenting children with index cards labelled with all of the ethnic words they said were about them (except American) and then asking them to choose the word that best described them.

Children were then asked three centrality measures. The first, based on Aboud and Skerry's (1983) measure, asked children to identify their most important identity. Specifically, children were asked "What is the most important thing about you, so important that without it you could no longer be yourself?" The results showed that best ethnic descriptor (chosen by 25% of the children), gender (23%), and son/daughter (23%) were the most likely to be chosen as the most important identity, and American was least likely (3%). Interestingly, what children meant by ethnicity was generally not their basic ethnicity (Dominican or Chinese) but rather their ethnic identity hyphenated with American (e.g., Chinese-American, Dominican-American). Open-ended responses suggested that children often selected these identities because it allowed them to combine their ethnic identity with their American identity.

The second measure involved an open-ended ranking procedure, where children were asked to rank order their social identities by placing numbers (1 through 7) on each of the index cards. The results of this ranking measure of centrality revealed a similar pattern: son/daughter, gender, and best ethnic descriptor were ranked highest; American was ranked the lowest. The third measure, adapted from Willer and Romney (1988), consisted of a paired-comparison ranking. In this procedure, children were asked a total of 15 paired-comparison questions in which they were given two social identities and asked,"which word is more important to you?" Even in this more stringent paired-comparison format children ranked the importance of their social identities similarly. In this case, however, when the different identities were clearly pitted against each other, son/daughter was chosen more often relative to gender or best ethnic descriptor.

In the Akiba et al. (2001b) study, centrality was assessed using a method, adapted from Erkut, Garcia Coll, and Alarcon (1998), in which children were asked to indicate which of a large number of descriptors (gender, religion, race, ethnicity, nationality) were "about them". They were then asked to rank order the selected labels in order of personal importance. The results showed that European-American (41%), African-American (37%), and Asian-American (33%) children selected boy or girl as the word that best described them, whereas Latino-American children (26%) were more likely to select an ethnic term (e.g., Latino). Not surprisingly, ethnicity was more "central" for immigrant children, whereas gender was more central for American-born children. For the next most important label, European-American children were most likely to select "American", whereas other children were more likely to select race or ethnicity-related words. Thus, in this study, like the Alvarez et al. study, both gender and race/ethnicity were viewed as quite central relative to other possible identity labels, and race and ethnic descriptors were particularly central for non-white children and for immigrant children.

Akiba et al. (2001a) used a somewhat different measure of centrality in their study of over 400 first- and fourth-grade children from immigrant (Portuguese, Dominican, and Cambodian) families. Specifically, they examined the proportion of minority (e.g., Latino, Cambodian) versus majority (e.g., white, American) labels the children selected when asked "are you —?". In addition, children ranked each label selected in terms of importance, as in the above two studies, and then weighted factors were created by adding the weights for minority- versus majority-related labels. Both measures showed an age by ethnicity interaction, as there was an age-related increase in the centrality of minority labels and a decrease in the centrality of majority labels only for Cambodian and Dominican children. Minority labels were less central to Portuguese children, and relative centrality did not change with age. In short, this study suggests that the centrality of basic ethnicity may increase between first and fourth grades, except perhaps for white (Portuguese) immigrant children who probably identify with American and white with increasing age.

In summary, across several different measures and samples, these studies indicate that gender and ethnicity are reasonably central to children during the early to middle years of school, relative to other social identities, suggesting that collective identity is a worthwhile focus of study prior to adolescence. Furthermore, these studies demonstrate that there is consistency in children's selection of the social identities that are the most important to them. Not surprisingly, however, exactly how central these collective identities were depended on a number of other factors. First, it depended on what other identities were available, and exactly how centrality was assessed. For example, when the role of son or daughter was directly pitted against other social identities in a paired-comparison format, as in the Alvarez et al. study, this identity was clearly more central. Second, white immigrant children judged ethnic labels as less central, possibly because outwardly they are similar to white majority children. Finally, consistent with predictions based on developmental changes in children's understanding of racial constancy, ethnicity but not gender centrality increased with age in certain immigrant groups.

Knowledge

Another important aspect of social identity development is children's growing awareness of social stereotypes, status differences, and discrimination. Virtually all children become aware of gender stereotypes, regardless of family beliefs and values, because the messages are so blatantly presented through the mass media and supported in peer interactions, especially at school (Maccoby, 2002; Martin & Fabes, 2001). The developmental trend of children's knowledge of gender stereotypes is well documented. Children show increasing knowledge about concrete (e.g., toys and activities) aspects of the stereotypes until 5–6 years of age, and subsequently show an increase in knowledge about traits associated with masculinity and femininity (Ruble & Martin, 1998). Surprisingly little research has examined the development of children's knowledge of status differences, however. Children older than 10 years appear aware of greater discrimination and restrictions for women

(Intons-Peterson, 1988), but the perceptions of younger children are not known. Young children do attribute greater power to males, as Kohlberg (1966) hypothesised, in the sense of viewing them as stronger, faster, and more aggressive (Ruble & Martin, 1998), but it is not clear that such beliefs reflect perceptions of higher status for males.

In contrast to the gender literature, there has been relatively little research specifically assessing children's racial and ethnic stereotypes, except in a global, evaluative sense (e.g., nice–mean). Beliefs about ethnicity or race are less likely to be as uniform as those about gender, as information is often presented implicitly and parents vary enormously on their racial/ethnic socialisation strategies (Garcia Coll & Pachter, in press; Hughes & Chen, 1999). Nevertheless, there is some research suggesting that young children may have a rudimentary understanding of status differences among racial groups (Averhart & Bigler, 1997; Katz & Kofkin, 1997). For instance, children are aware that in America, higher status is awarded to white people and that they are accorded more power, control, and prestige (Van Ausdale & Feagin, 1996); even 3-year-olds may be aware of societal values regarding race (Katz & Kofkin, 1997). Averhart and Bigler found that, even with novel occupations, elementary-school-aged children rated those occupations performed by blacks as lower in status than those performed by whites. In addition, Nesdale and Flesser (2001) found that even 5-year-olds were sensitive to status differences between their own and other groups and that this difference had an impact on children's group attitudes. Such findings have led some to suggest that the relative status that various groups hold in society may be reflected in children's feelings about their own group (Spencer, Brooklins, & Allen, 1985). For instance, "male children rarely wish to be female, and white children never want to be black" (Katz, 1983, p. 68). Although children do demonstrate some awareness of the status differences of racial groups, it is still unclear exactly when and how this knowledge affects their perceptions and evaluations of their own and other racial groups.

Evaluation

Even if two individuals label their social identity in the same way and with the same degree of salience, centrality, and knowledge, it may be perceived in terms of its positive qualities for one and its negative qualities for the other. This feature of identity is associated with a number of related terms, such as stereotypic knowledge and in-group/out-group evaluation, and it may also be linked to intergroup prejudice. Moreover, a particularly interesting and significant line of inquiry concerns the relation between group evaluation and personal self-esteem (see below).

The social psychological literature has distinguished between personal (private) regard and perceived public regard (Luhtanen & Crocker, 1992; Sellers et al., 1998). Private regard refers to personal positive/negative feelings about a social category (e.g., feeling that Latinos have made major accomplishments) and about being a member of that category (e.g., proud to be a woman). Public regard refers to perceptions of others' positive/negative feelings (e.g., feelings that men are highly regarded by others). Although these forms of social category evaluation might be expected to be highly related, the degree of relation varies across groups. For example, in one study, public and private regard were significantly associated for white and Asian-American students but not for African-American students (Crocker, Luhtanen, Blaine, & Broadnax, 1994). One explanation for these differences concerns the possibility that an explicit recognition of racism may help keep African-Americans from internalising negative messages from the broader society (Sellers et al., 1998). Moreover, depending on the specific group, some dimensions are more important than others in predicting well-being. For example, in the Crocker et al. study, neither private nor public regard predicted life satisfaction for European-American college students once personal self-esteem was controlled; but among African-American college students, private regard predicted life satisfaction, even with self-esteem controlled.

A few studies on children's perceptions of gender provide some relevant data about developmental trends. Interestingly, most of the available evidence suggests that young children show higher personal regard for females than for males (Ruble & Martin, 1998). For example, Yee and Brown (1994) found that although 3- to 11-year-olds showed the expected in-group favouritism (see next section), both boys and girls described boys in more negative terms overall. Ruble and Martin (1998) suggest that young children may be particularly attentive to attributes that reflect moral goodness or obedience, such as helpfulness, and that such attributes are more likely to be associated with females. Indeed, this form of positive evaluation of females continues into adulthood (Eagly, Mladinic, & Otto, 1991). Older children begin to view males more highly on competency and leadership attributes (e.g., Lockheed, Harris, & Nemceff, 1983). Thus, personal and public regard of males and females may depend on which attributes are salient or important to the evaluator, which probably varies as a function of age and context.

Developmental studies have typically not examined race or ethnic group evaluation in quite this way. Most of the developmental literature that has been interpreted in terms of evaluation refers to a comparison of in-group versus out-group choices and preferences, rather than feelings about one's own group, per se. This "in-group bias" literature will be discussed below with respect to consequences of social identity. This kind of evaluation is potentially quite different from private regard. In-group bias can emerge even if an identity is relatively trivial or transitory (wearing blue or yellow tee-shirts in a classroom: Bigler et al., 1997). Thus, one might favour one's own group over another without experiencing a strong sense of pride in group membership. It will be of great interest in future research to examine when distinct and stable feelings about one's group emerges in relation to the other components of collective identity. It will also be interesting to examine whether the relation between private and public regard, as well as certain differences across groups, as reported above, change in relation to emerging knowledge about the group's status in the broader culture.

CONSEQUENCES OF DEVELOPMENTAL CHANGES IN COLLECTIVE IDENTITY

Social identity theory, as proposed by Tajfel and Turner (1979, 1986), highlights the important role that social group membership plays in shaping individuals' self-conceptions (Turner, 1985) and interactions with both in-group and out-group members (Tajfel, 1979). Considerable empirical research with adults has demonstrated relations between social identity and self-evaluation, motivation, activity engagement, and relationships with others (e.g., Crocker et al., 1994; Sellers et al., 1998). In this section, we ask what the developmental literature has to say about possible consequences of collective identity development. Three broad types of consequences are examined: evaluative (in-group biases and self-esteem), motivational (information-seeking and personal choices), and interpersonal (evaluation of individual members of groups and prejudice towards out-groups).

Evaluative consequences

In-group biases

In their original formulations of social identity theory, Tajfel and Turner (1979) suggested that the basic process of social categorisation was sufficient to create intergroup discrimination in favour of the in-group and against the out-group. For example, in terms of social judgments it has been found that people evaluate their own group members more favourably (Allen & Wilder, 1975; Oaker & Brown, 1986; Perdue, Dovidio, Gurtman, & Tyler, 1990) and are less critical of in-group members' behaviours (Duncan, 1976; Hewstone, 1990). Particularly when their own identity is threatened, patterns of bias intensify and further in-group favouritism is manifested (Branscombe, Wann, Noel, & Coleman, 1993). Behavioural ramifications include rewarding out-group members to a lesser degree than in-group members (Brewer, 1979) and derogating out-group members, especially when self-regard has been threatened (Fein & Spencer, 1997).

In short, theory and research suggest that categorisation of persons into groups becomes an evaluative process through self-identification (e.g., identification with one ethnic group and disidentification with another ethnic group; see Hogg & Abrams, 1988, for a review). Thus, subsequent to categorisation, children should evaluate their own group positively and out-groups negatively. Research on gender-related in-group bias is consistent with this prediction (Ruble & Martin, 1998). For example, Yee and Brown (1994) found that by age 5, both boys and girls were more positive about their own sex than about the other sex, and even 3-year-old girls showed some evidence of in-group favouritism. Children also show greater liking for their own sex and they typically play with same-sex others after the age of 3 (Maccoby, 1998). Finally, children assign more positive than negative traits to their own sex during the early to middle school years (e.g., Albert & Porter, 1983; Powlishta, 1995).

Developmental trends for race- or ethnicity-related biases differ between children of majority versus minority status in the culture (see Aboud, 1988; Aboud & Amato, 2001; and J. A. Cameron et al., 2001, for reviews), but these findings provide some support for this basic hypothesis, especially for majority children. White children (examined only in white-majority cultures) show an in-group preference as early as 3–4 years of age, and in-group/out-group differentiation increases until 7–8 years of age, either stabilising or declining after that age (e.g., Corenblum & Annis, 1993; Doyle & Aboud, 1995). A similar in-group bias among young children has been observed for Asian children in an Asian society (Morland & Hwang, 1981). Children with minority status in the culture show a very different developmental pattern. Children under 7 years of age are less likely to show an in-group preference (e.g., Newman et al., 1983; Spencer & Markstrom-Adams, 1990; but see Semaj, 1980, for an exception), whereas after age 7, most (but not all) studies show in-group bias (e.g., Spencer, 1982). Thus, at about age 7, children in all groups are showing a clear in-group positive evaluation, a pattern that is in parallel with the emergence of racial constancy. Indeed, some research supports the idea that the achievement of constancy understanding is associated with greater in-group preferences, especially for ethnic/racial minority children (Rhee et al., 2003b). What is not clear is whether such trends are related to the different components of collective identity (e.g., centrality). Although there is some recent evidence of clear individual differences in the degree of in-group bias as early as preschool (Rhee, Alvarez, McGlynn, & Mull, 2003a), it is not known whether greater in-group bias is associated with either individual differences or developmental trends in, for example, centrality or knowledge. Moreover, although positive evaluation of one's group per se is obviously part of in-group bias, it is not even clear that this evaluative component of identity is necessarily related to in-group bias. For example, it seems possible that one could feel proud to be a woman without feeling women are superior to men.

Self-esteem

Social identity theory maintains that people strive for positive self-concepts and that the emotional and value significance of social identities greatly impacts the self-concept and self-esteem (Tajfel & Turner, 1979). By selectively comparing the in-group with the out-group on dimensions positive for the in-group, one's social identity is enhanced, thereby endowing one with a greater sense of well-being and higher self-esteem (Hogg & Abrams, 1998). Three issues regarding this relation between collective identity and self-esteem have dominated the literature and are relevant to a developmental analysis.

First, the question of how individuals construct positive personal identities that include a social identity associated with a lower status or stigmatised group has been a major focus of research for decades. Classic "doll studies" by Clark and Clark and others had suggested that black children identified with the black doll but were likely to choose the white doll when asked questions about desirable characteristics (e.g., nice, smart). These findings led to conclusions that societal stigmatisation of a racial group is internalised as "self-hatred" by black children, leading to lowered self-esteem. Such conclusions were instrumental in the Supreme Court decision of *Brown* v. *Board of Education*, which resulted in a social policy of racial integration.

Findings relating self-esteem to group membership have been equivocal, however. First, a series of important conceptual and empirical analyses have questioned the conclusion that identification with a stigmatised group leads inevitably to lowered self-esteem (Banks, 1976; Cross, 1991) (see Phinney, 1990, for a review concerning ethnic group membership). Instead, considerable research has shown that individuals have at their disposal a wide range of strategies to protect self-esteem, such as attributing negative feedback to prejudice and devaluing dimensions on which the group fares poorly while valuing those on which the group fares well (Crocker & Major, 1989). For example, Steele (1988) has suggested that "self-affirmation" processes may explain how African-American college students face stigmatisation. Because these students do not feel that they will ever be perceived as academically successful, they reject an identity as a hardworking student and adopt alternative identities. Such coping strategies may maintain self-esteem, but often at the cost of optimising the performance in valued domains of society and perhaps lowering a sense of self-efficacy in the long run (Jones, 1992). Nevertheless, research taking identity structure into account suggests that, for some individuals, membership in a stigmatised group may indeed affect self-evaluation (Rowley et al., 1998). Thus, it remains important to continue to examine if and how identification with a devalued group lowers personal self-esteem.

Second, despite the prevalent assumption that negative consequences stem from attaching importance to devalued groups, group status may not be the most important influence on the self-esteem associated with group membership. Instead, because of the significance of interpersonal connections and a sense of being accepted for self-esteem (Baumeister & Leary, 1995), identification with a group may foster well-being, regardless of group status. For example, some research suggests that stressful transitions may be buffered by a strong identification with one's own ethnic group (Ethier & Deaux, 1994). Similar stress-buffering effects of social identity have been found in daily diaries with adolescents (Yip & Fuligni, 2002). Collective identification may also act as a buffer for the experience of discrimination. For example, in a study of African-American college students, Branscombe, Schmitt, and Harvey (1999) found that the effect of making attributions of discrimination to prejudice varied depending on collective identification. Although attributions to prejudice showed a direct relation to lower personal and collective well-being, an indirect positive relation was also found: Attributions to prejudice led to an increase in minority group identification that, in turn, led to positive increases in personal and collective well-being.

Third, it follows from social identity theory that when a person's self-esteem is threatened, biased intergroup comparisons, intergroup discrimination, and prejudice are a likely result of self-esteem maintenance. Although this hypothesised relation between self-esteem and prejudice is central to social identity theory, the evidence for it has been equivocal (see Rubin & Hewstone, 1998; cf. Fein & Spencer, 1997).

A developmental approach may be able to shed some light on these controversial relations between group identification and self-esteem. To illustrate, one would expect that the impact of group membership on self-esteem would be problematic for children of devalued ethnic minority groups, whose ethnic identity is central, at least once they recognise that devaluation. In one study, for example, fifth- and sixth-grade Chinese-American children showed lower self-esteem than first- and second-grade Chinese-American children (Ou & McAdoo, 1999). The authors suggest that the decrease may be related to experiences interacting with the dominant culture, making them aware of the lower status of their racial group and affecting their sense of self-worth. It is also possible, however, that the finding reflects other age-related differences, because other research suggests that the self-esteem of ethnic minority children is generally not lower than that of majority white children (e.g., Aboud, 1988).

We would like to suggest three reasons why it may be productive to re-examine this relation from a developmental perspective. First, because most studies have not examined the developmental trajectory of children's learning of society's evaluations of their own and others' ethnic groups, there is still the possibility that they may not be capturing the key point at which there is a drop in self-esteem prior to children's development of coping mechanisms (see Crocker, Major, & Steele, 1999). Second, the measures of self-esteem employed in the past may not adequately capture the aspect influenced by being a member of a devalued ethnic group. For example, measures that specifically ask about wanting to change skin colour, wanting to fit in, and so on may be more appropriate to capture self-esteem losses due to devalued ethnic group membership (Alarcon, Szalacha, Erkut, Fields, & Garcia Coll, 2002). Moreover, it may be productive to look separately at subcomponents of self-esteem, such as physical and social self-worth, as well as at elements of group membership other than status, such as a sense of belonging. Finally, racial/ethnic socialisation in the family and schools can support the development of positive self-esteem even if the child learns about negative stereotypes applied to their group (Garcia Coll & Pachter, in press; Hughes & Chen, 1999). Future research should examine the possibility that the relation between self-esteem and knowledge is moderated by exposure to environments that contradict negative messages.

A social identity theory perspective has typically not been applied directly to understanding gender-related processes and self-esteem. Many studies show that females have somewhat lower self-esteem than males (Ruble & Martin, 1998), and sex differences in self-esteem and related constructs have been observed prior to the well-documented sex difference in depression that seems to emerge during adolescence (Ruble, Greulich, Pomerantz, & Gochberg, 1993). Other research has applied the concept of androgyny (Bem, 1974) or dualism (Spence & Helmreich, 1978) to the relation between gender and self-esteem. The idea is that flexibility with respect to masculine and feminine identity and behaviours is adaptive. Indeed, the literature has shown some support for this hypothesis (see Ruble & Ruble, 1982, for a review) but, more often, adjustment is more closely related to instrumental characteristics or masculinity for both sexes (Aube, Norcliffe, Craig, & Koestner, 1995; Spence & Hall, 1996). Assuming that masculinity or instrumentality are more highly valued by society, such findings seem consistent with the idea described above with respect to ethnicity (i.e., that negative consequences follow from identification with a less valued group).

Recently, however, such interpretations have been questioned, and approaches more directly relevant to social identity hypotheses have been offered (Egan & Perry, 2001). Specifically, Egan and Perry argued that if identification with a social group is partially in the service of self-esteem enhancement, then feeling particularly connected or compatible with one's biological sex should promote feelings of well-being. In support of this hypothesis, they found perceptions of gender typicality (e.g., "think you are a good example of being a girl") and gender contentedness (e.g., "like being a girl") were positively related to global self-worth in fourth- to eighth-graders. Moreover, these associations remained significant when children's perceptions of self-efficacy for gender-typed activities were controlled, implying that gender identity as operationalised in this way has implications for adjustment beyond gender-linked competencies. Interestingly, feeling pressured to engage in gender-typed activities and in-group favouritism were negatively related to self-esteem. This latter finding of a negative effect for in-group favouritism is intriguing because it is inconsistent with the social identity prediction that the value one places on one's group should positively affect self-esteem. It will be useful in future research to explore possible reasons for this apparent discrepancy.

Motivational consequences

When and in what ways do children's identification with and knowledge about social groups influence their interests, choices, and behaviours? There has been a fair amount of research related to these questions in the gender development literature. For example, numerous studies have examined children's knowledge of gender stereotypes and how that may influence their own characteristics and behaviours (see Aubry, Ruble, & Silverman, 1999, for a review). Little is known, however, about whether young children learn the "do's and don't's" of ethnicity in the same way. A further limitation is that consequences of identity have been examined only with fairly limited and unsophisticated measures of identity: simple knowledge of group distinctions, or one's placement in a group and knowledge about the stability or constancy of those placements. The implications of the other elements of identity, such as centrality or evaluation, have typically not been included. In this section, we examine this literature with respect to two classes of motivational consequences: (1) interest in and information-seeking about group norms; and (2) adherence to group norms in personal choices and behaviours.

Information-seeking and processing

Both cognitive theories regarding the development of social identity (Kohlberg, 1966; Martin et al., in press; Ruble, 1994) and social identity theory (Tajfel, 1978) predict that identification with a social category has a number of immediate consequences for children's orientation towards other members of the group. In particular, it should lead them to seek to be similar to other category members and to exaggerate differences from members of contrasting categories. Considerable evidence suggests that children actively seek out and construct their own rules about gender soon after they have learnt about gender categories and their placement in one of them (Martin et al., 2002). For example, once children have a stable conception of gender categories, they show increased interest in watching same-sex others (Luecke-Aleksa, Anderson, Collins, & Schmitt, 1995; Slaby & Frey, 1975, boys only). Moreover, young children pay increased attention to and remember more information about an activity when they believe it is something for their own sex than for the other sex (Bradbard, Martin, Endsley, & Halverson, 1986). Finally, there is evidence that early levels of gender identity are associated with a shift to same-sex play (Fagot, 1985; Smetana & Letourneau, 1984).

Some research has also suggested that once racial identity becomes solidified (i.e., attainment of constancy), children engage in information-seeking about the in-group (Aboud, 1977). It is only the previously mentioned study by Rhee et al. (2003b), however, that directly examined differences in information-seeking at different stages of racial constancy understanding. As expected, the results showed that when given a choice of books to read, children who understood the stability of their racial category were more interested in learning about in-group characters than children who did not have this level of understanding. In addition, African-American and Asian-American (but not European-American) children who understood the stability of their racial categorisation perceived themselves as more similar to other in-group members and liked them more than children who had not reached this level of understanding. This result implies that for racial minority children, the understanding that their racial categorisation is stable changed the meaning of their social category membership.

In short, studies on the initial development of real group self-categorisation are consistent with findings that manipulate assignment to arbitrary and artificial groups. Children who have some initial understanding of the permanence of their membership in racial and gender groups show a more positive orientation towards group members and seek to learn more about group norms. Future research should attempt to look at such consequences longitudinally and assess why such effects often occur for some groups only, for example, boys more than girls and racial/ethnic minority children more than majority children.

Personal choices and behaviours

Collective identity should not only lead individuals to seek information about group norms, but should also affect their desires to look and act in identity-consistent ways. The motivational consequences of social group membership take many forms and emerge from multiple pathways. For example, J. E. Cameron (1999) has argued that social identities created by group membership may guide the formation of motivationally important possible selves (Markus & Nurius, 1986). In addition, group membership may shape personal values and interests, which in turn influences effort and performance. For example, Eccles (1983; Wigfield & Eccles, 2000) argues that individuals whose sex role identity is central may value those tasks associated with their sex and devalue those tasks associated with the other sex. Similarly, Steele (1992, 1997) suggests that identifying with a group that is stereotyped for failing in a certain domain (e.g., academics) may lead an individual to dis-identify in that domain in order to protect self-esteem. Moreover, experimental work demonstrates that simply labelling an ambiguous activity as being performed by one sex or the other can affect performance (see Martin & Dinella, 2002, for a review). For example, in one study, both boys and girls performed better on a novel throwing game when they thought is was gender appropriate rather than gender inappropriate (Montemayor, 1974).

A developmental analysis of the processes linking personal choices and behaviours to the emergence of collective identity seems important for several reasons. First, identification with and knowledge about social groups emerge in tandem during early childhood, and thus represent a unique opportunity to examine the interplay of these two important processes. Second, the initial emergence of social category connections and beliefs, and the context in which they emerge, seem likely to set fundamental individual differences in motion. Many life-defining choices – such as willingness to pursue careers in science and math, engagement in school, orientation towards college – may have their origins at this time. To illustrate, Steele's research described above suggests reasons why African-Americans may perform less well in college. But these individuals have, at least, made it to college; many more do not. What about the children who, in essence, drop out of school as soon as they can because they perceive school success is not for people like them? Similarly, girls' apparent loss of interest in science and maths during adolescence may have already been predetermined by an identification with feminine attributes and expectations at a much earlier time.

Several studies provide evidence regarding such developmental links for gender categories. One set of studies has examined whether knowledge of gender stereotypes affects children's own activity preferences (see Martin et al., in press, and Ruble & Martin, 1998, for reviews). This research has yielded very mixed findings, indicating the inherent difficulty in examining the link between social identity and behaviour (see Aubry et al., 1999). For example, a large number of factors other than gender identity influence a person's activity choice in a particular situation, such as activity attractiveness, social desirability, personal skills, and familiarity. In addition, other aspects of identity, such as centrality and evaluation, are likely to influence the extent to which social identity guides one's choices. Finally, developmental level has not been carefully considered in most studies. Finding associations between knowledge of gender stereotypes and gender-typed behavioural preferences may be precluded by the very high levels of knowledge that most children exhibit about gender roles after the age of 5 years. It is thus noteworthy that several studies have found significant relations between stereotyped knowledge and behaviour/preferences (Coker, 1984; Martin, Fabes, Evans & Wyman, 1999; Serbin, Powlishta, & Gulko, 1993). Moreover, one longitudinal study found that many relations between knowledge and preferences involved lagged effects (i.e., knowledge predicting preferences 1 year later; Aubry et al., 1999).

A second set of studies has examined the impact of gender identity, as measured by children's recognition that they are girls or boys, or higher levels of gender identity understanding, namely stability and constancy. Consistent with social identity theory and cognitive theories of gender development, several studies suggest that level of understanding about one's gender category membership influences adherence to gender norms (see Lutz & Ruble, 1995; Martin et al., 2002, and Ruble & Martin, 1998, for reviews). There are many inconsistencies in the findings, however, and the exact conclusion to be drawn remains controversial (e.g., Bussey & Bandura, 1999). One promising direction for future research would be to examine identification more directly. For example, one could predict, in accordance with Kohlberg (1966), that understanding the permanence of social identity would make that identity more important or central. Another possible prediction is that the predicted links between constancy and adherence to norms would occur only for children who did in fact view their identity as central. It would also be of interest in future research to look jointly at the impact of identification and knowledge about the characteristics associated with the group. For example, one study found that girls who had attained gender constancy and who had considerable gender stereotypic knowledge showed less interest in computers than did all other groups of children, suggesting, perhaps that they had abandoned an attractive activity to comply with gender norms (Newman, Cooper, & Ruble, 1995).

There is little comparable research on the development of adherence to ethnic norms, perhaps because activities for children are not as clearly marked by ethnicity and race as they are for gender. One study, however, examined differences in children's friend and activity choices as a function of level of racial constancy understanding (Rhee et al., 2003b). As predicted, the results showed that children who had attained constancy were more likely to choose a same-race activity and same-race playmates. Similar to the findings reported above for information-seeking, these effects were stronger for the African-American and Asian-American children than for the European-American children.

In addition, Akiba et al. (2001a) examined the relations between social identity and engagement in school. They found that among the Dominican-American and Cambodian-American children, those whose "minority" identity (e.g., Dominican, Latino, Cambodian, Asian) was central tended to have lower school engagement scores, as measured by items assessing importance of getting good grades and importance of being liked by the teachers. These results appear consistent with notions of stereotype threat disidentification (Steele, Spencer, & Aronson, in press), as well as with ideas about an oppositional identity (Cross, 1995; Fordham, & Ogbu, 1986). Other findings, however, suggest that the proper interpretation of these relations may be more complex and involve culture-specific meanings of engagement (Akiba & Garcia Coll, in press). For example, Cambodian-American children with a strong "minority" identity scored higher on the conduct aspect (e.g., attendance) of school.

It will be useful in future research to examine more directly the implications of children's growing awareness of ethnicity-related ability stereotypes for their engagement, as well as the processes underlying such relations. Although stereotypes about the interests and characteristics of boys and girls are well known by the age of 8 years (Ruble & Martin, 1998), there is surprisingly little information about school-related ability stereotypes for either sex or ethnicity. Nevertheless, previous research on the development of children's understanding of ability (e.g., Dweck, 1999) and social comparison of abilities (Ruble & Frey, 1991) suggest that stereotype threat could appear during middle elementary school, as long as the relevant stereotypes were known. Indeed, recent research reported by Aronson and Good (in press) is consistent with this prediction.

Interpersonal consequences

Considerable effort in social psychology has been devoted to showing how identification with a particular social category (that involves a comparison with other social categories) may promote a sense of belonging and connectedness but can also lead to stereotyping of out-group members and to prejudice and intergroup conflict (Hewstone et al., 2002; Tajfel & Turner, 1979). Research in this area has been largely concerned with documenting when and how such effects occur (e.g., whether they are automatically elicited or can be controlled: Devine, 1989). Such research typically either examines differences among individuals who already have relatively well-developed social category representations or group identifications, or it varies the situation in some way, such as by increasing the salience of group distinctions. Curiously, despite the wide-ranging importance of the interpersonal consequences of social category beliefs, we know little about how these processes develop. In this section, we consider a few areas that seem of particular interest for a developmental analysis.

Evaluation of individual members of groups

Research with adults suggests that not all in-group members will necessarily be evaluated positively. Specifically, individuals who deviate from in-group social category norms are likely to be evaluated more negatively than those who support the norms (Marques, Abrams, Paez, & Martinez-Taboada, 1998). The logic underlying this research is based upon the self-categorisation theory idea that in-group norms represent what category members should do and be like, and that behaving in accordance with norms helps maintain the boundaries with other categories (Turner, Hogg, Oakes, Reicher, & Wetherell, 1987). Moreover, the group norms are legitimised by people who act in accordance with them and such people thereby facilitate what is, for social identity theory, a central goal of group identification: maintaining a positive social identity (Tajfel & Turner, 1986). An interesting corollary hypothesis is that not all out-group members will be evaluated negatively. Indeed, an out-group deviant may be liked more than an in-group deviant, even if their expression of norms is identical (Abrams, Marques, Bown, & Henson, 2000).

Although it is now well-documented that children show in-group biases from an early age, it is not clear when they might adopt this more discerning approach to interpersonal evaluation. Is there a point in development, for example, when children's evaluations depend on individual fit to group norms rather than just in-group/out-group membership? Some research on developmental changes in the inferences children draw from gender-related information provides a partial answer to this question. In this research, children are provided with categorical information (being male) and attribute (typicality) information (masculine or feminine interests). In two studies, children younger than third grade were influenced by categorical information only, whereas older children used both types of information (Biernat, 1991; Martin, 1989). These data suggest that children's judgments about individuals in a group may not be influenced by information about relative typicality or deviance until approximately 8 years of age or later. Future research should examine whether such developmental changes apply to perceptions of other groups and whether they are linked in systematic ways to the growth of social category understanding and the different dimensions of collective identity.

Out-group derogation and prejudice

As described earlier, decades of research have shown an in-group bias for both sex and race or ethnicity. On the basis of these results, it has been argued that children as young as 3 years old are prejudiced (see Aboud, 1988; Brand et al., 1974; Brown, 1995; Davey, 1983, for reviews). Indeed, in her review, Aboud suggested that, contrary to the recent reductions seen in adult prejudice, the prejudice seen in children has remained constant.

We have argued elsewhere (J. A. Cameron et al., 2001), however, that it is premature to conclude from this research that young children are exhibiting prejudice. Developmental researchers, in confounding attitudes towards in-groups and out-groups, have not incorporated recent propositions that positive in-group bias is not the same as prejudice (Brewer, 1999, 2001). In our review of the literature on prejudice in children, we found that much of the past research in this area relied on measures and/or statistical analyses that confounded in-group positivity and out-group negativity (J. A. Cameron et al., 2001). Thus, in these studies it was not possible to determine whether children's differential responses were the result of out-group derogation rather than simple in-group favouritism. The few studies that had employed measures that separately assessed evaluations towards the in-group and out-group demonstrated that evidence of out-group derogation was seen only in older children (12-year-olds). Therefore, it seems likely that young children, rather than expressing prejudice, are probably manifesting in-group favouritism.

The lack of an empirical relationship between in-group favouritism and out-group derogation suggests that these two aspects of intergroup behaviour may have different motivational origins (Brewer, 1999; Brown, 1995). Brewer (2001) suggests a hierarchy such that the principles of social categorisation and in-group positivity are most likely to be universal aspects of human social groups. Intergroup comparison and out-group hostility, in contrast, "require additional social-structural and motivational conditions that are not inherent in the processes of group formation itself" (Brewer, 2001, p. 19). For example, prejudice against women is more likely when they violate gender stereotypes or participate in male-dominated domains (Eagly & Mladinic, 1994). As Lutz and Ruble (1995) illustrate: "girls' efforts to 'beat the boys' in areas where boys may be tacitly expected to do better, such as playground athletics, are likely to provoke resentment and active attempts at exclusion on the part of boys" (p. 144).

We further suggest that future research should examine whether the developmental trajectory of intergroup attitudes may be described similarly to Brewer's (2001) hierarchical progression of relations between in-group formation and intergroup behaviour. That is, when children understand social categorisation, they exhibit in-group positivity. Only with sufficient social-cognitive development and specific social-structural and motivational conditions, however, will children exhibit intergroup comparisons and out-group hostility. According to this framework, prejudice would emerge as an interaction of developmental changes and social-contextual factors, such as the explicit socialisation of evaluations associated with particular groups or more implicit socialisation that membership in particular groups has a meaningful function.

In some cases, explicit socialisation practices may lead even young children to develop out-group derogation. Such messages might be conveyed to young children by racist parents or in mass media portrayals of conflict with other nationalities or ethnicities. Indeed, when examining ethnic attitudes in a country where clear ethnic friction results in explicit out-group derogation (e.g., the Arab–Israeli conflict), it becomes evident that children can be socialised to view certain groups in a prejudicial manner at a very young age. For instance, Bar-Tal (1996) found that Israeli children as young as 2½ years old rated a male photo more negatively when he was identified as an Arab than when the photo was not labelled. Similarly, Rutland (1999) found evidence of out-group derogation for children's evaluations of a group that has been depicted negatively in British society (Germans) (see also Bennett, Lyons, Sani, & Barrett, 1998). Thus, it is likely that young children exposed to frequent and overt negativity towards particular groups may develop out-group negativity as well as in-group positivity.

In addition, prejudicial attitudes could result from children learning that social categories have functional value (Bigler, 1995; Bigler et al., 1997). For instance, Bigler (1995) found that children exhibited more occupational stereotyping of men and women in a classroom when gender was made functional by the teacher. In more recent research, novel groups, unequal in status, were created and made salient by teachers. Children who were members of high-status groups developed in-group biased attitudes (Bigler, Spears-Brown, & Markell, 2001). These studies suggest that social conditions, such as the differences in social status and the extent to which group membership influences children's experiences, affect the extent to which children make competitive intergroup comparisons. Hence, when society makes functional use of racial/ethnic groups, prejudice is a conceivable consequence; but whether or not such conditions directly foster out-group hostility is a question that awaits future research.

In addition to context, researchers need to account for the role of social category understanding and multidimensionality of collective identity in determining when children might demonstrate out-group derogation (J. A. Cameron et al., 2001). Even though young children (under the age of 7 years) might demonstrate some out-group devaluation, these attitudes will be more rudimentary and unlike the prejudicial attitudes of older children and adults (see also Rhee et al., 2003a). That is, aspects that would underlie prejudice – that individuals belong to distinct, immutable racial groups with particular interests and proclivities that endure over time – are not likely to be available to young children until they have realised certain social-cognitive capacities such as racial constancy, an understanding of stable traits, and the ability to engage in social comparisons. Moreover, it will be of interest in future research to examine the interplay between context and the emergence of the different dimensions of collective identity as it influences the development of prejudicial attitudes.

SUMMARY AND CONCLUSIONS

Given the salience and consequences of group membership and social identi-fication during adolescence and young adulthood, the lack of attention to the development of collective identity during childhood is surprising and unfortunate. Our review of related developmental literatures suggests that identification with social groups, especially gender and ethnicity or race, is likely to be quite significant to children by middle childhood. First, develop-mental trends observed in research on children's development of a personal self implies that between 5 and 9 years of age, social categories – particularly gender and race – should change from being viewed in terms of overt physical characteristics (e.g., long hair, dark skin) to becoming a comparison of traits and behaviours and, in the process, take on evaluative meaning. Thus, collective identities may become quite significant to children's self-concept by middle childhood. Second, research on children's understanding of and iden-tification with social categories suggests that children are capable of a sense of "we" by preschool but that the nature and meaning of this identification changes dramatically during childhood and varies as a function of ethnic/ racial minority or majority status. Third, borrowing from social-psycho-logical research and theory, we further argued that simply labelling oneself as a member of a particular group is inadequate to fully capture the significance of collective identity. Instead, we adopted a multidimensional view in which salience, centrality, knowledge, and evaluation were viewed as integral but separable components of this identity. Although there is relatively little developmental work to date on the emergence of these components of col-lective identity, recent research suggests that gender and ethnicity are reason-ably central to children during the early to middle years of school, relative to other social identities, and that there is consistency in children's selection of the social identities that are the most important to them. It also appears that the relative importance of ethnicity increases with age in some groups. These conclusions about centrality are preliminary, however, and, with the excep-tion of clear evidence regarding the development of gender stereotypes by middle childhood, we do not yet know much about the development of the other components of collective identity. Given the clear personal and interpersonal consequences later in development, we view focusing on these different components of collective identity as a high priority for future research.

Acknowledgements

We appreciate the helpful comments and suggestions made on an earlier draft by Anna Akerman and Tracy McLauglin-Volpe. We are also grateful to Faith Greulich for providing support in manuscript preparation. Preparation of the chapter was facilitated by grants from the National Institute of Mental Health (MH37215), MacArthur Foundation, and Russell Sage Foundation.

REFERENCES

Aboud, F. E. (1977). Interest in ethnic information: A cross-cultural developmental study. *Canadian Journal of Behavioural Science, 9*, 134–146.

Aboud, F. E. (1984). Social and cognitive bases of ethnic identity. *Journal of Genetic Psychology, 145*, 217–230.

Aboud, F. E. (1988). *Children and prejudice*. Oxford: Basil Blackwell.

Aboud, F. E., & Amato, M. (2001). Developmental and socialization influences on intergroup bias. In R. Brown & S. Gaertner (Eds.), *Blackwell handbook in social psychology: Intergroup processes, Vol. 4*. Oxford: Blackwell.

Aboud, F., & Ruble, D. N. (1987). Identity constancy in children: Developmental processes and implications. In T. M. Honess & K. M. Yardley (Eds.), *Self and identity: Individual change in development* (pp. 95–107). London: Routledge & Kegan Paul.

Aboud, F. E., & Skerry, S. A. (1983). Self and ethnic concepts in relation to ethnic constancy. *Canadian Journal of Behavioral Science, 15*, 14–26.

Abrams, D., Marques, J. M., Bown, N., & Henson, M. (2000). Pro-norm and anti-norm deviance within and between groups. *Journal of Personality and Social Psychology, 78*, 906–912.

Akiba, D., DiMartino, L., & Rodriquez, S. (2001a). *The construction of self among children of color and children from immigrant families*. Paper presented at the biennial meeting of the Society for Research in Child Development in Minneapolis, MN.

Akiba, D., & Garcia Coll, C. (in press). Effective interventions with children of color and their families: An ecological systems approach. In T. B. Smith (Ed.), *Handbook of multicultural counseling: Internalizing and affirming diversity in counseling and psychology*. Boston: Allyn & Bacon.

Akiba, D., Garcia Coll, C., & Magnuson, K. (2001b). *Children of color and children from immigrant families: The development of social identities, school engagement and interethnic social attribution during middle childhood*. Manuscript under review.

Alarcon, O., Szalacha, L. A., Erkut, S., Fields, J. P., & Garcia Coll, C. T. (2002). The color of my skin: A measure to assess children's perceptions of their skin color. *Applied Developmental Science, 14*, 208–221.

Albert, A. A., & Porter, J. R. (1983). Age patterns in the development of children's gender-role stereotypes. *Sex Roles, 9*, 59–67.

Alejandro-Wright, M. N. (1985). The child's conception of racial classification: A socio-cognitive developmental model. In M. D. Spencer, G. K. Brookins, & W. R. Allen (Eds.), *Beginnings: The social and affective development of black children* (pp. 185–200). Hillsdale, NJ: Lawrence Erlbaum Associates, Inc.

Allen, V. L., & Wilder, D. A. (1975). Categorization, belief similarity, and intergroup discrimination. *Journal of Personality and Social Psychology, 32*, 971–977.

Alvarez, J. M., Cameron, J., Garfinkle, G. S., Ruble, D. N., & Fuligni, A. J. (2001, April). *Identity development in immigrant children.* Paper presented at the biennial meeting of the Society for Research in Child Development. Minneapolis, MN.

Alvarez, J. M., Ruble, D. N., & Bolger, N. (2001). The role of evaluation in the development of person perception, *Child Development, 72*, 1409–1425.

Aronson, J., & Good, C. (in press). The development and consequences of stereotype vulnerability in adolescents. In F. Pajaras & T. Urdan (Eds.), *Adolescence and education, Vol. 2: Academic motivation of adolescents.* Greenwich, CT: Information Age Publishing.

Ashmore, R. D., Jussim, L., Wilder, D., & Heppen, J. (2001). Toward a social identity framework for intergroup conflict. In R.D. Ashmore, L. Jussim, & D. Wilder (Eds.), *Social identity, intergroup conflict, and conflict reduction.* London: Oxford University Press.

Ashmore, R. D., & Ogilvie, D. M. (1992). He's such a nice boy . . . when he's with grandma: Gender and evaluation in self-with-other representations. In T. M. Brinthaupt & R. P. Lipka (Eds.), *The self: Definitional and methodological issues* (pp. 236–290). Albany, NY: State University of New York Press.

Aube, J., Norcliffe, H., Craig, J., & Koestner, R. (1995). Gender characteristics and adjustment-related outcomes: Questioning the masculinity model. *Personality and Social Psychology Bulletin, 21*, 284–295.

Aubry, S., Ruble, D. N., & Silverman, L. (1999). The role of gender knowledge in children's gender-typed preferences. In C. Tamis-LeMonda & L. Balter (Eds.), *Child psychology: A handbook of contemporary issues.* Philadelphia, PA: Psychology Press.

Averhart, C., & Bigler, R. (1997). Shades of meaning: Skin tone, racial attitudes, and constructive memory in African American children. *Journal of Experimental Child Psychology, 67*, 363–388.

Banks, W. C. (1976). White preference in blacks: A paradigm in search of a phenomenon. *Psychological Bulletin, 83*, 1179–1186.

Bar-Tal, D. (1996). Development of social categories and stereotyping in early childhood: The case of "the Arab" concept formation, stereotype and attitudes by Jewish children in Israel. *International Journal of Intercultural Relations, 20*, 341–370.

Baumeister, R. F., & Leary, M. R. (1995). The need to belong: Desire for interpersonal attachments as a fundamental human motivation. *Psychological Bulletin, 117*, 497–529.

Bem, S. L. (1974). The measurement of psychological androgyny. *Journal of Consulting and Clinical Psychology, 42*, 155–162.

Bem, S. L. (1981). Gender schema theory: A cognitive account of sex typing. *Psychological Review, 88*, 354–364.

Bem, S. L. (1983). Gender schema theory and its implication for child development: Raising gender-aschematic children in a gender-schematic society. *Signs, 8*, 598–616.

Bennett, M., Lyons, E., Sani, F., & Barrett, M. (1998). Children's subjective identification with the group and in-group favouritism. *Developmental Psychology*, *34*, 902–909.

Bennett, M., & Sani, F. (2001). *Children's social categorization: Evidence for automatic processing of ethnicity.* Paper presented at the biennial meeting of the SRCD in Minneapolis, MN.

Bennett, M., & Sani, F. (2003). The role of target gender and race in children's encoding of category-neutral person information. *British Journal of Developmental Psychology*, *21*, 99–112.

Bennett, M., Sani, F., Hopkins, N., Agostini, L., & Malucchi, L. (2000). Children's gender categorization: An investigation of automatic processing. *British Journal of Developmental Psychology*, *18*, 97–102.

Bernal, M. E., & Knight, G. P. (Eds.) (1993). *Ethnic identity: Formation and transmission among Hispanics and other minorities.* Albany, NY: State University of New York Press.

Bernal, M. E., & Knight, G. P. (1997). Ethnic identity of Latino children. In J. G. Garcia & M. C. Zea (Eds), *Psychological interventions and research with Latino populations* (pp. 15–38). Needham Heights, MA: Allyn & Bacon.

Bernal, M. E., Knight, G. P., Garza, C. A., Ocampo, K. A., & Cota, M. K. (1990). The development of ethnic identity in Mexican-American children. *Hispanic Journal of Behavioral Sciences*, *12*, 3–24.

Biernat, M. (1991). Gender stereotypes and the relationship between masculinity and femininity: A developmental analysis. *Journal of Personality and Social Psychology*, *61*, 351–365.

Bigler, R. S. (1995). The role of classification skill in moderating environmental influences on children's gender stereotyping: A study of the functional use of gender in the classroom. *Child Development*, *66*, 1072–1087.

Bigler, R. S. (1997). Conceptual and methodological issues in the measurement of children's sex typing. *Psychology of Women Quarterly*, *21*, 53–69.

Bigler, R. S., Jones, L. C., & Lobliner, D. B. (1997). Social categorization and the formation of intergroup attitudes in children. *Child Development*, *68*, 530–543.

Bigler, R. S., & Liben, L. S. (1993). Cognitive mechanisms in children's gender stereotyping: Theoretical and educational implications of a cognitive-based intervention. *Child Development*, *63*, 1351–1363.

Bigler, R. S., Spears-Brown, C., & Markell, M. (2001). When groups are not created equal: Effects of group status on the formation of intergroup attitudes in children. *Child Development*, *72*, 1151–1162.

Bowlby, J. (1980). *Attachment and loss: Vol. 1. Attachment* (original work published in 1969). New York: Basic Books.

Bradbard, M., Martin, C., Endsley, R., & Halverson, C. (1986). Influence of sex stereotypes on children's exploration and memory: A competence versus performance distinction. *Developmental Psychology*, *22*, 481–486.

Brand, E. S., Ruiz, R. A., & Padilla, A. M. (1974). Ethnic identification and preference: A review. *Psychological Bulletin*, *81*, 860–890.

Branscombe, N. R., Schmitt, M. T., & Harvey, R. D. (1999). Perceiving pervasive discrimination among African Americans: Implications for group identification and well-being. *Journal of Personality and Social Psychology*, *77*, 135–149.

Branscombe, N. R., Wann, D. L., Noel, J. G., & Coleman, J. (1993). In-group or out-group extremity: Importance of the threatened social identity. *Personality and Social Psychology Bulletin, 19*, 381–388.

Bretherton, I., McNew, S., & Beeghly-Smith, J. (1981). Early person knowledge as expressed in gestural and verbal communication: When do infants acquire a "theory of mind"? In M. E. Lamb & L. R. Sherrod (Eds.), *Infants' social cognition* (pp. 333–373). Hillsdale, NJ: Lawrence Erlbaum Associates, Inc.

Brewer, M. B. (1979). Ingroup bias in the minimal intergroup situation: A cognitive-motivational analysis. *Psychological Bulletin, 86*, 307–324.

Brewer, M. B. (1991). The social self: On being the same and different at the same time. *Personality and Social Psychology Bulletin, 17*, 475–482.

Brewer, M. B. (1999). The psychology of prejudice: Ingroup love or outgroup hate? *Journal of Social Issues, 55*: 429–444. (Special Issue: Prejudice and intergroup relations: Papers in honour of Gordon W. Allport's centennial.)

Brewer, M. B. (2001). Ingroup identification and intergroup conflict: When does ingroup love become out-group hate? In R. D. Ashmore, L. Jussim, & D. Wilder (Eds.), *Social indentity, intergroup conflict, and conflict reduction*. New York: Oxford University Press.

Brewer, M. B., & Brown, R. J. (1998). Intergroup relations. In D. T. Gilbert, S. T. Fiske et al. (Eds.), *The handbook of social psychology, Vol. 2* (4th ed.; pp. 554–594). New York: McGraw-Hill.

Brewer, M. B., & Gardner, W. (1996). Who is this we? Levels of collective identity and self representations. *Journal of Personality and Social Psychology, 71*, 83–93.

Brown, R. (1995). *Prejudice: Its social psychology*. Oxford: Blackwell.

Bussey, K., & Bandura, A. (1992). Self-regulatory mechanisms governing gender development. *Child Development, 63*, 1236–1250.

Bussey, K., & Bandura, A. (1999). Social cognitive theory of gender development and differentiation. *Psychological Review, 106*, 676–713.

Cameron, J. A., Alvarez, J. M., Ruble, D. N., & Fuligni, A. J. (2001). Children's lay theories about ingroups and outgroups: Reconceptualizing research on "prejudice". *Personality and Social Psychology Review, 5*, 118–128.

Cameron, J. E. (1999). Social identity and the pursuit of possible selves: Implications for the psychological well-being of university students. *Group Dynamics, 3*, 179–189.

Cameron, J. E. & Lalonde, R.N. (2001). Social identification and gender related ideology in men and women. *British Journal of Social Psychology, 40*, 59–77.

Carter, D. B., & Levy, G. D. (1988). Cognitive aspects of children's early sex-role development: The influence of gender schemas on preschoolers' memories and preferences for sex-typed toys and activities. *Child Development, 59*, 782–793.

Coker, D. R. (1984). The relationships among gender concepts and cognitive maturity in preschool children. *Sex Roles, 10*, 19–31.

Connolly, P. (1998). *Racism, gender identities and young children: social relations in a multi-ethnic, inner-city primary school*. New York: Routledge.

Cooley, C. H. (1902). *Human nature and the social order*. New York: Scribner.

Corenblum, B., & Annis, R. C. (1993). Development of racial identity in minority and majority children: An affect discrepancy model. *Canadian Journal of Behavioural Science, 25*, 499–521.

Crocker, J., Luhtanen, R., Blaine, B., & Broadnax, S. (1994). Collective self-esteem and psychological well-being among white, black, and Asian college students. *Personality and Social Psychology Bulletin, 20*, 503–513.

Crocker, J., & Major, B. (1989). Social stigma and self-esteem: The self-protective properties of stigma. *Psychological Review, 96*, 608–630.

Crocker, J., Major, B., & Steele, C. (1998). Social stigma. In D. T. Gilbert, S. T. Fiske, & G. Lindzey (Eds.), *Handbook of social psychology* (4th ed.; pp. 504–553). New York: McGraw-Hill.

Cross, W. E. (1978). The Thomas and Cross models of psychological nigrescence: A literature review. *Journal of Black Psychology, 5*, 13–31.

Cross, W. E. (1985). Black identity: Rediscovering the distinction between personal identity and reference group orientation. In M. B. Spencer, G. K. Brookins, & W. R. Allen (Eds.), *Beginnings: The social and affective development of black children* (pp. 155–171). Hillsdale, NJ: Lawrence Erlbaum Associates, Inc.

Cross, W. E. (1991). *Shades of black: Diversity in African American identity.* Madison, WI: University of Wisconsin Press.

Cross, W. E. (1995). Oppositional identity and African American youth: Issues and prospects. In W. Hawley & A. Jackson (Eds.), *Toward a common destiny: Improving race and ethnic relations in America* (pp. 185–204). San Francisco: Jossey-Bass.

Cross, W. E. Jr., & Fhagen-Smith, P. (2001). Patterns of African American identity development: A life span perspective. In B. Jackson & C. Wijeyesinghe (Eds.), *New perspectives on racial identity development.* New York: New York University Press.

Cross, W. E, Strauss, L., & Fhagen-Smith, P. (1999). African American identity development across the life span: Educational implications. In R. Hernandez & E. R. Hollins (Eds.), *Racial and ethnic identity in school practices: Aspects of human development* (pp. 29–47). Mahwah, NJ: Lawrence Erlbaum Associates, Inc.

Damon, W., & Hart, D. (1988). *Self-understanding in childhood and adolescence.* Cambridge: Cambridge University Press.

Davey, A. (1983). *Learning to be prejudiced: Growing up in multi-ethnic Britain.* London: Edward Arnold.

Deaux, K., & Martin, D. (2001). *Which context? Specifying levels of context in identity processes.* Paper presented at Indiana Conference on Identity Theory.

Devine, P. G. (1989). Stereotypes and prejudice: Their automatic and controlled components. *Journal of Personality and Social Psychology, 56*, 5–18.

Doyle, A. B., & Aboud, F. E. (1995). A longitudinal study of white children's racial prejudice as a social-cognitive development. *Merrill-Palmer Quarterly, 41*, 209–228.

Duncan, B. L. (1976). Differential social perception and attribution of intergroup violence: Testing the lower limits of stereotyping of blacks. *Journal of Personality and Social Psychology, 34*, 590–598.

Durkin, K. (1995). *Developmental social psychology: From infancy to old age.* Cambridge, MA: Blackwell Publishers.

Dweck, C. S. (1999). *Self-theories: Their role in motivation, personality, and development (Essays in Social Psychology).* Philadelphia, PA: Psychology Press.

Eagly, A. H., & Mladinic, A. (1994). Are people prejudiced against women? Some answers from research on attitudes, gender stereotypes, and judgments of competence. In W. Stroebe & M. Hewstone (Eds.), *European Review of Social Psychology: Vol. 5* (pp. 1–35). New York: John Wiley & Sons.

Eagly, A. H., Mladinic, A., & Otto, S. (1991). Are women evaluated more favourably than men? An analysis of attitudes, beliefs, and emotions. *Psychology of Women Quarterly, 15*, 203–216.

Eccles, J. (1983). Expectancies, values, and academic behaviors. In J. T. Spence (Ed.), *Achievement and achievement motives.* San Francisco, CA: W. H. Freeman.

Eder, R. A. (1990). Uncovering young children's psychological selves: Individual and developmental differences. *Child Development, 61,* 849–863.

Egan, S. K., & Perry, D. G. (2001). Gender identity: A multidimensional analysis with implications for psychosocial adjustment. *Developmental Psychology, 37,* 451–463.

Erikson, E. H. (1963). *Childhood and society* (2nd ed.). New York: Norton.

Erkut, S., Garcia Coll, C., & Alarcon, O. (1998). *Ethnic self-identity. A measure to assess children's conceptualization of race and ethnicity.* Manuscript in preparation.

Ethier, K. A., & Deaux, K. (1994). Negotiating social identity when contexts change: Maintaining identification and responding to threat. *Journal of Personality and Social Psychology, 67,* 243–251.

Fagan, J. F., & Singer, L. T. (1979) The role of simple feature differences in infants' recognition of faces. *Infant Behavior and Development, 2,* 39–45.

Fagot, B. I. (1985). Changes in thinking about early sex role development. *Developmental Review, 5,* 83–98.

Fein, S., & Spencer, S. (1997). Prejudice as self-image maintenance: Affirming the self through derogating others. *Journal of Personality and Social Psychology, 73,* 31–44.

Fordham, C., & Ogbu, J. (1986). Black students' school success: Coping with the burden of "acting white". *Urban Review, 18,* 176–206.

Garcia Coll, C. T., & Pachter, L. (in press). Ethnic and minority parenting. In M. H. Bornstein (Ed.), *Handbook of parenting* (2nd ed.). Mahwah, NJ: Lawrence Erlbaum Associates, Inc.

Gelman, S. A., & Markman, E. M. (1986). Categories and inductions in young children. *Cognition, 23,* 183–209.

Harrison, A. O., Wilson, M. N., Pine, C. J., Chan, S. Q., & Buriel, R. (1990). Family ecologies of ethnic minority children. *Child Development, 61,* 347–362.

Harter, S. (1983). Developmental perspectives on the self-system. In E. M. Hetherington (Ed.), *Handbook of child psychology: Vol. 4. Socialization, personality, and social development.* New York: John Wiley & Sons.

Harter, S. (1998). The development of self-representations. In W. Damon & N. Eisenberg (Eds.), *Handbook of child psychology: Vol. 3. Social, emotional, and personality development* (pp. 553–617). New York: John Wiley & Sons.

Hewstone, M. (1990). The "ultimate attribution error"? A review of the literature on intergroup causal attribution. *European Journal of Social Psychology, 20,* 311–335.

Hewstone, M., Rubin, M., & Willis, H. (2002). Intergroup bias. *Annual Review of Psychology, 53,* 575–604.

Higgins, E. T. (1991). Development of self-regulatory and self-evaluative processes: Costs, benefits, and tradeoffs. In M. R. Gunnar & L. A. Sroufe (Eds.), *Self processes and development: The Minnesota Symposium on Child Psychology: Vol. 23,* pp. 125–166. Hillsdale, NJ: Lawrence Erlbaum Associates, Inc.

Higgins, E. T., & Parsons, J. E. (1983). Social cognition and the social life of the child: Stages as subcultures. In E. T. Higgins, D. N. Ruble, & W. W. Hartup (Eds.), *Social cognition and social development* (pp. 15–62). New York: Cambridge University Press.

Hirschfeld, L. A. (1995). Do children have a theory of race? *Cognition, 54,* 209–252.

Hogg, M. A. (2000). Social identity and social comparison. In J. Suls & L. Wheeler (Eds), *Handbook of social comparison: Theory and research. The Plenum series in social/clinical psychology* (pp. 401–421). New York: Kluwer Academic/Plenum Publishers.

Hogg, M. A., & Abrams, D. (1988). *Social identifications: A social psychology of intergroup relations and group processes.* London: Routledge.

Holmes, R. M. (1995). *How young children perceive race.* Thousand Oaks, CA: SAGE Publications.

Hughes, D., & Chen, L. (1999). The nature of parents' race-related communications to children: A developmental perspective. In L. Balter & C. S. Tamis-LeMonda (Eds.), *Child psychology: A handbook of contemporary issues* (pp. 467–490). Philadelphia, PA: Psychology Press/Taylor & Francis.

Intons-Peterson, M. J. (1988). *Gender concepts of Swedish and American youth.* Hillsdale, NJ: Lawrence Erlbaum Associates, Inc.

Jones, J. M. (1992). Understanding the mental health consequences of race: Contributions of basic social psychological processes. In D. N. Ruble, P. R. Costanzo, & M. E. Oliveri (Eds.), *The social psychology of mental health: Basic mechanisms and applications* (pp. 199–240). New York: Guilford Press.

Katz, P. A. (1983). Developmental foundations of gender and racial attitudes. In R. L. Leahy (Ed.), *The child's construction of social inequality* (pp. 41–78). New York: Academic Press.

Katz, P. A., & Kofkin, J. A. (1997). Race, gender, and young children. In S. S. Luthar, J. A. Burack, D. Cicchetti, & J. Weisz (Eds.), *Developmental psychopathology: Perspectives on adjustment, risk, and disorder* (pp. 51–74). New York: Cambridge University Press.

Kohlberg, L. A. (1966). A cognitive-developmental analysis of children's sex role concepts and attitudes. In E. E. Maccoby (Ed.), *The development of sex differences* (pp. 82–173). Stanford, CA: Stanford University Press.

Kohlberg, L. (1969). Stage and sequence: The cognitive-developmental approach to socialization. In D. A. Goslin (Ed.), *Handbook of socialization theory and research* (pp. 347–480). Chicago, IL: Rand McNally.

Leinbach, M. D., & Fagot, B. I. (1986). Acquisition of gender labelling: A test for toddlers. *Sex Roles, 15,* 655–666.

Leinbach, M. D., & Fagot, B. I. (1993). Categorical habituation to male and female faces: Gender schematic processing in infancy. *Infant Behavior and Development, 16,* 317–332.

Levy, G. D. (2000). Individual differences in race schematicity as predictors of African American and white children's race-relevant memories and peer preferences. *The Journal of Genetic Psychology, 16,* 400–419.

Levy, G. D., & Carter, D. B. (1989). Gender schema, gender constancy, and gender-role knowledge: The roles of cognitive factors in preschoolers' gender-role stereotype attributions. *Developmental Psychology, 25,* 444–449.

Lewis, M. (1990). Social knowledge and social development. *Merrill-Palmer Quarterly, 36,* 93–116.

Livesley, W., & Bromley, D. (1973). *Person perception in childhood and adolescence.* London: John Wiley & Sons.

Lockheed, M. E., Harris, A. M., & Nemceff, W. P. (1983). Sex and social influence: Does sex function as a status characteristic in mixed-sex groups of children? *Journal of Educational Psychology, 75,* 877–888.

Luecke-Aleksa, D., Anderson, D. R., Collins, P. A., & Schmitt, K. L. (1995). Gender constancy and television viewing. *Developmental Psychology, 31,* 773–780.

Luhtanen, R., & Crocker, J. (1992). A collective self-esteem scale: Self-evaluation of one's social identity. *Personality and Social Psychology Bulletin, 18,* 302–318.

Lutz, S. E., & Ruble, D. N. (1995). Children and gender prejudice: Context, motivation, and the development of gender concepts. *Annals of Child Development, 10*, 131–166.

Maccoby, E. E. (1988). Gender as a social category. *Developmental Psychology, 24*, 755–765.

Maccoby, E. E. (1998). *The two sexes: Growing up apart, coming together.* Cambridge, MA: Harvard University Press.

Maccoby, E. E. (2002). Gender and group process. *Current Directions in Psychological Science, 11*, 54–58.

Marcia, J. (1988). Identity, cognitive/moral development, and individuation. In D. K. Lapsley & F. C. Power (Eds.), *Self, ego, and identity: Integrative approaches* (pp. 211–225). New York: Springer-Verlag.

Markus, H., & Nurius, P. (1986). Possible selves. *American Psychologist, 41*, 954–969.

Marques, J., Abrams, D., Paez, D., & Martinez-Taboada, C. (1998). The role of categorization and in-group norms in judgments of groups and their members. *Journal of Personality and Social Psychology, 75*, 976–988.

Marques, J. M., Robalo, E. M., & Rocha, S. A. (1992). Ingroup bias and the "black sheep" effect: Assessing the impact of social identification and perceived variability on group judgments. *European Journal of Social Psychology, 22*, 331–352.

Martin, C. L. (1989). Children's use of gender-related information in making social judgments. *Developmental Psychology, 25*, 80–88.

Martin, C. L., & Dinella, L. M. (2001). Children's gender cognitions, the social environment, and sex differences in cognitive domains. In A. M. Lisi & R. D. Lisi (Eds.), *Biology, society, and behavior: The development of sex differences in cognition* (pp. 207–239). Westport, CT: Ablex.

Martin, C. L., & Dinella, L. M. (2002). Children's gender cognitions, the social environment, and sex differences in cognitive domains. In A. V. McGillicuddy-De Lisi & R. De Lisi (Eds.), *Biology, society, and behavior: The development of sex differences in cognition. Advances in applied developmental psychology, Vol. 21* (pp. 207–239). Westport, CT: Ablex.

Martin, C. L., & Fabes, R. A. (2001). The stability and consequences of young children's same-sex peer interactions. *Developmental Psychology, 37*, 431–446.

Martin, C. L., Fabes, R. A., Evans, S. M., & Wyman, H. (1999). Social cognition on the playground: Children's beliefs about playing with girls versus boys and their relations to sex segregated play. *Journal of Social and Personal Relationships, 16*, 751–771.

Martin, C. L., & Halverson, C. F. (1981). A schematic processing model of sex typing and stereotyping in children. *Child Development, 52*, 1119–1134.

Martin, C. L., Ruble, D. N., & Szkrybalo, J. (2002). Cognitive theories of early gender development. *Psychological Bulletin, 128*, 903–933.

McGuire, W. J., McGuire, C. V., Child, P., & Fujioka, T. (1978). Salience of ethnicity in the spontaneous self-concept as a function of one's ethnic distinctiveness in the social environment. *Journal of Personality and Social Psychology, 36*, 511–520.

Mead, G. H. (1934). *Mind, self, and society: From the standpoint of social behaviorist.* Chicago, IL: University of Chicago Press.

Montemayor, R. (1974). Children's performance in a game and their attraction to it as a function of sex-typed labels. *Child Development, 45*, 152–156.

Morland, J. K., & Hwang, C. H. (1981). Racial/ethnic identity of preschool children. *Journal of Cross-Cultural Psychology, 12*, 409–424.

Nesdale, D., & Flesser, D. (2001). Social identity and the development of children's group attitudes. *Child Development, 72,* 506–517.

Newman, L. S., Cooper, J., & Ruble, D. N. (1995). Gender and computers: II. The interactive effects of gender knowledge and constancy on gender-stereotyped attitudes. *Sex Roles, 33,* 325–351.

Newman, M. A., Liss, M. B., & Sherman, F. (1983). Ethnic awareness in children: Not a unitary concept. *The Journal of Genetic Psychology, 143,* 103–112.

Newman, L. S., & Ruble, D. N. (1988). Stability and change in self-understanding: The early elementary school years. *Early Child Development and Care, 40,* 77–99.

Oaker, G., & Brown, R. (1986). Intergroup relations in a hospital setting: A further test of social identity theory. *Human Relations, 39,* 767–778.

Ocampo, K. A., Bernal, M. E., & Knight, G. P. (1993). Gender, race, and ethnicity: The sequencing of social constancies. In M. E. Bernal & G. P. Knight (Eds.), *Ethnic identity: Formation and transmission among Hispanics and other minorities* (pp. 11–59). New York: State University of New York Press.

Ogilvie, D. M., & Ashmore, R. D. (1991). Self-with-other representation as a unit of analysis in self-concept research. In R. C. Curtis (Ed.), *The relational self: Theoretical convergences in psychoanalysis and social psychology* (pp. 282–314). New York: Guilford Press.

Ou, Y., & McAdoo, H. P. (1999). The ethnic socialization of Chinese American children. In H. P. McAdoo (Ed.), *Family ethnicity: Strength in diversity* (2nd Ed., pp. 252–276). Thousand Oaks, CA: SAGE Publications.

Parke, R. D., & Buriel, R. (1998). Socialization in the family: Ethnic and ecological perspectives. In W. Damon & N. Eisenberg (Eds.), *Handbook of child psychology: Vol. 3, Social emotional and personal development* (pp. 553–617). New York: John Wiley & Sons.

Perdue, C. W., Dovidio, J. F., Gurtman, M. B., & Tyler, R. B. (1990). Us and them: Social categorization and the process of intergroup bias. *Journal of Personality and Social Psychology, 59,* 475–486.

Phinney, J. S. (1989). Stages of ethnic identity development in minority group adolescents. *Journal of Early Adolescence, 9,* 34–49.

Phinney, J. S. (1990). Ethnic identity in adolescents and adults: Review of research. *Psychological Bulletin, 108,* 499–514.

Phinney, J. S. (1992). The multigroup ethnic identity measure: A new scale for use with diverse groups. *Journal of Adolescent Research, 7,* 156–176.

Phinney, J. (1993). A three-stage model of ethnic identity development. In M. Bernal & G. Knight (Eds.), *Ethnic identity: Formation and transmission among Hispanics and other minorities* (pp. 61–79). Albany, NY: State University of New York Press.

Phinney, J. (1996). When we talk about American ethnic groups: What do we mean? *American Psychologist, 51,* 918–926.

Phinney, J. S., & Chavira, V. (1992). Ethnic identity and self-esteem: An exploratory longitudinal study. *Journal of Adolescence, 15,* 271–281.

Powlishta, K. K. (1995). Gender bias in children's perception of personality traits. *Sex Roles, 32,* 17–28.

Quintana, S. M. (1998). Children's developmental understanding of ethnicity and race. *Applied and Preventive Psychology, 7,* 27–45.

Ramsey, P. G. (1991). The salience of race in young children growing up in an all-white community. *Journal of Educational Psychology, 83,* 28–34.

Ramsey, P. G., & Myers, L. C. (1990). Salience of race in young children's cognitive, affective, and behavioral responses to social environments. *Journal of Applied Developmental Psychology, 11*, 49–67.

Rhee, E., & Ruble, D. N. (1997). Development of gender and racial constancy. Poster session presented at the biannual meeting of the Society for Research in Child Development, Washington, DC.

Rhee, E., Cameron, J. A., & Ruble, D. N. (2002). *Development of gender and racial constancy in European American and racial minority children.* Manuscript in preparation.

Rhee, E., Alvarez, J. M., McGlynn, E. A., & Mull, E. (2003a). *Variation in European American children's racial attitudes and race-related perceptions and preferences.* Manuscript submitted for publication.

Rhee, E., Ruble D. N., Alvarez, J. M., Stangor, C., & Jones, J. M. (2003b). *Relationship between racial constancy and judgments about racial groups in African American, Asian American, and European American children.* Manuscript submitted for publication.

Rholes, W. S., Newman, L. S., & Ruble, D. N. (1990). Understanding self and other: Developmental and motivational aspects of perceiving people in terms of invariant dispositions. In E. T. Higgins & R. Sorrentino (Eds.), *Handbook of motivation and cognition: Foundations of social behavior, Vol. II.* New York: Guilford Press.

Rowley, S. J., Sellers, R. M., Chavous, T. M., & Smith, M. A. (1998). The relationship between racial identity and self-esteem in African American college and high school students. *Journal of Personality and Social Psychology, 74*, 715–724.

Rubin, M., & Hewstone, M. (1998). Social identity theory's self-esteem hypothesis: A review and some suggestions for clarification. *Personality and Social Psychology Review, 2*, 40–62.

Ruble, D. N. (1994). A phase model of transitions: Cognitive and motivational consequences. In M. Zanna (Ed.), *Advances in experimental social psychology, Vol. 26*, (pp. 163–214). New York: Academic Press.

Ruble, D. N., & Dweck, C. (1995). Self-conceptions, person conceptions, and their development. In N. Eisenberg (Ed.), *Review of personality and social psychology: Social development, Vol. 15.* Thousand Oaks, CA: SAGE Publications.

Ruble, D. N., & Frey, K. S. (1991). Changing patterns of comparative behavior as skills are acquired: A functional model of self-evaluation. In J. Suls & T.A. Wills (Eds.), *Social comparison: Contemporary theory and research.* Hillsdale, NJ: Lawrence Erlbaum Associates, Inc.

Ruble, D. N., & Goodnow, J. (1998). Social development from a lifespan perspective. In D. Gilbert, S. Fiske, & G. Lindzey (Eds.), *Handbook of social psychology.* New York: McGraw-Hill.

Ruble, D. N., Greulich, F., Pomerantz, E. M., & Gochberg, B. (1993). The role of gender-related processes in the development of sex differences in self-evaluation and depression. *Journal of Affective Disorders, 29*, 97–128.

Ruble, D. N., & Martin, C. L. (1998). Gender development. In D. W. Damon (Ed.), *Handbook of Child Psychology, Vol. 3* (5th ed.). New York: John Wiley & Sons.

Ruble, D. N., & Ruble, T. L. (1982). Sex-role stereotypes. In A. G. Miller (Ed.), *In the eye of the beholder: Contemporary issues in stereotyping.* New York: Holt, Rinehart, & Winston.

Ruble, D. N., & Seidman, E. (1996). Social transitions: Windows into social psychological processes. In E. T. Higgins & A. Kruglanski (Eds.), *Handbook of social processes*. New York: Guilford Press.

Ruble, D. N., & Stangor, C. (1986). Stalking the elusive schema: Insights from developmental and social analyses of gender schemas. *Social Cognition*, *4*, 227–261.

Rutland, A. (1999). The development of national prejudice, in-group favouritism and self-stereotypes in British children. *British Journal of Social Psychology*, *38*, 55–70.

Sani, F., & Bennett, M. (2001). Contextual variability in young children's gender in-group stereotypes. *Social Development*, *10*, 221–229.

Sellers, R. M., Rowley, S. A. J., Chavous, T. M., Shelton, J. N., & Smith, M. A. (1997). Multidimensional inventory of black identity: A preliminary investigation of reliability and construct validity. *Journal of Personality and Social Psychology*, *73*, 805–815.

Sellers, R. M., Smith, M., Shelton, J. N., Rowley, S. A. J., & Chavous, T. M. (1998). Multidimensional model of racial identity: A reconceptualization of African American racial identity. *Personality and Social Psychology Review*, *2*, 18–39.

Semaj, L. T. (1980). The development of racial evaluation and preference: A cognitive approach. *The Journal of Black Psychology*, *6*, 59–79.

Semaj, L. T. (1985). Afrikanity, cognition, and extended self-identity. In M. B. Spencer, G. K. Brookins, & W. R. Allen (Eds.), *Beginnings: The social and affective development of black children* (pp. 173–184). Hillsdale, NJ: Lawrence Erlbaum Associates, Inc.

Serbin, L. A., Powlishta, K. K., & Gulko, J. (1993). The development of sex-typing in middle childhood. *Monographs of the Society for Research in Child Development*, *58*, Serial No. 232 (Whole issue).

Serbin, L. A., & Sprafkin, C. (1986). The salience of gender and the process of sex-typing in three- to seven-year old children. *Child Development*, *57*, 1188–1199.

Serbin, L. A., Sprafkin, C., Elman, M., & Doyle, A. B. (1984). The early development of sex differentiated patterns and social influence. *Canadian Journal of Social Science*, *14*, 350–363.

Sigelman, C. K., & Singleton, L. C. (1986). Stigmatization in childhood: A survey of developmental trends and issues. In G. Becker, L. M., Colemena, & S. Ainley (Eds.), *The dilemma of difference: A multidisciplinary view of stigma*. New York: Plenum Press.

Signorella, M. L., Bigler, R. S., & Liben, L. S. (1993). Developmental differences in children's gender schemata about others: A meta-analytic review. *Developmental Review*, *13*, 147–183.

Slaby, R. G., & Frey, K. S. (1975). Development of gender constancy and selective attention to same-sex models. *Child Development*, *52*, 849–856.

Smetana, J. G., & Letourneau, K. J. (1984). Development of gender constancy and children's sex-typed free play behavior. *Developmental Psychology*, *20*, 691–695.

Spence, J. T., & Hall, S. K. (1996). Children's gender-related self-perceptions, activity preferences, and occupational stereotypes: A test of three models of gender constructs. *Sex-Roles*, *35*, 659–692.

Spence, J. T., & Helmreich, R. (1978). *Masculinity and femininity: Their psychological dimensions, correlates, and antecedents*. Austin, TX: University of Texas Press.

Spencer, M. B. (1982). Personal and group identity of black children: An alternative synthesis. *Genetic Psychology Monograph*, *106*, 59–84.

Spencer, M. B. (1984). Black children's race awareness, racial attitudes and self-concept: A reinterpretation. *Journal of Child Psychology and Psychiatry, 24*, 433–441.

Spencer, M. B. (1985). Cultural cognition and social cognition as identity factors in black children's personal-social growth. In M. B. Spencer, G. K. Brookins, & W. R. Allen (Eds.), *Beginnings: The social and affective development of black children.* Hillsdale, NJ: Lawrence Erlbaum Associates, Inc.

Spencer, M. B. (1988). Self-concept development. In D. Slaughter (Ed.), *Black children and poverty: A developmental perspective* (pp. 59–72). San Francisco: Jossey-Bass.

Spencer, M. B., Brooklins, G. K., & Allen, W. R. (1985). *Beginnings: The social and affective development of black children.* Hillsdale, NJ: Lawrence Erlbaum Associates, Inc.

Spencer, M. B. & Markstrom-Adams, C. (1990). Identity processes among racial and ethnic minority children in America. *Child Development, 61*, 290–310.

Stangor, C., & Ruble, D. N. (1987). Development of gender role knowledge and gender constancy. In L. S. Liben & M. L. Signorella (Eds.), *New directions for child development: Vol. 39. Children's gender schemata* (pp. 5–22). San Francisco: Jossey-Bass.

Steele, C. (1992). Race and the schooling of black Americans. *The Atlantic Monthly, 269*, 68–78.

Steele, C. M. (1997). A threat in the air: How stereotypes shape the intellectual identities and performance of women and African Americans. *American Psychologist, 52*, 613–629.

Steele, C. M. (1988). The psychology of self-affirmation: Sustaining the integrity of the self. *Advances in Experimental Social Psychology, 21*, 261–302.

Steele, C. M., Spencer, S., & Aronson, J. (in press). Stereotype threat. In M. Zanna (Ed.), *Advances in Experimental Social Psychology.* New York: Academic Press.

Stephan, W. G., & Rosenfield, D. (1979). Black self-rejection: Another look. *Journal of Educational Psychology, 71*, 708–716.

Stipek, D., Gralinski, H., & Kopp, C. (1990). Self-concept development in the toddler years. *Developmental Psychology, 26*, 972–977.

Szkrybalo, J., & Ruble, D. N. (1999). "God made me a girl": Gender constancy judgements and explanations revisited. *Developmental Psychology, 35*, 392–402.

Tajfel, H. (1978). Social categorization, social identity and social comparison. In H. Tajfel (Ed.), *Differentiation between social groups: Studies in the social psychology of intergroup relations* (pp. 61–76). London: Academic Press.

Tajfel, H. (1979). Individuals and groups in social psychology. *British Journal of Social Psychology, 18*, 183–90.

Tajfel, H., & Turner, J. (1979). An integrative theory of intergroup conflict. In W. Austin & S. Wochel (Eds.), *The social psychology of intergroup relations* (pp. 33–47). Monterey, CA: Brooks/Cole.

Tajfel, H., & Turner, J. C. (1986). The social identity theory of intergroup behavior. In S. Worchen & W. G. Austin (Eds), *Psychology of intergroup relations* (pp. 7–24). Chicago, IL: Nelson Hall.

Taylor, S. E., Fiske, S. T., Etcoff, N. L., & Ruderman, A. J. (1978). Categorical and contextual bases of person memory and stereotyping. *Journal of Personality and Social Psychology, 36*, 778–793.

Thoits, P. A., & Virshup, L. K. (1997). Me's and we's: Forms and functions of social identities. In R. D. Ashmore & L. J. Jussim (Eds.), *Self and identity: Fundamental issues. Rutgers series on self and social identity, Vol. 1* (pp. 106–133). New York: Oxford University Press.

Thompson, S. K. (1975). Gender labels and early sex-role development. *Child Development, 46*, 339–347.

Turner, J. C. (1982). Towards a cognitive redefinition of the social group. In H. Tajfel (Ed.), *Social identity and intergroup relations* (pp. 15–40). Cambridge: Cambridge University Press.

Turner, J. C. (1985). Social categorization and the self-concept: A social cognitive theory of group behaviour. In E. J. Lawler (Ed.), *Advances in group processes, Vol. 2* (pp. 77–121). Greenwich, CT: JAI Press.

Turner, J. C., Hogg, M. A., Oakes, P. J., Reicher, S. D., & Wetherell, M. S. (1987). *Rediscovering the social group: A self-categorization theory*. Oxford: Basil Blackwell.

Van Ausdale, D. V., & Feagin, J. R. (1996) Using racial and ethnic concepts: The critical case of very young children. *American Sociological Review, 61*, 779–793.

Vaughan, G. M. (1963). Concept formation and the development of ethnic awareness. *Journal of Genetic Psychology, 103*, 93–103.

Wellman, H. (1990). *The child's theory of mind*. Cambridge, MA: MIT Press.

Weinraub, M., Clemens, L. P., Sockloff, A., Ethridge, R., Gracely, E., & Myers, B. (1984). The development of sex role stereotypes in the third year: Relationships to gender labelling, gender identity, sex-typed toy preferences, and family characteristics. *Child Development, 55*, 1493–1503.

Wigfield, A., & Eccles, J. S. (2000). Expectancy-value theory of achievement motivation. *Contemporary Educational Psychology, 25*, 68–81.

Willer, S. C., & Romney, A. K. (1988). *Systematic data collection*. Newbury Park, CA: Sage Publications.

Yee, M. D., & Brown, R. J. (1988). *Children and social comparisons*. Final report to the ESRC, University of Kent.

Yee, M. D., & Brown, R. (1992). Self-evaluations and intergroup attitudes in children aged three to nine. *Child Development, 63*, 619–629.

Yee, M., & Brown, R. (1994). The development of gender differentiation in young children. *British Journal of Social Psychology, 33*, 183–196.

Yip, T., & Fuligni, A. J. (2002). Daily variation in ethnic identity, ethnic behaviors, and psychological well-being among American adolescents of Chinese descent. *Child Development, 73*, 1557–1572.

3 Developmental aspects of social identity

Fabio Sani and Mark Bennett

Our interest is in the development of social identities and children's understanding of those identities. In this chapter we present a series of studies emerging from this interest, studies that are part of a wider research programme on developmental aspects of self and identity. To start with, we discuss qualitative developmental change in children's conception of normative features of members of social groups. Essentially, the question we try to address is: Can we assume that, when thinking about the normative features of group members, children focus on the same aspects of their identities as adults do? Social identity and self-categorisation theorists tend to equate, at least implicitly, normative aspects of group members with the beliefs, values, and attitudes of group members (e.g., Bar-Tal, 1998). However, we will suggest that children's understanding of normative aspects of group members, and therefore children's knowledge of group identities, moves through age-related stages, and that a focus on identity-related beliefs and attitudes may be a relatively late achievement.

Following this, we investigate whether children's representation of the content of in-group identity varies according to changes within the intergroup context in which an identity is construed, and when this starts to happen. In particular, we consider the possible contextual variability of both national and gender identities. The likelihood that there may be variations in conceptualisations of identities as a function of the comparative context has important implications for the way in which children's stereotypes are understood; indeed, it may pose a challenge to widely held cognitive-structural views of stereotypes.

Finally, we discuss developmental aspects of the inclusion of a group in the self. Thus, the question we address is: When do children start subjectively identifying with social groups? When do they intentionally embrace the group norms and represent the self in a stereotypical fashion (i.e., in terms of the group prototype)? In sum, when do children start behaving, thinking, and feeling in terms of a collective self?

We conclude by suggesting that there are many specifically developmental issues that need to be addressed by the social identity approach. In particular, we make the case that more attention should be directed to the particular difficulties associated with the investigation of children's subjective identification with the group. Finally, we note that although social identity theory and self-categorisation theory have considerable heuristic potential for developmentalists, it is nonetheless important to observe that, as theories proposed for adult behaviour, they make a variety of assumptions that may constrain their developmental application.

CHILDREN'S CONCEPTION OF SOCIAL IDENTITIES

People's understanding of the normative aspects of group members' identities can be based on many types of information. For instance, ethnicity can be conceived in terms of skin colour, facial features, appearance based on dress, psychological properties, values, beliefs, and culture. Clearly, adults may draw upon any or indeed all of these different characteristics in conceptualising social groups. However, we suggest that children's conceptualisations of the normative features of group members are likely initially to be quite limited and may undergo substantial elaboration with increasing age. Specifically, we suggest that young children may conceive of group members' normative features in terms of actions and dispositions; only later might they also consider identity-related beliefs. Our hypotheses are based upon work concerning children's person perception (including self-perception) and explanations for interpersonal events.

First of all, in their descriptions of self and other, although there is much evidence that young children are interested in actions (Bartsch & Wellman, 1995) and dispositions (e.g., Damon & Hart, 1988; Eder, 1990), the same is not true with respect to identity-relevant beliefs (e.g., "I believe in world peace because I don't think wars solve anything"; from Damon & Hart, 1988, p. 69). References to such beliefs typically do not appear until late childhood or adolescence. Considered together, these findings are perhaps unsurprising in the sense that where actions and dispositions may have a reasonable degree of predictive utility in terms of future behaviour, the same is not true with respect to identity-related beliefs. As such, it is understandable that, developmentally, priority is given to actions and dispositions.

Going further, we propose that during middle to late childhood there may be a progression from an individualistic to a more collective conception of the normative features of group members that also recognises the role of supra-individual phenomena, such as shared values and belief systems. In a pilot study of children's conceptions of their national identity (Sani, Lyons, & Barrett, 1996), we found evidence broadly consistent with this proposal, such that there was a move from conceptions that emphasised dispositional and concrete aspects of national identity ("English people like football"; "Scotland has nice countryside") to those that emphasised belief-based and collective aspects of national identity ("We believe in democracy"; "We value fair play"). Lambert and Klineberg (1967), too, looking at conceptions of nationality, found that it was not until late childhood that references were made to political and religious belief. Such findings, coupled with the general observation of a move in children's cognition from the concrete to the abstract, suggest the proposal that in representing normative features of group members, young children are likely to focus on features such as behavioural, physical, and dispositional attributes (which have concrete and specifiable manifestations). Only later might they start conceiving of normative features in terms of socially shared beliefs and values (which are abstract and lacking clear behavioural implications). In order to examine this proposal, we conducted three separate studies, which we now outline.

Study 1: Children's understanding of normative features in the context of the Northern Irish conflict

Our first study (Sani, Bennett, Agostini, Malucchi, & Ferguson, 2000; Study 1) looked at Northern Irish children's explanations for the conflict that has long existed between Catholic and Protestant communities in Northern Ireland. What we were interested in was whether, in accounting for group members' behaviour, children would appeal to intrapsychic dispositions ("They're mean and like to start a fight") or to socially shared values and beliefs ("Catholics won't give up their belief that it should just be one country"). We decided to use an intergroup situation as the stimulus for the production of behavioural explanations because, in accordance with the social identity approach, we assume that human groups and their relevant features become cognitively salient and meaningful through intergroup comparisons (Tajfel, 1981; Turner, Hogg, Oakes, Reicher, & Wetherell, 1987). The Northern Irish context was selected because the serious and chronic form of conflict found in that province is likely to provide a high level of experience of issues of group membership; as such, it provides a strict test of our proposals concerning cognitive-developmental limitations, in that "poor" performance might not be readily ascribed to a lack of relevant experience.

Six-, nine-, and twelve-year-olds (with approximately equal numbers of boys and girls and Roman Catholics and Protestants at each age level) were asked semistructured questions that focused upon the relationship between Catholics and Protestants in Northern Ireland. Specifically, the children were first asked: "*Do you think there are any problems between Catholics and Protestants in this country?*" In case of affirmative answers, they were then asked, "*What do you think causes the problems?*"

The 12-year-old children were found to be significantly more inclined than the 6- and 9-year-olds to acknowledge the conflict between the two religious groups: Nearly all the oldest children recognised the conflict, but surprisingly only about half of the two younger groups did so.

Concerning the causes of conflict, we found a very strong association between age group and type of explanation provided, which provided evidence of a progression from a tendency to use individualistic explanations to a willingness to describe the genesis of the events in terms of collective beliefs. The younger children had a propensity to use individualistic explanations, the 9-year-olds could be viewed as transitional, in that some already used belief-based accounts, (though many still employed individualistic accounts), whereas nearly all 12-year-olds explained category members' actions in terms of supra-individual features.

The unexpected feature of the data was that so many children, particularly the younger ones, failed to acknowledge the existence of conflict between the communities of Northern Ireland. This could reflect a general failure to understand conflict at the level of relatively abstract social groups such as those studied here; alternatively it may be the result of parents' and teachers' efforts to shield children from the conflict. Regardless of why these findings emerged, the data relevant to our hypothesis about developments in children's thinking in this domain were limited by the fact that sample sizes were substantially reduced; moreover, in looking only at children who were aware of the conflict, we may have had an atypical subsample. In order to address these problems, we conducted a further study in which we ensured that all participants possessed requisite knowledge about the existence of a specified conflict.

Study 2: Children's understanding of normative features in the context of a fictional intergroup conflict.

This study (Sani et al., 2000; study 2) involved 8-, 10-, and 12-year-old Italian children. Unfortunately, 5-year-old children were not recruited because in the course of a pilot study it became clear that many of them were unable to cope with the memory demands of the task.

Children were shown a story in the form of cartoons. At the beginning of the story a specific group, called "People of the Mountains", was presented. Then, information about (1) external, physical characteristics, (2) psychological/behavioural characteristics, and (3) socially shared beliefs of the group members was provided. For each of the foregoing three aspects, two pieces of information – one conflict-relevant and one conflict-irrelevant – were provided. (The purpose of the inclusion of both relevant and irrelevant information for each of the three aspects was to ensure that children's preference for specific levels of explanations over others reflected a proper understanding of the relation between *particular* antecedents and consequences, rather than a general preference for one level of explanation over others.) So, for instance, concerning psychological/behavioural characteristics, it was stated that the members of one group were "rather aggressive" (relevant information) and that "they tend to be very quiet" (irrelevant information). Finally, a social conflict with the out-group (the "People of the Valley") was described: it was specified that the People of the Mountains invaded the village in the plains surrounding the mountains, where the People of the Valley lived, and forced them to worship their gods in the temple.

We found significant associations between age and types of explanation provided for the conflict. Explanations based on beliefs systems were used by one third of the 12-year-old children, but by very few 10- and 8-year-olds. On the other hand, the majority of 10- and 8-year-olds used explanations based on psychological/behavioural characteristics; these groups invoked such explanations significantly more frequently than did 12-year-olds. (None of the children used explanations that included conflict-irrelevant information. Therefore, within a particular level of explanation, it appears that children's selection of particular explanations is appropriate.)

As in the previous study, there was evidence of a progression from explanations based on the individualistic features of group members to explanations based on supra-individual aspects. However, it is noteworthy that the overall proportion of the oldest children referring to belief systems was markedly lower in this study than in the initial study (34% vs. 94%). This discrepancy between the studies may reflect the fact that the initial study, unlike the present study, involved genuine conflict about which, over a period of years, the older children were likely to have gathered a wealth of information from many diverse sources (Cairns, 1990). More generally, we should also note that, over both studies, explanation in terms of shared belief emerged slightly later than we had predicted. Conceivably this may have been due to a *preference* for explaining aggressive behaviour in terms of corresponding dispositions, rather than to a lack of *understanding* of belief-based aspects of behaviour. Thus, in the study that follows, we move away from children's explanations for conflict and instead rely on direct questioning about social identities.

Study 3: Children's descriptions of group identities

In the studies described thus far we investigated how children account for group members' behaviour and looked in particular at their explanations for intergroup conflict. Although the data were broadly consistent with our predictions, a weakness of these studies, which may have given rise to "noisy" data, is that they tackled the issue of children's conception of the normative features of social group members in an oblique manner: Rather than asking directly about the characteristics of group members, such information was sought in the explanations offered for conflict. Thus, Study 3, using direct questioning, aimed to cast light on the way in which children and adults represent the identity of several types of group, including both in-groups and out-groups.

This study involved more than 250 Scottish participants: 5-, 8-, 11-, and 14-year-olds, and adults. Initially participants were presented with cards, each with a descriptor of a particular social identity (e.g., child, adult, Christian, Muslim, Scottish, English, Girl Guide, Cub, Socialist, Scottish Nationalist, boy, girl, white, black, etc.), and were asked to select those identities that described themselves. The selected cards were then rank-ordered in terms of their subjective importance. Finally, participants were required to consider their two most important social identities and in randomised order, and for each identity, were asked: "What are [boys/children/Scottish people/etc.] like?"; "What do [. . .] do?"; "What do [. . .] want?"; "What do [. . .] believe?". Thus, we asked a broad range of open-ended questions in order to generate a data set that might reflect participants' conceptions of social identities. In addition, and in order to address the possibility that children may have knowledge of belief-based groups but not judge those groups as subjectively important (and thus not be asked about them), we also asked about two such groups likely to be familiar to them: Christians and Scottish Nationalists. (The research was conducted at the same time as the election of Members of the Scottish Parliament (MSPs) to the then newly established Scottish Parliament and debates concerning Scottish Nationalism were conspicuous and vigorous at the time.)

Responses were content-analysed. The unit of analysis was the response to each specific question asked. So, for instance, the answer to the question "What are [. . ..] like?" constituted a unit to be allocated to a category. Six theoretically relevant categories were used in coding responses to each of the questions. The first category was concerned with behavioural/psychological attributes (e.g., "kind", "likes sharing", "don't like boys", "go shopping") that were judged by coders to be identity-relevant for the members of that particular group. For example, if boys were described as liking football, fighting, and fishing, this was considered as identity-relevant for boys. The second category was concerned with behavioural/psychological attributes that are irrelevant to identity. So, for instance, responses in which boys were described as friendly or pet-loving were allocated to this category; that is, while these attributes may be true of particular cases, they are not consistent with general, category-based expectations in this instance. The third category included responses based on beliefs that are relevant but not defining for the group that is described. For example, when Christians were described as "charitable" this may be seen as a relevant belief for this group, but not as defining. The fourth category was concerned with responses based on beliefs that are both relevant and defining for a given group. For example, when Christians were described as believing in God, it is clear that this description is concerned with something that is central for members of the Christian group (but it would not be crucial for members of the groups of children, Socialists, and whites). The fifth category concerned responses based on beliefs that are irrelevant to the group to be judged (and so cannot be defining either). Finally, category six was a residual category, *other*.

The data set is extremely rich and many analyses remain to be conducted. However, our hypotheses were largely supported. Young children's conceptions of social identities were principally concerned with personal and behavioural attributes; little reference was made to belief-based attributes. Among the youngest children, preferred identities related to gender and age and were seen as characterised by behavioural and dispositional features (e.g., "boys like to play football"). Only among the older children, adolescents, and adults was there a clear recognition of the role of beliefs in some social identities (e.g., "to be a Christian means believing in God", "the nationalists want independence for Scotland"). This is not to say that young children entirely failed to understand belief-based identities; rather, their view is partial. For example, younger children recognised that Scottish Nationalists hold very positive views of Scotland, but failed to provide evidence of understanding that they are defined by their beliefs concerning Scottish independence.

Looking at the data in more detail, what emerges is that all age groups made reference to identity-relevant psychological attributes, so that even 5-year-olds identified at least one relevant attribute per group considered (for example, commenting that, "girls like going shopping"). Eight-, eleven-, and fourteen-year-olds identified significantly more such attributes (typically around 1.6 per group). Adults on average noted more still (around 2 identity-relevant psychological attributes per group).

Turning to identity-defining beliefs, 5-year-olds, as we had predicted, made no reference to such attributes. Eight-, eleven-, and fourteen-year-olds made significantly more references to them and did not differ from each other with, on average, a total of 1.2 such attributes over the four groups considered. Adults offered significantly more examples than did 8-year-olds, typically 1.5 identity-defining beliefs over the four groups considered. Although the age differences are broadly as we had predicted, it is noteworthy that when directly asked about beliefs, even 8-year-olds provide evidence of comprehension, suggesting that our previous method underestimated ability in this respect. It is also noteworthy that even among adults the mean number of references to social identity-defining beliefs was quite small. The fact that means for behavioural/psychological attributes were larger than those for beliefs probably reflects the fact that while all social identities are associated with the former, not all are associated with the latter. For example, the groups "teenagers", "children", "boys", "girls", "whites", "blacks", and "Scottish" (to name but a few) have no identity-defining beliefs associated with them. Thus, differences over the coding categories considered here need to be viewed with this caution in mind.

A nearly identical pattern of findings emerged for identity-relevant beliefs as for identity-defining beliefs. Thus, means for all groups were relatively low compared to those for behavioural/psychological attributes, but predicted age trends nonetheless emerged.

Finally, looking at identity-irrelevant references to both behavioural/psychological attributes and beliefs, what is striking is the *absence* of age differences. We had expected that younger children's conceptions of social identities would be "noisy", incorporating information that both agreed with and diverged from the adult conception. As we saw it, children's developmental task would be both to gather relevant information and to sift out irrelevant information. Our data, however, appear not to support this proposal. In this respect, the difference between young children and adults would appear to be in the extent, rather than the clarity, of their knowledge about social identities, suggesting that from a very early age children may be especially sensitive to identity-relevant information – indeed, a claim central to schematic models of identity, such as gender-schematic processing theory (Martin & Halverson 1981).

Summary

Overall, what emerges from these studies is that, as predicted, younger children conceive of social identities primarily in terms of group members' behavioural and dispositional attributes. Not until later do they come to recognise the importance (for some identities at least) of shared beliefs and values[1]. This is not to suggest that there are no important developments prior to the age of 5 years. Indeed, Quintana (1998) has suggested that among 3- to 5-year-old children, ethnic groups may be conceived primarily in physical terms (e.g., with reference to skin tone, facial morphology, etc.). Such a tendency may be found for other types of group, too. Regardless of such a possibility, our findings suggest that belief-based forms of social identity may not be fully grasped until mid to late childhood.

For many identities, it is plainly inconsequential that belief-based attributes are not understood. For example, gender identities appear to be based primarily on behavioural and dispositional attributes; there are no beliefs that can be taken as necessary and sufficient for gender group membership. The same is self-evidently not the case with respect to identities such as "Christian", "Muslim", "Socialist", and "animal rights activist". For such identities, beliefs play a definitional role. Our assumption in this chapter has been that owing to cognitive-developmental limitations, children experience difficulties in conceiving of abstract entities such as socially shared beliefs. However, we accept that a further explanation for this progression may be that belief-based identities involve personal choice; that is, they reflect agents' commitments. Interestingly, the sorts of identities children understand well (e.g., gender identity, age-based identity, ethnic identity, etc.) are de facto identities – identities about which they have little choice. To the extent that such identities are largely immutable and are significant across diverse social contexts, we speculate that parents, in socialising children, may give these identities priority; ascribed identities, virtually by definition, may be "scaffolded" to a greater degree than those reflecting personal choice. With this in mind, we recognise the possibility that the developmental progression we have

---

1 Theory of mind researchers may find this puzzling. After all, a wealth of evidence now shows that even 4-year-olds understand belief (e.g., see Perner, 1999). However, it is important to point out that the sorts of beliefs considered here differ from those investigated by theory of mind researchers. For example, in the latter tradition beliefs are empirical in nature and involve a world-to-mind "direction of fit" (Searle, 1983); the beliefs considered here are essentially ideological and cannot be seen as driven by the empirical facts of the world.

identified may not primarily be a cognitive-developmental phenomenon, but instead one based on domain-related increments in expertise (Chi & Rees, 1983). It remains for future research to address the relative contributions of experience and cognitive development in children's understanding of social identities.

Finally, then, a general point to note is that social identities differ. This is not something that has been widely addressed by the social identity approach. Deaux, Reid, Mizrahi, and Cotting (1999) have speculated that "this neglect reflects a concern with general psychological processes that are assumed to characterize a variety of specific forms of identification" (p. 93). From a developmental perspective, we suggest that the evidence provided by our work points to a need to examine diverse types of social identity, the challenges of conceptualisation that they pose for children, and the challenges of socialisation that they pose for adults.

THE FLEXIBILITY OF CHILDREN'S UNDERSTANDING OF IN-GROUP IDENTITY

Thus far we have considered general *developmental* change in the conceptual-isation of social identity. However, it is important, too, to consider possible *contextual* variation in this domain. That is, to what extent are children's conceptions of particular groups context-specific? In what follows we shall introduce some of our own studies, which suggest that children, like adults, may judge a given group on the basis of the *particular* intergroup situation in which a judgment is made. First, however, to place this work within a broader theoretical context, we turn to social psychological work demonstrating that adults' conceptions of social identities (as expressed in stereotypes) are subject to contextual variation.

Within contemporary social psychology, a stereotype is widely conceived as a set of beliefs about attributes and behaviours of members of a social category (Hamilton & Trolier, 1986; Stangor & Shaller, 1996). Stereotypes are viewed as stored in memory, and automatically assigned to people who are categorised as members of the social category associated to those specific stereotypes (e.g., Fiske & Neuberg, 1990). Clearly, this view implies a con-ceptualisation of stereotypes as essentially fixed and rigid mental structures, which, as asserted by Stangor (1995, p. 631), may change only through inter-action with individuals from the stereotyped group, which disconfirm existing stereotypes, or because the perceiver does not consider the stereotype as useful or desirable any longer.

An obvious implication of this position is that the content of a stereotype is unaffected by the nature of the intergroup context within which the stereo-type is invoked. So, for instance, according to this position my conception of psychologists in terms of, say, their methodological orientation (e.g., whether they are rigorous, objective, imaginative, etc.) will remain the same, regardless of whether I am thinking about psychologists in comparison to historians or whether I am thinking about them in comparison to chemists.

More recently, this cognitive-structural view of stereotypes has been criticised by self-categorisation theorists (Oakes, Haslam, & Turner, 1994), who have rejected the notion that a stereotype is a stored concept "waiting-to-be-activated". They contend that (1) a stereotype is always formed within a specific intergroup context, either explicit or implicit, as stereotypes are used to explain, describe, and justify the nature of intergroup relations, and that (2) in forming stereotypes, people make use of all cognitive resources that are available to them. This implies that a change in the intergroup context within which a given stereotype is used is likely to lead to a change in the nature of the stereotype itself. Therefore, the substantive content of a stereotype (regardless of whether the stereotyped group is an in-group or an out-group) is inherently comparative, flexible, and variable.

However, self-categorisation theorists do not just emphasise stereotype variability; they also contend that the different understandings of a certain group that may arise in different intergroup contexts arise systematically, and not merely haphazardly. It is argued that in each particular context a group's definition is based on an accentuation of its differences from the other groups on relevant dimensions of comparison. The function of this process of accentuation is that of allowing the perceiver to structure the social environment and to make sense of the situation (Oakes et al., 1994; Turner & Oakes, 1997).

Self-categorisation theorists have supported their position with strong evidence. For instance, Haslam, Turner, Oakes, McGarty, and Hayes (1992) found that the way in which Australians described Americans during the Gulf War changed as a function of the number and type of nations included in the comparative context, and that changes occurred particularly on dimensions that were relevant to the ongoing military conflict. Thus, Americans were characterised as more "aggressive" when the context included the USSR than when it did not, indicating that subjects perceived differences between America and the USSR in their approach to the war and to East–West relations in general.

These general findings, which have been replicated by other studies looking at further identities (e.g., Haslam & Turner, 1992; Hopkins & Murdoch, 1999; Hopkins, Regan, & Abell, 1997; Sani & Thomson, 2001), have important implications for developmental studies on stereotypes, as developmental psychologists seem to subscribe, at least implicitly, to a view of stereotypes as endemically rigid and fixed. Researchers have assumed that at any point in development children's understanding of social categories is based on a specific and cross-situationally stable stereotypical content, which may change only through more general social-cognitive development. Thus, attempts have been made to specify, at different points in development, children's stereotypes of national groups (Barrett & Short, 1992; Lambert & Klineberg, 1967), gender groups (Best et al., 1977; Serbin & Sprafkin, 1986), age groups (Edwards, 1984), and ethnic groups (Davey, 1983). However, results emerging from the research conducted by self-categorisation theorists suggest the desirability of investigating the issue of stereotype variability from a developmental perspective.

From the perspective of the social identity approach, the process of stereotyping clearly rests on a capacity to engage in social comparison. That is, "we" may seem easygoing when compared to Group X, but when compared to Group Y, may appear quite formal. Interestingly, Ruble and her colleagues (Pomerantz, Ruble, Frey, & Greulich, 1995; Ruble, 1983; Ruble & Flett, 1988; Ruble & Frey, 1991) have found that only at around 7 years old do children draw upon social comparison information in order to make judgments about the self. Thus, contextual variability of stereotype content may be a relatively late development.

A further developmental consideration is that young children have relatively compartmentalised notions about the self, reflecting "a rudimentary ability to intercoordinate concepts" about the self (Harter, 1999, p. 41). Only by mid childhood does there appear to be the sort of cognitive flexibility in self-concepts that is presupposed by the account of stereotyping presented by self-categorisation theory. In the light of such considerations, we assume that contextual variability in stereotyping is likely to emerge in children aged around 7 years. Clearly, this assumption has important implications for the developmental study of social identity. As we have already mentioned, in-group identity can be legitimately seen as based on a stereotypical representation of in-group members, including self. As a result, once applied to the in-group, stereotype variability is conceptually equivalent to social identity variability.

In an initial study, we investigated children's national stereotypes (Sani, Bennett, & Joyner, 1999), adapting the procedure used by social psychologists (e.g., Haslam et al., 1992). That is, we solicited stereotypes of the national in-group following consideration of two distinct out-groups (Spanish/Germans). Contrary to expectation, in-group stereotypes were unaffected by the comparative context. That is, children described the in-group in the same way irrespective of whether it was described following consideration of Spanish people or of German people. (Interestingly, Barrett, Wilson, & Lyons, (2003), using a different methodology, obtained similar findings to ours.) Conceivably, however, rather than reflecting essentially fixed stereotypes, these results may have been due to two main weaknesses of the study. First, this study was concerned with an aspect of social identity, that is, nationality, which may not be salient for many young children (Bennett, Lyons, Sani, & Barrett, 1998a). Second, since children were presented with a brief and ready-made (rather than solicited) description of the out-group, this procedure may have failed to establish a comparative context. These considerations formed a basis for the design of Study 4.

Study 4: On the flexibility of children's gender identity

In this study (Sani & Bennett, 2001), we explored possible contextual variability in 6- and 7-year-old children's gender stereotypes, using a simple trait selection procedure (i.e., children were required to select from a large set of cards those which best described a specified group) as in the Sani et al. (1999) study. Two experimental conditions were employed. In the first condition the out-group was represented by adult "men" if participants were boys, or by adult "women" if participants were girls. In the second condition the out-group was represented by "girls" if participants were boys, or by "boys" if participants were girls. Obviously, in both conditions, the in-group was either "girls" or "boys", depending on the participants' sex.

Importantly, there were clear indications that some stereotypical traits attributed to the in-group changed significantly as the frame of reference changed. Girls selected "friendly" more often when describing the in-group after describing boys than after describing adult women, and boys selected "strong" and "brave" more often when stereotyping the in-group after describing girls than after describing adult men. Moreover, consistent with SCT, the dimensions that varied according to changes in the comparative context were those dimensions that seemed to maximise perceived intergroup difference.

However, despite being consistent with predictions, the effects of the comparative context were not as strong as expected: Only 2 adjectives used by males and 1 used by girls, out of 27 adjectives that each group considered, varied cross-situationally. This may have reflected methodological limitations of the study. In particular, we suspect that adjective selection was an unduly "noisy" measure. First, when children are presented with a large number of adjectives, they might make their selections based not on a consideration of the entire set, but upon those adjectives that are noticed either early or late in the task. Second, children may tend to select positive and highly accessible adjectives, for instance "friendly", "happy", and "nice", at the expense of more neutral and slightly less accessible adjectives such as "greedy", "talkative", and "loud", whatever the nature of the intergroup context. That implies that, if some of the more neutral or slightly negative adjectives were seen as characterising many in-group members in a given intergroup context, but only some in-group members in a different intergroup context, predicted effects would be hard to observe. Finally, we should note that this study looked only at an age group that had been predicted to show the predicted effects of comparative context on stereotype content. In the following study, younger children are included in the sample in order to address the hypothesis that their responses would *not* show the predicted effects of comparative context. Moreover, a different method was employed.

Study 5: A further investigation into the flexibility of children's gender identity

Study 5 (Sani, Bennett, Mullally, & MacPherson, 2003), using a sample of 5- and 7-year-old children, retained the same design as Study 4 but addressed the limitations of that study. First of all, we reduced the number of adjectives, selecting 18 of the original 27. (We discarded those adjectives that were never used by more than one child in any of the experimental conditions in Study 4.) Second, we investigated children's stereotypes by means of a rating task. Children were asked to look at each card in the set and decide whether the adjective written on the card was applicable to *most* girls/boys/grown-up women/grown-up men, *some*, or *none*.

Results provided clear evidence that 7-year-old children conceive the in-group identity in a flexible fashion. Boys' conceptions of the in-group were more likely to draw attention to being "brave", "big", and "strong" in the context of girls than of men, but "talkative" in the context of men, rather than girls. Girls' in-group descriptions emphasised cleverness and hardwork-ingness more strongly in the context of boys than of women, but greediness, loudness, and smallness in the context of women, rather than boys. Therefore, results seem to show that a stereotype is not an unchanging representation of a social group but a representation of a group in relation to one or more other groups. Also, results suggest that the adjectives that are rated in differ-ent ways according to changes in the comparative context are those that maximise perceived intergroup differences. So, this is why boys indicated, for instance, that the adjectives "clean", "happy", and "kind" are applicable to the same number of in-group members in both conditions, but that "brave", "big", and "strong" are applicable to a higher number of in-group members in comparison to girls than in comparison to men. Clearly, reference to such qualities in the context of girls is a way to accentuate aspects of the in-group that can be used to differentiate it from the relevant out-group on specific dimensions.

Contrary to our initial predictions, even among the 5-year-olds there appears to be some degree of flexibility in the construction of their gender identity, though only among boys. Thus, boys described in-group members as being more dirty and loud in the context of men than in the context of girls, and as being tougher in the context of girls than in the context of men. Again, the dimensions that varied according to changes in the intergroup context appear to be those dimensions that maximise perceived differences between the two groups. This indicates that 5-year-olds may possess, at least in rudimentary form, the cognitive competencies necessary to demonstrate sensitivity to comparative context[2].

2 A puzzling aspect of the data is the gender difference observed among 5-year-olds in the present study. An explanation for this difference may be that although gender is a highly significant aspect of both boys' and girls' identities (Eckes & Trautner, 2000), socialisation agents' gender-related expectations of boys are more sharply defined than those of girls (Fagot & Hagan, 1991). As a consequence, boys may have a more coherent set of gender-related self-beliefs than girls, and may be more motivated to affirm these self-beliefs when their gender identity is made salient. Consistent with this is Premack and Premack's (1995) contention that boys may be more sensitive than girls to group-based distinctions.

Summary

The results of our studies on gender identity (though not national identity) demonstrate that conceptions of in-group identity vary as a function of the comparative context. In characterising gender in-group identity, children do not appeal to identical descriptors regardless of intergroup context. These results are consistent with Banerjee and Lintern's (2000) finding that 4- to 6-year-old boys' self-descriptions were significantly more gender-stereotypical when before a group of same-sex peers than when alone.

These findings are surprising insofar as they indicate that even young children provide evidence of sensitivity to comparative context, contrary to what we had predicted. Thus, 5-year-olds appear to possess, to some degree, the cognitive competencies necessary to demonstrate sensitivity to comparative context, at least in the case of gender identity. That such competencies are not seen in the domain of national identity is perhaps unsurprising. First of all, as a highly abstract and inclusive category, nationality has significantly lower utility than does gender. Whereas gender is an effective basis for distinguishing between people within one's typical social contexts, the same is not true of nationality since the overwhelming majority of one's peers, relatives, teachers, and so on are likely to be of the same nationality as oneself. Given its relatively low utility, nationality will be less salient than gender, and in consequence, less is likely to be known about nationality-appropriate characteristics than about gender-appropriate characteristics. Thus, although young children appear to know the national labels (e.g., American, Italian; see Barrett, Lyons, & del Valle, Chapter 6), they do not yet have the wealth of knowledge about the content of the categories to provide a basis for the metacontrasts assumed by self-categorisation theory.

A general question raised by our results is whether children's representations of stereotypes, and group identities in general, can be considered as stored concepts waiting to be activated, as is widespread within developmental psychology. Researchers in the social identity tradition propose two different responses to the issue. On the one hand, Turner and Onorato (1999) suggest that in-group stereotypes are "created as they are used, on the spot, and brought into being as they are brought into sight" (p. 32). Although these authors do not deny that knowledge that is used to construe specific stereotypes is stored in our cognitive system, they do not believe that this knowledge is stored in the same form as the stereotype that is phenomenally experienced. Instead, it exists as complex theoretical knowledge about ourselves and the world in which we live, and is used flexibly to create specific in-group stereotypes on the basis of current needs, expectations, and sociostructural constraints.

In opposition to this view, Hogg (2001) contends that people have a stored set of group stereotypes (including stereotypes of in-groups) that are situationally adjusted. That is, stereotypes are not created on the spot, but are carried in people's heads and modified at the moment in which they are employed on the basis of the nature of the intergroup context. Clearly, this is a key issue inasmuch as it speaks to the question of whether we should see stereotypes and identities essentially as structures or as processes. (See David, Grace, & Ryan, Chapter 5, for a fuller discussion of this matter.) Furthermore, it is an issue that is amenable to empirical inquiry. But as a subtle and complex matter, and one that will mobilise strong (and competing) theoretical commitments, it is unlikely to see an easy resolution. Regardless of such grand-scale debates, an important focus of inquiry should be the further investigation of the social and developmental factors affecting the extent of contextual variability in children's identities.

THE EMERGENCE OF SOCIAL IDENTITY

Irrespective of developmental and contextual variations in children's conceptions of social identity, a key issue that remains is the matter of the internalisation of social identities. That is, children may have knowledge of identities, and may use that knowledge flexibly, but they may not *subjectively experience* themselves as members of particular collectivities. Thus, as Ruble et al. (Chapter 2) put it, we need to address "the developmental course of children's sense of 'we' ".

Previous developmental researchers have often equated the social self with the description of oneself in terms of particular social categories ("I am a girl"; "I am a boy scout"; "I'm Scottish", etc.). Although this is an important first step in the development of social identity, it is no more than that: a first step. We would make the case that merely describing oneself in terms of social categories is not equivalent to social identity as conceived within the social identity approach. As Turner, Oakes Haslam, and McGarty (1994) point out, "social identity can be distinguished from personal identity in terms of self-referential cognitions that identify 'we' and 'us' rather than 'I' and 'me' " (p. 454). Among adults, it is reasonable to assume that social self-descriptions, such as Democrat, Catholic, or whatever, imply subjective identification with the particular collectivity. Indeed, much research provides evidence to this effect (e.g., see Abrams & Hogg, 2001; Tyler, Kramer, & John, 1999). However, we suggest that in a developmental context it becomes important to question whether children's early self-referential descriptions such as "I'm a boy" and "I'm Italian" connote that sense of "we" and "us" that properly constitute social identity. Might they instead be derived merely by reference to 'objective' indices (in the case of gender, that is, clothing, behaviour, genitals, etc.; in the case of nationality, place of birth, passport held, etc.)?

Central here is that a fully-fledged social identity requires recognition that the self may be defined through relationship with other category members. (Other features, too, are required; see Ruble et al., Chapter 2.) With this in mind, we explored the initial development of the social self by means of two studies. First, extending Bennett, Yuill, Banerjee, and Thomson's (1998b) work on identity in dyadic contexts, we examined children's sense of responsibility for actions committed by unknown in-group members. Second, we explored how far, if at all, children evince a cognitive tendency to accentuate self-stereotypical characteristics when relevant social identities are made salient (as has been found among adults).

Study 6: Feelings of responsibility for in-group members' actions

As Doosje, Branscombe, Spears, and Manstead (1998) have noted, an important consequence of a social identity is that many aspects of self-perception result not from one's *own* actions, but from those of others who share one's social identity. For example, Doosje et al. note the sense of collective guilt experienced by many Germans born following Word War II. Since these individuals could in no way have personally influenced the events of 1939–45, their sense of guilt and responsibility can be understood only in terms of their social identity, that is, as Germans.

Previous research by Bennett et al. (1998b) has shown that not until around 7–8 years of age do children feel compromised by the wrongdoings of another person with whom they are closely associated (mother or best friend); prior to this they assert that others' perceptions of them will be based only on those actions for which they are personally responsible (e.g., "They'll still think I'm nice. He did it, it wasn't me"). Although this study looked only at interpersonal contexts, rather than the intergroup contexts required to examine social identity, it nevertheless suggests the possibility that a fully-fledged social identity may be a considerably later development than previously assumed.

Using a method based on that of Bennett et al. (1998b), in collaboration with Wendy Gibson, we investigated when children start to feel compromised by the wrongdoings of in-group members. Participants (5-, 7-, and 9-year olds) were asked to consider hypothetical scenarios in which either they personally were responsible for a particular negative outcome (personal condition), or in which it was stated that a member of the same social category committed the action (social condition). For example, children were asked to consider a context in which, during a sporting visit to another school, either they or another (unknown) child from their school commit a normative transgression. Following this, children were asked a variety of questions about their likely responses to the events depicted. Interestingly, whereas in the personal condition majorities in all age groups indicated that they would want to apologise for the transgression, in the social condition the desire to offer apology was present only in the 7- and 9-year-olds. Similarly, only among the two older age groups was there a recognition of how the unknown in-group member's action would colour out-group members' perceptions of the in-group. These findings, like those of Bennett et al. (1998b), suggest that the youngest children may have an essentially individualistic perspective:

That is, they may see actions as reflecting only upon their particular per-petrators, rather than upon the groups of which those perpetrators are members. Given this, one may question the widely held assumption that young children's references to social-categorical memberships carry the same meaning as those of older children and adults.

Study 7: The emergence of self-stereotyping

As we noted earlier, a crucial issue to be addressed is when it is that children become able to redraw the boundaries of the self in order to include other people within the self. Study 5, conducted in collaboration with Georgina Ferrier, investigated this issue in the context of gender identity. That is, we studied when children begin to include the characteristics of their gender in-group in the self. The inclusion of the in-group in the self was operationalised as self-stereotyping, that is, as the perception of self in terms of the stereo-typical characteristics of the gender in-group.

Our study included two experimental conditions. In both, the child was asked to judge the self by specifying the extent to which a set of adjectives (e.g., nice, friendly, brave, loud, clever, dirty, etc.) applied to him/her. More precisely, the child had to say whether he/she was "not at all", "quite", or "very" nice, friendly, brave, kind, and so on. However, in the first condition the child had to describe only the self ("only self" condition), while in the second condition he/she initially described the relevant gender out-group in general – that is "girls' if the child was a male, or "boys" if the child was a female – and then subsequently the self ("out-group then self" condition). Thus, this was a repeated measures design; the second condition was run 2 weeks after the first, to ensure that in the second condition participants would not remember their previous judgments.

The central assumption of this study, then, was that if participants assign more gender-stereotypical characteristics to themselves in the second than in the first condition, then we can infer that the nature of the intergroup context has made children's social identity salient, and in turn, social identity has led to important changes in self-perception and self-stereotyping. That is, we can infer that the group has become part of the self.

Results show that 5-year-olds tended to describe themselves in a consistent fashion across conditions: in-group identification does not seem to lead younger children to a more gender-stereotypical perception of the self. However, there is clear evidence that older males described the self in a more gender-stereotypical fashion in the out-group then self than in the "only self" condition. To start with, 7-year-old males defined self as bigger, tougher, stronger, and more hardworking when judging it after judging the group of girls than when judging it alone. Similarly, 10-year-old males saw the self as dirtier and bigger in the out-group then self than in the "only self" condition. Among girls, effects were less marked: As was the case for 5-year-olds boys, the youngest group of girls provided the same sorts of self-descriptions regardless of condition. However, for both 7- and 10-year-old females there was a marginal effect for the adjective "talkative", in the sense that they described the self as less talkative when gender identity was salient. In sum, results indicate that by 7 years of age children become cognitively able to include the in-group in the self. (The lack of clear effects for girls may reflect the possibility that the adjectives used in the study better reflected male than female identity, a possibility we are currently addressing.)

Summary

Interestingly, the results of the two studies reported in this section, though using quite different methodologies, seem to yield similar findings. Both suggest that it is not until around 7 years of age, at the earliest, that children internalise particular social identities. (And of course, the internalisation of many identities, especially those based on belief, is likely to come rather later.) Although we accept that much work is needed to substantiate this suggestion properly, it points to the necessity to reconsider previous claims concerning the early appearance of social identities. In particular, future research should seek to distinguish between mere labelling of the self in social categorical terms and internalisation of social categories in self-conception, in that it may be that initial self-categorisation serves to direct attention to those aspects of the environment that facilitate the subsequent internalisation of an identity.

Despite convergence between the findings of the two studies, it may be worth noting that the studies' foci differ in at least one important way that may transpire to be significant. The first study deals with phenomena that are contingent upon having internalised a social identity whereas the second perhaps deals more directly with presence or absence of an internalised identity. Thus, in the former study we examined beliefs about out-group members' views of the in-group, the desire to apologise, and so on. In the second study we looked directly at self-conception. We speculate that more fine-grained work may reveal the need to distinguish between the initial internalisation of an identity and the subsequent coupling of internalisation to identity-related processes (such as facework, social role-taking, social emotions, etc.). Such a pattern of findings is well-documented in other domains. For example, "theory of mind" research has shown that an understanding of false belief precedes an appreciation of false belief-related emotions (e.g., feeling happy because one falsely believes something positive has transpired; Harris, Johnson, Hutton, Andrews, & Cooke, 1989). Thus, future research on social identity should seek to distinguish measures of basic processes from those contingent upon basic processes.

So far in our discussion we have spoken of the internalisation of social identities as an all-or-none affair, and indeed, our measures, too, imply a dichotomous conception in this respect. Inevitably, initial research on a particular problem must make simplifying assumptions, and this is a case in point. We fully accept, therefore, that future research should examine the *extent* of identification with particular social categories. Indeed, not only may identification vary quantitatively (i.e., in that children may feel more or less identified with a group), but also qualitatively, in the sense that there are likely to be age-related changes in category *meaning* (e.g., along the sorts of lines implied by the first subsection of this chapter).

GENERAL SUMMARY AND CONCLUSIONS

The fundamental message of the three subsections of this chapter is that social identity-related phenomena are subject to important developmental changes. We have suggested that developments take place in conceptualising identities. In particular, we propose that younger children conceive of identities largely in terms of particular behaviours, practices, and dispositions, and that only later do they also consider socially shared beliefs. Second, we suggest that children's conceptualisation of identities is likely, with increasing age, to vary with the comparative context in which conceptualisations are instantiated. Finally, we propose that children's internalisation of particular social identities may be a somewhat later development than previous researchers have supposed.

The work that we have outlined here represents only a start on these questions and much remains to be done in terms of detailed confirmation (or not!) of our claims and their implications. We consider that the first two areas (i.e., conceptualisations of identities and their contextual variability) are fairly tractable methodologically and lend themselves readily to further empirical inquiry. More problematic, in our view, is the assessment of the extent to which social identities have penetrated children's self-conception. In looking at children's subjective sense of themselves as group members we would advocate (for the time being at least) the abandonment of conventional methods, such as verbal self-description, on the grounds that categorical labels can be applied with reference merely to public criteria, without necessarily indicating subjective identification with a particular group. (See too David et al., Chapter 5, who note also that social identification, though not mere self-labelling, necessarily involves recognition of within-group similarity and between-group difference.) Similarly, we have reservations about methods that require children to rank-order identities, since these *presuppose* that those identities are internalised (e.g., a child may rank-order the identity "American" high not because it is one that is central to her current sense of herself, but because this represents an identity *aspiration*, one that others have marked out for her as desirable). In our own work on this topic we have outlined two methods that we believe better assess the internalisation of social identities. A key goal for future research is to extend the range of methodologies that address this matter. We suggest that the social psychological literature represents a rich resource in terms of methodologies that might be adapted for developmental inquiry.

Like others in this volume, we propose that mid to late childhood may be a particularly important time in terms of the understanding and internalisation of many social identities, particularly those that are ascribed rather than chosen (the latter perhaps being more characteristic of adolescence, e.g., Eckert, 1989). In addition to burgeoning cognitive developments that underlie categorical differentiation, it is clear that during this period children acquire a social "face" (Bennett et al., 1998b; Miller, 1996) and recognise that others make expectations in line with that face. Importantly, too, the shelter afforded by the domestic arena of family life is to some extent diminished by children's participation in school life, and particularly the peer group. The peer group, marked by greater heterogeneity than the family unit, inevitably highlights issues of *difference* and increasingly calls attention to social identities. Where social identities may have been relatively taken for granted (or even invisible) within the family, they are likely to be subject to extensive negotiation and even contestation within the peer group (see Connolly, 1998). Such experiences may contribute not only to the development of the social self but also to the *personal* self, inasmuch as, for example, children's commitments to public claims about the social self may sharpen their sense of private selfhood.

In conclusion, we take the view that the heuristic value of the social identity approach to developmentalists is considerable, both in terms of empirical predictions and conceptual illumination. The chapters of this book largely attest to this contention. However, it is important to note that there are many specifically developmental questions that are thrown up by this approach – some of which we have tackled here, albeit relatively superficially, given that our efforts have been largely descriptive rather than explanatory (that is, we have said little of the possible *causes* underlying observed developments). It is important, too, to reiterate the obvious but vital observation that these theories were developed with *adult* behaviour in mind. As such, they may reflect assumptions that are untenable in a developmental context, thereby limiting the theories' developmental application[3]. Moreover, we suggest that there are questions about the development of social identity that lie beyond the scope of the social identity approach. For example, in considering the *origins* of social identities, an essentially cognitive account, based on the individual child's capacity for categorisation of social stimuli, is likely to neglect

---

3 For example, social identity theory's distinction between permeable and impermeable group boundaries is predicated on an adult conception. From a developmental perspective it may be a potentially problematic distinction in that, lacking ethnic/gender/and so on constancy, young children are unlikely to respond to it in the same way, seeing all boundaries as in some sense permeable. Similarly, concerning self-categorisation theory, the calculation of comparative fit cannot be taken for granted in that the cognitive capacity to partition stimuli into sets and subsets and reason about their interrelations is not apparent in young children.

important social sources of identity. As Jenkins (1996) has adeptly expressed it, "if identity is a prerequisite for social life, the reverse is also true" (p. 20). With this in mind, and drawing upon a Vygotskian analysis, we suggest that it may be fruitful to conceive of the origins of social identities in terms of co-construction (i.e., between novice and elder), rather than in terms of purely individual cognitive construction. Drawing upon this approach, one could then usefully think about the activities through which the social enactment of identities, and the affirmation of those identities by others, contributes to their internalisation. In turn, this raises the need to extend the range of methodologies employed that have been used to date, to include, for example, ethnographic and other qualitative techniques (Connolly, 2001).

Acknowledgements

The research reported in this chapter was largely funded by a grant from the Economic and Social Research Council, UK (grant reference R000222801).We are extremely grateful for the constructive comments made by Martyn Barrett on an earlier version of this chapter.

REFERENCES

Abrams, D., & Hogg, M. (2001). Collective self. In M. A. Hogg & S. Tindale (Eds.), *Blackwell handbook of social psychology: Vol. 3. Group processes* (pp. 425–461). Oxford: Blackwell.

Banerjee, R., & Lintern, V. (2000). Boys will be boys: The effect of social evaluation concerns on gender typing. *Social Development, 9*, 397–408.

Barrett, M., & Short, J. (1992). Images of European people in a group of 5–10-year-old English schoolchildren. *British Journal of Developmental Psychology, 10*, 339–363.

Barrett, M., Wilson, H., & Lyons, E. (2003). The development of national ingroup bias: English children's attributions of characteristics to English, American and German people. *British Journal of Developmental Psychology, 21*, 193–220.

Bar-Tal, D. (1998). Group beliefs as expressions of social identity. In S. Worchel, J. Francisco Morales, D. Paez, & J.-C. Deschamps (Eds.), *Social identity: International perspectives* (pp. 93–113). London: SAGE Publications.

Bartsch, K., & Wellman, H. M. (1995). *Children talk about the mind.* Oxford: Oxford University Press.

Bennett, M., Lyons, E., Sani, F., & Barrett, M. (1998a). Children's subjective identification with the group and in-group favoritism. *Developmental Psychology, 34*, 902–909.

Bennett, M., Yuill, N., Banerjee, R., & Thomson, S. (1998b). Children's understanding of extended identity. *Developmental Psychology, 34*, 322–331.

Best, D. L., Williams, J. E., Cloud, M. J., Robertson, L. S., Edwards, J. R., Giles, H., & Fowles, J. (1977). Development of sex-trait stereotypes among young children in the United States, England and Ireland. *Child Development, 48*, 1375–1384.

Cairns, E. (1990). Impact of television news on children's perceptions of violence in Northern Ireland. *Journal of Social Psychology, 130,* 447–452.

Chi, M. T. H., & Rees, E. T. (1983). A learning framework for development. In M. T. H. Chi (Ed.), *Trends in memory development.* Basel: Karger.

Connolly, P. (1998). *Racism, gender identities and young children: Social relations in a multi-ethnic inner-city primary school.* New York: Routledge.

Connolly, P. (2001). Qualitative methods in the study of children's racial attitudes and identities. *Infant and Child Development, 4,* 219–233.

Damon, W., & Hart, D. (1988). *Self-understanding in childhood and adolescence.* New York: Cambridge University Press.

Davey, A. (1983). *Learning to be prejudiced.* London: Edward Arnold.

Deaux, K., Reid, A., Mizrahi, K., & Cotting, D. (1999). Connecting the person to the social: The functions of social identification. In T. R. Tyler, R. M. Kramer, & O. P. John (Eds.), *The psychology of the social self* (pp. 91–114). Mahwah, NJ: Lawrence Erlbaum Associates, Inc.

Doosje, B., Branscombe, N. R., Spears, R., & Manstead, A. S. R. (1998). Guilty by association: When one's group has a negative history. *Journal of Personality and Social Psychology, 75,* 872–886.

Eckert, P. (1989). *Jocks and burnouts: Social categories and identity in the high school.* Columbia, SC: Teachers College Press.

Eckes, T., & Trautner, H. M. (Eds.) (2000). *The developmental social psychology of gender.* Mahwah, NJ: Lawrence Erlbaum Associates, Inc.

Eder, R. A. (1990). Uncovering young children's psychological selves: Individual and developmental differences. *Child Development, 61,* 849–863.

Edwards, C. P. (1984). The age group labels and categories of preschool children. *Child Development, 55,* 440–452.

Fagot, B. L., & Hagan, R. (1991). Observations of parents reactions to sex-stereotyped behaviors. *Child Development, 62,* 1617–1628.

Fiske, S. T., & Neuberg, S. L. (1990). A continuum of impression formation, from category-based to individuating processes: Influences of information and motivation on attention and interpretation. In M. P. Zanna (Ed.), *Advances in experimental social psychology, Vol. 23* (pp. 1–74). New York: Academic Press.

Hamilton, D. L., & Trolier, T. K. (1986). Stereotypes and stereotyping: An overview of the cognitive approach. In J. F. Dovidio & S. Gaertner (Eds.), *Prejudice, discrimination and racism* (pp. 127–163). London: Academic Press.

Harris, P., Johnson, C. N., Hutton, D., Andrews, G., & Cooke, T. (1989). Young children's theory of mind and emotions. *Cognition and Emotion, 3,* 379–400.

Harter, S. (1999). *The construction of the self: A developmental perspective.* New York: Guilford Press.

Haslam, S. A., & Turner, J. C. (1992). Context-dependent variation in social stereotyping 2: The relationship between frame of reference, self-categorization and accentuation. *European Journal of Social Psychology, 22,* 251–278.

Haslam, S. A., Turner, J. C., Oakes, P. J., McGarty, C., & Hayes, B. K. (1992). Context-dependent variation in social stereotyping 1: The effects of intergroup relations as mediated by social change and frame reference. *European Journal of Social Psychology, 22,* 3–20.

Hogg, M. (2001). Social identity and social comparison. In J. Suls & L. Wheeler (Eds.), *Handbook of social comparison* (pp. 401–421). Hingham, MA: Kluwer Academic Publishers.

Hopkins, N., & Murdoch, N. (1999). The role of the "other" in national identity: Exploring the context-dependence of the national in-group stereotype. *Journal of Community and Applied Social Psychology, 9,* 321–338.

Hopkins, N., Regan, M., & Abell, J. (1997). On the context dependence of national stereotypes: Some Scottish data. *British Journal of Social Psychology, 36,* 553–563.

Jenkins, R. (1996). *Social identity.* London: Routledge.

Lambert, W. E., & Klineberg, O. (1967). *Children's views of foreign peoples.* New York: Appleton-Century-Crofts.

Martin, C. L., & Halverson, C. F. (1981). A schematice processing model of sex typing and streoptyping in children. *Child Development, 52,* 1119–1134.

Miller, R. E. (1996). *Embarrassment: Poise and peril in everyday life.* New York: Guilford Press.

Oakes, P. J., Haslam, A., & Turner, J. C. (1994). *Stereotyping and social reality.* Oxford: Blackwell.

Perner, J. (1999). Theory of mind. In M. Bennett (Ed.), *Developmental psychology: Achievements and prospects.* New York: Psychology Press.

Pomerantz, E. M., Ruble, D., Frey, K. S., & Greulich, F. (1995). Meeting goals and confronting conflict: Children's changing perceptions of social comparison. *Child Development, 66,* 723–738.

Powlishta, K. K. (2002). *Perceived similarity of boys and girls: Contextual variations in the salience of gender.* Manuscript under review.

Premack, D., & Premack, A. J. (1995). Origins of human social competence. In M. S. Gazzaniga (Ed.), *The cognitive neurosciences* (pp. 205–218). Cambridge, MA: MIT Press.

Quintana, S. M. (1998). Children's developmental understanding of ethnicity and race. *Applied and Preventive Psychology, 7,* 27–45.

Ruble, D. N. (1983). The development of social comparison processes and their role in achievement-related self-socialization. In E. T. Higgins, D. N. Ruble, & W. W. Hartup (Eds.), *Social cognition and social development: A socio-cultural perspective.* Cambridge: Cambridge University Press.

Ruble, D. N., & Flett, G. L. (1988). Conflicting goals in self-evaluative information seeking. *Child Development, 59,* 97–106.

Ruble, D., & Frey, K. (1991). Changing patterns of comparative behavior as skills are acquired. In J. Suls & T. A. Wills (Eds.), *Social comparison: Contemporary theory and research* (pp. 70–112). Hillsadale, NJ: Lawrence Erlbaum Associates, Inc.

Sani, F., & Bennett, M. (2001). Contextual variability in young children's gender ingroup stereotype. *Social Development, 10,* 221–229.

Sani, F., Bennett, M., Agostini, L., Malucchi, L., & Ferguson, N. (2000). Children's conception of characteristic features of category members. *Journal of Social Psychology, 140,* 227–239.

Sani, F., Bennett, M., & Joyner, L. (1999, 13–15 September). *Developmental aspects of contextual variability in the stereotype of the ingroup: The case of Scottish children.* Paper presented at the Annual Conference of the Social Psychology Section of the British Psychological Society, Lancaster.

Sani, F., Bennett, M., Mullally, S., & MacPherson, J. (2003). On the assumption of fixity in children's stereotypes: A reappraisal. *British Journal of Developmental Psychology, 21,* 113–124.

Sani, F., Lyons, E., & Barrett, M. (1996). *The child's discovery of the collective self.* Paper presented at the Annual Conference of the Social Section of the British Psychological Society, University of Oxford.

Sani, F., & Thomson, L. (2001). We are what we wear: The emergence of consensus in stereotypes of students and managers' dressing style. *Social Behaviour and Personality*, *29*, 695–700.

Searle, J. (1983). *Intentionality: An essay in the philosophy of mind.* Cambridge: Cambridge University Press.

Serbin, L. A., & Sprafkin, C. (1986). The salience of gender and the process of sex-typing in three- to seven-year-old children. *Child Development*, *57*, 1188–1199.

Stangor, C. (1995). Stereotyping. In A. S. R. Manstead & M. Hewstone (Eds.), *The Blackwell encyclopedia of social psychology* (pp. 628–633). Oxford: Blackwell.

Stangor, C., & Shaller, M. (1996). Stereotypes as individual and collective representations. In C. N. Macrae, C. Stangor, & M. Hewstone (Eds.), *Stereotypes and stereotyping* (pp. 3–37). New York: Guilford Press.

Tajfel, H. (1981). *Human groups and social categories.* Cambridge: Cambridge University Press.

Turner, J. C., Hogg, M. A., Oakes, P. J., Reicher, S. D., & Wetherell, M. (1987). *Rediscovering the social group: A self-categorisation theory.* Oxford: Blackwell.

Turner, J. C., & Oakes, P. J. (1997). The socially structured mind. In C. McGarty & S. A. Haslam (Eds.), *The message of social psychology* (pp. 355–373). Oxford: Blackwell.

Turner, J. C., & Onorato, R. S. (1999). Social identity, personality, and the self-concept: A self-categorization perspective. In T. R. Tyler, R. M. Kramer, & O. P. John (Eds.), *The psychology of the social self* (pp. 11–46). Mahwah, NJ: Lawrence Erlbaum Associates, Inc.

Turner, J. C., Oakes, P. J., Haslam, S. A., & McGarty, C. (1994). Self and collective: Cognition and social context. *Personality and Social Psychology Bulletin*, *20*, 454–463.

Tyler, T. R., Kramer, R. M., & John, O. P. (Eds.) (1999). *The psychology of the social self* (pp. 11–46). Mahwah, NJ: Lawrence Erlbaum Associates, Inc.

Part II
Identities

4   Gender as a social category: Intergroup processes and gender-role development

Kimberly K. Powlishta

"All boys push! All boys push!" is a chant I recall from my childhood, as a group of girls on the playground during recess at school tried to convince those "other creatures" to push the merry-go-round. Boys too seem to view the sexes as members of distinct groups, as illustrated in the following lunchroom scene:

> a fourth-grade boy pointed at one of the white squares that alternated with green squares on the linoleum floor. "That's kook territory . . . girl's territory," he said loudly, tiptoeing in an exaggerated way from one green square to another. "If you step on the white you change into a girl." He tiptoed around a girl and then leaned up against the wall. "This is boys' territory by the wall," he said.
>
> (Thorne, 1987, p. 10)

With this sense that boys and girls are very different from each other, having separate responsibilities and territories, often comes the belief that one's own sex is better. The other sex "has cooties" and should be avoided. For example, the boy quoted above equated girls with "kooks". Similarly, an 11-year-old girl told Maccoby and Jacklin (1987) that "Nobody who had any care of status would sit next to a boy if they could sit next to a girl . . . It is sort of like being in a lower rank or peeing in your pants" (p. 245).

More formal research evidence supports these observations that boys and girls tend to exaggerate differences between the sexes and to show strong biases favouring their own sex. The current chapter will review this evidence and propose that generic intergroup processes (i.e., in-group favouritism, the accentuation of within-group similarities and between-group differences, social stereotyping, and out-group homogenisation) contribute to children's beliefs about, attitudes towards, and interactions with, other males and females. The extent to which developmental factors, individual and group differences, and variations in social context may influence the salience of gender as a social category and the subsequent activation of these intergroup processes also will be discussed. Finally, the ways in which gender may differ from other social categories will be described.

INTERGROUP PROCESSES

Numerous social psychological studies, conducted primarily with adolescents and adults, have demonstrated that mere assignment to a social category can lead people to favour members of their own groups. In the original studies by Tajfel and colleagues (e.g., Tajfel, 1970; Tajfel, Billig, Bundy, & Flament, 1971), participants were assigned at random to one of two groups defined on some apparently trivial basis (e.g., did the person over- or underestimate the number of dots in an array?). Even though group membership is anonymous, and group members have no conflicts of interest, pre-existing hostilities, or face-to-face contacts, individuals placed in these sorts of "minimal groups" show favouritism towards in-group members (e.g., a fellow "dot underestimator"). They display this bias when allocating rewards, making ratings on positive and negative traits, or evaluating group products (Brown, 2000; Messick & Mackie, 1989). In other words, as a mere result of being categorised, evaluative perceptions are distorted. According to social identity theory (Tajfel & Turner, 1979), individuals seek to differentiate their own groups positively from others in this way in order to enhance their own self-esteem (i.e., to achieve a positive social identity).

Although studied less frequently, children also display in-group favouritism in laboratory minimal group situations. In one of the earliest studies, 7- to 11-year-olds divided randomly into groups, supposedly on the basis of the type of art they preferred, allocated more money to in-group than to out-group others. In fact, they showed as much favouritism as when asked to divide the rewards between their "best friend" and someone they did not like (Vaughan, Tajfel, & Williams, 1981). Similar minimal group in-group favouritism effects have been obtained with European, Maori, and Samoan 8-year-olds in New Zealand (Wetherell, 1982) and with 10- to 12-year-old English boys (Moghaddam & Stringer, 1986).

More recently, Bigler and colleagues (Bigler, 1995; Bigler, Jones, & Lobliner, 1997) found that 6- to 11-year-old children showed favouritism towards members of their own, randomly assigned "colour groups" (e.g., red vs. green), at least if the group distinction was made salient through the functional use of groupings by teachers in the classroom. They displayed this favouritism in a variety of ways, for example by being unwilling to change groups, by predicting that their own group would win contests, by choosing more in-group than out-group members to go on a field trip, and by estimating that in-group children had received more rewards for good behaviour than had out-group children. In addition, when the grouping distinction was made perceptually salient through the use of coloured tee shirts (Bigler et al., 1997), children reported liking individual in-group classmates more than out-group classmates. Relative to a control condition, children whose teachers made functional use of the colour groupings also showed more in-group favouritism in their positive and negative trait attributions.

Using a minimal group paradigm in which children were assigned at random to higher (fast) or lower (slow) status teams, Yee and Brown (1992) also demonstrated in-group favouritism. Children reported liking their own team more than the other as early as 3 years of age, regardless of status. Five-year-olds were particularly biased, rating their own team as faster than the other even when assigned to the "slow" team. Nesdale and Flesser (2001) demonstrated consistent in-group favouritism in the liking ratings of children in a minimal group paradigm as well. The extent of this favouritism varied, however, depending on the relative status of the in-group and out-group, the permeability of group boundaries, and the availability of non-status-related dimensions on which to compare the groups, consistent with earlier studies of adults.

In addition to in-group favouritism, social categorisation also leads to distorted perceptions of variability (Brown, 2000; Messick & Mackie, 1989). In particular, people tend to exaggerate differences between and similarities within groups along non-evaluative as well as evaluative dimensions. In fact, it has been argued that these perceptual distortions (i.e., cognitive differentiation) may contribute to in-group favouritism, above and beyond the need for self-esteem maintenance posited by social identity theory (Doise & Sinclaire, 1973; Wilder, 1981). In other words, perceptual accentuation of between-group differences and within-group similarities, when coupled with positive views of the self, would lead to in-group favouritism. This perceptual accentuation effect also may encourage the formation and use of social stereotypes, as stereotypes are based on the notion that members of a particular social category are alike in some way, a way that distinguishes them from other groups (Brown, 2000). The exaggeration of within-group similarities is often especially pronounced when evaluating groups to which one does not belong ("they're all alike, but we're individuals"). That is, out-groups are believed to be more homogeneous than in-groups (Quattrone, 1986), at least on some dimensions (Brown, 2000).

As with in-group favouritism, although most of the research concerning the impact of mere social categorisation on perceptions of variability has been conducted with adults, there has been some research with children. Bigler et al. (1997) reported that, relative to a control group, children whose teachers made functional use of experimentally created groups perceived greater between-group differences. These children also made more extreme judgments concerning the in-group than the out-group. However, because the judgments all involved evaluative trait ratings, the apparent accentuation of between-group differences (in-group ratings higher on positive traits and lower on negative traits than out-group ratings) and homogenisation of the in-group ("all of us have positive traits; none of us have negative traits") are confounded with in-group favouritism. Nesdale and Flesser (2001) measured perceptions of similarity in a minimal group situation more directly, finding that in general, 5- and 8-year-olds rated themselves as more similar to the in-group than to the out-group.

In summary, even in the absence of any pre-existing attitudes based on direct experience or environmental teachings, the mere act of placing people into categories can set in motion intergroup processes whereby the in-group is favoured, differences between and similarities within groups are exaggerated, and the out-group is often homogenised.

These same sorts of phenomena also can be seen with naturally occurring groups (Brown, 2000; Messick & Mackie, 1989). Children begin to notice such real-world social categories at a very early age. Cognitively grouping people allows for the efficient processing of large amounts of information, while at the same time helping the child to establish a self-identity (Martin & Halverson, 1981; Serbin, Powlishta, & Gulko, 1993). During childhood, one of the most salient groupings is based on gender (Powlishta, 2002b; Serbin et al., 1993). There are a number of reasons why this may be so. First, people in general (Allport, 1954), but especially young children (Livesley & Bromley, 1973), tend to focus on perceptually salient characteristics. As Allport (1954) put it nearly 50 years ago:

> Visibility and identifiability aid categorization . . . All our experience teaches us that when things look different they usually are different. A black cloud in the sky has very different significance from a white cloud. A skunk is not a cat. Our comfort and sometimes our lives depend on learning to act differently in the face of unlike objects.
>
> (pp. 129, 131)

Like black and white clouds, the distinction between males and females is perceptually salient. Actual differences between the sexes make gender group-ings useful for predicting and monitoring behaviour. By definition, males and females play different roles in reproduction. Sex also is a stable, dichotomous, exhaustive, biological, "natural kind" basis for categorisation. Furthermore, the gender distinction is emphasised by both adults and peers in the child's environment. Hence, it is not surprising that sex-based categorisation is so prevalent during childhood (Bigler al., 1997; Martin & Halverson, 1981; Serbin et al., 1993), typically occurring at a much earlier age than other more abstract forms of social categorisation, such as those based on nationality (Rutland, 1999).

If children are treating boys and girls as members of distinct groups, then the same sort of generic intergroup processes demonstrated in minimal group studies might influence children's perceptions, beliefs, attitudes, and behaviours towards the sexes as well. In other words, viewing males and females as "us" versus "them" may lead children to favour their own sex, exaggerate differences between and similarities within each sex, hold stereo-typic beliefs and expectations, and view the other sex as more homogeneous than their own. In this way, generic intergroup processes may contribute to gender-role development.

THE DEVELOPMENT OF GENDER CATEGORIES

The first prerequisite for intergroup processes to contribute to gender-role development is that children must be able to categorise themselves and others into male and female groups. The groundwork for this categorisation is laid in infancy. A number of studies have demonstrated that infants will lose interest in a particular novel face or voice that is presented repeatedly (habituation). When the face or voice is changed, interest is regained (dishabituation), but only if the sex of the new target is different from the original. In other words, even dissimilar targets fail to elicit distinctive reactions if they are of the same sex. However, a male and a female are treated as different by the middle of the first year, suggesting the existence of rudimentary gender categories among these infants (Fagan & Shepherd, 1981; Fagan & Singer, 1979; Katz, 1996; Leinbach & Fagot, 1993; Miller, 1983).

Not long after showing the ability to recognise gender categories in this way, children more actively begin to divide the world into males and females. For example, Johnston, Madole, Bittinger, and Smith (2001) gave toddlers a set of male and female dolls and examined the sequence in which the dolls were touched. Touching dolls from a single gender category in succession more than would be expected by chance was used to infer gender categorisation. Such categorisation showed a sharp increase between 18 and 22 months of age.

These gender categories soon become even more explicit. Children are able to sort photographs on the basis of gender by 2 to 3 years of age (Katz, 1996; Sen & Bauer, 2002; Thompson, 1975; Weinraub, Clemens, Sockloff, Ethridge, Gracely, & Meyers, 1984; Yee & Brown, 1994). Two-year-olds often begin to use gender labels appropriately as well, becoming experts at labelling themselves and others by the time they are three years old (Katz, 1996; Leinbach & Fagot, 1986; Levy, 1999; Sen & Bauer, 2002; Thompson, 1975; Weinraub et al., 1984).

Gender appears to be quite salient at this age. For example, Serbin and Sprafkin (1986) presented young children with a target male or female (e.g., a photo of a man stirring a pot) and asked them to select another photo that "goes with" the first from among three options: one that matched the target in terms of gender (e.g., a man reading), one that matched on some other dimension such as activity, body stance, or facial expression (e.g., a woman rolling dough), and a third that did not match on any obvious dimension (e.g., a woman sweeping). Three-year-olds tended to make gender-based matches.

Although children became more likely to focus on alternative dimensions rather than gender as they got older in this study (Serbin & Sprafkin, 1986), other methodologies (and everyday experience) suggest that gender remains a salient basis for categorisation throughout childhood. For example, two studies using a release from a proactive interference paradigm have demonstrated that elementary-school-aged children encode the gender connotations of words in memory. That is, when presented either with all masculine or all feminine words to remember on a series of trials, children (especially girls) show an increase in recall on a subsequent trial in which the words are drawn from the other gender category (Kail & Levine, 1976; Perez & Kee, 2000).

When it comes to categorising people (as opposed to words), both sexes show evidence of spontaneously invoking gender in their automatic processing of social information during mid and late childhood. Bennett and colleagues (Bennett, Sani, Hopkins, Agostini, & Malucchi, 2000) presented children with a series of statements attributed to individual boys and girls depicted in photographs. When asked to recall "who said what?", children were more likely to be confused about which boy or girl made a particular statement than about whether the statement was made by a boy or a girl. The children thus seemed to be categorising the people and their statements in terms of gender.

Additional evidence that children of this age spontaneously form gender-based person categories comes from a study in which 6- to 12-year-olds were presented with photographs of people and asked to rate the similarity of each pair (Powlishta, 2002b). A multidimensional scaling procedure was used to obtain a spatial configuration of the photographs, with pairs receiving higher similarity ratings placed closer together in space. The features presumably influencing similarity judgments are thus represented as dimensions in the resulting configuration. Four such dimensions were revealed – gender, age, facial expression, and hair colour – with gender being the most salient. Once again, then, there is evidence that gender is ubiquitous as a social category (Maccoby, 1988).

EXAGGERATION OF BETWEEN-SEX DIFFERENCES AND WITHIN-SEX SIMILARITIES

Given that children do seem to treat gender as an important basis for categorising their social world, is there evidence that the same sorts of intergroup processes seen in minimal group studies of children and adults also influence children's perceptions, attitudes, and behaviours regarding males and females? Children do often treat the sexes as very different from each other, while emphasising the ways in which all boys or all girls are similar. For example, elementary-school-aged children rate unfamiliar people as more similar to themselves (Brewer, Ho, Lee, & Miller, 1987; Powlishta, 1995c) or two unfamiliar people as more similar to each other (Powlishta, 2002b) when they are of the same sex.

Children also tend to assume that same-sex peers will have similar interests to their own. For example, Martin, Eisenbud, and Rose (1995) showed preschoolers unfamiliar, non-sex-typed toys and asked them to rate how much they and other children would like each toy. Despite the fact that boys and girls showed a similar liking of the toys in their self-ratings (confirming that the toys were not traditionally sex-typed), their self and other ratings were more similar when the others were of their own sex. In other words, children made the gender-based inference that "What I like, children of my sex will also like, and children of the other sex will not like" (p. 1453).

More generally, children seem quite ready to form new gender-based stereotypes. In fact, this tendency may even begin in infancy. When presented with a series of male or female faces paired with objects, 10-month-olds increase their attention to a new face–object pairing only when a face of one sex is paired with an object previously associated with the other sex. These findings suggest that infants can detect correlations between gender and other attributes, in a sense forming primitive gender stereotypes (Levy & Haaf, 1994).

This readiness to attach new characteristics to gender becomes even more apparent in the preschool years. Gelman, Collman, and Maccoby (1986) taught 4-year-olds new sex-linked properties (e.g., "This boy has little seeds inside; this girl has little eggs inside"). When shown another labelled boy or girl, children were able to infer sex-linked properties (e.g., that a new "boy" would also have seeds inside). Similarly, Bauer and Coyne (1997) assigned a different, traditionally gender-neutral preference to a boy and a girl figure. When asked about the preference of a new ambiguous-looking target labelled as either a boy or girl, 3½-year-olds made stereotypical inferences (i.e., that the "boy" target would prefer an object similar to the one liked by the original boy and the "girl" target would prefer an object similar to the one liked by the original girl).

In addition to readily attaching new characteristics to gender categories, children also have extensive knowledge of traditional gender stereotypes. This knowledge can be seen as early as the toddler years. Using a visual preference paradigm in a series of studies, Serbin, Poulin-Dubois, and colleagues have demonstrated that 18- to 24-month-olds have at least some awareness of toy, activity, and metaphorical (e.g., bears are masculine) gender associations (Eichstedt, Serbin, Poulin-Dubois, & Sen, in press; Poulin-Dubois, Serbin, Eichstedt, & Sen, in press; Serbin, Poulin-Dubois, Colburne, Sen, & Eichstedt, 2001). Knowledge of activity stereotypes is also seen in 2-year-olds when they choose a "sex-appropriate" doll to imitate gender-stereotyped actions (e.g., shaving the face, putting on lipstick; Poulin-Dubois et al., in press).

When children are asked more directly whether certain toys, objects, activities, occupations, or clothing are associated with males or females, their stereotype knowledge exceeds chance levels by 2 to 2½ years of age and increases rapidly throughout the preschool (Blaske, 1984; Edelbrock & Sugawara, 1978; Helwig, 1998; Katz, 1996; Kuhn, Nash, & Brucken, 1978; Leinbach, Hort, & Fagot, 1997; Martin & Little, 1990; Ruble & Martin, 1998; Thompson, 1975; Vener & Snyder, 1966; Weinraub et al., 1984) and elementary-school-aged years (Carter & Patterson, 1982; Nadleman, 1974; Ruble & Martin, 1998; Trautner, Helbing, Sahm, & Lohaus, 1989; Vener & Snyder, 1966). In fact, knowledge of these sorts of stereotypes reaches ceiling on many measures during early childhood (Serbin et al., 1993; Signorella, 1987).

Awareness of the gender stereotyping of personality traits lags behind the more concrete object and activity stereotypes, but even 2½- to 3-year-olds show at least minimal awareness of them (Albert & Porter, 1983; Cowan & Hoffman, 1986; Etaugh & Riley, 1979; Haugh, Hoffman, & Cowan, 1980; Reis & Wright, 1982). Substantial increases in personality stereotype knowledge occur between the ages of 5 and 11 years, so that adult-like levels of knowledge are shown by late childhood (Beere, 1990; Best, 1982; Best et al., 1977; Serbin et al., 1993; Williams, Bennett, & Best, 1975).

Children's knowledge and acceptance of gender stereotypes also can be seen in the sorts of inferences they make about other people. Even preschoolers can use information about the stereotyped preferences and characteristics of a gender-unspecified target to predict that the target would like other toys and clothing consistent with that stereotype (e.g., someone who likes a toy soldier would probably also like cars; someone who is a librarian would probably wear a two-piece bathing suit rather than swimming trunks; Bauer, Liebl, & Stennes, 1998; Martin, Wood, & Little, 1990). Older children make increasingly complex inferences, using a person's gender or gender-typed characteristics to make predictions about competencies, behaviours, toy preferences, personality traits, physical characteristics, roles, and occupations (Berndt & Heller, 1986; Biernat, 1991; Cann & Palmer, 1986; Martin, 1989; Martin et al., 1990; Powlishta, 1995c, 2000).

The fact that children are so knowledgeable about and willing to make use of traditional gender stereotypes suggests that they may be showing the same sort of exaggeration of between-group differences and within-group similarities seen in minimal group experiments. On the other hand, it is possible that children are reporting actual differences and similarities involving males and females, rather than exaggerating them.

On average, boys and girls certainly do differ in many ways. They tend to be more similar than they are different, however (see Powlishta, Sen, Serbin, Poulin-Dubois, & Eichstedt, 2001, and Ruble & Martin, 1998, for recent reviews). As Maccoby (1998) points out, most existing sex differences reflect highly overlapping distributions, with extensive within-sex variability in the sorts of preferences, interests, aspirations, traits, skills, and interpersonal styles children display. Only a few behaviours are highly differentiated by sex (i.e., playmate preferences, rough-and-tumble play, direct aggression, and the themes enacted in pretend play). Similarly, Ruble and Martin (1998) note that on average boys are more aggressive, assertive, and active, less socially oriented and sensitive, better at physical activities, and have higher self-esteem than girls. But they found little evidence to support other gender stereotypes, such as those involving prosocial behaviour, moral reasoning, passivity, or dependence.

Nevertheless, young children often treat gender stereotypes as if they are rigidly binding absolutes. We've seen that they are quite willing to learn or create new stereotypes (e.g., that boys have little seeds inside), stereotypes that they are unlikely to have encountered in their everyday world. Carol Martin (2000) reports an anecdote in which her 4-year-old niece even created a stereotype (girls but not boys have eyelashes) that obviously contradicts reality. My 3½-year-old nephew similarly informed me recently that he likes "boy songs" but not "girl songs". He was unable to describe the difference, and when I asked him to define "boy songs", all he could tell me is that "they're not girl songs". He also let me know that because he's a boy I should refer to him as "handsome" rather than "cute", apparently generalising from the more common handsome/pretty distinction.

Once they are formed, children's gender stereotypes tend to be highly resistant to change (Katz, 1986). The fact that children show better memory for information that is consistent rather than inconsistent with their stereotypes, even distorting information so that it becomes stereotype-consistent (e.g., relabelling a male nurse as a doctor), may contribute to this resistance (Cordua, McGraw, & Drabman, 1979; Martin & Halverson, 1983; Stangor & Ruble, 1987). Children also tend to evaluate negatively anyone who violates stereotyped norms, particularly in early to mid childhood (Damon, 1977; Levy, Taylor, & Gelman, 1995; Martin, 1989). This ready acceptance of new gender stereotypes and resistance to stereotypic changes or violations suggests that children's stereotypes represent more than a truthful reflection of their world. Instead, children do seem to be exaggerating similarities within and differences between the sexes.

Very little research has examined whether children perceive the other sex to be more homogeneous than their own. With adults, anecdotal evidence suggests that other-sex homogenisation sometimes occurs. One often hears people making generalised statements about the other sex (e.g., a man saying "I don't understand women"; a woman saying that "Men are so—") but rarely about their own sex. Research evidence backs up this observation. In a series of studies, Park and Rothbart (1982) found that stereotypic characteristics were viewed as more prevalent in a given sex when members of the other sex were doing the rating. Counterstereotypic trait ratings showed the reverse pattern. These findings indicate that people have a more complex and varied image of their own gender group than they do of the other.

The extent to which this phenomenon is seen in children is not entirely clear. One study has provided some tentative evidence for other-sex homogenisation in childhood. In this study, children viewed unfamiliar boys and girls in videotaped segments and rated the extent to which they thought each target possessed a series of traits. A measure reflecting the variability in ratings given to the three targets of each sex was created. For male targets only, this measure was higher among boys than among girls. That is, there was some evidence for other-sex homogenisation by girls (Powlishta, 1995c).

OWN-SEX FAVOURITISM

In addition to exaggerating between-sex differences and within-sex similarities, extensive evidence indicates that children show own-sex favouritism in
their behaviours, attitudes, and perceptions (see Glick & Hilt, 2000, for a
recent review of "gender prejudice"). For example, even 2½- to 3-year-olds
have begun to prefer same-sex playmates. This gender segregation becomes
more prevalent with age, at least through early or mid childhood (see
Maccoby, 1998, for a review). In fact, in one study children were observed
with same-sex playmates 11 times as often as with other-sex playmates
(Maccoby & Jacklin, 1987). When asked to name their friends, older children
rarely list someone of the other sex (Hayden-Thomson, Rubin, & Hymel,
1987; Powlishta, 2001; Powlishta, Serbin, Doyle, & White, 1994; Serbin et al.,
1993). They also report liking same-sex classmates more than other-sex
classmates (Powlishta & Vartanian, 1999). And in one study, both boys and
girls estimated that classmates of their own sex had performed better on a
series of games than had classmates of the other sex (Deschamps & Doise,
1978). In other words, the preference for same-sex peers is so pervasive that it
is found seemingly no matter what the measure. When I have carried out
research with groups of children and have looked back as they are following
me from the classroom to the testing room, they typically are walking in
a gender-segregated fashion. That is, I see anecdotal evidence for own-sex
favouritism even before the research has officially begun.

At least in the elementary-school-aged years, this preference for one's own
sex extends beyond children's attitudes and behaviours toward familiar peers.
Children also show biases towards male and female strangers. For example,
when asked to rate their liking for boys and girls depicted in pictures, videotapes, or short verbal descriptions, children give higher ratings to targets of
their own sex (Martin, 1989; Powlishta, 1995c, 2001; Powlishta et al., 1994).
They also predict that such targets will have more positive traits and fewer
negative traits than targets of the other sex (Powlishta, 1995c, 2001; Zalk &
Katz, 1978). When shown drawings depicting unfamiliar boy–girl or man–
woman pairs and asked to choose who they would like to play with, children
again show a significant bias in favour of their own sex (Powlishta et al., 1994;
Serbin & Sprafkin, 1986).

In addition to favouring both familiar and unfamiliar same-sex individuals,
children of this age also believe that their own sex is better in general. This
effect can be seen when children are asked to provide global ratings of how
they feel about boys and girls (Yee & Brown, 1994). Children also show
earlier knowledge of personality trait stereotypes that portray their own sex
in a favourable light (Serbin et al., 1993). Furthermore, they attribute more
positive and fewer negative characteristics to their own sex than to the other
(Deschamps & Doise, 1978; Parish & Bryant, 1978; Powlishta, 1995a;
Powlishta et al., 1994; Powlishta & Vartanian, 1999; Silvern, 1977; Yee &
Brown, 1994).

Of course, it is possible that children's own-sex favouritism does not reflect biased perceptions, per se. Instead, as with gender stereotypes, such preferences may result from actual differences between boys and girls. For example, children may seek out same-sex playmates not because they are biased against the other sex, but instead because sex differences in the interests or play styles of boys and girls make same-sex playmates more compatible (Maccoby, 1998; Powlishta, 1995b; Serbin, Moller, Gulko, Powlishta, & Colburne, 1994). Such compatibility may lead them to have more friendships with and greater liking for familiar same-sex peers. Rational inferences based on these past experiences could then lead children to predict that they would like same-sex strangers more than other-sex strangers and to develop more positive general attitudes about their own sex.

Although actual experiences with boys and girls undoubtedly do contribute to children's own-sex preferences (Maccoby, 1998), there is good evidence that perceptions are also distorted by in-group favouritism. For example, boys and girls generally agree on what traits are positive or negative. Yet the very same trait is rated as more masculine/less feminine by boys than by girls if it is positive (e.g., strong; gentle), and by girls than by boys if it is negative (e.g., messy; cries; Powlishta, 1995a; Silvern, 1977). In other words, "children do not simply like what they see in members of their own sex; they see what they like" (Powlishta et al., 2001, p. 124).

THE IMPACT OF SOCIAL CONTEXT ON THE SALIENCE OF GENDER

According to the more recent elaboration of social identity theory known as self-categorisation theory (Turner, Hogg, Oakes, Reicher, & Wetherell, 1987; Turner & Onorato, 1999), the way in which the self is categorised depends on the social context. That is, some contexts heighten the salience of personal identity, wherein the self is defined in terms of personal or idiosyncratic attributes. Other contexts heighten the salience of social identity, wherein the self is defined in terms of membership in social categories. Intergroup processes (i.e., in-group favouritism, exaggeration of intragroup similarities and intergroup differences, social stereotyping) should be most apparent in the latter contexts.

Which social categories are salient can also vary with context. "People who are categorized and perceived as different in one context (e.g., biologists and physicists in a science faculty) can be recategorized and perceived as similar in another contest (e.g., scientists rather than social scientists in a university) without any actual change in their own positions" (Turner & Onorato, 1999, p. 23). Or as Taylor (1981) put it:

> An apple is less likely to be categorized as a fruit if it is with the objects: beach ball, cube, cardboard box, and ball bearing than if it is with the objects: orange, carrot, bean, and pear. Likewise, a black woman may be

more likely to be perceived as black if she is in a group dominated by white people, but more likely to be seen as a woman in a group dominated by men.

(p. 85)

Extensive research evidence supports the context-dependent nature of intergroup processes, especially among adults. Contexts that make group membership diagnostic (e.g., through the actual or anticipated presence of an out-group) or accessible (e.g., by priming group membership through labelling) lead to an intensification of intergroup processes. These context effects have been shown to influence perceptions of similarity between group members (Doise, Deschamps, & Meyer, 1978; Wilder, 1984), stereotypical descriptions of self (Charters & Newcomb, 1958) and others (Doosje, Haslam, Spears, Oakes, & Koomen, 1998; Hopkins, Regan, & Abell, 1997), and in-group favouritism (Doise & Sinclair, 1973; Dustin & Davis, 1970; Janssens & Nuttin, 1976; Rabbie & Wilkens, 1971; Stephenson, Skinner, & Brotherton, 1976; Turner, 1975).

Relatively few studies have examined the effect of context on intergroup processes in children. Katz and Seavey (1973) asked elementary-school-aged students to judge the similarity of pairs of faces that varied in terms of colour (purple, green) and facial expression (smiling, frowning). When the colour or expression grouping was made salient through the use of novel labels, perceived differences between the groups increased, at least for white children. Bigler et al. (1997) found that children divided into "blue" and "yellow" groups designated by coloured tee shirts showed more in-group favouritism in their attribution of positive and negative traits if their teacher made the group distinction salient (e.g., by having the children sit according to group membership or by using verbal group labels).

It seems likely that the salience of gender would vary considerably with context as well. Deaux and Major (1987) suggest that some events (e.g., having just watched the Miss America pageant; participating in a mixed-sex group) may prime us to focus on the gender of other people. Indeed, numerous studies have shown that the extent to which adults show own-sex favouritism (Hogg & Turner, 1987; McKillip, DiMiceli, & Luebke, 1977; Schmitt, Silvia, & Branscombe, 2000; Starer & Denmark, 1974; Todor, 1980) or use gender stereotypes when describing themselves (Hogg & Turner, 1987; Onorato & Turner, 1996, 1997, as cited in Turner & Onorato, 1999) or others (McKillip et al., 1977) increases in contexts designed to enhance the salience of gender.

A few studies have examined the impact of contextual variations on gender-based intergroup processes among children. Thorne (1987) describes an incident in which a group of fourth-graders, who were typically quite gender-segregated on the playground, came together in a mixed-sex group to defend and discuss the plight of a classmate who had been unjustly punished by a teacher. The children united on the basis of classroom membership, which temporarily appeared to become more salient than gender.

Quantitative research evidence supports the importance of context as well. In one of my own studies (Powlishta, 2002a), boy–girl pairs depicted in photographs were seen as more similar to each other when they were surrounded by photos of adults and explicitly labelled as children than when the very same pairs were surrounded by photographs of other children. Focusing attention on a characteristic that boys and girls share (i.e., childhood) appeared to make gender less salient, reducing children's tendency to see males and females as different sorts of creatures. Sani and Bennett (2001) similarly found that children attributed different traits to their gender-based in-group ("boys" or "girls") depending on whether they had first been asked to describe an age-based out-group (i.e., a same-sex adult) or a gender-based out-group (i.e., a child of the other sex). Bigler (1995) also showed that gender stereotyping can vary with context. A subgroup of children whose teachers made gender salient (e.g., through seating arrangements and labelling) were more likely than those in a control condition to view occupations in a stereotypical fashion.

Finally, at least one study has examined the impact of context on children's own-sex favouritism (Deschamps & Doise, 1978). Groups of six boys and six girls were seated so that each sex occupied two adjacent sides of a table. For half of the groups, three of the boys and three of the girls were given blue pens and labelled the "blue group" with the remaining children given red pens and labelled the "red group". Thus, for this crossed-category condition there were two potential ways of making an in-group–out-group distinction (boys vs. girls; blues vs. reds). The other half of the twelve-person groups were not further divided (the simple category condition), so that gender was the only salient basis for group formation. Each child then individually completed a series of paper-and-pencil games and estimated how well the other children did at these games. Only in the simple category condition did children predict that individuals of their own sex had done better than the other sex. In other words, a context designed to reduce the salience of gender through the introduction of an alternative basis for categorisation (blue vs. red) reduced gender-based in-group favouritism.

INDIVIDUAL AND GROUP DIFFERENCES IN GENDER-BASED INTERGROUP PROCESSES

Gender schematicity

In addition to varying with context, the salience of gender may also vary from person to person. Although not focusing on individual differences, self-categorisation theory (Turner & Onorato, 1999) nevertheless proposes that one factor determining the salience of a particular social category is its accessibility, that is, the readiness of a person to use a particular categorisation. In addition to varying with the situation, such accessibility or readiness is thought to depend on past experience, which can influence the extent to which a person identifies with a group or sees the group as central or valued.

With respect to gender, Bem (1981) similarly proposed that, because of past exposure to differing social environments, gender should be more chronically salient for some individuals than for others. In other words, people vary in their level of gender schematicity, that is, their readiness to encode and organise information in a gender-based manner (Martin & Halverson, 1981).

Research evidence has revealed individual differences in gender schematicity as early as the preschool years. Levy and colleagues (Carter & Levy, 1988; Levy, 1994; Levy & Carter, 1989) measured gender schematicity by asking children to indicate their toy preferences when presented with pairs of toys. Those who displayed longer reaction times when asked to choose between two masculine or two feminine toys, or who displayed shorter reaction times when asked to choose between a masculine and a feminine toy, relative to other choice options, were considered to be highly gender schematic. Compared to low-schematic children, those with high-gender schematicity had poorer memory for stereotype-inconsistent information, were more likely to make memory errors that distorted information so as to be stereotype-consistent, showed more gender-typed toy preferences, were more likely to attribute activities to males and females in a stereotypic fashion, and showed a greater improvement in recall when items to be remembered shifted from same-sex gender-typed toys to gender-neutral animals (i.e., "release from proactive interference"). In other words, not only are some individual children more gender-schematic than others, but such schematicity or salience is related to other aspects of gender-role development.

If children's gender-based attitudes and beliefs are influenced by the activation of generic intergroup processes, and if there are individual differences in the salience of gender (and hence the likelihood that or extent to which these processes are activated) then we might expect to see correlations among the various component processes. Indeed, such correlations have been found. In one study, 8- to 10-year-olds were asked to rate unfamiliar boys and girls depicted in videotaped vignettes in terms of positive, negative, masculine, and feminine traits, predicted liking, and similarity to self. Results revealed that individual differences in the tendency to favour members of one's own sex, to use gender stereotypes, to emphasise similarities between the self and same-sex others, and to homogenise the other sex in these ratings were significantly correlated with each other (Powlishta, 1995c).

Among adults, there is even more direct evidence that individual differences in gender salience or schematicity are related to gender-based intergroup processes. In an intergroup context, female college students with high levels of gender group identification gave more favourable evaluations of a same-sex target than did students with low levels of gender group identification (Schmitt et al., 2000).

Self-esteem

Another individual difference variable related to intergroup processes, and in particular in-group favouritism, is self-esteem. According to social identity theory (Tajfel & Turner, 1979), in-group favouritism arises from a desire to achieve a positive social identity in order to enhance or maintain self-esteem. Although this theory has been used to predict both negative correlations (low self-esteem motivates in-group bias) and positive correlations (successful intergroup discrimination enhances self-esteem) between self-esteem and in-group favouritism, a recent meta-analysis revealed more support for the latter prediction. That is, among adults, high self-esteem individuals tend to exhibit more pro-in-group bias than do low self-esteem individuals (Aberson, Healy, & Romero, 2000).

This pattern is seen among children as well. Bigler and colleagues found that when classmates were assigned to "blue" or "yellow" groups, those with high self-esteem were more likely than those with low self-esteem to favour their own groups in their positive and negative trait attributions (Bigler et al., 1997).

If children's own-sex favouritism results, at least in part, from the generic tendency to positively evaluate in-groups, then such favouritism should be related to self-esteem in a similar manner. This hypothesis was tested in a recent study involving both children and early adolescents (Powlishta & Vartanian, 1999). Own-sex favouritism was assessed in two ways: the extent to which participants gave higher liking ratings to same-sex than to other-sex classmates and the extent to which they attributed positive traits to their own sex more than to the other. Self-esteem was assessed using Harter's Self-Perception Profile for Children (Harter, 1982), which measures perceptions of one's own competency in six different domains (scholastic, social acceptance, athletic, physical appearance, behavioural conduct, and global self-worth). Self-esteem (in the domain of social acceptance) was positively related to own-sex favouritism on both measures as predicted, but only for girls.

Sex differences

The previous finding highlights another common and somewhat puzzling pattern in the literature on children's gender-based intergroup processes. Not only are there individual differences in the extent to which these processes are seen, but there are also fairly consistent sex differences. In general, both sexes display own-sex favouritism, but girls display stronger biases than do boys. These sex differences are seen using a wide variety of assessment techniques. For example, in the study just described, girls favoured their own sex more than did boys on both measures (liking of classmates, attribution of evaluative traits), and the two favouritism measures were significantly correlated with each other only for girls (Powlishta & Vartanian, 1999). Other studies also have found greater own-sex favouritism among girls than boys in their attribution of traits to the sexes in general (Egan & Perry, 2001; Parish & Bryant, 1978; Powlishta, 1995a; Powlishta et al., 1994; Silvern, 1977) or to individual unfamiliar boys and girls depicted in photographs or videotapes (Heyman, 2001; Powlishta, 1995c; Zalk & Katz, 1978). Yee and Brown (1994) found greater bias among girls than boys when asking children to rate how they felt about each sex, to name "nice" and "mean" things about each sex, and to award prizes to groups of girls and boys who allegedly had made collages varying in quality. Girls also display more own-sex favouritism when naming classmates they dislike or when rating their predicted liking of unfamiliar peers (Powlishta et al., 1994). Only when it comes to time spent with same-sex playmates (i.e., gender segregation) do boys often show stronger own-sex preferences than girls (Maccoby, 1998).

Although most sex differences in gender-based intergroup processes involve own-sex favouritism, there is some indication that such processes are stronger more generally for girls than for boys. In a meta-analysis, girls were found to be more knowledgeable about gender stereotypes than were boys (Signorella, Bigler, & Liben, 1993). Preliminary evidence indicates that girls also may show a greater tendency to homogenise the other sex (Powlishta, 1995c) and to encode the gender connotation of words in memory (Perez & Kee, 2000).

One of the most likely explanations for sex differences in gender-based intergroup processes, particularly own-sex favouritism, has to do with status or power differences between males and females (Glick & Hilt, 2000; Powlishta et al., 1994). Children know that males are considered to be of higher status than females (Glick & Hilt, 2000; Lockheed & Klein, 1985; see also David, Grace, & Ryan, Chapter 5). In fact, the first trait stereotypes they learn in the preschool years portray males as powerful and females as fearful and helpless (Ruble & Martin, 1998). Perhaps reflecting this difference, mas-culine stereotyped traits are considered more adult-like/less child-like than are feminine stereotyped traits by both children and adults (Powlishta, 2000). In addition, boys are often resistant to influence attempts by girls, enabling them to dominate cross-sex interactions (Charlesworth & LaFreniere, 1983; Powlishta & Maccoby, 1990; Serbin, Sprafkin, Elman, & Doyle, 1984). This dominance may lead to resentment of the other sex among girls (Glick & Hilt, 2000). More generally, lower status groups show heightened in-group favouritism under some circumstances, particularly on dimensions not dir-ectly related to the status difference (Brown, 2000; Van Knippenberg, 1984). The elevated own-sex favouritism in girls, then, may be a direct reaction to their lower status and power.

A second possible cause of the sex difference in own-sex favouritism is that boys may be more concerned with gender stereotypicality than with own-sex favouritism. Indeed, children are well aware that it is considered worse to be a sissy than a tomboy (Levy et al., 1995; Martin, 1990), perhaps explaining in part why gender-typed interests and occupational aspirations tend to become more flexible for girls but not boys in later childhood (Powlishta et al., 2001).

Adults, too, are particularly unwilling to attribute feminine stereotyped traits to males (Powlishta, 2000). Hence, boys may be willing to accept traditionally masculine characteristics even if they are negative and to reject traditionally feminine characteristics even if they are positive, yielding less apparent own-sex favouritism. Once again, status differences between the sexes may account for the differential willingness of boys and girls to deviate from gender norms.

A third factor that may account for the sex differences in own-sex favouritism is acceptance of the overarching stereotypes that girls are "sugar and spice and everything nice" whereas boys are "snakes and snails and puppy dog tails" (Serbin et al., 1993). Consistent with this interpretation, Serbin et al. found that children had greatest knowledge of positive feminine (e.g., gentle) and negative masculine (e.g., fights) trait stereotypes, intermediate knowledge of negative feminine stereotypes (e.g., weak), and least knowledge of positive masculine stereotypes (e.g., adventurous). In fact, it is even possible that boys may be willing to attribute negative characteristics to their own sex because they believe it is "cool to be bad". Heyman (2001) also found evidence for a "boys are bad" bias. When shown photographs of unfamiliar peers described as having performed ambiguous behaviours, children were more likely to interpret and remember the behaviours in an unfavourable way when the peer was male rather than female. Both boys and girls showed this pattern, even though boys predicted they would like the male peers more than did girls.

A fourth factor that may contribute to the greater own-sex favouritism typically seen in girls than in boys is a sex difference in the salience of gender as a grouping characteristic. Yee and Brown (1994) suggested that such a difference could account for the greater gender bias shown by girls in selecting prizes for group products, such that boys were rewarding prizes based on performance (i.e., the best prize to the best product) whereas girls were rewarding prizes based on gender (i.e., the best prize to girls, regardless of performance). In other words, boys may have been more attuned to a performance schema and girls to a gender schema.

Evidence for sex differences in schema activation can be seen in studies using a release from proactive interference paradigm. As noted earlier, Perez and Kee (2000) found that girls but not boys seemed to encode the gender connotation of words in memory. This finding was consistent with an earlier study of adults (Mills & Tyrrell, 1983) in which women consistently displayed evidence of encoding the gender connotation of occupations. Men, however, showed release from proactive interference when shifting from feminine to masculine occupations but not vice versa, suggesting that masculine occupations were treated simply as "occupations" unless a gender schema was first activated by the presentation of feminine items.

Using a different paradigm, Hurtig and Pichevin (1990) also found evidence for asymmetry in gender salience. Adults were asked to describe another person using as few cues as possible. Gender was more often used as a cue when the target was a woman rather than a man and when the target was seen in a traditionally feminine rather than a neutral situation. Further-more, female participants more often used gender as the first cue than did male participants. The authors proposed that the greater salience of "female" than of "male" results from status differences between the sexes. Because the higher-status "male" is the default or generic group, it is less likely to cause gender-schema activation (also see David et al., Chapter 5). Once again, if gender is more salient for females than for males, this pattern may explain the greater own-sex favouritism seen among girls.

One final potential explanation for girls' greater own-sex favouritism has to do with the way in which favouritism has typically been measured. Perhaps trait attributions and liking ratings do a better job of capturing how in-group biases are displayed for girls than for boys. In one minimal group study of adults, women favoured the in-group by giving more favourable interpersonal evaluations to in-group members whereas men favoured the in-group by overevaluating in-group products (Dion, 1979). Consistent with this pattern, when Deschampes and Doise (1978) used performance predictions as an index of own-sex favouritism (i.e., asking children to guess how well their male and female classmates had performed on a novel task), both boys and girls showed the expected gender biases. However, in this study (unlike most others) boys were more biased than girls. Additional research including both trait/liking ratings and performance evaluations to measure children's own-sex favouritism is warranted.

Nevertheless, based on the research to date, it appears that girls are more generally prone to gender-based intergroup processes than are boys. If so, then why do boys show just as much if not more gender segregation in their choice of playmates? One possibility is that they are reacting to behavioural differences between males and females more than to the sex of the playmate, per se. That is, boys may be seeking out playmates who have similar or com-patible play styles to their own (e.g., a similar enjoyment of roughhousing); because of sex differences in play style, such playmates may frequently end up being other boys (Maccoby, 1998; Powlishta, 1995b; Serbin et al., 1994). Boys also may avoid playing with other girls for fear of being seen as feminine.

Age/Developmental differences

In addition to individual and sex differences, there may also be age or devel-opmental differences in the activation of gender-based intergroup processes. First, there is reason to suspect that gender is particularly salient during early childhood. As noted previously, except in infancy, gender is almost always visually apparent; it represents a stable, dichotomous, and exhaustive way of classifying the self and others. Because young children tend to focus on con-crete, external attributes and have difficulty dealing with multiple classifica-tions simultaneously, they may attend to the simplest, most salient basis for classification, such as gender, rather than to more complex classification systems. They also may be particularly attentive to gender when they are first trying to learn about gender roles. As children become older, they are more likely to focus on internal attributes. Mastering multiple classification skills should enable them to make finer differentiations among people and to realise that people can simultaneously be "the same" in some ways (e.g., gender) and "different" in others (e.g., interests, abilities, traits). Attention to gender also may become less important as gender role expertise is developed. As a result, gender may become a less salient basis for classification in later childhood (Martin & Halverson, 1981; Powlishta et al., 1994; Serbin & Sprafkin, 1986).

Indeed, research supports the notion that gender salience declines somewhat with age (Serbin & Sprafkin, 1986). For example, Yee and Brown (1994) found that 5-year-olds were more likely to sort photographs on the basis of gender than were either younger or older children. In another study described previously, Bennett et al. (2000) attributed a series of statements to boys and girls depicted in photographs, and then asked children to recall who said what. In general, children made more within-gender errors (i.e., attributed a statement made by one boy to another boy or a statement made by one girl to another girl) than between-gender errors, indicating that they had categorised the information according to gender. This pattern was stronger for younger than for older children, perhaps suggesting that gender was more salient for the younger group. In a study comparing children and adults, when asked to rate the similarity of pairs of photographed people varying in terms of gender, age, and facial expression, both age groups attended to all three dimensions. However, the salience of gender and age was lower and the salience of facial expression was higher for adults than for children (Powlishta, 2002b).

In addition to this decline in gender salience, there is a second reason that there may be developmental changes in the activation of gender-based intergroup processes. Young children have been shown to display more favouritism towards experimentally created minimal groups than have older children, with such favouritism peaking around 5 years of age (Yee & Brown, 1992). To the extent that generic intergroup processes influence children's attitudes towards males and females, then young children may be particularly prone to own-sex favouritism as well.

Consistent with this decline in gender salience and in the general tendency to show in-group favouritism, as noted above, a number of studies have found a reduction in gender-based intergroup processes in later childhood. For example, although knowledge of gender stereotypes increases and reaches ceiling, older children (especially girls) often become more flexible in their use of stereotypes. By the end of the elementary-school-aged years, children more often acknowledge that "both" males and females can engage in similar activities and possess similar traits. The inferences they make about other people become more flexible as well, increasingly influenced by individuating information (e.g., current behaviour, stated preferences or traits, labels such as "tomboy" or "sissy"). That is, older children predict that a person with one feminine characteristic will have others as well, even if the person is a boy, whereas a person with one masculine characteristic is predicted to have others, even if the person is a girl (see Powlishta et al., 2001).

Evidence suggests that this age-related decline in gender stereotyping is tied to cognitive development. Bigler (1995) found that even after controlling for age, children who were less able to classify people along multiple dimensions (e.g., gender, age, race) were more stereotypical in their beliefs about whether men, women, or both should perform various occupations. And when placed in an experimental condition in which teachers emphasised gender grouping in the classroom, only children with poor classification skills gave more extreme gender stereotypical ratings of their classmates relative to a control condition. Of course, this doesn't mean that the use of gender stereotypes disappears with age; even adults make stereotypical inferences, especially in their perceptions of children (Powlishta, 2000).

Age patterns for own-sex favouritism are somewhat less consistent than they are for stereotyping. Although preference for same-sex playmates remains strong or even increases from early to late childhood (Maccoby, 1998; Powlishta, 2001; Powlishta et al., 1994, 2001; Serbin et al., 1993), other measures of own-sex favouritism, such as the attribution of positive traits to one's own sex, typically decline with age as expected during this period (Parish, Bryant, & Prawat, 1977; Powlishta et al., 1994; Zalk & Katz, 1978).

Not surprisingly, the decline in own-sex favouritism continues into adolescence. Several studies have found a reduced tendency to attribute more favourable traits to one's own sex in adolescence relative to childhood (Egan & Perry, 2001; Parish & Bryant, 1978; Powlishta & Vartanian, 1999). In fact, in one study, adolescent boys actually rated the other sex more favourably than their own (Parish & Bryant, 1978). Young adolescents show less own-sex favouritism than children in their liking of classmates as well; but despite these reductions, even early adolescents continue to show some degree of own-sex favouritism, both in their general perception of the sexes and in their attitudes towards familiar individuals (Powlishta & Vartanian, 1999). Glick and Hilt (2000) suggest that in adolescence, the hostile intergroup attitudes characteristic of childhood do not simply disappear, but are combined with a new "benevolent sexism", particularly on the part of boys towards girls. This benevolent sexism is a patronising form of prejudice in which perceivers believe that their attitudes towards the target group are favourable, but at the same time view the other group as inferior to their own.

HOW IS GENDER DIFFERENT FROM OTHER SOCIAL CATEGORIES?

The decline in own-sex favouritism seen during adolescence highlights one important difference between gender and other social categories. As Williams and Giles (1978) point out, the "psychological and physiological dependencies between men and women, their numerical balance in the population and their positive affect for each other" (p. 431) distinguish gender from many other social groupings. Given that taboos against cross-sex interaction start to weaken in most Western societies between 11 and 13 years of age (Maccoby, 1998), it is not surprising that gender-based biases decline in early adolescence as sexual attraction begins to compete with own-sex favouritism (at least for heterosexual individuals).

Own-sex favouritism does not disappear even in adulthood, however. It does become more unpredictable, though, in that in some studies people favour their own sex (Starer & Denmark, 1974) and in others they show a general pro-male or pro-female bias or no bias at all (McKillip et al., 1977; Todor, 1980). Such variations exemplify the ambivalence and complexity that characterises adolescent and adult gender relations (Glick & Hilt, 2000). The discrepancies in research findings may be accounted for, at least in part, by contextual variations that heighten the salience of gender in-groups and out-groups (leading to own-sex favouritism or traditional stereotyping) versus sexuality (leading to more benevolent attitudes towards the other sex). Consistent with this interpretation, Hogg and Turner (1987) found that female participants favoured men in a point allocation task when tested in mixed-sex dyads (which might be expected to make sexuality salient) but favoured women when tested in mixed-sex groups (which might be expected to make gender in-groups and out-groups salient).

The discrepancy in findings of own-sex favouritism among adults may also be accounted for by the influence of gender stereotypes. For example, when women were asked to evaluate products that might be considered tradition-ally masculine ("published journal articles" on various academic topics), they gave more favourable ratings when the products were attributed to male rather than female authors (Goldberg, 1968). But when women read articles on more traditionally feminine topics (marriage, child discipline, and special education), there was a nonsignificant trend to evaluate the "female-authored" articles more highly than the very same "male-authored" articles (see Pheterson, Kiesler, & Goldberg, 1971).

These latter findings point to a second factor that sets gender apart from other social categories, and particularly from the sorts of minimal groups created in laboratory settings. Existing stereotypes (positive and negative) about each sex and actual behavioural differences between the sexes can influence children's attitudes and behaviours in ways that sometimes run counter to and sometimes enhance generic intergroup processes. We have already seen that children have extensive knowledge about traditional gender stereotypes. Some of these stereotypes portray their own sex in a negative fashion. For example, boys are aware that males are considered to be messier than females; girls are aware that females are considered to be weaker than males. Acknowledging these stereotypes reduces the appearance of own-sex favouritism. Yet if examined carefully, the influence of in-group bias can nevertheless be seen in children's gender stereotyped attitudes. Girls believe that traits like messiness are very masculine whereas boys see them as only somewhat so; likewise, boys view traits such as weakness as more feminine than do girls. The reverse pattern is seen for positive gender-stereotyped traits, where each sex will acknowledge that the other has positive stereotypical characteristics (e.g., that girls are gentle and boys are strong), yet have more extreme beliefs about the positive own-sex stereotypes (Powlishta, 1995a). In other words, just as with national groups (Bennett, Lyons, Sani, & Barrett, 1998), children's gender-related attitudes may reflect the expression of socially shared knowledge (i.e., stereotypes) in addition to any generic in-group bias.

In fact, as with national groups where children sometimes show in-group favouritism even before subjective identification with the in-group has occurred (Bennett et al., 1998), very young children may display gender-segregated play before they are fully aware of the relationship between sex of self and others (Maccoby, 1998). This pattern could arise from biologically and/or environmentally determined sex differences in play styles, coupled with a preference for playmates with similar or compatible styles. In other words, as noted earlier, children may not always be reacting to the sex of a potential playmate per se, but instead to the sorts of positive experiences they have had during face-to-face contacts with individual children of their own sex. That is, children's same-sex preferences are probably influenced by biological and social-environmental factors as well as by generic intergroup processes.

Perceived differences between and similarities within the sexes are also most likely determined by more than generic intergroup processes. Children encounter models of gender-typed behaviour in their homes, schools, and the media (see Powlishta et al., 2001). For example, despite changes in recent years, men and women often continue to divide household and child-care tasks along traditional gender lines. Men are more likely to work, and work longer hours, outside of the home. Women are more often teachers and men more often administrators in elementary schools. Stereotypical portrayals are perhaps even more extreme in television programmes, commercials, video games, and books. When children describe males and females as being different, then, they may not simply be exaggerating intragroup similarities and intergroup differences. Instead, as Glick and Hilt (2000) put it, "Gender-related attitudes exaggerate, but also reflect (and help to reinforce), social realities" (p. 266).

In sum, gender groups are different from experimentally created minimal groups in that males and females *do* have pre-existing differences, experiences, hostilities (or attractions), and face-to-face contacts. Thus, although generic intergroup processes most likely contribute to children's beliefs and preferences about the sexes, such processes do not fully explain gender-role development. Cognitive-developmental, social-environmental, and biological factors must also be taken into account. The complex patterns seen in children's gender-related attitudes and behaviours also have broader implications for those studying intergroup processes. In particular, the social identity approach could give greater attention to the fact that social categories differ from one another in ways that may have significant consequences, especially in a developmental context.

CONCLUSIONS AND IMPLICATIONS FOR IMPROVING CROSS-SEX RELATIONS

In summary, the same phenomena that are seen in social psychological studies of natural and experimentally created groups of adults are found with respect to children's attitudes and beliefs about males and females. Children favour their own sex in their choice of playmates, in their liking and trait ratings of males and females both individually and globally, and in their evaluations of male and female performance. In other words, consistent with social identity theory, children believe that their own sex is better than the other. At least for girls, such own-sex favouritism is linked to heightened self-esteem, as expected.

This in-group favouritism is accompanied by other intergroup phenomena. Namely, children exaggerate differences between and similarities within the gender groups, show a readiness to learn and create new gender stereotypes, and resist stereotypic changes or violations. Although not yet studied extensively, there also may be a tendency to view the other sex as particularly homogeneous. These distorted perceptions of variability are correlated with own-sex favouritism, consistent with a common origin in gender-based social categorisation.

As predicted by self-categorisation theory, these gender-based intergroup processes are elevated in contexts designed to enhance the salience of gender and among individuals for whom gender seems to be chronically salient. Such processes tend to be stronger in girls than in boys, perhaps reflecting the sort of status effects that have been found with experimentally created groups as well. And despite the sexual attraction and increased cognitive maturity that is most likely to account for the decline in gender-based intergroup processes with age, even adults sometimes favour their own sex and make use of gender stereotypes.

These findings suggest that a tendency to categorise the world into male and female groups, viewing same-sex individuals as "us" as opposed to "them", contributes to children's gender-role development above and beyond any domain-specific processes (e.g., biological sex differences, gender-differentiated socialisation). Children may view their own sex as superior in order to achieve a positive social identity, which in turn should motivate them to adopt gender-typed characteristics and prefer same-sex playmates. The resulting gender-segregated play exposes boys and girls to different socialisation contexts, potentially creating or amplifying sex differences (Martin & Fabes, 2001). The generic tendency to exaggerate between-group differences and within-group similarities may contribute to gender stereotypes, further encouraging boys and girls to adopt different behaviours and roles.

This intergroup perspective on gender role development has implications for how one might encourage boys and girls to have more positive attitudes about each other. Rather than attempting to change children's behaviours and beliefs directly, for example by rewarding cross-sex interactions (Serbin, Tonick, & Sternglanz, 1977) or by providing training that contradicts gender stereotypes (Bigler & Liben, 1992), a more promising approach may be to inhibit the formation of gender-based categories. Of course, one cannot block the basic human tendency to form social categories that help us make sense of the world and feel good about ourselves. And we have seen that, relative to other potential grouping characteristics, gender is a rather chronically salient basis for social categorisation among young children. However, we also have seen that it is possible to create contexts that focus attention on characteristics other than gender, for example situations that require the cooperation of boys and girls to achieve goals or that introduce explicit groupings that cross-cut gender. By encouraging children to categorise themselves, at least temporarily, in some manner other than gender, this approach shows promise for reducing children's biases against the other sex and their tendency to view each other in a rigidly stereotypical fashion.

REFERENCES

Aberson, C. L., Healy, M., & Romero, V. (2000). Ingroup bias and self-esteem: A meta-analysis. *Personality and Social Psychology Review, 4*, 157–173.

Albert, A. A., & Porter, J. R. (1983). Age patterns in the development of children's gender-role stereotypes. *Sex Roles, 9*, 59–67.

Allport, G. (1954). *The nature of prejudice*. Cambridge, MA: Addison-Wesley.

Bauer, P. J., & Coyne, M. J. (1997). When the name says it all: Preschoolers' recognition and use of the gendered nature of common proper names. *Social Development, 6*, 271–291.

Bauer, P. J., Liebl, M., & Stennes, L. (1998). Pretty is to dress as brave is to suitcoat: Gender-based property-to-property inferences by 4½-year-old children. *Merrill-Palmer Quarterly, 44*, 355–377.

Beere, C. A. (1990). *Gender roles: A handbook of tests and measures*. New York: Greenwood.

Bem, S. L. (1981). Gender schema theory: A cognitive account of sex typing. *Psychological Review, 88*, 354–364.

Bennett, M., Lyons, E., Sani, F., & Barrett, M. (1998). Children's subjective indentification with the group and in-group favouritism. *Developmental Psychology, 34*, 902–909.

Bennett, M., Sani, F., Hopkins, N., Agostini, L., & Malucchi, L. (2000). Children's gender categorization: An investigation of automatic processing. *British Journal of Developmental Psychology, 18*, 97–102.

Berndt, T. J., & Heller, K. A. (1986). Gender stereotypes and social inferences: A developmental study. *Journal of Personality and Social Psychology, 50*, 889–898.

Best, D. L. (1982). An overview of findings from children studies of sex-trait stereo-types in 23 countries. In R. Rath, H. S. Asthana, D. Sinha, & J. B. H. Sinha (Eds.), *Diversity and unity in cross-cultural psychology* (pp. 261–271). Amsterdam: Swets.

Best, D. L., Williams, J. E., Cloud, J. M., Davis, S. W., Roberston, L. S., Edwards, J. R., Giles, H., & Fowles, J. (1977). Development of sex-trait stereotypes among young children in the United States, England, and Ireland. *Child Development, 48,* 1375–1384.

Biernat, M. (1991). Gender stereotypes and the relationship between masculinity and femininity: A developmental analysis. *Journal of Personality and Social Psychology, 61,* 351–365.

Bigler, R. S. (1995). The role of classification skill in moderating environmental influences on children's gender stereotyping: A study of the functional use of gen-der in the classroom. *Child Development, 66,* 1072–1087.

Bigler, R. S., Jones, L. C., & Lobliner, D. B. (1997). Social categorization and the formation of intergroup attitudes in children. *Child Development, 68,* 530–543.

Bigler, R. S., & Liben, L. S. (1992). Cognitive mechanisms in children's gender stereo-typing: Theoretical and educational implications of a cognitive-based intervention. *Child Development, 63,* 1351–1363.

Blaske, D. M. (1984). Occupational sex-typing by kindergarten and fourth-grade children. *Psychological Reports, 54,* 795–801.

Brewer, M. B., Ho, H., Lee, J., & Miller, N. (1987). Social identity and social distance among Hong Kong school children. *Personality and Social Psychology Bulletin, 13,* 156–165.

Brown, R. (2000). Social identity theory: Past achievements, current problems and future challenges. *European Journal of Social Psychology, 30,* 745–778.

Cann, A., & Palmer, S. (1986). Children's assumptions about the generalizability of sex-typed abilities. *Sex Roles, 15,* 551–558.

Carter, D. B., & Levy, G. D. (1988). Cognitive aspects of early sex-role development: The influence of gender schemas on preschoolers' memories and preferences for sex-typed toys and activities. *Child Development, 59,* 782–792.

Carter, D. B., & Patterson, C. J. (1982). Sex roles as social conventions: The develop-ment of children's conceptions of sex-role stereotypes. *Developmental Psychology, 18,* 812–824.

Charlesworth, W. R., & LaFreniere, P. (1983). Dominance, friendship, and resource utilization in preschool children's groups. *Ethology and Sociobiology, 4,* 603–615.

Charters, W. W., & Newcomb, T. M. (1958). Some attitudinal effects of experimentally increased salience of a membership group. In E. E. Maccoby, T. M. Tewcomb, & E. L. Hartley (Eds.), *Readings in social psychology* (pp. 276–281). New York: Henry Holt.

Cordua, G. D., McGraw, K. O., & Drabman, R. S. (1979). Doctor or nurse: Children's perception of sex typed occupations. *Child Development, 50,* 590–593.

Cowan, G., & Hoffman, C. D. (1986). Gender stereotyping in young children: Evidence to support a concept-learning approach. *Sex Roles, 14,* 211–224.

Damon, W. (1977). *The social world of the child.* San Francisco: Jossey-Bass.

Deaux, K., & Major, B. (1987). Putting gender into context: An interactive model of gender-related behavior. *Psychological Review, 94,* 369–389.

Deschamps, J. C., & Doise, W. (1978). Crossed category memberships in intergroup relations. In H. Tajfel (Ed.), *Differentiation between social groups* (pp. 141–158). London: Academic Press.

Dion, K. L. (1979). Status equity, sex composition of group, and intergroup bias. *Personality and Social Psychology Bulletin, 5*, 240–244.

Doise, W., Deschamps, J.-C., & Meyer, G. (1978). The accentuation of intra-category similarities. In H. Tajfel (Ed.), *Differentiation between social groups* (pp. 159–168). London: Academic Press.

Doise, W., & Sinclair, A. (1973). The categorisation process in intergroup relations. *European Journal of Social Psychology, 3*, 145–157.

Doosje, B., Haslam, S. A., Spears, R., Oakes, P. J., & Koomen, W. (1998). The effect of comparative context on central tendency and variability judgments and the evaluation of group characteristics. *European Journal of Social Psychology, 28*, 173–184.

Dustin, D. S., & Davis, H. P. (1970). Evaluative bias in group and individual competition. *European Journal of Social Psychology, 80*, 103–108.

Edelbrock, C., & Sugawara, A. I. (1978). Acquisition of sex-typed preferences in preschool-aged children. *Developmental Psychology, 14*, 614–623.

Egan, S. K., & Perry, D. G. (2001). Gender identity: A multidimensional analysis with implications for psychosocial adjustment. *Developmental Psychology, 37*, 451–463.

Eichstedt, J. A., Serbin, L. A., Poulin-Dubois, D., & Sen, M. G. (in press). Of bears and men: Infants' knowledge of conventional and metaphorical gender stereotypes. *Infant Behavior and Development*.

Etaugh, C., & Riley, S. (1979). Knowledge of sex stereotypes in preschool children. *Psychological Reports, 44*, 1279–1282.

Fagan, J. F., & Shepherd, P. A. (1981). Theoretical issues in the early development of visual perception. In M. Lewis & L. Taft (Eds.), *Developmental disabilities in preschool children* (pp. 9–34). New York: Spectrum.

Fagan, J. F., & Singer, L. T. (1979). The role of simple feature differences in infants' recognition of faces. *Infant Behavior and Development, 2*, 39–45.

Gelman, S., Collman, P., & Maccoby, E. (1986). Inferring properties from categories versus inferring categories from properties: The case of gender. *Child Development, 57*, 396–404.

Glick, P., & Hilt, L. (2000). Combative children to ambivalent adults: The development of gender prejudice. In T. Eckes & H. M. Trautner (Eds.), *The developmental social psychology of gender* (pp. 243–272). Mahwah, NJ: Lawrence Erlbaum Associates, Inc.

Goldberg, P. (1968). Are women prejudiced against women? *Transaction, 5*, 28–30.

Harter, S. (1982). The Perceived Competence Scale for Children. *Child Development, 53*, 87–97.

Haugh, S. S., Hoffman, C. D., & Cowan, G. (1980). The eye of the very young beholder: Sex typing of infants by young children. *Child Development, 51*, 598–600.

Hayden-Thomson, L., Rubin, K. H., & Hymel, S. (1987). Sex preferences in sociometric choices. *Developmental Psychology, 23*, 558–562.

Helwig, A. A. (1998). Gender-role stereotyping: Testing theory with a longitudinal sample. *Sex Roles, 38*, 403–423.

Heyman, G. D. (2001). Children's interpretation of ambiguous behavior: Evidence for a "boys are bad" bias. *Social Development, 10*, 230–247.

Hogg, M. A., & Turner, J. C. (1987). Intergroup behaviour, self-stereotyping and the salience of social categories. *British Journal of Social Psychology, 26*, 325–340.

Hopkins, N., Regan, M., & Abell, J. (1997). On the context dependence of national stereotypes: Some Scottish data. *British Journal of Social Psychology, 36*, 553–563.

Hurtig, M.-C., & Pichevin, M.-F. (1990). Salience of the sex category system in person perception: Contextual variations. *Sex Roles, 22,* 369–395.

Janssens, L., & Nuttin, J. R. (1976). Frequency perception of individual and group successes as a function of competition, coaction, and isolation. *Journal of Personality and Social Psychology, 34,* 830–836.

Johnston, K. E., Madole, K. L., Bittinger, K., & Smith, A. (2001). Developmental changes in infants' and toddlers' attention to gender categories. *Merrill-Palmer Quarterly, 47,* 563–584.

Kail, R. V. Jr., & Levine, L. E. (1976). Encoding processes and sex-role preferences. *Journal of Experimental Child Psychology, 21,* 256–263.

Katz, P. A. (1986). Modification of children's gender-stereotyped behavior: General issues and research considerations. *Sex Roles, 14,* 591–602.

Katz, P. A. (1996). Raising feminists. *Psychology of Women Quarterly, 20,* 323–340.

Katz, P. A., & Seavey, C. (1973). Labels and children's perception of faces. *Child Development, 44,* 770–775.

Kuhn, D., Nash, S., & Brucken, L. (1978). Sex role concepts of two- and three-year-olds. *Child Development, 49,* 445–451.

Leinbach, M. D., & Fagot, B. I. (1986). Acquisition of gender labels: A test for toddlers. *Sex Roles, 15,* 655–667.

Leinbach, M. D., & Fagot, B. I. (1993). Categorical habituation to male and female faces: Gender schematic processing in infancy. *Infant Behavior and Development, 16,* 317–332.

Leinbach, M. D., Hort, B. E., & Fagot, B. I. (1997). Bears are for boys: Metaphorical associations in young children's gender stereotypes. *Cognitive Development, 12,* 107–130.

Levy, G. D. (1994). High and low gender schematic children's release from proactive interference. *Sex Roles, 30,* 93–108.

Levy, G. D. (1999). Gender-typed and non-gender-typed category awareness in toddlers. *Sex Roles, 41,* 851–873.

Levy, G. D., & Carter, D. B. (1989). Gender schema, gender constancy, and gender-role knowledge: The roles of cognitive factors in preschoolers' gender-role stereotype attributions. *Developmental Psychology, 25,* 444–449.

Levy, G. D., & Haaf, R. A. (1994). Detection of gender-related categories by 10-month-old infants. *Infant Behavior and Development, 17,* 457–459.

Levy, G. D., Taylor, M. G., & Gelman, S. A. (1995). Traditional and evaluative aspects of flexibility in gender roles, social conventions, moral rules, and physical laws. *Child Development, 66,* 515–531.

Livesley, W. J., & Bromley, D. B. (1973). *Person perception in childhood and adolescence.* London: John Wiley & Sons.

Lockheed, M., & Klein, S. (1985). Sex equity in classroom organization and climate. In S. Klein (Ed.), *Handbook for achieving sex equity through education* (pp. 189–217). Baltimore, MD: Johns Hopkins University Press.

Maccoby, E. E. (1988). Gender as a social category. *Developmental Psychology, 24,* 755–765.

Maccoby, E. E. (1998). *The two sexes: Growing up apart, coming together.* Cambridge, MA: Harvard University Press.

Maccoby, E. E., & Jacklin, C. N. (1987). Gender segregation in childhood. In H. Reese (Ed.), *Advances in child development and behavior, Vol. 20* (pp. 239–288). New York: Academic Press.

Martin, C. L. (1989). Children's use of gender-related information in making social judgments. *Developmental Psychology, 25*, 80–88.

Martin, C. L. (1990). Attitudes and expectations about children with nontraditional and traditional gender roles. *Sex Roles, 22*, 151–165.

Martin, C. L. (2000). Cognitive theories of gender development. In T. Eckes & H. M. Trautner (Eds.), *The developmental social psychology of gender* (pp. 91–121). Mahwah, NJ: Lawrence Erlbaum Associates, Inc.

Martin, C. L., Eisenbud, L., & Rose, H. (1995). Children's gender-based reasoning about toys. *Child Development, 66*, 1453–1471.

Martin, C. L., & Fabes, R. A. (2001). The stability and consequences of young children's same-sex peer interactions. *Developmental Psychology, 37*, 431–446.

Martin, C. L., & Halverson, C. F. Jr. (1981). A schematic processing model of sex typing and stereotyping in children. *Child Development, 52*, 1119–1134.

Martin, C. L., & Halverson, C. F. Jr. (1983). The effects of sex-typing schemas on young children's memory. *Child Development, 54*, 563–574.

Martin, C. L., & Little, J. K. (1990). The relation of gender understanding to children's sex-typed preferences and gender stereotypes. *Child Development, 61*, 1427–1439.

Martin, C. L., Wood, C. H., & Little, J. K. (1990). The development of gender stereotype components. *Child Development, 61*, 1891–1904.

McKillip, J., DiMiceli, A. J., & Luebke, J. (1977). Group salience and stereotyping. *Social Behavior and Personality, 5*, 81–85.

Messick, D. M., & Mackie, D. M. (1989). Intergroup relations. *Annual Review of Psychology, 40*, 45–81.

Miller, C. (1983). Developmental changes in male/female voice classification by infants. *Infant Behavior and Development, 6*, 313–330.

Mills, C. J., & Tyrrell, D. J. (1983). Sex-stereotypic encoding and release from proactive interference. *Journal of Personality and Social Psychology, 45*, 772–781.

Moghaddam, F. M., & Stringer, P. (1986). "Trivial" and "important" criteria for social categorization in the minimal group paradigm. *Journal of Social Psychology, 126*, 345–354.

Nadleman, L. (1974). Sex identity in American children: Memory, knowledge and preference tests. *Developmental Psychology, 10*, 413–417.

Nesdale, D., & Flesser, D. (2001). Social identity and the development of children's group attitudes. *Child Development, 72*, 506–517.

Parish, T. S., & Bryant, W. T. (1978). Mapping sex group stereotypes of elementary and high school students. *Sex Roles, 4*, 135–140.

Parish, T. S., Bryant, W. T., & Prawat, R. S. (1977). Reversing effects of sexism in elementary school girls through counterconditioning. *Journal of Instructional Psychology, 4*, 11–16.

Park, B., & Rothbart, M. (1982). Perception of out-group homogeneity and levels of social categorization: Memory for the subordinate attributes of in-group and out-group members. *Journal of Personality and Social Psychology, 42*, 1051–1068.

Perez, S. M., & Kee, D. W. (2000). Girls not boys show gender-connotation encoding from print. *Sex Roles, 42*, 439–447.

Pheterson, G. I., Kiesler, S. B., & Goldberg, P. A. (1971). Evaluation of the performance of women as a function of their sex, achievement, and personal history. *Journal of Personality and Social Psychology, 19*, 114–118.

Poulin-Dubois, D., Serbin, L. A., Eichstedt, J. A., & Sen, M. G. (in press). Men don't put on make-up: Toddlers' knowledge of the gender stereotyping of household activities. *Social Development*.

Powlishta, K. K. (1995a). Gender bias in children's perception of personality traits. *Sex Roles, 32*, 17–28.

Powlishta, K. K. (1995b). Gender segregation among children: Understanding the "cootie phenomenon". *Young Children, May*, 61–69.

Powlishta, K. K. (1995c). Intergroup processes in childhood: Social categorization and sex role development. *Developmental Psychology, 31*, 781–788.

Powlishta, K. K. (2000). The effect of target age on the activation of gender stereotypes. *Sex Roles, 42*, 271–282.

Powlishta, K. K. (2001, April). *Own-sex favouritism and gender-role development*. Poster presented at the Biennial Meeting of the Society for Research in Child Development, Minneapolis, MN.

Powlishta, K. K. (2002a). *Perceived similarity of boys and girls: Contextual variations in the salience of gender*. Manuscript submitted for publication.

Powlishta, K. K. (2002b). *The salience of gender in social perception*. Manuscript submitted for publication.

Powlishta, K. K., & Maccoby, E. E. (1990). Resource utilization in mixed-sex dyads: The influence of adult presence and task type. *Sex Roles, 29*, 723–737.

Powlishta, K. K., Sen, M. G., Serbin, L. A., Poulin-Dubois, D., & Eichstedt, J. A. (2001). From infancy through middle childhood: The role of cognitive and social factors in becoming gendered. In R. K. Unger (Ed.), *Handbook of the psychology of women and gender* (pp. 116–132). New York: John Wiley & Sons.

Powlishta, K. K., Serbin, L. A., Doyle, A., & White, D. C. (1994). Gender, ethnic, and body type biases: The generality of prejudice in childhood. *Developmental Psychology, 30*, 526–536.

Powlishta, K. K., & Vartanian, L. R. (1999, April). *Self-esteem and own-sex favouritism in middle childhood and early adolescence*. Poster presented at the Biennial Meeting of the Society for Research in Child Development, Albuquerque, NM.

Quattrone, G. A. (1986). On the perception of a groups' variability. In S. Worchel & W. G. Austin (Eds.), *Psychology of intergroup relations* (pp. 25–48). Chicago, IL: Nelson-Hall Publishers.

Rabbie, J. M., & Wilkens, G. (1971). Intergroup competition and its effect on intra-group and intergroup relations. *European Journal of Social Psychology, 2*, 215–234.

Reis, H. T., & Wright, S. (1982). Knowledge of sex-role stereotypes in children aged 3 to 5. *Sex Roles, 8*, 1049–1056.

Ruble, D. N., & Martin, C. L. (1998). Gender development. In N. Eisenberg (Ed.), W. Damon (Series Editor), *Handbook of child psychology. Vol. 3: Social, emotional and personality development* (5th ed., pp. 933–1016). New York: John Wiley & Sons.

Rutland, A. (1999). The development of national prejudice, in-group favouritism and self-stereotypes in British children. *British Journal of Social Psychology, 38*, 55–70.

Sani, F., & Bennett, M. (2001). Contextual variability in young children's gender ingroup stereotype. *Social Development, 10*, 221–229.

Schmitt, M. T., Silvia, P. J., & Branscombe, N. R. (2000). The intersection of self-evaluation maintenance and social identity theories: Intragroup judgment in intergroup and interpersonal contexts. *Personality and Social Psychology Bulletin, 26*, 1598–1606.

Sen, M. G., & Bauer, P. J. (2002). *Cognitive correlates of two-year-old children's differential memory for own-gender-stereotyped information.* Manuscript submitted for publication.

Serbin, L. A., Moller, L. C., Gulko, J., Powlishta, K. K., & Colburne, K. A. (1994). The emergence of gender segregation in toddler playgroups. In C. Leaper (Ed.), *Childhood gender segregation: Causes and consequences. New directions for child development, Vol. 65* (pp. 7–17). San Francisco: Jossey-Bass.

Serbin, L. A., Poulin-Dubois, D., Colburne, K. A., Sen, M. G., & Eichstedt, J. A. (2001). Gender stereotyping in infancy: Visual preferences for and knowledge of gender-stereotyped toys in the second year. *International Journal of Behavioral Development, 25*, 7–15.

Serbin, L. A., Powlishta, K. K., & Gulko, J. (1993). The development of sex-typing in middle childhood. *Monographs of the Society for Research in Child Development, 58* (Serial No. 232).

Serbin, L. A., & Sprafkin, C. (1986). The salience of gender and the process of sex-typing in three- to seven-year-old children. *Child Development, 57*, 1188–1199.

Serbin, L. A., Sprafkin, C., Elman, M., & Doyle, A. B. (1984). The early development of sex differentiation patterns and social influence. *Canadian Journal of Social Science, 14*, 350–368.

Serbin, L. A., Tonick, I. J., & Sternglanz, S. H. (1977). Shaping cooperative cross-sex play. *Child Development, 48*, 924–929.

Signorella, M. L. (1987). Gender schemata: Individual differences and context effects. In L. S. Liben & M. L. Signorella (Eds.), *Children's gender schemata* (pp. 23–37). London: Jossey-Bass.

Signorella, M. L., Bigler, R. S., & Liben, L. S. (1993). Developmental differences in children's gender schemata about others: A meta-analytic review. *Developmental Review, 13*, 147–183.

Silvern, L. E. (1977). Children's sex-role preferences: Stronger among girls than boys. *Sex Roles, 3*, 159–171.

Stangor, C., & Ruble, D. N. (1987). Development of gender role knowledge and gender constancy. In L. S. Liben & M. L. Signorella (Eds.), *Children's gender schemata* (pp. 5–22). London: Jossey-Bass.

Starer, R., & Denmark, F. (1974). Discrimination against aspiring women. *International Journal of Group Tensions, 4*, 65–70.

Stephenson, G. M., Skinner, M., & Brotherton, C. J. (1976). Group participation and intergroup relations: An experimental study of negotiation groups. *European Journal of Social Psychology, 6*, 51–70.

Tajfel, H. (1970). Experiments in intergroup discrimination. *Scientific American, November*, 96–102.

Tajfel, H., Billig, M. G., Bundy, R. P., & Flament, C. (1971). Social categorization and intergroup behaviour. *European Journal of Social Psychology, 1*, 149–178.

Tajfel, H., & Turner, J. (1979). An integrative theory of intergroup conflict. In W. G. Austin & S. Worchel (Eds.), *The social psychology of intergroup relations* (pp. 33–47). Monterey, CA: Brooks/Cole.

Taylor, S. E. (1981). A categorization approach to stereotyping. In D. L. Hamilton (Ed.), *Cognitive processes in stereotyping and intergroup behavior* (pp. 83–114). Hillsdale, NJ: Lawrence Erlbaum Associates, Inc.

Thompson, S. K. (1975). Gender labels and early sex role development. *Child Development, 46*, 339–347.

Thorne, B. (1987, February). *Children and gender: Constructions of difference.* Paper presented at the Conference on Theoretical Perspectives on Sexual Difference, Stanford University, Stanford, CA.

Todor, N. L. (1980). The effect of the sexual composition of a group on discrimination against women and sex-role attitudes. *Psychology of Women Quarterly*, 5, 292–310.

Trautner, H. M., Helbing, N., Sahm, W. B., & Lohaus, A. (1989, April). *Beginning awareness-rigidity-flexibility: A longitudinal analysis of sex-role stereotyping in 4- to 10-year-old children.* Paper presented at the meeting of the Society for Research in Child Development, Kansas City.

Turner, J. (1975). Social comparison and social identity: Some prospects for intergroup behaviour. *European Journal of Social Psychology*, 5, 5–34.

Turner, J. C., Hogg, M. A., Oakes, P. J., Reicher, S. D., & Wetherell, M. S. (1987). *Rediscovering the social group: A self-categorization theory.* Oxford: Basil Blackwell.

Turner, J. C., & Onorato, R. (1999). Social identity, personality, and the self-concept: A self-categorization perspective. In T. R. Tyler, R. M. Kramer, & O. P. John (Eds.), *The psychology of the social self* (pp. 11–46). Mahwah, NJ: Lawrence Erlbaum Associates, Inc.

Van Knippenberg, A. F. M. (1984). Intergroup differences in group perceptions. In H. Tajfel (Ed.), *The social dimension: European developments in social psychology, Vol. 2* (pp. 560–578). Cambridge: Cambridge University Press.

Vaughan, G., Tajfel, H., & Williams, J. A. (1981). Bias in reward allocation in an intergroup and an interpersonal context. *Social Psychology Quarterly*, 44, 37–42.

Vener, A. M., & Snyder, C. A. (1966). The preschool child's awareness and anticipation of adult sex-roles. *Sociometry*, 29, 159–168.

Weinraub, M., Clemens, L. P., Sockloff, A., Ethridge, T., Gracely, E., & Meyers, B. (1984). The development of sex role stereotypes in the third year: Relationship to gender labelling, identity, sex-typed toy preference, and family characteristics. *Child Development*, 55, 1493–1503.

Wetherell, M. (1982). Cross-cultural studies of minimal groups: Implications for the social identity theory of intergroup relations. In H. Tajfel (Ed.), *Social identity and intergroup relations* (pp. 207–240). Cambridge: Cambridge University Press.

Wilder, D. A. (1981). Perceiving persons as a group: Categorization and intergroup behavior. In D. L. Hamilton (Ed.), *Cognitive processes in stereotyping and intergroup behavior* (pp. 213–257). Hillsdale, NJ: Lawrence Erlbaum Associates, Inc.

Wilder, D. A. (1984). Predictions of belief homogeneity and similarity following social categorization. *British Journal of Social Psychology*, 23, 323–333.

Williams, J. E., Bennett, S. M., & Best, D. L. (1975). Awareness and expression of sex stereotypes in young children. *Developmental Psychology*, 11, 635–642.

Yee, M., & Brown, R. (1992). Self-evaluations and intergroup attitudes in children aged three to nine. *Child Development*, 63, 619–629.

Yee, M., & Brown, R. (1994). The development of gender differentiation in young children. *British Journal of Social Psychology*, 33, 183–196.

Zalk, S. R., & Katz, P. A. (1978). Gender attitudes in children. *Sex Roles*, 4, 349–357.

5 The gender wars: A self-categorisation theory perspective on the development of gender identity

Barbara David, Diana Grace, and Michelle K. Ryan

"Who am I?" might be said to be the pre-eminent question of childhood. After telling us their name, the answer most children will give is that they are a child, and a girl or a boy (Brooks & Lewis, 1976; Fiske, 1992; Harris, 1995). If they live in a social context of high ethnic, religious, or national conflict, the child might also tell us that they are Serbian or Croatian, Catholic or Protestant, Israeli or Palestinian (Hirschfeld, 1993; Stevenson & Stevenson, 1960; see also Nesdale, Chapter 8, and Verkuyten, Chapter 7).

Empirical evidence confirms that the dimensions of age, gender, and, in some cases, race, are those on which children's first social identities are based. Of these, some researchers have claimed that "gender is the most fundamental" (Banaji & Prentice, 1994, p. 315) and there is certainly evidence that it is one of the earliest of which children show awareness: Infants are able to make categorical distinctions between males and females even before they have the language to articulate the differences (Leinbach & Fagot, 1993; Walker-Andrews, Bahrick, Raglioni, & Diaz, 1991). By the age of 2 to 3 years, most children not only distinguish between males and females but can tell us that they, themselves, are a boy or a girl, and will exhibit some distress if an adult assigns them to the wrong sex (Bussey, 1986; Money & Ehrhardt, 1972).

Correctly applying the label for one's biological sex, however, only answers the opening question in part for, without a meaning, the label is a long way from being an identity. It is obtaining that meaning, the process of gender socialisation, that will be the major focus of this chapter. We will first outline what is known about the developmental sequence of gender socialisation, and address the nature of the knowledge being acquired: What *does* it mean to be male or female in Western society? Second, we will outline and evaluate the major theoretical approaches. In the third section we will explicate what we see as the fundamental difference between an understanding of the self as an individual product – the concept underlying the major developmental theories – and one that sees the self as an ongoing *process* – the basic concept of self-categorisation (for recent summaries see Onorato & Turner, 2001; Turner, 1999a). In the final section we will suggest ways in which a more fluid and collective conceptualisation of self might address some of the short-comings and add to the rich insights already gained through the classic approaches to gender development.

THE DEVELOPMENTAL SEQUENCE

The importance of the category labels

Anyone who has attempted to buy a congratulatory card for the birth of a child will be aware of the necessity of choosing between one that is pink and one that is blue, between one that trumpets "It's a BOY!" or "Congratulations on the birth of your baby girl". Classic developmental studies show us that the importance adults place on labelling a newborn as male or female is reflected in their tendency to interpret babies' behaviour differently (Condry & Condry, 1976) and to treat babies in very different ways (Lewis, 1972), depending on their sex.

Whether or not they are reflecting adult preoccupations, infants themselves appear to be aware of the male/female dichotomy (Fagot & Leinbach, 1994; Leinbach & Fagot, 1993) and their preverbal awareness of categorical sex differences is expressed as soon as they can speak. By the time they are 2 years old, children are beginning to apply sex category labels correctly, to themselves and to other people (Fagot & Leinbach, 1989, 1993; Thompson, 1975), and by the time they are in primary school, boys and girls begin to practise sex segregation, eschewing voluntary contact with the other sex and engaging in enthusiastic derogation of it (Maccoby, 1988, 1990; Maccoby & Jacklin, 1987; Serbin, Sprafkin, Elmian, & Doyle, 1984; Thorne, 1993; see also Powlishta, Chapter 4). As one 11-year-old girl expressed it, "It's like the boys and girls are on different sides" (Thorne, 1993, p.63).

The primary school years, the period during which the sexes are most overtly "at war", is also the period during which they cling most determinedly to sex stereotypes for themselves and others. Preschoolers may know which category of objects, behaviours, and characteristics are "girl things" and which are "boy things", but they are not overly concerned if they or another child engages in cross-gender behaviour. On the other side of the "war zone", by mid adolescence girls and boys begin to use criteria such as athletic prowess, artistic, social, and academic interests, and race and ethnicity as the basis of their social groupings (Brown, Mounts, Lamborn, & Steinberg, 1993; Eckert, 1989; Schofield, 1981; see also the section on age/developmental differences in Powlishta, Chapter 4) and, with this association of self with other social categories, adolescents adopt a more flexible attitude to gender stereotypes (Katz & Ksansnak, 1994; Welch-Ross & Schmidt, 1996). It is the content of the stereotypes with which primary school children so strongly align themselves to which we will now turn our attention.

Stereotype content

What do we believe it means to be male or female? Williams and Best (1990) found that, nearly universally, males are seen as adventurous, forceful, and independent, and females as sentimental, submissive, and superstitious. In the more than 30 countries studied, males were characterised as more intelligent, stronger, and more active than females or, to put it in the words of an Australian children's playground chant, "Stupid, stupid gi-irls, stupid, stupid gi-irls! Girls are weak (chuck 'em in the creek). Boys are strong (like King Kong)".

In one of the classic studies to which we have already referred, parents showed evidence of fostering a reactive/proactive distinction in newborn children, gently constraining and talking quietly to their infant daughters, and encouraging alertness and exploratory activity in their sons (Lewis, 1972). Caretakers also tend to be more responsive to boys when they are assertive and girls when they are communicative (Fagot, Hagan, Leinbach, & Knonsberg, 1985). The reactive/proactive distinction is further fostered through the toys and the environment that adults provide for children (Pomerleau, Bolduc, Malcuit, & Cossette, 1990; Reingold & Cook, 1975.

By school age, children have learnt the stereotype-consistent ways to behave. Girls' groups are characterised by games in which there is little evidence of gross motor activity and an emphasis on "grown-up" social niceties such as turn-taking and making sure everyone is having a good time. Boys' groups, on the other hand, are characterised by rough, often aggressive, hierarchically organised physical activity (Maccoby, 1988, 1990; Maccoby & Jacklin, 1987; Serbin et al., 1984; Thorne, 1993).

While both boys and girls very quickly learn how each sex is supposed to play, dress, and behave, and while both sexes usually act in ways that are consistent with their gender, this is much more prescriptive for boys than for girls. More than girls, boys are both evaluated negatively (Feinman, 1981), and sanctioned severely (Fagot, 1977) for cross-sex behaviour, so it is not surprising that they are more rigid in their adherence to gender-stereotypical behaviour for themselves and more damning of others who fail to observe the "rules" (Jackson & Tein, 1998; Signorella, Bigler, & Liben, 1993). The differential rigidity in gender stereotypes is at its height, as we might expect, during the gender wars of primary school, but continues to a relative extent throughout the lifespan (as shown, for example, by Caldera, Huston, & O'Brien, 1989; Delk, Madden, Livingston, & Ryan, 1986; Rubin, Provenanzo, & Luria, 1974).

Why is it more important for males than for females to adhere to gender-appropriate norms? Why is it worse to be a "sissy" than a "tomboy"? Why is the most damning judgment that can be made of a boy is that he is like a girl? A recent United Nations publication provides a compelling answer in noting that ... "women constitute half the world's population, perform nearly two-thirds of its work hours, receive one-tenth of the world's income, and own less than one-hundredth of the world's property" (1991, p. 3). It is understandable that wealthy landlords should not want to be mistaken for indigent tenants!

Of course, this is not to say that children are aware of the statistics of sexual inequality; indeed, few adults are fully cognisant of them. Children do observe, however, that their fathers' jobs are more valued than their mothers' jobs (Catalyst, 1999; Gutek & Larwood, 1989), that females are more likely than males to be interrupted when they are speaking (Blakemore, Larue, & Oljenic, 1979 cited in Bussey, 1986), and from the hours children typically spend in front of television (up to one third of their waking hours according to Nielsen Media Research, 1989) they will observe that males have more authority and are more likely to be mature, materially well-off, professional, competent, and powerful than females (Signorielli & Bacue, 1999; see also Bussey & Bandura, 1999).

The importance for boys of avoiding any taint of femininity was illustrated in the first study of a now-classic report (Bussey & Bandura, 1984) in which children were shown a video of a team of men and a team of women playing a game in which each team performed a different sequence of ritualised actions. When invited to play the game themselves, while most girls copied the women's actions, a substantial number copied the men's actions. Boys copied the men's actions almost exclusively. That children are sensitive to the gender power differential became apparent in a second study, in which the authors preceded the game video with one that showed either the men's team or the women's team owning and having control over all the toys. When men were seen to have power there was little change in children's modelling of the game, but when women were seen to have power there was a significant increase in boy's modelling of the women's actions. Thus, it would appear that even more important as a cue for gender-appropriate behaviour than physical appearance (which we know to be extremely important to children) was the display of power, which children saw as the province of males.

There is also emerging evidence (David, 2003) that boys are aware of another abstract element of the sexual status quo: The idea that "people" are male. When asked to select, from pictures of items such as guns and dolls, those they would show to a Martian to describe human beings, girls chose a mixture of female and male items, while boys chose almost exclusively male items.

In sum, girls and boys are perceived as being different and are treated differently from birth, in ways that encourage expressive reactivity in girls and competent proactivity in boys. Children tend to conform to their assigned roles, with a sharp increase in conformity when they begin primary school and a decrease when, with adolescence, they begin to form friendship groups based on criteria other than sex. Throughout, boys are more strongly confined than girls by gender stereotypes, since it is vitally important that they learn not only to be boys, but *not* to be girls. It is to the theorised form this learning takes that we will now direct our attention.

THEORIES OF GENDER DEVELOPMENT

From the preceding section it will be clear that there is a strong correspondence between the gender stereotypes that children learn and apply to
themselves and social reality. Thus classic *psychoanalytic accounts* of gender
identity development are less than satisfactory in that they ignore social
factors and place all the emphasis on intra-individual factors such as the
resolution of infant sexual attraction to the opposite-sex parent (Freud, 1925/
1989) or the consequences of identification with the primary care-giver
(Chodorow, 1978, 1979). The only way social reality can be accounted for
within the framework of these theories is to posit that it is a reflection of
fundamentally and irrevocably different male and female personalities. As
such, the status quo cannot and will not change. This is not only pessimistic,
but flies in the face of sociological and historical evidence. (For a fuller critique of psychoanalytic theories, see Tavris, 1994, and for a discussion of the
social consequences of individualistic theories, see Turner, 1999b).

Looking at gender identity as taking the opposite direction from that
proposed by psychoanalytic theories – that is, seeing it as something which
goes from the outside to the inside, from society to the individual – is *social
learning theory* (Bandura, 1969, 1986; Bussey & Bandura, 1999; Mischel,
1966, 1993). An extension and modification of the traditional learning theory
postulated by B. F. Skinner, social learning theory proposes that gender
knowledge is gained from observation of many models of both sexes and
extrapolation of within-category similarities and between-category differences. Thus both girls and boys learn what is appropriate for both sexes. The
decision to adopt one or the other set of behaviours is also determined by
observation, in this case, of the rewards or punishments associated with it for
different protagonists. Children observe, for example, that females are
rewarded for being nurturant and taking care of their appearance, and disap-
proved of when they act too assertively, while male displays of aggression
meet with approval and male displays of nurturance or concern for appearance are met with at best, derision and at worst, violent abuse. Thus, girls
model their behaviour such as dress, activity choice, and manner on other
girls and women, while boys model their behaviour on boys and men.

Gender identity fits towards the end of the process outlined by social
learning theory: Children model their behaviour on similar others whom
they observe being rewarded for the behaviour, then observe their own
behaviour and conclude they are doing girl or boy things, therefore they must
be a girl or a boy. *Cognitive-developmental theory* (Kohlberg, 1966) turns this
around and posits that children must first know that they are a boy or a girl,
that is, they must achieve gender constancy, and will then seek out what
society defines as boy-appropriate or girl-appropriate behaviour because
consistency between identity and behaviour is rewarding in itself. Thus,
while both theories explain how the social reality of sex differences is
internalised, social learning theory proposes that society socialises children,

while cognitive-developmental theory proposes that children actively socialise themselves.

Gender schema theory simply proposes that children organise information about gender in a specific gender schema – ". . . a cognitive structure, a network of associations that organises and guides an individual's perceptions" (Bem, 1981, p. 355). Some children are believed to have more highly developed schemas than others – that is, they are gender-schematic – and they will be more likely to understand the world in gendered terms, to remember gender-consistent information better than gender-inconsistent information, and even to distort memory to make it fit the gender stereotypes contained in the schema (Stangor & Ruble, 1987). Their gender schema is incorporated by children into a broad, more inclusive self-schema.

From the perspective of the authors of this chapter, gender schema theory stands out by virtue of its explicitly stated concept of the self as a *structure*, and of people as being fixed *types* as a result of the nature of the structure. We will address the problems we see with such a static concept of self at the end of the following section, but first will address the more general issues raised by the dominant theories of gender.

MATCHING THE THEORIES AND THE EVIDENCE

Linda Brannon (2002) states that, "Each of the theories of gender development presents an orderly pattern of development, but the research shows a complex pattern with many components that do not necessarily match the theories. That is, none of the theories is able to explain all the data from research on gender development" (p. 146).

The insurmountable problem for cognitive-developmental theory is its predication of gender constancy as the initiator of children's search for gender-consistent behaviour. A substantial number of studies have shown that gender constancy develops later than the appearance of many other components of gender knowledge (e.g., Bussey & Bandura, 1984; Grace & David, 2001, 2003): Children typically do not reach gender constancy until they begin primary school, but by this time they are well able to correctly identify males and females and to sort objects into gender-appropriate categories, and they have a very well-developed sense of what is the "right" way for a girl or a boy to behave.

However, the very thing that is a problem for the cognitive-developmental approach underlies its main strength: The articulation of a strong motive for children to seek gendered behaviour – the implicitly rewarding fit between self-category labels and behaviour. In contrast to this, social learning theory has been criticised for portraying children as passive objects of societal conditioning (e.g., Bem, 1985). Children show signs of more active pursuit and enthusiastic embracing of gender-consistent behaviour than social learning would predict. Moreover, rather than a smooth, gradual accumulation of knowledge, children show distinct patterning of knowledge acquisition, for example being able to make category distinctions before fleshing out their content knowledge.

On the "plus" side for social learning theory is the fact that it can account for the sex differences in gender development, with boys cleaving more strongly than girls to strict gender-appropriate guidelines. Children's understanding that power is a male prerogative (Bussey & Bandura, 1984) explains why boys should be so determined not to be mistaken for a girl.

In the eyes of the authors of the current chapter, more important than any of the above problems is the fact that none of the dominant theories provide a rationale for the virulence of the primary school separatist "war". Maccoby (1990) suggests that children may keep to same-sex play groups because the girls find the high-energy, rough-and-tumble of boys' play aversive, and are put off by the fact that they can exert no influence in mixed-sex groups. There is ample evidence to back up Maccoby's claim, but while such a benign explanation accounts for separatism, it does not explain the enthusiastic derogation of the opposite sex, such dramatic assertions as that "boys have cooties" or "girls have girl germs" (Thorne, 1993; for a social identity explanation, see Powlishta, Chapter 4).

We will be proposing that self-categorisation theory provides a compelling account of this, and other aspects of gender development that are only poorly explained by the dominant theories. Before attempting this, however, it is necessary to address the fundamental difference between self-categorisation and the other theories – its conceptualisation of the self.

THE SELF AS A PROCESS

Gender schema theory explicitly defines the self as a cognitive structure. While neither social learning nor cognitive-developmental theory make such a concrete assertion, implicit in both is the idea that the gender knowledge children are gaining accumulates in some unitary, stable construct that constitutes their gender identity, part of a larger, stable construct that is the self.

In contrast to this, self-categorisation theory conceives of the self as a labile, context-dependent process (Onorato & Turner, 2001; Turner, 1985, 1988, 1999a, 1999b). The self is whatever an individual means when, at any time, they call themselves or think of themselves as "I", "me", "us", or "we". The primary determinant of the meaning is the social comparative context. For example, when, in conversation with her sister, a woman says "I", this may mean "the person you grew up with, the one who lent you pocket money, stole your Barbie doll, taught you to use make-up". If the same woman uses the first-person singular in conversation with a work colleague, "I" will mean something very different, perhaps "the person whose office is next to yours, whose paper-clips you are always borrowing, who is going to get promoted before you".

Thus, even the individual self is labile and socially determined. The meaning is determined both by the social context and the reservoir of memories and knowledge that will inform the content. This knowledge is what many theorists believe *is* the self. When contemporary theorists do make allowance for some fluidity of self-awareness, they see the "working self" (Markus & Wurf, 1987) as part of a system composed of many situation-specific selves: the relational self (Markus & Kitayama, 1991), the remembered self (Neisser & Jopling, 1997), even the false self (Harter, 1997, 1998). Self-categorisation theory sees this as lacking in parsimony. Since social contexts are potentially infinite in number, so are the selves that will be determined by them. The specific knowledge one brings to bear in a particular circumstance may never have been part of the self-concept before and may never be again. It seems wasteful, then, that having been part of the self, the knowledge should be stored on the "self" side of some cognitive barrier. Surely it is more parsimonious to see the self as being only what is brought into consciousness at any particular time, and to propose that in bringing to consciousness a current "I" or "me", one has access to *all* one's knowledge, memories, and understandings, not only those contained in a hypothetical "self" enclosure or system?

If the individual self is a social process, the collective self is much more so. When thinking or speaking of oneself as a woman or a man, an Australian, or an American, part of the meaning of "us" or "we" is gained from, and shared by, the other "selves" included in the first-person plural pronoun. To know what "us girls" means, a child must know what is typical or normative for girls – what "we" have in common that distinguishes us from "them". As outlined earlier in the chapter, social learning theorists found that gender knowledge (as distinct from behaviour) is gained through observation of males and females, and the making of judgments of within-sex similarity and between-sex difference (Perry & Bussey, 1979). In the classic modelling study described previously (Bussey & Bandura, 1984), it was observed that children did not copy the behaviour of a single same-sex adult, but waited until they had seen most of the team and could conclude that the actions were not idiosyncratic, but rather the normative way for males or females to behave in the circumstances. Thus a parent, no matter how loving or loved, cannot be a model for appropriate gender behaviour, unless the child's exposure to the wider world (for example, through friendship groups and the media) suggests that the parent is a *representative* or prototypical male or female (see Harris, 1995, for an extended review and discussion of peer group versus parental influence).

Importantly, a child's understanding of what it means to be a girl or a boy will be what they have worked out is typical, based on the exemplars to which they have had exposure. Since the number and variety of the exemplars will increase with age, a child's concept of "typical" will also change, presumably in the direction of becoming less prescriptive. Thus a self-categorisation conception of self is consistent with the findings that some children's gender stereotypes are more strongly influenced by their parents than others, and that children's gender stereotypes become more flexible with age.

While knowledge of the nature of other self-category members is one determinant of the meaning of a particular social identity, knowledge of the out-group is also necessary, since the meaning of "us" is as context-dependent as the meaning of "I". For example, "us girls" in a girl/woman context may mean "the ones who are noisy and boisterous", but in a "girl/boy" context may have the opposite meaning of "the ones who are quiet and mannerly".

Recent and ongoing studies at The Australian National University have shown the flexibility of the self-concept. Onorato and Turner (1996, 1997) required participants to complete a screening questionnaire that identified them as "independent schematics" or "dependent schematics" (after Markus, 1977). Some men and some women identified themselves as dependent schematics and some as independent schematics. In single-sex groups the participants were then required to discuss the extent to which the traits of tact, cautiousness, and dependency characterised women as distinct from men (women's groups) or the extent to which the traits of independence, dominance, and aggressiveness characterised men as distinct from women (men's groups). Participants then described themselves on a social-self rating task, and women, including those who had rated "me" as independent in the first task, indicated that "we" were dependent, while men, including those who had rated "me" as dependent, indicated that "we" were independent.

Critics could perhaps claim that Onorato and Turner's results do not necessarily illustrate flexibility of the self-concept, merely that people have an individual self and a number of collective selves that may differ from each other in content. The same cannot be said of Ryan and David's (2002) study, which tested the proposal that men have separate self-construals and women connected self-construals (after Cross & Madson, 1997). All participants completed a self-description questionnaire in which they indicated the extent to which they perceived their individual selves as connected to, or separate from, others. This was preceded by a supposedly different study in which they were required to think about either groups to which they belonged (the in-group condition), groups to which they did not belong (the out-group condition), or about gender. When gender had been made salient, participants responded to the self questionnaire in the gender-stereotypical way, with women indicating that they were connected, and men that they were separate individuals. When self-description was preceded by thinking about groups to which they belonged, both female and male participants indicated that they were connected individuals. When self-description was preceded by thinking about groups to which they did not belong, both female and male participants indicated that they were separate individuals. As well as showing (a) that the way people experience themselves as individuals is effected by a feeling of connectedness with in-group others and separation from out-group others, and (b) that when gender is salient, women experience themselves as connected to others, and men think of themselves as separate, this study shows very clearly that the self is not a fixed construct.

This brings us to consideration of the final aspect of self-categorisation to be discussed here: salience. We have already outlined our understanding of the self as a context-dependent process. Context plays its part, not in the simplistic way it has sometimes been seen to (context A calls forth self-category B, while context X awakens self-category Y), but as part of an interactive process.

In order to understand this, imagine that a child is contemplating an unknown group of children. The children have hair of different lengths, from virtually none to waist-length, but there seems to be a discontinuity at about the level of the ears: many children have hair lengths ranging from crew-cut, to ear-length, while others have hair that ranges from shoulder-blade to waist-length. There is less difference in the crew-cut-to-ear range and the shoulder-blade-to-waist range than there is between the short and the long, and the boy observing the group probably perceives even greater within-category similarity and between-category difference than actually exists (see Tajfel & Wilkes, 1963). Thus, the group meets the good *comparative fit* criterion for being perceived as two distinct categories (i.e., within-category similarity and between-category difference, Oakes, 1987; for the metacontrast principle, see Turner, 1985). Because the boy's father is always telling him to "act like a man", because his school teacher refers to her class, not as "children", but as "boys and girls", because his group of friends at school are currently mounting a terror campaign against a "sissy", and because his own male identity is very important to him (see Doosje & Ellemers, 1997), the gender categories have *high relative accessibility* for him (he is "perceiver ready" to call the categories "boys and girls", see Oakes, 1987). One more condition must be met before gender will be salient: The two categories must have good *normative* (Oakes, 1987), as well as the good comparative fit they have already displayed. In other words, the categories must display the qualities that are typically associated with them. Thus, if most of the "short-hairs" are wearing skirts and most of the "long-hairs" are wearing football boots, gender will have poor normative fit, despite good comparative fit and high relative accessibility. In this context, in other words, gender will not be salient. The categories will not be understood to be boys and girls, and the observer's own male identity will thus not be salient (he may think of himself as a "normal" child in comparison to the strange ones he is watching).

From the earlier part of the chapter we know that such poor normative fit is highly unlikely. Children, particularly between the ages of 4 years and early adolescence, religiously follow the dictates of gender appropriateness. "Short-hairs" are unlikely to wear skirts, or "long-hairs" football boots. Thus, in real life, children's behaviour has excellent normative fit with the gender categories. It also has good comparative fit because of the rigidity with which they adhere to same-sex modes of being in the world, avoiding at all costs looking or acting like the opposite sex. Also, because their world is one in which, rather than being called by their own name, they are so often referred to as one of the boys or the girls who can "tip-toe out quietly", "line up by the door", "go out to little lunch", and so on, the gender categories are highly accessible. In sum, gender is very salient for children.

Of course, we already know this as an empirical fact. Indeed, it is difficult to imagine any other stage in life when a single social category is as salient as gender is for primary school children. This does not mean, however, that we can assume that their gender is the only social category with which children can, or do, identify. We cannot take the lazy option of saying that gender salience is "chronic" for children (thus falling prey to speaking of gender differences as if they were part of the "personality", and taking on board all the problems associated with seeing the self as a fixed structure). One of the studies in our current research programme (David, in preparation) illustrates very clearly that, while gender is salient for children, it is not always so. The participants (aged 6 to 7 years old) allotted picture stimuli to the "girls' box" or the "boys' box" (gender condition) or to the girls' box, the boys' box or the "grown-ups' box" (age condition). Other than by the provision of the boxes, no attempt was made to make them conscious of either the dimension of age or of gender. In the gender condition, both boys and girls sorted the stimuli along gender-stereotypical lines (dolls for the girls, guns for the boys, etc.). In the age condition, although boys' stereotyping scores were significantly higher than girls', both girls and boys had significantly lower gender stereo-typing scores for their "boy" and "girl" boxes than did children in the gender condition. Identification measures supported what the stereotyping scores suggested: Children in the gender condition were thinking of themselves as girls and boys, but in the age condition, they were primarily aware of themselves as "children".

It is difficult to see how any of the dominant theories of gender develop-ment, embracing the fixed model of the self as they do, could explain this data. Self-categorisation theory, with its detailed analysis of salience and fluid understanding of the self, as well as explaining this data, could perhaps address some of the other questions of complexity that, as Brannon (2002) pointed out, the major theories have thus far been unable to answer. By the same token, the predictably high salience of gender for children makes gender identity a potentially rich vein of inquiry for self-categorisation researchers. In the following section we direct our attention to both of these assertions.

SELF-CATEGORISATION, THE DOMINANT THEORIES, AND GENDER DEVELOPMENT

Adopting the self-categorisation concept of the self as a process provides a different perspective on the dominant theories of gender development. When social learning theorists propose that children observe males and females and make evaluations of intracategorical similarity and intercategorical difference, we would propose that children are assessing the *comparative fit* of the gender categories. When children accumulate knowledge about what is "appropriate" for each category we would see them as laying down a store of information from which they will make decisions about *normative fit*, and on which they will base their own behaviour when gender is salient. The fact that, as social learning theorists compellingly point out, so much of what children observe tells them that gender *matters* (because it determines what they can wear, how long their hair should be, what and who they can play with, how they should talk, what school subjects they are good at, what jobs they do, what sports they play), we would see as meaning that gender will be highly *accessible* for children.

Framed this way, the social learning account of gender development no longer appears to characterise children as passive (Bem's, 1985, criticism). We see them as active participants whose current knowledge and level of cognitive ability determine what they mean when, at any time, they refer to themselves as a boy or a girl, which in turn determines how they will behave in that context.

While (with most other contemporary theorists) we reject Piaget's proposal of 8–9 years as the age at which children can competently categorise, we do accept that children are not born with fully developed cognitive skills and capacities, and we cannot ignore the findings that they are able to deal with simple and concrete processes before complex and abstract ones. The calculation of comparative fit would have to qualify as complex, and since it is a necessary part of the process of social identification, we would speculate that early use of gender labels and preference for gender-appropriate toys are not driven by the social self-process as outlined in the previous section. In their early use of "girl" or "boy" to describe themselves, we would suggest that children are simply applying a personal label, like "Jill" or "John", that it is part of the knowledge they have available to use in the personal self-process. When growing cognitive sophistication enables the perception of social categories, of similarities within and differences between the categories, and of identification with one of the categories, the same knowledge can be used to provide meaning in the social self-process. Because self-categorisation posits that the self-process draws on all the memories, knowledge, and skills that are available to an individual, rather than seeing these resources *as* the self, changes in children's cognitive capacities and content are not problematic.

The problem remains for social learning theory, which proposes that children's observation of intrasex similarities and intersex differences forms the basis of their gender knowledge and that only when they observe themselves behaving in a way that is consistent with one of the categories do they deduce that they are boys or girls. Children's gender-consistent labelling, toy and clothing preferences, and general behaviour prior to making this deduction can only be seen in this formulation as a series of passive-conditioned responses, unrelated to gender identity.

Although, as already stated, we disagree with his underlying rationale and proposed timing, we would endorse Kohlberg's assertion that children are not passive and will be motivated to seek identity-consistent behaviour. Where we differ from Kohlberg is that we believe the meaning of self is constantly changing, that a less complex understanding, or one that has less correspondence with social or physical reality, is no less "genuinely" self than a more complex one, or one that reflects the physical and social world more closely. Thus we would see Jill's claim that she is a girl because she is wearing her new frilly socks as a genuine expression of her gender identity, not merely a preparation for it.

Of course, we cannot ignore the fact that important and dramatic changes occur in girls' and boys' behaviour when they reach school age. Whereas, however, for social learning and cognitive-developmental theories, this change is the gaining of "real" gender identity, self-categorisation theorists would see it as the beginning of gender as a *social* identity. Prior to the age of 5 or 6 years, children cannot make complex categorical comparisons, nor are they typically treated as group members. With developments in their cognitive sophistication, and exposure to a social context that makes gender highly salient, most boys and girls will, for the first time, experience themselves as "us". Being a girl or a boy is no longer simply synonymous with being Jill or John; its meaning is determined by a perception of sameness with others of the same sex, and differences from those of the opposite sex.

An important consequence of identifying with a social category is that "we" are motivated to perceive "us" as being better than "them", or to use the terminology of social identity theory (Tajfel, 1972; Turner, 1975, 1978), there will arise ". . . a need for positive social identity, expressed through a desire to create, maintain, or enhance the positively-valued distinctiveness of ingroups compared to outgroups" (Turner & Onorato, 1999, p. 18). The form this commonly takes is that intragroup similarity and intergroup difference is perceptually exaggerated in a direction that favours the in-group (for evidence of this in the original minimal group paradigm see Tajfel, Flament, Billig, & Bundy, 1971; and for a full discussion see Powlishta, Chapter 4). Thus, when gender is salient – *not* when the individual self or a social category other than gender is salient – school-age children will tend to perceive all boys as the same, all girls as the same, and boys and girls as fundamentaly different from each other. Girls see the difference as favouring them, while boys see it as favouring them.

If we apply the Piagetian idea that children rehearse new cognitive processes in a way that can seem obsessive to adults, we would predict that, armed with new social gender identities, primary school children will practise intergroup skills, and will devote much effort to creating, maintaining, and exaggerating ways in which girls/boys are better than boys/girls – as of course we know they do. Thus both the gender separatism and the intergroup hostility of childhood are explained as simply an illustration of the social psychology of intergroup relations, albeit a very clear and dramatic one.

By the time the skills are well learnt and can become a less focal part of the repertoire, children are beginning to have a broader and more varied social world, access to dimensions other than gender on which to base social identities, and have reached puberty, which gives the heterosexual majority strong motivation to perceive members of the opposite sex as potential partners rather than as enemies. Thus, gender loses its appearance of "chronic" salience, it becomes less important to "maximise the difference", and gender stereotypes become less prescriptive.

We suggest that there are other important facts that need to be considered concerning the gender intergroup hostility of childhood. Earlier we drew attention to the fact that people are motivated to gain collective self-esteem from intergroup encounters. Overt social competition is not, however, possible when the status quo assigns one of the categories to an inferior position (Tajfel, 1978). In this case, members of the low-status group do not employ the empty rhetoric of "we are better than them", but employ any one of a number of individual or collective strategies, choice of which is determined by their perceptions of the stability and legitimacy of the status differential and of the permeability of the boundaries between the groups (for a summary see Tajfel & Turner, 1979). Since it is clear that the status quo places women in an inferior position to men, it should follow that girls will not enagage in direct social competition with boys – yet we know that they do, and are in fact more likely than boys to engage in gender in-group favouritism. To understand this, we need to consider a number of developmental factors that make girls' situation different from that of women.

First, girls develop earlier than boys, so for most of the primary school years they are at least as big as, if not bigger than, members of their gender out-group (Wong, 2000). Girls are also boys' equals or, in the case of language skills, their betters in school work (Halpern, 1997). Thus when boys assert that girls are "weak" and "stupid", this may be backed up by societal attitudes, but not by the daily reality of girls' lives. To use Tajfelian terminology, girls will perceive the status differential as *illegitimate*. Since most have been protected from the cruelty of the real world, they will probably also perceive the status differential as *unstable*. Girls, therefore, do not initially perceive themselves as deserving lower status than boys, and respond to the status quo by direct competition for positive distinctiveness.

With time, however, girls' perceptions of legitimacy and stability will change. They will observe, for example, that while most primary teachers are women, senior teachers are usually men, and that high school teachers of the "objective" subjects like science and maths are men, leaving the less valued "expressive" subjects like language, music, and art, to women (American Association of University Women, 1992). Girls will begin to notice that teachers pay more attention to boys, and that boys respond to this by dominating the classroom: Calling out, demanding help or attention, and being praised by teachers, while girls themselves receive praise mainly for being compliant (Epperson, 1988; Sadker & Sadker, 1986). As young adolescents, girls will come to realise that being popular is determined by how decorative they are, rather than how intelligent, interesting, friendly, or funny (Suitor & Reavis, 1995). Thus feisty female children will internalise the social reality of sexual inequality and become disempowered young women. In Tajfelian terms, they perceive their status as legitimate and realise that the status boundaries are stable. They stop fighting (at least most of them do!).

The strategies older females subsequently use to gain positive distinctiveness for their female identity represent a field of inquiry largely unexplored by self-categorisation theorists, but one we predict would be rich in content and perhaps in theoretical insights. Anecdotally, we believe that some women identify with the female role as defined by the status quo (feminists call these "male-identified" women, on the basis that the status quo is male-dominated, male-defined, and male-serving), and gain self-esteem from being good mothers, daughters, and wives, while others genuinely identify with males and gain self-esteem from running a successful business, having professional status, and in other ways not being like "stupid women". For most, we suggest, it is not as straightforward as either of these options, since their female identity will not always be salient and, when it is, it will mean different things to them in different contexts. Thus potential researchers will need to take into account complex interactions of comparative fit, perceived normative fit, and, importantly, the myriad factors that contribute to perceiver readiness, which determine not only when the female social identity is salient but what the identity means, for any particular woman at any particular time (see Breinlinger & Kelly, 1994).

We believe that there are also developmental changes for males, perhaps not as much in the meaning of their gender category (for we have seen that the male stereotype is comparatively less flexible than the female), but in its salience. As we have seen in this chapter, being male seems to be more important for boys than being female is for girls. Evidence suggests, on the other hand, that while gender is highly salient for women, men are more likely to think of themselves as "people", "humans", or whatever the generic category of salience happens to be (Hurtig & Pichevin, 1990). The adult situation is a logical outcome of a society in which the generic "man" *is* male (Spender, 1985). In an elegant illustration of this, Eagly and Kite (1987) asked participants to describe people of specific nationalities, then men, then women of those nationalities. Descriptions of men of each nationality matched descriptions of people of that nationality. Descriptions of women did not match those of men or people of their nationality, but were similar to women of other nationalities. In other words, men were characterised as people (of French, Italian, British, or American nationality), while women were characterised primarily as women.

Thus we suggest that changes in the salience of gender, as well as reflecting the different circumstances of individuals' lives, reflect developmental changes in adaptation to the social reality of a world in which females and males are not equal. We therefore do not agree with Powlishta's conclusion (Chapter 4) that better gender relations can be engendered by encouraging children to self-categorise on a dimension other than gender. The self-categorisations that are relevant to us, we believe, are not simply a matter of choice but rather a direct consequence of the genuine economic, political, and social circumstances of our lives.

SUMMARY AND SUGGESTIONS

To summarise gender development from the perspective of self-categorisation theory, we first emphasise that gender is one aspect of the flexible, changing, context-dependent self-process. What it means to a child to be a girl or a boy will change with context, as it does for adults, but the changes will be more dramatic due to developmental growth in cognitive skills and knowledge, the latter which children will accumulate through direct and indirect reinforcement and self-directed observation.

As a reflection of their cognitive limitations, early gender identity will simply be one aspect of a child's personal identity: They will learn that Jill/girl plays with dolls or that John/boy is going to be a truck driver when he grows up. John/boy will come to understand that he meets with approval when he does things like his father and brother but is ignored, shunned, or punished when he does things like his sister or mother.

As growing cognitive sophistication allows children to extrapolate from their observations that, on gender-relevant dimensions, most females have certain things in common, most males have certain things in common, and that there is little common ground between females and males, they will form cognitive representations of the gender categories. Identification with one of the categories will come with the recognition that they (as Jill/girl or John/boy) share not just the name, but also the characteristics of one of the gender categories. In their new world of school, Jill and John will frequently be referred to, and required to act, as one of "the girls" or "the boys" rather than as Jill or John; thus the connection between gender category and self will be reinforced. Boys will receive validation from other in-group members of their earlier decision to eschew all things female, and both boys and girls will enthusiastically practise maximising the difference between the sexes.

As they approach adolescence, children's social worlds will broaden and they will begin to specialise in activities that suit their unique skills and enthusiasms. The discovery of similarities between themselves and others in the choir, the football team, the debating club, the ballet class, and so on, will increase the dimensions on which they can base social identities, and gender will lose its prepotency. Intergroup hostility between girls and boys will lessen as girls adapt to the adult status quo, and as romantic and sexual partnerships become a possibility.

For girls, since the world will continue to treat them primarily as female, their gender will continue to be highly salient. While their masculinity will always be important to them, boys will become the generic or "default option" adult category members and may even come to deny the revelance of gender in everyday social interactions.

A substantial body of self-categorisation and social identity research supports many of the premises on which this speculative account of gender development are based: the flexibility and context-dependent nature of the self-process; the role of fit and accessibility in determining the salience of self-categorisations; the motivation to seek collective self-esteem in intergroup encounters; the fact that lower-status category members use strategies other than overt social competition to gain positive distinciveness. Similarly, developmental research confirms such aspects as children's growing ability to form cognitive representations of categories, sex differences in the rigidity of gender stereotypes and in their application to self, and the broadening social context of adolescents' lives.

Many aspects, however, need to be investigated and questions remain to be answered: Is there support for our speculation that there is a developmental "switch" in the comparative salience of gender as girls and boys become women and men?; Are young females less aware (or simply less accepting) than older females, of the gender status quo?; What strategies do adolescent girls and older women use to gain positive distinctiveness, and how do these relate to perception of stability, legitimacy, and permeability of the group boundaries?; What specific variables feed into "perceiver readiness" to employ gender self-categorisation?; How does self-categorisation as "generic" effect perceptions and treatment of nongeneric category members?

Regardless of future answers to these questions, self-categorisation theory can make a valuable contribution to the field. At the practical theoretical level, we conceptualise the self (and therefore gender identity) as a process, and understand the descriptive content of a current identity as drawing on all one's cognitive resources. Thus we do not have the problems of both cognitive-developmental and social learning theories in accounting for gendered behaviour in infants and preschoolers (for cognitive-developmental theory, the problem is that there is no motivation for gendered behaviour to exist at all prior to gender constancy; for social learning theory, the problem is that it can only be seen as a passive conditioned response). Equally importantly, our understanding of intergroup behaviour as an outcome of social identity provides an explanation for the hostility of primary school gender interactions, and for its cessation in adolescence.

At a more abstract theoretical level, because we do not see the descriptive content of self-awareness *as* the self, we are able to make a distinction between the content and the social-psychological process by which individuals apply the content to their ever-changing self-awareness and through which the content of gender knowledge informs their behaviour. Thus, while we continue to investigate the ways in which males and females adapt and respond to the status quo, we do not see their responses as being the outcome of stable differences in the "personalities" or "selves" of males and females. In fact, we would suggest that commonly found sex differences in behaviour and personality are common human responses to different, established positions in the social hierarchy. While not referring to the gender categories, Reynolds and Turner (2001) express this point when they say that ". . .both groups are engaged in the same psychology; . . . their respective perspectives stem from the same categorical process in interaction with intergroup relations and social structural factors" (p. 173).

In our society, gender is arguably "the first socialization" (Bussey, 1986) and girls and boys are different. Not only do they characterise themselves in ways that are diametrically opposed (although some would claim complementary), but there are also sex differences in the intensity with which they adhere to the characterisations, and in their readiness to invoke gender identity. We have presented here a perspective that could logically be extended to suggest that if some other social category, for example class or race, was the primary dimension on which a society was divided, it would form the basis for children's first social identity and possibly the content of the stereotypes children learnt to apply to themselves would bear the familiar reactive/expressive versus proactive/competent characterisations of the stereotypes based on sexual inequality, as Celia Ridgeway's (2001) argument suggests might be the case.

The development of gender identity, we thus suggest, should not be approached as a field of inquiry with its own unique, psychological processes and specialist theories, but as a field that offers a rich and complex example of the way children develop self-awareness as members of the society in which they live.

REFERENCES

American Association of University Women (1992). *The AAUW report: How schools short-change girls*. Washington, DC: American Association of University Women Education Foundation and National Educational Association.

Banaji, M. R., & Prentice, D. A. (1994). The self in social contexts. *Annual Review of Psychology, 45*, 297–332.

Bandura, A. (1969). *Principles of behavior modification*. Stanford, CA: Stanford University Press.

Bandura, A. (1986). *Social foundations of thought and action: A social cognitive theory*. Englewood Cliffs, NJ: Prentice-Hall.

Bem, S. L. (1981). Gender schema theory: A cognitive account of sex-typing. *Psychological Review, 88*, 354–364.

Bem, S. L. (1985). Androgeny and gender schema theory: A conceptual and empirical integration. In T. B. Sonderegger (Ed.), *Nebraska symposium on motivation, 1984: Psychology and gender* (pp. 179–226). Lincoln, NE: University of Nebraska Press.

Blakemore, J. E. O., Larue, A. A., & Oljenik, A. B. (1979). Sex-appropriate toy preferences and the ability to conceptualize toys as sex-role related. *Developmental Psychology, 15*, 339–340.

Brannon, L. (2002). *Gender: Psychological perspectives* (3rd ed.) Boston, MA: Allyn & Bacon.

Breinlinger, S., & Kelly, C. (1994). Women's responses to status inequality. *Psychology of Women Quarterly, 18*, 1–16.

Brooks, J., & Lewis, M. (1976). Infants' responses to strangers: Midget, adult and child. *Child Development, 47*, 323–332.

Brown, B. B., Mounts, N., Lamborn, S. D., & Steinberg, L. (1993). Parenting practices and peer group affiliation in adolescence. *Child Development, 64*, 467–482.

Bussey, K. (1986). The first socialization. In N. Grieve & A. Burns (Eds.), *Australian women: New feminist perspectives*. Melbourne, Australia: Oxford University Press.

Bussey, K., & Bandura, A. (1984). Influence of gender constancy and social power on sex-linked modeling. *Journal of Personality and Social Psychology, 47*, 1292–1302.

Bussey, K., & Bandura, A. (1999). Social cognitive theory of gender development and differentiation. *Psychological Review, 106*, 676–713.

Caldera, Y. M., Huston, A. C., & O'Brien, M. (1989). Social interactions and play patterns of parents and toddlers, with feminine, masuline, and neutral toys. *Child Development, 60*, 70–76.

Catalyst (1999). Catalyst census of women corporate officers and top earners. Retrieved July 12, 2001, from http://www.catalystwomen.org/press

Chodorow, N. (1978). *The reproduction of mothering: Psychoanalysis and the sociology of gender*. Berkeley, CA: University of California Press.

Chodorow, N. (1979). Feminism and difference: Gender, relation, and difference in psychoanalytic perspective. *Socialist Review, 46*, 42–64.

Condry, J., & Condry, S. (1976). Sex differences: A study of the eye of the beholder. *Child Development, 47*, 812–818.

Cross, S. E., & Madson, L. (1997). Models of the self: Self-construals and gender. *Psychological Bulletin, 122*, 5–37.

David, B. (2003). *Children's gender stereotypes and the salience of gender, age and "human" identities*. Manuscript in preparation.

Delk, J. L., Madden, R. B., Livingston, M., & Ryan, T. T. (1986). Adult perceptions of the infant as a function of gender labelling and observed gender. *Sex Roles, 15*, 57–534.

Doosje, B., & Ellemers, N. (1997). Stereotyping under threat: The role of group identification. In R. Spears, P. J. Oakes, N. Ellemers, & S. A. Haslam (Eds), *The social psychology of stereotyping and group life* (pp. 257–272). Oxford: Blackwell.

Eagly, A. H., & Kite, M. E. (1987). Are stereotypes of nationalities applied to both women and men? *Journal of Personality and Social Psychology, 53*, 451–462.

Eckert, P. (1989). *Jocks and burnouts: Social categories and identity in the high school*. New York: Teachers College Press.

Epperson, S. E. (1988, September 16). Studies link subtle sex bias in schools with women's behavior in the workplace. *Wall Street Journal*, p. 27.

Fagot, B. I. (1977). Consequences of moderate cross-gender behavior in preschool children. *Child Development, 48*, 902–907.

Fagot, B. I., & Leinbach, M. D. (1989). The young child's gender schema: Environmental input, internal organization. *Child Development, 60*, 663–672.

Fagot, B. I., & Leinbach, M. D. (1993). Gender-role development in young children: From discrimination to labelling. *Developmental Review, 13*, 205–224.

Fagot, B. I., & Leinbach, M. D. (1994). Gender-role development in young children. In M. R. Stevenson (Ed.), *Gender roles throughout the lifespan: A multi-disciplinary perspective* (pp. 3–24). Muncie, IN: Ball State University.

Fagot, B. I., Leinbach, M. D., & O'Boyle, C. (1992). Gender labelling, gender stereotyping, and parent behaviors. *Developmental Psychology, 28*, 225–230.

Fagot, B. I., Hagan, R., Leinbach, M. D., & Knonsberg, S. (1985). Differential reactions to assertive and communicative acts of toddler boys and girls. *Child Development, 56*, 1499–1505.

Feinman, S. (1981). Why is cross-sex-behavior more appropriate for girls than for boys? A status characteristic approach. *Sex Roles, 10*, 445–456.

Fiske, S. T. (1992). Thinking is for doing: Portraits of social cognition from daguerreotype to laserphoto. *Journal of Personality and Social Psychology, 63*, 877–889.

Freud, S. (1989). Some psychical consequences of the anatomical distinction between the sexes. In P. Gay (Ed.), *The Freud reader* (pp. 670–678). New York: Norton. (Original work published 1925)

Grace, D., & David, B. (2001, July). *Sources of influence in preschoolers' use of gender categories.* Paper presented at the seventh annual meeting of the Society of Australasian Social Psychologists, Melbourne, Australia.

Grace, D., & David, B. (2003). *Sources of influence in preschoolers' use of gender categories.* Manuscript in preparation: PhD thesis, Australian National University, Canberra, Australia.

Gutek, B. A., & Larwood, L. (1989). Introduction: Women's careers are important and different. In B. A. Gutuk & L. Larwood (Eds.), *Women's career development* (pp. 7–14). Newbury Park, CA: SAGE Publications.

Halpern, D. F. (1997). Sex differences in intelligence: Implications for education. *American Psychologist, 52*, 1091–1102.

Harris, J. R. (1995). Where is the child's environment?: A group socialization theory of development. *Psychological Bulletin, 102*, 458–489.

Harter, S. (1997). The personal self in social context: Barriers to authenticity. In R. Ashmore & L. Jussim (Eds.), *Self and identity: Fundamental issues*. New York: Oxford University Press.

Harter, S. (1998). The development of self-representations. In W. Damon (Series Ed.), N. Eisenberg (Vol. Ed.), *Handbook of child psychology: Vol. 3, Social, emotional and personality development* (5th ed.), New York: John Wiley & Sons.

Hirschfeld, L. A. (1993). Discovering social difference: The role of appearance in the development of racial awareness. *Cognitive Psychology, 25*, 317–350.

Hurtig, M. C., & Pichevin, M. F. (1990). Salience of the sex category system in person perception: Contextual variations. *Sex Roles, 22*, 369–395.

Jackson, D. W., & Tein, J.-Y. (1998). Adolescents' conceptualization of adult roles: Relationships with age, gender, work goal, and maternal employment. *Sex Roles, 38*, 987–1008.

Katz, P. A., & Ksansnak, K. R. (1994). Developmental aspects of gender role flexibility and traditionality in middle childhood and adolescence. *Developmental Psychology, 30*, 272–282.

Kohlberg, L. (1966). A cognitive-developmental analysis of children's sex-role concepts and attitudes. In E. Maccoby (Ed.), *The development of sex differences* (pp. 52–173). Stanford, CA: Stanford University Press.

Leinbach, M. D., & Fagot, B. I. (1993). Categorical habituation to male and female faces: Gender schematic processing in infancy. *Infant Behavior and Development, 16*, 317–332.

Lewis, M. (1972). State as an infant–environment interaction: An analysis of mother–infant interaction as a function of sex. *Merril-Palmer Quarterly, 18,* 58–69.

Maccoby, E. E. (1988). Gender as a social category. *Developmental Psychology, 24,* 755–765.

Maccoby, E. E. (1990). Gender and relationships. *American Psychologist, 45,* 513–520.

Maccoby, E. E., & Jacklin, C. N. (1987). *The psychology of sex differences.* Stanford, CA: Stanford University Press.

Markus, H. R. (1977). Self-schemata and processing information about the self. *Journal of Personality and Social Psychology, 35,* 63–78.

Markus, H. R., & Kitayama, S. (1991). Culture and the self: Implications for cognition, emotion and motivation. *Psychological Review, 98,* 224–253.

Markus, H. R., & Wurf, E. (1987). The dynamic self-concept: A social psychological perspective. *Annual Review of Psychology, 38,* 299–337.

Mischel, W. (1966). A social-learning view of sex differences in behavior. In E. E. Maccoby (Ed.), *The development of sex differences* (pp. 56–81). Stanford, CA: Stanford University Press.

Mischel, W. (1993). *Introduction to personality* (5th ed.). Fort Worth, TX: Harcourt Brace Jovanovich.

Money, J., & Ehrhardt, A. (1972). *Man and woman, boy and girl.* Baltimore, MD: Johns Hopkins University Press.

Neisser, U., & Jopling, D. (1997). *The conceptual self in context: Culture, experience, self-understanding.* New York: Cambridge University Press.

Nielsen Media Research (1989). *'89 Nielson report of television.* Northbrook, IL: Author.

Oakes, P. J. (1987). The salience of social categories. In J. C. Turner, M. A. Hogg, P. J. Oakes, S. D. Reicher, & M. S. Wetherell (Eds.), *Rediscovering the social group: A self-categorization theory.* Oxford: Blackwell.

Onorato, R. S., & Turner, J. C. (1996, May). *Fluidity in the self-concept: A shift from personal to social identity.* Paper presented at the second meeting of the Society of Australasian Social Psychologists, Canberra, Australia.

Onorato, R. S., & Turner, J. C. (1997, April). *Individual differences and social identity: A study of self-categorization processes in the Markus paradigm.* Paper presented at the third meeting of the Society of Australasian Social Psychologists, Woolongong, Australia.

Onorato, R. S., & Turner, J. C. (2001). The "I", the "me" and the "us": The psychological group and self-concept maintenance and change. In C. Sedikedes & M. Brewer (Eds.), *Individual self, relational self, collective self.* Philadelphia, PA: Psychology Press.

Perry, D. G., & Bussey, K. (1979). The social learning theory of sex differences: Imitation is alive and well. *Journal of Personality and Social Psychology, 37,* 1699–1712.

Pomerleau, A., Bolduc, D., Malcuit, G., & Cossette, L. (1990). Pink or blue: Environmental stereotypes in the first two years of life. *Sex Roles, 22,* 359–367.

Reingold, H. L., & Cook, K. V. (1975). The content of boys' and girls' rooms as an index of parents' behavior. *Child Development, 46,* 510–513.

Reynolds, K. J., & Turner, J. C. (2001). Prejudice as a group process: The role of social identity. In M. Augostinos & K. J. Reynolds (Eds.), *Understanding prejudice, racism, and social conflict* (pp. 159–178). London: SAGE Publications.

Ridgeway, C. (2001, July). *Status and the content of stereotypes.* Paper presented at the seventh annual meeting of the Society of Australasian Social Psychologists, Melbourne, Australia.

Rubin, J. Z., Provenanzo, F. J., & Luria, Z. (1974). The eye of the beholder: Parents' views on sex of newborns. *American Journal of Orthopsychiatry, 44*, 512–519.

Ryan, M., & David, B. (2002). *A gendered self or a gendered context: A self-categorization approach to independence and interdependence.* Manuscript submitted for publication.

Sadker, M., & Sadker, D. (1986, March). Sexism in the classroom: From grade school to graduate school. *Phi Delta Kappan*, 512–515.

Schofield, J. W. (1981). Complementary and conflicting identities: Images and inter-actions in an inter-racial school. In S. R. Asher & J. M. Gottman (Eds.), *The development of children's friendships* (pp. 53–90). Cambridge: Cambridge University Press.

Serbin, L. A., Sprafkin, C., Elmian, M., & Doyle, A. (1984). The early development of sex differentiated patterns of social influence. *Canadian Journal of Social Science, 14*, 350–363.

Signorella, M. L., Bigler, R. L., & Liben, L. S. (1993). Developmental differences in children's gender schemata about others: A meta-analytic review. *Developmental Review, 13*, 147–183.

Signorielli, N., & Bacue, A. (1999). Recognition and respect: A content analysis of prime-time television characters across three decades. *Sex Roles, 40*, 527–544.

Spender, D. (1985). *Man made language.* London: Routledge & Kegan Paul.

Stangor, C., & Ruble, D. (1987). Development of gender role knowledge and gender constancy. In L. S. Liben & M. L. Signorella (Eds.), *Children's gender schemata* (pp. 5–22). San Francisco: Jossey-Bass.

Stevenson, H. W., & Stevenson, N. G. (1960). Social interaction in an interracial nursery school. *Genetic Psychology Monographs, 61*, 41–75.

Suitor, J. J., & Reavis, R. (1995). Football, fast cars, and cheerleading: Adolescent gender norms. *Adolescence, 30*, 265–272.

Tajfel, H. (1972). La categorisation sociale. In S. Moscovici (Ed.), *Introduction a la psychologie sociale* (pp. 272–302). Paris: Larousse.

Tajfel, H. (1978). *The social psychology of minorities* (Report No. 38). London: Minority Rights Group.

Tajfel, H., Flament, C., Billig, M. G., & Bundy, R. F. (1971). Social categorization and intergroup behaviour. *European Journal of Social Psychology, 1*, 149–177.

Tajfel, H., & Turner, J. C. (1979). An integrative theory of intergroup conflict. In W. G. Austin & S. Worchell (Eds.), *The social psychology of intergroup relations* (pp. 33–47). Monterey, CA: Brooks/Cole.

Tajfel, H., & Wilkes, A. L. (1963). Classification and quantitative judgment. *British Journal of Psychology, 54*, 101–114.

Tavris, C. (1994). Reply to Brown and Gilligan. *Feminism and Psychology, 4*, 350–352.

Thompson, S. K. (1975). Gender labels and early sex role development. *Child Development, 46*, 605–608.

Thorne, B. (1993). *Gender play: Girls and boys in school.* New Brunswick, NJ: Rutgers University Press.

Turner, J. C. (1975). Social comparison and social identity: Some prospects for intergroup behaviour. *European Journal of Social Psychology, 5*, 5–34.

Turner, J. C. (1978). Social categorization and social discrimination in the minimal group paradigm. In H. Tajfel (Ed.), *Differentiation between social groups: Studies in the social psychology of intergroup relations* (pp. 101–140). London: Academic Press.

Turner, J. C. (1985). Social categorization and the self-concept: A social-cognitive theory of group behaviour. In E. J. Lawlor (Ed.), *Advances in group processes: Theory and research, Vol. 2* (pp. 77–122). Greenwich, CT: JAI Press.

Turner, J. C. (1988). Comments on Doise's "Individual and social identities in intergroup relations". *European Journal of Social Psychology, 18,* 113–116.

Turner, J. C. (1999a). Some current issues in research on social identity and self-categorization theories. In N. Ellemers, R. Spears, & B. Doosje (Eds.), *Social identity: Context, commitment, content* (pp. 6–34). Oxford: Basil Blackwell.

Turner, J. C. (1999b, July) *The prejudiced personality and social change: A self-categorization perspective. The Tajfel lecture.* European Association of Experimental Social Psychology, Oxford.

Turner, J. C., & Onorato, R. S. (1999). Social identity, personality and the self-concept: A self-categorization perspective. In T. Tyler, R. M. Kramer, & O. P. John (Eds.), *The psychology of the social self.* Mahwah, NJ: Lawrence Erlbaum Associates, Inc.

United Nations. (1991). *The world's women 1970–1990: Trends and statistics.* New York: United Nations Publications.

Walker-Andrews, A. S., Bahrick, L. E., Raglioni, S. S., & Diaz, I. (1991). Infants' bimodal perception of gender. *Ecological Psychology, 3,* 55–75.

Welch-Ross, M. K., & Schmidt, C. R. (1996). Gender-schema development and children's constructive story memory: Evidence or a developmental model. *Child Development, 67,* 820–835.

Williams, J. E., & Best, D. L. (1990). *Measuring sex stereotypes: A multination study* (Rev. ed.) Newbury Park, CA: SAGE Publications.

Wong, D. L. (2000). *Essentials of pediatric nursing* (6th ed.). St. Louis, MO: Mosby.

6 The development of national identity and social identity processes: Do social identity theory and self-categorisation theory provide useful heuristic frameworks for developmental research?

Martyn Barrett, Evanthia Lyons, and Arantza del Valle

This chapter is concerned with the development of national identity in children and adolescents, and the possible utility of social identity theory (SIT) and self-categorisation theory (SCT) as heuristic frameworks for the investigation of developmental processes in this domain. It is noteworthy that, while there has been a large amount of research over the years into the development of both gender and ethnic identity (see, for example, Aboud, 1988; Bernal & Knight, 1993; Eckes & Trautner, 2000; Phinney & Rotheram, 1987; Ruble & Martin, 1998), comparatively little research has been conducted into the development of national identity. In addition, SIT and SCT have proven to be fertile sources of hypotheses for the study of gender and ethnic identity development. By contrast, that research which has been conducted into the development of national identity has tended to be rather descriptive and atheoretical by comparison. The aim of the present chapter is to examine whether SIT and SCT might also provide useful heuristic frameworks for the investigation of the development of national identity, by providing a range of hypotheses for empirical investigation in this domain.

The chapter will proceed in the following way. After a brief overview of some of the principal phenomena that characterise the development of national identity, the relevance of both SIT and SCT to these phenomena will be noted. A number of empirical predictions suggested by these two theories will then be articulated, and these predictions will be examined, primarily using data drawn from a large multinational study that investigated the sense of national identity in 6-, 9-, 12-, and 15-year-old British, Spanish, and Italian children (Barrett et al., 1997). It will be seen that the data are actually much more complex than might have been anticipated from the perspectives of SIT and SCT.

To anticipate the conclusions, it will be argued that while SIT and SCT are useful for the articulation of some key questions for empirical investigation, it is an open question as to whether these theories themselves provide satisfactory answers to those questions. No simple solutions or answers will be offered in this chapter. Instead, the present chapter will caution against resorting to oversimplistic theoretical solutions when addressing what are, in fact, extremely complex developmental and theoretical issues.

We begin with a brief overview of some of the principal phenomena that characterise the development of national identity, in order to provide an initial orientation to some of the issues in this field, and to illustrate why SIT and SCT might potentially be useful heuristic frameworks for investigating children's development in this domain.

THE PRINCIPAL PHENOMENA THAT CHARACTERISE THE DEVELOPMENT OF NATIONAL IDENTITY

Existing research into the development of children's sense of national identity indicates that, before about 5 years of age, children have little knowledge of their own country or national group (Piaget & Weil, 1951). However, from about 5 years of age onwards, children can usually state the name of their own country, and they also begin to classify themselves as members of their own national group (Barrett, 1996; Wilson, 1998). During mid childhood, children's knowledge of the people who belong to their own national group expands considerably, and by 10 years of age they are able to describe many of the stereotypical characteristics that are attributed to the members of their own national group (Barrett, in press; Lambert & Klineberg, 1967; Piaget & Weil, 1951).

Studies investigating how children feel about their own country and national group have produced a mixed set of findings. In some studies, it has been found that children do not have a systematic preference for their own country or for members of their own national group until 7 years of age or even later (e.g., Jaspers, Van de Geer, Tajfel, & Johnson, 1972; Middleton, Tajfel, & Johnson, 1970; Piaget & Weil, 1951). However, other studies have found a systematic preference for the child's own country from at least 5–6 years of age (Bennett, Lyons, Sani, & Barrett, 1998; Lambert & Klineberg, 1967; Tajfel, Jahoda, Nemeth, Campbell, & Johnson, 1970; Wilson, 1998). At whatever age this preference for the in-group is first acquired, once it has been established, it typically persists through into adolescence (Lambert & Klineberg, 1967). The importance that children attribute to their national identity, as well as their degree of identification with their national group, also tend to increase between 5–6 and 11–12 years of age (Barrett, 2001, in press).

As far as knowledge of foreign countries and national groups is concerned, children's ability to name other countries is poor before about 5 years of age, and young children also have great difficulty in understanding the concept of a foreign country (Piaget & Weil, 1951). Knowledge about other countries begins to develop from about 5 years of age onwards (Barrett & Farroni, 1996; Bourchier, Barrett, & Lyons, 2002; Jahoda, 1962; Piaget & Weil, 1951). The growth of geographical knowledge in mid childhood is accompanied by the acquisition and elaboration of stereotypes of the people who live in other countries and beliefs about their lifestyles and behavioural habits (Barrett & Short, 1992; Jahoda, 1962; Lambert & Klineberg, 1967; Piaget & Weil, 1951).

Children sometimes acquire very strong feelings about particular groups of foreign people before they have acquired any concrete knowledge about those groups (Barrett & Short, 1992; Johnson, 1973; Johnson, Middleton, & Tajfel, 1970). Despite the general tendency to prefer their own national group over all others, children can nevertheless feel very positively about some national out-groups (Barrett, in press; Barrett & Short, 1992; Johnson et al., 1970; Lambert & Klineberg, 1967; Middleton et al., 1970). The relative order of preference for other countries, once it is established (perhaps by 6 years of age), seems to remain fairly stable and consistent across the remaining childhood years (Barrett & Short, 1992; Jaspers et al., 1972; Johnson et al., 1970). However, the overall degree of liking for all national out-groups tends to increase between 5 and 11 years of age (Barrett & Short, 1992; Lambert & Klineberg, 1967). After 11 years of age, this general increase in positive regard for other national groups usually levels out (Lambert & Klineberg, 1967).

Thus, the studies that have been conducted in this field indicate that, during mid childhood, children acquire a preference for their own national group, do not always exhibit out-group denigration, display an increase in positive regard for national out-groups, and construct stereotypes of the national in-group and of salient national out-groups. Furthermore, although national identity may not be especially important to 5-year-old children, it does become much more important over the course of mid childhood. Children's degree of national identification also increases at this time of life, and national identity typically remains important throughout the adolescent years.

THE RELEVANCE OF SIT AND SCT TO THE STUDY OF NATIONAL IDENTITY DEVELOPMENT

SIT and SCT both postulate that in-group favouritism, out-group prejudice, and the stereotyping of in-groups and out-groups can sometimes occur as psychological consequences of knowing that one belongs to a particular social group. These theories posit that these effects may be most pronounced either when that particular social group membership is subjectively important to the individual (SIT) or when the prevailing social context renders that social group membership especially salient to the individual (SCT). There is thus a prima facie case that these two theories might be able to contribute to the elucidation of the phenomena of in-group favouritism, prejudice, and stereotyping as these are exhibited by children and adolescents in relationship to national groups. In order to examine this possibility in more detail, we first need to identify some of the principal postulates of these two theories.

Social identity theory

In brief, SIT (Tajfel, 1978; Tajfel & Turner, 1986) is based upon the observation that individuals belong to many different social groups (e.g., gender, national, ethnic, occupational, social class, etc.) and that these social group memberships may sometimes be internalised as part of an individual's self-concept. SIT postulates that, when this occurs, individuals strive to obtain a sense of positive self-worth from these social identities. Consequently, in constructing representations of in-groups and relevant out-groups, dimensions of comparison are chosen that produce more favourable representations of in-groups than of out-groups, resulting in in-group favouritism or out-group denigration or both. The positive distinctiveness that is ascribed to the in-groups produces positive self-esteem.

However, in order for these effects to occur, the individual needs to have internalised a social group membership as part of his or her self-concept, that is, the individual must subjectively identify with that category. If an individual's subjective identification with a particular social group is weak or absent, these effects will not occur. Furthermore, in certain cases (e.g., when one belongs to a group which has a low social status), it may be difficult to achieve positive in-group distinctiveness. Under these circumstances, other strategies (such as changing one's social group membership, or changing the existing social order to improve the status of the in-group) may be used instead to try to achieve a more favourable in-group representation.

SIT also postulates that there is a cognitive processing bias that affects people's categorical judgments. This bias attenuates within-category differences and accentuates between-category differences. Thus, the knowledge that one belongs to a particular social group produces intragroup homogeneity effects in which the variation among the members of in-groups and out-groups is underestimated, and the differences between members of the in-group and members of out-groups are overestimated. It is this mechanism that results in the stereotyping of in-groups and out-groups.

Thus, SIT suggests that in-group favouritism, out-group prejudice, and stereotyping can occur as psychological consequences of internalising social group memberships. Over the years, researchers (e.g., Bigler, Brown, & Markell, 2001; Bigler, Jones, & Lobliner, 1997; Branscombe & Wann, 1994; Grant, 1992, 1993; Hinkle & Brown, 1990; Kelly, 1988; Mummendey, Klink, & Brown, 2001; Nesdale & Flesser, 2001; Perreault & Bourhis, 1998; Powlishta, 1995; Verkuyten, 2001; Yee & Brown, 1992) have drawn a number of empirical predictions from SIT (although see Turner, 1999, and Haslam,

2001, who have disputed that SIT actually makes such direct predictions, a point that will be revisited towards the end of this chapter). The predictions that have been explored by researchers include the following: (1) Representations of in-groups and out-groups will be based upon dimensions of comparison that produce in-group distinctiveness and in-group favouritism. (2) The strength of identification will correlate either with the positivity of the in-group evaluation, or with the negativity of out-group evaluations, or with the positive distinctiveness that is ascribed to the in-group. (3) In-group favouritism will be a consequence of subjective identification with the in-group.

Self-categorisation theory

SCT was developed from SIT in order to account for a number of additional findings that emerged from social-psychological research with adults, especially the findings that the presence and degree of both in-group bias and in-group homogeneity are affected by the salience of the relevant social categorisation in a given setting (Oakes, Haslam, & Turner, 1994; Turner, Hogg, Oakes, Reicher, & Wetherell, 1987). Elaborating on the basic SIT paradigm, SCT postulates that individuals have a multiplicity of personal and social identities, which are organised in the form of a category hierarchy. The level in the hierarchy at which the self is categorised at any given moment depends on: the specific social context in which the individual finds him- or herself; a cognitive process that is driven by the principle of metacontrast (whereby categorisation occurs at that level in the hierarchy which maximises between-category differences while minimising within-category differences in the given context); the fit between the perceiver's normative beliefs about the particular categories that are involved and the actual stimuli contained in the current social situation; and the readiness of the individual to use a particular categorisation.

When a social identity becomes salient through this mechanism, for example when the social context contains members of both the in-group and a relevant out-group, there is a depersonalisation of self-perception (i.e., self-stereotyping occurs), group behaviour appropriate to the social identity is elicited, and in-group homogeneity increases. However, when the social context contains only members of the in-group, self-categorisation typically occurs at a lower level in the hierarchy than that of the in-group, and in-group homogeneity decreases. In addition, any other factor that enhances the salience of the social identity for the individual may increase perceptions of in-group homogeneity. For example, when the in-group is a minority group perceived as being chronically under threat from a majority out-group, the salience of the in-group category, the strength of subjective identification, and in-group homogeneity may be particularly high for those individuals within intergroup situations.

SCT also proposes that the prevailing comparative context can affect stereotype content, including the content of the in-group stereotype. The dimensions used to define the stereotype for a particular social group, as well as the relative prototypicality of the various group members, can change according to the comparative context in which the group is being judged. However, stereotypical variation will be constrained by what the individual perceiver knows and understands about the particular in-groups and out-groups that are involved, and about the nature of the intergroup relationships.

Thus, SCT suggests that in-group bias, the perceived homogeneity of the in-group, and the content of the in-group stereotype will change as a function of the prevailing comparative context. However, all of these effects will only occur if the individual has internalised the relevant social group membership as part of his or her self-concept. As in the case of SIT, if an individual's subjective identification with a group is weak or absent, these various effects will not occur.

Once again, researchers have drawn a number of empirical predictions from these various postulates (e.g., Branscombe, Ellemers, Spears, & Doosje, 1999; Brown & Wootton-Millward, 1993; Ellemers, Doosje, Van Knippenberg, & Wilke, 1992; Ellemers, Kortekaas, & Ouwerkerk, 1999; Haslam, Oakes, Turner, & McGarty, 1995; Haslam, Turner, Oakes, McGarty, & Hayes, 1992; Hopkins & Cable, 2001; Hopkins, Regan, & Abell, 1997; Oakes et al., 1994; Simon, 1992; Simon & Brown, 1987; Simon & Hamilton, 1994). These predictions include the following: (1) In-group homogeneity will be lower in contexts in which only the in-group is present, and higher in contexts in which relevant out-groups are also present. (2) In-group stereotype content will change in conjunction with changes in comparative context, with different dimensions being selected depending on the comparison out-groups that are available in the prevailing context. (3) The strength of identification will correlate with in-group homogeneity. (4) The strength of identification with the in-group may be higher in members of minority groups than in members of majority groups. (5) In-group homogeneity may be higher in members of minority groups than in members of majority groups.

THE APPLICATION OF SIT AND SCT TO THE DEVELOPMENT OF NATIONAL IDENTITY

Thus, a number of predictions have been drawn from both SIT and SCT by researchers. These predictions may all be tested against the data that are available from studies into the development of national identity during childhood and adolescence. In these studies, data are typically collected from children at a variety of ages. By examining whether the predicted phenomena occur at particular ages, it should be possible in principle to obtain some insight into the developmental process. For example, if the data indicate that the predicted phenomena do not occur in children of a particular age, then the full set of social identity processes that are postulated by the relevant theory as being responsible for the production of those phenomena are either not yet operative in children of that age, or are being overridden by other competing factors or processes that are simultaneously operative in those children. If, however, the data indicate that all of the phenomena predicted by the relevant theory do indeed occur in children of a given age, then there is good evidence that the social identity processes postulated by that theory have begun to operate in children of that age. A more complex outcome would be one in which some of the predicted phenomena occur, and others do not, in children of a given age. Such an outcome would be rather more difficult to interpret theoretically in terms of identifying which particular processes may be operating in children at that age (although examination of the phenomena themselves may provide us with some clues). However, for present purposes, it is sufficient to note that testing these predictions against the data collected from children at different ages may help to delineate the sequence in which the various component processes postulated by SIT and/or SCT begin to operate during the course of development. In the discussion that follows, each of the eight predictions identified above will be evaluated in turn against evidence that has been collected on the development of national identity.

EVALUATION OF THE PREDICTIONS

Representations of in-groups and out-groups will be based upon dimensions of comparison that produce in-group distinctiveness and in-group favouritism

As noted earlier in this chapter, existing studies have revealed a somewhat mixed pattern of findings concerning the age at which a systematic preference for the national in-group first emerges. These discrepancies may be due to either of two factors. First, different studies have used different measures of in-group preference. For example, some studies have measured global affect, that is, how much the child "likes" the national in-group versus various comparison out-groups (e.g., Middleton et al., 1970), others have measured how much the child "likes" particular in-group versus out-group members as depicted in photographs (e.g., Jaspers et al., 1972), others have asked children to assign positive and negative adjectives to the in-group and to comparison out-groups (e.g., Bennett et al., 1998), while others have used open-ended interviewing (Piaget & Weil, 1951). In addition, different studies have examined children belonging to different national groups, including Swiss (Piaget & Weil, 1951), Dutch (Jaspers et al., 1972), English (Middleton et al., 1970), and British (Bennett et al., 1998) children. It is possible that preference for the in-group varies from group to group.

Not all of the measures used in these studies are relevant to testing the prediction. It is most appropriately tested by examining the contents of children's descriptions of national groups; SIT predicts that more positive descriptions will be produced of the national in-group than of comparison out-groups. This prediction is not appropriately tested using global measures of how much children like or dislike particular national groups, which merely assess children's affect for, and not their representations of, national groups.

In the multinational study conducted by Barrett et al. (1997), data were collected from 1700 children aged 6, 9, 12, and 15 years old living in England, Scotland, Catalonia, Southern Spain, Northern Italy, and Central Italy. Each of these six subgroups of children was asked to assign descriptive adjectives both to their own national group and to a number of national out-groups. The children were instructed to reject adjectives that they considered to be inapplicable to an individual national group when describing that group. Because the adjectives consisted of both positive and negative adjectives (e.g., *friendly* and *unfriendly*, *clean* and *dirty*), an overall evaluation score could be computed for each national group based upon the relative proportion of positive and negative adjectives that had been assigned to each group. The children's evaluations of their own national in-group were then compared with their evaluations of each individual out-group. The prediction is that the evaluation of the in-group should be higher than the evaluations of the out-groups.

The findings are summarised in Table 6.1. This table shows the results broken down according to whether the children were British (which includes both the Scottish and the English children together), Spanish (which includes both the Catalan and the Southern Spanish children together), or Italian (which includes all of the Italian children together). In the case of the British and Catalan children, however, it is possible that the British and Spanish national groups are not the psychologically most relevant groups with which these children identify, and that these children identify with the English, Scottish, and Catalan groups instead. Consequently, Table 6.1 also includes the findings for these three groups of children on their own. The findings are also broken down according to age.

To start with the youngest children, the table shows that in-group favouritism is clearly exhibited by the Spanish, Italian, English, and Catalan 6-year-olds; however, in-group favouritism is not exhibited by the 6-year-old Scottish children, and is not consistently exhibited by the 6-year-old British children overall. At 9 years of age, in-group favouritism is exhibited by the Spanish and Catalan children, and by the English children in relationship to all of the national out-groups except the Scottish out-group. However, at 9 years of age, the Italian children no longer exhibit in-group favouritism, whereas the Scottish children are beginning to show some evidence of this phenomenon, but not consistently so (and while it might be argued that the Italian out-group is probably not relevant to Scottish children's self-definitions, it would be rather more difficult to argue this for the English out-group). At 12 years of age, the Spanish and Catalan children still consistently display in-group

Table 6.1 Significant differences in the evaluations of the national in-group versus various national out-groups by 6-, 9-, 12-, and 15-year-old British, Spanish, and Italian children

British	Brit vs. Fren	Brit vs. Span	Brit vs. Ital	Brit vs. Ger
6-yr-olds	ns	Brit > Span	ns	Brit > Ger
9-yr-olds	ns	ns	Brit > Ital	Brit > Ger
12-yr-olds	ns	ns	ns	Brit > Ger
15-yr-olds	Brit > Fren	ns	Ital > Brit	Brit > Ger

Spanish	Span vs. Fren	Span vs. Brit	Span vs. Ital	Span vs. Ger
6-yr-olds	Span > Fren	Span > Brit	Span > Ital	Span > Ger
9-yr-olds	Span > Fren	Span > Brit	Span > Ital	Span > Ger
12-yr-olds	Span > Fren	Span > Brit	Span > Ital	Span > Ger
15-yr-olds	Span > Fren	ns	Span > Ital	Span > Ger

Italian	Ital vs. Fren	Ital vs. Brit	Ital vs. Span	Ital vs. Ger
6-yr-olds	Ital > Fren	Ital > Brit	Ital > Span	Ital > Ger
9-yr-olds	ns	Brit > Ital	ns	ns
12-yr-olds	Fren > Ital	Brit > Ital	Span > Ital	ns
15-yr-olds	Fren > Ital	Brit > Ital	Span > Ital	ns

English	Eng vs. Fren	Eng vs. Span	Eng vs. Ital	Eng vs. Ger	Eng vs. Scot
6-yr-olds	Eng > Fren	Eng > Span	Eng > Ital	Eng > Ger	Eng > Scot
9-yr-olds	Eng > Fren	Eng > Span	Eng > Ital	Eng > Ger	ns
12-yr-olds	ns	ns	Ital > Eng	Eng > Ger	Scot > Eng
15-yr-olds	Eng > Fren	ns	Ital > Eng	Eng > Ger	ns

Scottish	Scot vs. Fren	Scot vs. Span	Scot vs. Ital	Scot vs. Ger	Scot vs. Eng
6-yr-olds	ns	ns	ns	ns	ns
9-yr-olds	Scot > Fren	Scot > Span	ns	Scot > Ger	ns
12-yr-olds	ns	Scot > Span	ns	Scot > Ger	Scot > Eng
15-yr-olds	Scot > Fren	Scot > Span	ns	Scot > Ger	Scot > Eng

Catalan	Cat vs. Fren	Cat vs. Brit	Cat vs. Ital	Cat vs. Ger
6-yr-olds	Cat > Fren	Cat > Brit	Cat > Ital	Cat > Ger
9-yr-olds	Cat > Fren	Cat > Brit	Cat > Ital	Cat > Ger
12-yr-olds	Cat > Fren	Cat > Brit	Cat > Ital	Cat > Ger
15-yr-olds	Cat > Fren	Cat > Brit	Cat > Ital	Cat > Ger

Source: Barrett et al., 1997.

Notes
ns = no significant difference in the evaluations of the two groups.
Brit = British; Fren = French; Span = Spanish; Ital = Italian; Ger = German; Eng = English; Scot = Scottish; Cat = Catalan.

favouritism, but now the English children no longer do so, while the Scottish children still only display partial evidence of in-group favouritism. The 12-year-old Italian children actually display a tendency towards in-group denigration, as they still do at 15 years of age. And at 15 years of age, the Spanish and Catalan children are still presenting strong evidence of in-group favouritism (with just a single exception), as are the Scottish children, while the English 15-year-olds present little consistent evidence of the phenomenon.

Thus, the overall picture that emerges is that in-group favouritism is exhibited to a different extent by different national groups of children at different ages, and only Spanish and Catalan children behave in a manner consistent with the prediction of SIT at all ages. Furthermore, different developmental patterns are exhibited by children who are growing up in different national contexts. For example, while Italian children exhibit in-group favouritism at 6 years of age but not at later ages, Scottish children do not exhibit this phenomenon at 6 years of age, but do tend to do so by 15 years of age. Such differential patterns of development are difficult to explain in terms of there being particular ages or points in development at which particular identity processes begin to operate in children.

Barrett et al. (1997) also administered a second measure to assess the children's affect towards the various national groups. This took the form of a pair of questions: "*Do you like or dislike X people?*" followed by "*How much? Do you like/dislike them a lot or a little?*", with the children's responses then being scored on a 5-point scale ranging from "*like a lot*" to "*dislike a lot*". Once again, the children's scores for the in-group were compared with the scores for each of the out-groups. The results are shown in Table 6.2. A very different picture emerges from this table. Here, there is clear and consistent evidence of in-group preference in virtually all subgroups of children. However, while such affective preference for the in-group is interesting as a phenomenon in its own right, it is not strictly relevant to testing the prediction made by SIT. Comparing Table 6.1 with Table 6.2, it is clear that different findings can be obtained concerning children's in-group bias depending on the particular measure used, while Table 6.1 indicates that different findings can be obtained depending on the particular national population that is being studied. These observations must be borne in mind when interpreting the evidence from single nation studies that have utilised single measures.

The strength of identification will correlate either with the positivity of the in-group evaluation, or with the negativity of out-group evaluations, or with the positive distinctiveness that is ascribed to the in-group

In the study by Barrett et al. (1997), two measures were made of the strength of the children's national identifications: one that measured the importance which the children ascribed to their national identity relative to their other social identities, and one that measured the children's degree of identification

Table 6.2 Significant differences in the affect expressed towards the national in-group versus various national out-groups by 6-, 9-, 12-, and 15-year-old British, Spanish, and Italian children

British	Brit vs. Fren	Brit vs. Span	Brit vs. Ital	Brit vs. Ger	
6-yr-olds	ns	ns	Brit > Ital	Brit > Ger	
9-yr-olds	Brit > Fren	Brit > Span	Brit > Ital	Brit > Ger	
12-yr-olds	Brit > Fren	Brit > Span	Brit > Ital	Brit > Ger	
15-yr-olds	Brit > Fren	Brit > Span	Brit > Ital	Brit > Ger	
Spanish	**Span vs. Fren**	**Span vs. Brit**	**Span vs. Ital**	**Span vs. Ger**	
6-yr-olds	Span > Fren	Span > Brit	Span > Ital	Span > Ger	
9-yr-olds	Span > Fren	Span > Brit	Span > Ital	Span > Ger	
12-yr-olds	Span > Fren	Span > Brit	Span > Ital	Span > Ger	
15-yr-olds	Span > Fren	Span > Brit	Span > Ital	Span > Ger	
Italian	**Ital vs. Fren**	**Ital vs. Brit**	**Ital vs. Span**	**Ital vs. Ger**	
6-yr-olds	Ital > Fren	Ital > Brit	Ital > Span	Ital > Ger	
9-yr-olds	Ital > Fren	Ital > Brit	Ital > Span	Ital > Ger	
12-yr-olds	Ital > Fren	ns	Ital > Span	Ital > Ger	
15-yr-olds	Ital > Fren	ns	ns	Ital > Ger	
English	**Eng vs. Fren**	**Eng vs. Span**	**Eng vs. Ital**	**Eng vs. Ger**	**Eng vs. Scot**
6-yr-olds	Eng > Fren	Eng > Span	Eng > Ital	Eng > Ger	Eng > Scot
9-yr-olds	Eng > Fren	Eng > Span	Eng > Ital	Eng > Ger	Eng > Scot
12-yr-olds	Eng > Fren	Eng > Span	Eng > Ital	Eng > Ger	Eng > Scot
15-yr-olds	Eng > Fren	Eng > Span	Eng > Ital	Eng > Ger	Eng > Scot
Scottish	**Scot vs. Fren**	**Scot vs. Span**	**Scot vs. Ital**	**Scot vs. Ger**	**Scot vs. Eng**
6-yr-olds	Scot > Fren	ns	Scot > Ital	Scot > Ger	Scot > Eng
9-yr-olds	Scot > Fren	Scot > Span	Scot > Ital	Scot > Ger	Scot > Eng
12-yr-olds	Scot > Fren	Scot > Span	Scot > Ital	Scot > Ger	Scot > Eng
15-yr-olds	Scot > Fren	Scot > Span	Scot > Ital	Scot > Ger	Scot > Eng
Catalan	**Cat vs. Fren**	**Cat vs. Brit**	**Cat vs. Ital**	**Cat vs. Ger**	
6-yr-olds	Cat > Fren	Cat > Brit	Cat > Ital	Cat > Ger	
9-yr-olds	Cat > Fren	Cat > Brit	Cat > Ital	Cat > Ger	
12-yr-olds	Cat > Fren	Cat > Brit	Cat > Ital	Cat > Ger	
15-yr-olds	Cat > Fren	Cat > Brit	Cat > Ital	Cat > Ger	

Source: Barrett et al., 1997.

Notes
ns = no significant difference in the affect expressed towards the two groups.
Brit = British; Fren = French, Span = Spanish; Ital = Italian; Ger = German; Eng = English;
Scot = Scottish; Cat = Catalan.

with their national group (i.e., whether they felt *"very British/Spanish/Italian"*, *"a little bit British/Spanish/Italian"* or *"not at all British/Spanish/Italian"*, etc.). The correlations between each of these two scores and the children's evaluations of their national in-group and the various national out-groups were examined. The results are summarised in Table 6.3.

This table provides little support for the prediction that the strength of national identification will correlate with the evaluation of national in-groups and out-groups. Only the Spanish children's evaluations of their own national in-group produced consistent evidence supporting this prediction. In addition, the older Catalan children's evaluations of their national in-group indicate that a similar correlation emerges during adolescence in these children. However, the other significant correlations exhibited by the Catalan children's data also indicate that the stronger their sense of national identity, the more *positive* their evaluations of some national out-groups at certain ages, contrary to prediction.

The data were also examined to ascertain whether the strength of national identification was related to the *difference* between the evaluation of the in-group and the evaluations of the out-groups, in other words, to the *positive distinctiveness* of the in-group vis-à-vis each individual out-group. Consequently, the correlations between the differences between the various in-group–out-group evaluations (i.e., the positive distinctiveness of the in-group over each individual out-group) and the two strengths of national identification scores were also examined. The results of these analyses are shown in Table 6.4. This table reveals that the predicted relationship only applies in the case of the Spanish children. In addition, there is partial evidence that this relationship might apply in some Catalan children as far as their Catalan identity is concerned, but there is no real evidence that it applies in Italian, English, or Scottish children.

Next, the correlations between the strength of identification measures and the affect that was expressed towards each individual national group (in response to the *like/dislike* questions) were examined. The results are shown in Table 6.5. First, it is of interest to note that strength of identification with the in-group does not appear to be related to affect towards national out-groups. Second, Table 6.5 suggests that the strength of in-group identification tends to be positively related to the affect expressed towards the national in-group in the case of the British, Spanish, Italian, and Catalan identities. However, this relationship was largely absent in the case of the English and Scottish children as far as their English and Scottish identities were concerned.

Last, the data were examined to ascertain whether the strength of national identification was related to the *difference* between the affect expressed towards the in-group and the affect expressed towards the out-groups, in other words, to the *affective distinctiveness* of the in-group vis-à-vis each individual out-group. The results are shown in Table 6.6. This table reveals that the predicted relationship applies consistently only in the case of the

Table 6.3 Correlations between the evaluation of each individual national group and either the importance of national identity (Imp) or the degree of national identification (Deg)

British	Brit	Span	Ital	Ger	Fren	
6-yr-olds	ns	ns	ns	ns	ns	
9-yr-olds	ns	ns	ns	ns	ns	
12-yr-olds	ns	Deg –	ns	ns	ns	
15-yr-olds	ns	ns	ns	ns	ns	

Spanish	Span	Brit	Ital	Ger	Fren	
6-yr-olds	Imp +, Deg +	ns	ns	ns	ns	
9-yr-olds	Imp +, Deg +	Deg –	ns	ns	ns	
12-yr-olds	Imp +, Deg +	Imp –, Deg –	Deg –	ns	ns	
15-yr-olds	Imp +, Deg +	ns	ns	ns	ns	

Italian	Ital	Brit	Span	Ger	Fren	
6-yr-olds	Imp +	ns	ns	ns	ns	
9-yr-olds	ns	ns	ns	ns	ns	
12-yr-olds	ns	ns	ns	ns	ns	
15-yr-olds	ns	ns	ns	ns	ns	

English	Span	Ital	Ger	Fren	Scot	
6-yr-olds	ns	ns	ns	ns	ns	ns
9-yr-olds	ns	ns	ns	ns	ns	ns
12-yr-olds	ns	ns	ns	ns	ns	ns
15-yr-olds	ns	ns	ns	ns	ns	ns

Scottish	Span	Ital	Ger	Fren	Eng	
6-yr-olds	ns	ns	ns	ns	ns	ns
9-yr-olds	ns	ns	ns	ns	ns	ns
12-yr-olds	ns	ns	ns	ns	ns	Imp –
15-yr-olds	ns	ns	ns	ns	ns	ns

Catalan	Cat	Brit	Ital	Ger	Fren	
6-yr-olds	ns	ns	ns	ns	ns	
9-yr-olds	ns	Imp +	ns	Imp +	ns	
12-yr-olds	Deg +	ns	ns	Imp +, Deg +	ns	
15-yr-olds	Imp +, Deg +	ns	ns	ns	Deg +	

Source: Barrett et al., 1997.

Notes
ns = no significant correlations; + = positive correlation; – = negative correlation.
Brit = British; Fren = French, Span = Spanish; Ital = Italian; Ger = German; Eng = English; Scot = Scottish; Cat = Catalan.

Table 6.4 Correlations between the positive distinctiveness of the national in-group (as measured against each individual out-group) and either the importance of national identity (Imp) or the degree of national identification (Deg)

British	Brit vs. Fren	Brit vs. Span	Brit vs. Ital	Brit vs. Ger	
6-yr-olds	ns	Deg +	ns	Deg +	
9-yr-olds	ns	Deg +	ns	ns	
12-yr-olds	ns	Imp −	ns	ns	
15-yr-olds	ns	ns	ns	ns	

Spanish	Span vs. Fren	Span vs. Brit	Span vs. Ital	Span vs. Ger	
6-yr-olds	Imp +	Imp +, Deg +	Imp +	Imp +	
9-yr-olds	ns	Imp +, Deg +	Imp +, Deg +	ns	
12-yr-olds	Imp +, Deg +	Imp +, Deg +	Imp +, Deg +	Imp +, Deg +	
15-yr-olds	Imp +, Deg +	Imp +, Deg +	Imp +, Deg +	Imp +, Deg +	

Italian	Ital vs. Fren	Ital vs. Brit	Ital vs. Span	Ital vs. Ger	
6-yr-olds	ns	Imp +	ns	ns	
9-yr-olds	ns	ns	ns	ns	
12-yr-olds	ns	ns	ns	ns	
15-yr-olds	ns	ns	ns	ns	

English	Eng vs. Fren	Eng vs. Span	Eng vs. Ital	Eng vs. Ger	Eng vs. Scot
6-yr-olds	ns	ns	ns	ns	ns
9-yr-olds	ns	ns	ns	ns	ns
12-yr-olds	ns	ns	ns	ns	ns
15-yr-olds	ns	ns	ns	ns	ns

Scottish	Scot vs. Fren	Scot vs. Span	Scot vs. Ital	Scot vs. Ger	Scot vs. Eng
6-yr-olds	ns	ns	Imp −	ns	ns
9-yr-olds	ns	ns	ns	ns	ns
12-yr-olds	ns	ns	ns	ns	Imp +
15-yr-olds	ns	ns	ns	ns	ns

Catalan	Cat vs. Fren	Cat vs. Brit	Cat vs. Ital	Cat vs. Ger	
6-yr-olds	Deg +	ns	Deg +	Deg +	
9-yr-olds	ns	ns	ns	ns	
12-yr-olds	Deg +	ns	ns	ns	
15-yr-olds	ns	Imp +, Deg +	ns	ns	

Source: Barrett et al., 1997.

Notes
ns = no significant correlations; + = positive correlation; − = negative correlation.
Brit = British; Fren = French, Span = Spanish; Ital = Italian; Ger = German; Eng = English; Scot = Scottish; Cat = Catalan.

Table 6.5 Correlations between the affect expressed towards each individual national group and either the importance of national identity (Imp) or the degree of national identification (Deg)

British	Brit	Span	Ital	Ger	Fren
6-yr-olds	Imp +	ns	ns	Imp +	ns
9-yr-olds	Imp +, Deg +	ns	ns	ns	ns
12-yr-olds	Deg +	ns	ns	ns	ns
15-yr-olds	Imp +, Deg +	ns	ns	ns	ns

Spanish	Span	Brit	Ital	Ger	Fren
6-yr-olds	Imp +, Deg +	ns	Imp –	ns	ns
9-yr-olds	Imp +, Deg +	ns	ns	ns	ns
12-yr-olds	Imp +, Deg +	Deg –	Deg –	ns	ns
15-yr-olds	Imp +, Deg +	ns	ns	ns	ns

Italian	Ital	Brit	Span	Ger	Fren
6-yr-olds	Imp +, Deg +	ns	ns	ns	ns
9-yr-olds	ns	Deg +	ns	ns	ns
12-yr-olds	Imp +	ns	ns	ns	ns
15-yr-olds	Deg +	ns	ns	ns	ns

English	Eng	Span	Ital	Ger	Fren	Scot
6-yr-olds	ns	ns	ns	ns	ns	ns
9-yr-olds	ns	ns	ns	ns	ns	ns
12-yr-olds	Deg +	ns	ns	ns	ns	ns
15-yr-olds	ns	ns	ns	ns	ns	ns

Scottish	Scot	Span	Ital	Ger	Fren	Eng
6-yr-olds	ns	ns	ns	ns	ns	ns
9-yr-olds	ns	ns	ns	ns	ns	ns
12-yr-olds	ns	ns	ns	ns	ns	ns
15-yr-olds	ns	ns	ns	ns	ns	ns

Catalan	Cat	Brit	Ital	Ger	Fren
6-yr-olds	ns	ns	ns	ns	ns
9-yr-olds	Deg +	ns	ns	ns	ns
12-yr-olds	Imp +, Deg +	ns	ns	Deg +	Imp +
15-yr-olds	Imp +, Deg +	ns	ns	ns	Deg +

Source: Barrett et al., 1997.

Notes
ns = no significant correlations; + = positive correlation; – = negative correlation.
Brit = British; Fren = French, Span = Spanish; Ital = Italian; Ger = German; Eng = English; Scot = Scottish; Cat = Catalan.

Table 6.6 Correlations between the affective distinctiveness of the national in-group (as measured against each individual out-group) and either the importance of national identity (Imp) or the degree of national identification (Deg)

British	*Brit vs. Fren*	*Brit vs. Span*	*Brit vs. Ital*	*Brit vs. Ger*
6-yr-olds	ns	ns	Imp +	ns
9-yr-olds	Imp +, Deg +	Deg +	ns	Imp +, Deg +
12-yr-olds	ns	ns	Imp +	ns
15-yr-olds	Imp +, Deg +	Imp +, Deg +	ns	Imp +, Deg +

Spanish	*Span vs. Fren*	*Span vs. Brit*	*Span vs. Ital*	*Span vs. Ger*
6-yr-olds	Imp +, Deg +	Imp +, Deg +	Imp +, Deg +	Imp +, Deg +
9-yr-olds	Imp +	Imp +, Deg +	Imp +, Deg +	Imp +, Deg +
12-yr-olds	Imp +, Deg +	Imp +, Deg +	Imp +, Deg +	Imp +, Deg +
15-yr-olds	Imp +, Deg +	Imp +, Deg +	Imp +, Deg +	Imp +, Deg +

Italian	*Ital vs. Fren*	*Ital vs. Brit*	*Ital vs. Span*	*Ital vs. Ger*
6-yr-olds	ns	ns	ns	ns
9-yr-olds	ns	ns	ns	ns
12-yr-olds	Imp +	Imp +	Deg +	ns
15-yr-olds	ns	Deg +	Deg +	ns

English	*Eng vs. Fren*	*Eng vs. Span*	*Eng vs. Ital*	*Eng vs. Ger*	*Eng vs. Scot*
6-yr-olds	ns	ns	ns	ns	ns
9-yr-olds	ns	ns	ns	ns	ns
12-yr-olds	ns	ns	ns	ns	Deg +
15-yr-olds	ns	ns	ns	ns	ns

Scottish	*Scot vs. Fren*	*Scot vs. Span*	*Scot vs. Ital*	*Scot vs. Ger*	*Scot vs. Eng*
6-yr-olds	ns	ns	ns	ns	ns
9-yr-olds	ns	ns	ns	ns	ns
12-yr-olds	ns	ns	ns	ns	ns
15-yr-olds	ns	ns	ns	ns	ns

Catalan	*Cat vs. Fren*	*Cat vs. Brit*	*Cat vs. Ital*	*Cat vs. Ger*
6-yr-olds	ns	ns	ns	Imp +
9-yr-olds	ns	ns	ns	ns
12-yr-olds	Deg +	Imp +, Deg +	Imp +, Deg +	ns
15-yr-olds	ns	Imp +, Deg +	ns	ns

Source: Barrett et al., 1997.

Notes
ns = no significant correlations; + = positive correlation; – = negative correlation.
Brit = British; Fren = French, Span = Spanish; Ital = Italian; Ger = German; Eng = English; Scot = Scottish; Cat = Catalan.

Spanish children at all ages. In addition, there is partial evidence that this relationship applies among some British, older Italian, and older Catalan children as well, but there is little evidence that it applies in the case of the English and Scottish children in relationship to their English and Scottish identities at any age.

Thus, once again, there are differences in findings according to the precise method that is used to assess in-group bias, and according to which particular national group is being investigated. Overall, Tables 6.3–6.6 suggest only limited empirical support for the second theoretical prediction, with different developmental patterns being exhibited by children who are growing up within different national contexts.

In-group favouritism will be a consequence of subjective identification with the in-group

SIT postulates that in-group favouritism occurs as a consequence of subjective identification with the in-group. When an individual internalises a social group membership as part of his or her self-concept, that individual is motivated by the need for positive self-esteem to construct more positive representations of that in-group than of out-groups. Thus, in-group favouritism is a consequence of subjective identification; if the individual does not identify with that group, then there is no motivation to evaluate the group more positively than other groups.

Bennett et al. (1998) examined the British data collected by Barrett et al. (1997), in order to ascertain whether or not subjective identification is, in fact, a necessary precondition for in-group favouritism. Using the degree of identification task, they found that 30% of the British children failed to identify with being British, and 14% of the children failed to identify with being either English or Scottish, even though they were all, de facto, both British and either English or Scottish (these nonidentifying children tended to be the younger children in the samples). Focusing upon the data of these nonidentifying children, Bennett et al. looked to see whether these children nevertheless exhibited in-group favouritism. They found that the children who failed to identify as being British in fact assigned more positive adjectives to the British national group than to any other national group in the adjective evaluation task, and expressed more positive affect towards British people than towards Italian and German people (although French and Spanish people were liked just as much as British people). In addition, the children who failed to identify as being English or Scottish assigned more positive adjectives to the English or Scottish national group than to any other national group, and expressed more positive affect towards the English or Scottish national group than towards any other national groups.

These findings indicate that nonidentifying children may exhibit favouritism towards their own national group, even though they do not categorise themselves as being members of that group. From a developmental perspective, this finding is important, as it implies that such favouritism must, at least in some cases, stem from factors other than subjective identification with the in-group coupled to the motivation for positive self-esteem.

In-group homogeneity will be lower in contexts in which only the in-group is present, and higher in contexts in which relevant out-groups are also present

SCT differs in its emphasis from SIT, insofar as it predicts that the salience of an individual's national identity, and therefore the perceived homogeneity of the in-group, will be higher in contexts in which relevant out-groups are present than in contexts in which only the in-group is present. It is postulated that the latter kind of situation encourages intragroup comparisons, which therefore enhance the salience of lower-level (personal or subgroup) categories between which the differences are accentuated, thereby increasing the perceived variability of the in-group. By contrast, in intergroup comparative contexts that contain both the in-group and a relevant out-group, intergroup comparisons occur and intragroup differentiations within the in-group become less salient, with the result that the perceived variability of the in-group decreases and the salience of the in-group category increases.

In order to examine whether these effects occur in children in relationship to their national identity, Barrett, Wilson, and Lyons (1999) conducted an experiment with 5- to 11-year-old English children. The children were asked to attribute adjectives to their own national group either on its own or in conjunction with attributing characteristics to one of two national out-groups, either Americans or Germans. From the attribution of adjectives, a perceived variability score for each of the target national groups was derived. This was essentially a measure of how variable each of those national groups was perceived to be on those descriptive dimensions that the children themselves had used for attributing the adjectives to those groups. In addition, the importance that the children ascribed to their own English national identity in relationship to their other social identities was assessed immediately after the administration of the attribution task.

It was found that the younger children attributed less variability to all of the national groups than the older children. In addition, the younger children ascribed less importance to their national identity than the older children. However, judging the in-group in the presence of an American or German out-group did *not* reduce the perceived variability of the national in-group compared with when that in-group was judged on its own. The presence of a comparative out-group also did not increase the importance that was ascribed to the national identity relative to other identities (such as gender and age). In other words, in-group homogeneity was not lower in the non-comparative context than in the two comparative contexts, and the relative importance of the national identity was also not lower in the noncomparative condition than in the comparative conditions.

Interestingly, this study did find that in-group favouritism (as indexed using an evaluation measure) was exhibited by the English children at all ages in relationship to both Germans and Americans. It will be recalled that in-group favouritism was also displayed by the English children in relationship to Germans in the study by Barrett et al. (1997; see Tables 6.1 and 6.2). However, there were no significant correlations between the importance of the English national identity and either the in-group evaluation, the two out-group evaluations, or the positive distinctiveness of the English in-group vis-à-vis either the American or the German out-group (which is consistent with the lack of such relationships among the English children in the study by Barrett et al., 1997; see Tables 6.3 and 6.4).

In-group stereotype content will change in conjunction with changes in comparative context, with different dimensions being selected depending on the comparison out-groups that are available in the prevailing context

In the study by Barrett et al. (1999), the adjectives that the children attributed to the English in-group in the three different conditions (i.e., evaluating English people on their own, evaluating English people in relationship to Germans, and evaluating English people in relationship to Americans) were also examined to see whether the children attributed different characteristics to the in-group in the three conditions. It was anticipated that different characteristics would be attributed to English people when they were being compared to Americans and to Germans (e.g., it was expected that "friendly" would be used less frequently in the American context, and "peaceful" would be used more frequently in the German context, because English children typically perceive Americans as "friendly" and Germans as "aggressive": Barrett, Day, & Morris, 1990; Barrett & Short, 1992; Wilson, Barrett, & Lyons, 1995). However, there were no effects of comparative context upon the contents of the children's in-group stereotype. That is to say, irrespective of the out-group against which the children were comparing the English, they attributed very similar adjectives to the English in-group. Thus, 5- to 11-year-olds do not appear to be sensitive to the comparative context when attributing characteristics to national groups. Similar findings have also been obtained by Sani, Bennett and Joyner (1999), who also failed to find any effect of comparative context on the in-group national stereotypes of Scottish 7- to 11-year-old children.

Thus, national in-group stereotype content does not appear to change in conjunction with changes in comparative context in 5- to 11-year-old children, contrary to prediction. Insofar as these effects of comparative context upon national stereotype content clearly do occur in adults aged 18 years and older (e.g., Haslam et al., 1992, 1995; Hopkins et al., 1997), it would be useful to ascertain the age at which these effects begin to occur (currently, no data are available on 12- to 17-year-olds as far as their national identity is concerned).

The strength of identification will correlate with perceived in-group homogeneity

SCT postulates that, when an individual has internalised a social group membership as part of his or her self-concept, then when that social identity becomes salient to that individual (perhaps as a function of the prevailing social context), there is a depersonalisation of the perception of self and others, the perceived homogeneity of the in-group increases, self-stereotyping occurs, and group behaviour that is appropriate to the social identity is elicited. This increase in in-group homogeneity is therefore one of the consequences of subjective identification; if an individual does not subjectively identify with a group, then that particular group membership will not be so salient for that individual in the intergroup context, and in-group homogeneity will not be so pronounced in such an individual compared with an individual for whom that social group membership is subjectively important. Thus, SCT predicts that in-group homogeneity will be higher in individuals who subjectively identify with the group compared with individuals who do not identify with the group; in other words, in an intergroup situation, the strength of identification should correlate with in-group homogeneity.

The data from Barrett et al. (1997) were used to test this prediction. Using the data from the task in which the children were asked to assign descriptive adjectives to their own national group and to a number of national out-groups (in which an intergroup frame of reference had been established), a perceived variability score for each of the target national groups was derived. This score was a measure of how variable each national group was perceived to be on those descriptive dimensions that the children themselves had used for assigning the adjectives to that group; a high score meant that a group was perceived to be highly variable, while a low score meant that a group was perceived to be highly homogeneous. In addition, two measures of the children's strength of identification with the national in-group were available: the importance that the children ascribed to their national identity relative to their other social identities, and the children's degree of identification with their national group. The correlations between each of these two identification measures and the perceived variability of each individual national group are summarised in Table 6.7.

This table shows that only the Spanish 6- and 12-year-olds and the Catalan 6- and 15-year-olds provided evidence consistent with the prediction that there will be a negative correlation between the strength of identification with the national in-group and the perceived variability of that group. In addition, the stronger the 6- and 12-year-old Spanish children's national identification, the more they perceived the British, Italian, and French national out-groups as being homogeneous. However, these trends were not exhibited by the

Table 6.7 Correlations between the perceived variability of each individual national group and either the importance of national identity (Imp) or the degree of national identification (Deg)

British	Brit	Span	Ital	Ger	Fren	
6-yr-olds	Imp +	ns	ns	Deg +	ns	
9-yr-olds	ns	ns	ns	ns	ns	
12-yr-olds	ns	Imp +	ns	ns	ns	
15-yr-olds	ns	ns	ns	ns	ns	

Spanish	Span	Brit	Ital	Ger	Fren	
6-yr-olds	Imp –	Imp –	Imp –	ns	Imp –, Deg –	
9-yr-olds	ns	ns	Imp –	ns	ns	
12-yr-olds	Imp –, Deg –	Deg –	Deg –	ns	Imp –	
15-yr-olds	ns	ns	ns	ns	ns	

Italian	Ital	Brit	Span	Ger	Fren	
6-yr-olds	ns	ns	ns	ns	ns	
9-yr-olds	ns	ns	ns	ns	ns	
12-yr-olds	ns	ns	ns	ns	ns	
15-yr-olds	ns	ns	Deg –	ns	ns	

English	Eng	Span	Ital	Ger	Fren	Scot
6-yr-olds	ns	ns	ns	ns	ns	ns
9-yr-olds	ns	ns	ns	ns	ns	Deg –
12-yr-olds	ns	ns	ns	Imp +	ns	ns
15-yr-olds	ns	ns	Imp –	ns	ns	ns

Scottish	Scot	Span	Ital	Ger	Fren	Eng
6-yr-olds	ns	ns	ns	ns	ns	ns
9-yr-olds	ns	ns	ns	ns	ns	ns
12-yr-olds	ns	Deg –	Deg –	ns	ns	ns
15-yr-olds	ns	ns	ns	ns	ns	ns

Catalan	Cat	Brit	Ital	Ger	Fren	
6-yr-olds	Imp –	ns	ns	ns	ns	
9-yr-olds	ns	ns	ns	ns	ns	
12-yr-olds	ns	ns	ns	ns	ns	
15-yr-olds	Imp –	ns	ns	Imp –	ns	

Source: Barrett et al., 1997.

Notes
ns = no significant correlations; + = positive correlation; – = negative correlation.
Brit = British; Fren = French, Span = Spanish; Ital = Italian; Ger = German; Eng = English; Scot = Scottish; Cat = Catalan.

children growing up in other national contexts. Overall, it would appear from Table 6.7 that the degree of stereotyping of both national in-groups and out-groups is not consistently related to the strength of national identification in children aged between 6 and 15 years of age.

The strength of identification with the in-group may be higher in members of minority groups than in members of majority groups

The data collected by Barrett et al. (1997) were also examined to ascertain whether individuals who belong to a minority national group exhibit a higher level of identification with their in-group than do the members of a majority national group. The analyses here initially focused upon the data from the English and Scottish children. Within the British context, the English national group is both politically and economically more powerful than the Scottish national group; the English national group is also numerically much larger. Thus, the Scottish nation is a subordinate group within Britain in terms of its power, wealth, and size. Under these circumstances, one might expect Scottish people to display higher levels of identification with their national in-group than English people (cf. Branscombe et al., 1999; Simon, 1992).

In order to examine this possibility, both the importance of the national identity and the degree of identification with the national group were compared in the English and Scottish children. The results are summarised in the upper half of Table 6.8 (first two columns). This shows that only the

Table 6.8 Significant differences in the importance of national identity, the degree of national identification, and the perceived variability of the national in-group, in Scottish versus English children, and in Catalan versus Spanish (Andalusian) children

	Importance of national identity	*Degree of national identification*	*Perceived variability of the national in-group*
English vs. Scottish			
6-yr-olds	Eng > Scot	Eng > Scot	ns
9-yr-olds	ns	Eng > Scot	ns
12-yr-olds	ns	ns	Eng > Scot
15-yr-olds	Scot > Eng	ns	Eng > Scot
Catalan vs. Spanish[a]			
6-yr-olds	ns	Cat > Span	Cat > Span
9-yr-olds	ns	ns	Cat > Span
12-yr-olds	ns	Span > Cat	Cat > Span
15-yr-olds	ns	ns	ns

Notes
ns = no significant difference.
[a] In Andalusian children.

15-year-old children displayed the expected pattern (and then only on one of the two measures of the strength of national identification). Developmentally, this outcome does make sense, as it is probable that only the older children would have acquired sufficient knowledge concerning the political, economic, and minority status of Scotland for the predicted effects to occur. However, this explanation does not account for the fact that the *opposite* pattern was exhibited by the younger children (where the English children actually exhibited a *stronger* sense of national identification than the Scottish children).

Similar analyses were also conducted on the data collected from the Catalan children in relationship to their Catalan identity and from the non-Catalan Spanish (Andalusian) children in relationship to their Spanish identity. In this case, the Spanish national group is numerically much larger than the Catalan national group. However, Catalonia has achieved a high level of political autonomy from the rest of Spain, has control of its own educational, health, and social services, and uses Catalan as the official language of education. Thus, the Spanish context is very different from the British context in terms of the political influence and power exercised by the Catalan people, and this needs to be borne in mind when interpreting the findings from the Spanish context. The results of the analyses are shown in the lower half of Table 6.8 (first two columns). It can be seen that a very different picture emerges from the Catalan and Spanish children compared to the Scottish and English children. And it is noteworthy that there is no real evidence (except, counterintuitively, from the 6-year-olds) to support the notion that the members of a minority group will identify with their national group more strongly than the members of a majority group.

In-group homogeneity may be higher in members of minority groups than in members of majority groups

Finally, the data from Barrett et al. (1997) were also examined to explore whether the members of minority national groups perceive their national in-group as being more homogeneous than members of majority national groups. The expectation is that, within the British context, Scottish people, as the minority and politically and economically subordinate group, should perceive their national in-group as being more homogeneous and less variable than should English people.

Lyons et al. (1997) used the data from the Scottish and English children in order to test this idea. The findings are shown in the final column of Table 6.8 (upper half). It can be seen that, in the two younger age groups, there was no difference in the perceived variabilities of the two in-groups. However, in the 12- and 15-year-olds, the predicted effect *did* occur: In both cases, the Scottish children perceived their in-group to be more homogeneous than the English children. Once again, the fact that this trend was exhibited only by the older children, and not by the younger children, does make sense in terms of it being only the older children who are likely to have acquired sufficient knowledge concerning the political, economic, and minority status of Scottish people within Britain for this effect to occur. This finding underlines the point that knowledge about relative group size and status are likely to mediate the impact of social identity processes in children just as much as in adults (cf. Bigler et al., 2001; Nesdale & Flesser, 2001).

However, the empirical findings are rather more complex than even this might suggest. The comparable data from the Spanish context are shown in the final column of Table 6.8 (lower half). A very different picture emerges here. In this case, it is the *younger* members of the *majority* national group who see their in-group as being more homogeneous; there is no significant difference between the perceptions of the Catalan and Andalusian children at 15 years of age. Despite the necessary caveats concerning these data drawn from the Spanish context, it is difficult to avoid the conclusion that the effects of minority status do not occur consistently across children who are growing up in different national contexts, and that different developmental patterns may be exhibited depending on the specific national group to which the child belongs.

SO DO SIT AND SCT PROVIDE USEFUL HEURISTIC FRAMEWORKS FOR DEVELOPMENTAL RESEARCH?

Earlier in this chapter, it was noted that although SIT and SCT are not developmental theories, it might nevertheless be possible to obtain some insight into the development of national identity by examining whether particular phenomena are exhibited by children at particular points in development; the presence of these phenomena could then be interpreted as evidence that the social identity processes postulated by SIT or SCT as being responsible for the production of those phenomena have become operative in these children. However, as we have seen, the findings are actually more complex than this. Rather than there being evidence that particular phenomena start to be exhibited by children at particular points in development, pervasive differences have been found in the developmental patterns of phenomena that are exhibited by children who are growing up in different national contexts.

Thus, even the most basic phenomenon of in-group favouritism reveals different developmental patterns in children who are growing up in Catalonia, Scotland, and Italy (see Table 6.1). Similarly, while the strength of national identification does indeed correlate with both positive and affective distinctiveness in Spanish children at all ages, it does not do so consistently in other national groups that have been studied, and in some national groups, such a correlation does not appear to be present at any age (see Tables 6.4 and 6.6). Furthermore, differences (in strength of national identification, and in perceptions of in-group homogeneity) between children who belong to minority and majority national groups also seem to vary as a function of age in different ways in different national contexts (see Table 6.8). In fact, the only finding which seems to appear consistently in all national groups is affective preference for the national in-group (see Table 6.2), which appears to be present from 6 years of age onwards.

So do SIT and SCT provide useful heuristic frameworks for research into identity development? If we are concerned with a close match between the concrete predictions that many researchers have construed these theories as making and the specificities of the data collected to date, and in using the developmental patterns in these data to help delineate a general model of identity development, the answer would appear to be no. However, if we are concerned with the articulation of further hypotheses for empirical investigations in the future, the answer is, perhaps somewhat paradoxically, yes. That is to say, SIT and SCT may still prove to be useful theoretical frameworks for the articulation of further hypotheses concerning the development of national identity, for the following reasons.

Turner (1999; Turner & Onorato, 1999) has recently argued that the core social identity processes postulated by SIT and SCT (as summarised earlier in this chapter) are likely to interact with a number of other factors, including the individual's motives, values, needs, goals, expectations, background knowledge, theories and beliefs concerning the specific social groups involved, and theories and beliefs about the prevailing intergroup relations and the relative status and position of the in-group within the social system. Furthermore, it seems plausible that all of these factors would be especially important in the case of real-world social groups (as opposed to artificial, experimenter-imposed, social groups). Thus, the extent to which particular identity phenomena are exhibited may actually be a product of a much more complex interaction between, for example, the strength of subjective identification with the in-group, the individual's beliefs about the nature of the group boundaries (e.g., whether they are legitimate or illegitimate) and about the status of the different groups within that system (e.g., whether the in-group is high or low status, and whether this status is secure or insecure), and the individual's own personal motivations, values, needs, and expectancies in relationship to these beliefs. In other words, Turner has argued that it may actually be inappropriate to look for simple correlations between pairs of variables.

Turner's suggestion may help to explain why the identity phenomena that are exhibited by children in the national identity domain vary so dramatically according to the specific national context within which the children are growing up. For example, as has been noted already in this chapter, the political realities of the intergroup relationships differ in Britain and in Spain. Furthermore, the collective ideologies and shared beliefs concerning intergroup relations (between Scotland and England within Britain, and between Catalonia and Castilian Spain within Spain) also differ between the two countries (e.g., language use – Catalan vs. Castilian – is one of the key issues within the Catalan context, but is far more marginal within the Scottish context, where the political and economic subordination of Scotland to England is probably the most significant issue). Therefore children who are growing up in these different countries will be exposed to, and hence may internalise, quite different beliefs about the prevailing intergroup relations and about the relative status and position of their own in-group within the national system. If, however, identity phenomena are a product of an inter-action between, for example, the intensity of in-group identification and the individual's beliefs about the prevailing intergroup relations, then this might explain the different patterns of development that are exhibited by the children living in these two different national contexts.

If Turner is correct concerning the number of factors that are actually responsible for eliciting particular identity phenomena, then there are two implications for the future investigation of national identity development in children. One of these implications is positive and the other is negative as far as the utility of SIT and SCT as heuristic frameworks for developmental research is concerned. The positive implication is that the research agenda opens up dramatically. If identity phenomena really are an interactive product of so many factors, then there are clearly many more variables that need to be measured in developmental studies than have been measured to date in any study. And it will be imperative for researchers conducting such research to develop suitable methods of operationalising and measuring all of these different variables in children, and to use a much more complex multivariate approach to analysis, in order to explore properly the implications of SIT and SCT.

However, the negative implication of Turner's most recent formulations is that they potentially render SIT and SCT impervious to empirical evaluation. If negative findings that run counter to prediction are obtained, it is possible that such findings can now always be explained post hoc by reference to some kind of cognitive or motivational factor. In other words, precisely because so many loosely specified psychological factors (i.e., motives, values, needs, goals, expectations, background knowledge, theories, and beliefs) have now been flagged as possible influences upon identity phenomena, and because both SIT and SCT appear to have been augmented by a number of auxiliary hypotheses that seem to form a protective belt around the key ideas contained within these theories, it is possible that these two theories have now been rendered invulnerable to empirical refutation.

Certainly, the complexities of the existing data, alongside Turner's most recent statements, should caution us against drawing any oversimplistic interpretations and conclusions concerning the role of social identity and self-categorisation processes as far as the development of national identity is concerned. It will be an issue for future researchers to decide, with the advantage of hindsight, whether SIT and SCT have proved to be helpful and productive heuristic theoretical frameworks for developmental research.

Acknowledgements

The study by Barrett, Lyons, Bennett, Vila, Giménez, Arcuri, and de Rosa (1997), upon which this chapter has been largely based, was supported by a grant received from the Commission of the European Communities DGXII, Human Capital and Mobility (Networks) Programme (Grant No. CHRX-CT94-0687), which was awarded to the Universities of Surrey, Dundee, Girona, Málaga, Padova, and Roma "La Sapienza". The following colleagues contributed to the design of the research: Mark Bennett, Fabio Sani, Ignasi Vila, Santi Perera, Almudena Giménez de la Peña, Luciano Arcuri, Anna Emilia Berti, Annamaria Silvana de Rosa, and Anna Silvia Bombi. We are extremely grateful to all of these individuals for their contributions to this study. However, none of them should be blamed for the theoretical speculations that have been put forward in this chapter.

REFERENCES

Aboud, F. (1988). *Children and prejudice*. Oxford: Blackwell.

Barrett, M. (1996). English children's acquisition of a European identity. In G. Breakwell & E. Lyons (Eds.), *Changing European identities: Social psychological analyses of social change* (pp. 349–369). Oxford: Butterworth-Heinemann.

Barrett, M. (2001). The development of national identity: A conceptual analysis and some data from Western European studies. In M. Barrett, T. Riazanova, & M. Volovikova (Eds.), *Development of national, ethnolinguistic and religious identities in children and adolescents* (pp. 16–58). Moscow: Institute of Psychology, Russian Academy of Sciences (IPRAS).

Barrett, M. (in press). *Children's knowledge, beliefs and feelings about nations and national groups*. Hove, UK: Psychology Press.

Barrett, M., Day, J., & Morris, E. (1990, June). *English children's conceptions of European people: a pilot study*. Paper presented at the Conference on Perception and Cognitive Processes, Trieste, Italy.

Barrett, M., & Farroni, T. (1996). English and Italian children's knowledge of European geography. *British Journal of Developmental Psychology, 14*, 257–273.

Barrett, M., Lyons, E., Bennett, M., Vila, I., Giménez, A., Arcuri, L., & de Rosa, A. S. (1997). *Children's beliefs and feelings about their own and other national groups in Europe*. Final Report to the Commission of the European Communities, Directorate-General XII for Science, Research and Development, Human Capital and Mobility (HCM) Programme, Research Network No. CHRX-CT94-0687.

Barrett, M., & Short, J. (1992). Images of European people in a group of 5–10-year-old English school children. *British Journal of Developmental Psychology, 10*, 339–363.

Barrett, M., Wilson, H., & Lyons, E. (1999). *Self-categorization theory and the development of national identity in English children*. Poster presented at Biennial Meeting of SRCD, Albuquerque, USA.

Bennett, M., Lyons, E., Sani, F., & Barrett, M. (1998). Children's subjective identification with the group and in-group favoritism. *Developmental Psychology, 34*, 902–909.

Bernal, M. E., & Knight, G. P. (Eds.) (1993). *Ethnic identity: Formation and transmission among Hispanics and other minorities*. Albany, NY: State University of New York Press.

Bigler, R. S., Brown, C. S., & Markell, M. (2001). When groups are not created equal: Effects of group status on the formation of intergroup attitudes in children. *Child Development, 72*, 1151–1162.

Bigler, R. S., Jones, L. C., & Lobliner, D. B. (1997). Social categorization and the formation of intergroup attitudes in children. *Child Development, 68*, 530–543.

Bourchier, A., Barrett, M., & Lyons, E. (2002). The predictors of children's geographical knowledge of other countries. *Journal of Environmental Psychology, 22*, 79–94.

Branscombe, N. R., Ellemers, N., Spears, R., & Doosje, B. (1999). The context and content of social identity threat. In N. Ellemers, R. Spears, & B. Doosje (Eds.), *Social identity* (pp. 35–58). Oxford: Blackwell.

Branscombe, N. R., & Wann, D. L. (1994). Collective self-esteem consequences of out-group derogation when a valued social identity is on trial. *European Journal of Social Psychology, 24*, 641–657.

Brown, R., & Wootton-Millward, L. (1993). Perceptions of group homogeneity during group formation and change. *Social Cognition, 11*, 126–149.

Eckes, T., & Trautner, H. M. (Eds.) (2000). *The developmental social psychology of gender*. Mahwah, NJ: Lawrence Erlbaum Associates, Inc.

Ellemers, N., Doosje, B. J., Van Knippenberg, A., & Wilke, H. (1992). Status protection in high status minorities. *European Journal of Social Psychology, 22*, 123–140.

Ellemers, N., Kortekaas, P., & Ouwerkerk, J. (1999). Self-categorization, commitment to the group and social self-esteem as related but distinct aspects of social identity. *European Journal of Social Psychology, 29*, 371–389.

Grant, P. R. (1992). Ethnocentrism between groups of unequal power in response to perceived threat to valued resources and to social identity. *Canadian Journal of Behavioural Science, 24*, 348–370.

Grant, P. R. (1993). Reactions to intergroup similarity: Examination of the similarity-differentiation and similarity-attraction hypothesis. *Canadian Journal of Behavioural Science, 25*, 28–44.

Haslam, S. A. (2001). *Psychology in organizations: The social identity approach*. London: SAGE Publications.

Haslam, S. A., Oakes, P. J., Turner, J. C., & McGarty, C. (1995). Social categorization and group homogeneity: Changes in the perceived applicability of stereotype content as a function of comparative context and trait favourableness. *British Journal of Social Psychology, 34*, 139–160.

Haslam, S. A., Turner, J. C., Oakes, P. J., McGarty, C., & Hayes, B. K. (1992). Context-dependent variation in social stereotyping 1: The effects of intergroup relations as mediated by social change and frame of reference. *European Journal of Social Psychology, 22*, 251–278.

Hinkle, S., & Brown, R. (1990). Intergroup comparisons and social identity: Some links and lacunae. In D. Abrams & M. A. Hogg (Eds.), *Social identity theory: Constructive and critical advances*. Hemel Hempstead, UK: Harvester Wheatsheaf.

Hopkins, N., & Cable, I. (2001). Group variability judgments: Investigating the context-dependence of stereoypicality and dispersal judgments. *British Journal of Social Psychology, 40*, 455–470.

Hopkins, N., Regan, M., & Abell, J. (1997). On the context-dependence of national stereotypes: Some Scottish data. *British Journal of Social Psychology*, *36*, 553–563.

Jahoda, G. (1962). Development of Scottish children's ideas and attitudes about other countries. *Journal of Social Psychology*, *58*, 91–108.

Jaspers, J. M. F., Van de Geer, J. P., Tajfel, H., & Johnson, N. (1972). On the development of national attitudes in children. *European Journal of Social Psychology*, *2*, 347–369.

Johnson, N. (1973). Development of English children's concept of Germany. *Journal of Social Psychology*, *90*, 259–267.

Johnson, N., Middleton, M., & Tajfel, H. (1970). The relationship between children's preferences for and knowledge about other nations. *British Journal of Social and Clinical Psychology*, *9*, 232–240.

Kelly, C. (1988). Intergroup differentiation in a political context. *British Journal of Social Psychology*, *27*, 321–327.

Lambert, W. E., & Klineberg, O. (1967). *Children's views of foreign peoples: a cross-national study*. New York: Appleton-Century-Crofts.

Lyons, E., Barrett, M., Bennett, M., Sani, F., Vila, I., Giménez de la Peña, A., Arcuri, L., de Rosa, A. S., & Bombi, A. S. (1997, September). *Intragroup homogeneity effects in the development of national identity: A cross-national study*. Paper presented at the 8th European Conference on Developmental Psychology, Rennes, France.

Middleton, M., Tajfel, H., & Johnson, N. (1970). Cognitive and affective aspects of children's national attitudes. *British Journal of Social and Clinical Psychology*, *9*, 122–134.

Mummendey, A., Klink, A., & Brown, R. (2001). Nationalism and patriotism: National identification and out-group rejection. *British Journal of Social Psychology*, *40*, 159–172.

Nesdale, D., & Flesser, D. (2001). Social identity and the development of children's group attitudes. *Child Development*, *72*, 506–517.

Oakes, P. J., Haslam, S. A., & Turner, J. C. (1994). *Stereotyping and social reality*. Oxford: Blackwell.

Perreault, S., & Bourhis, R. Y. (1998). Social identification, interdependence and discrimination. *Group Processes and Intergroup Relations*, *1*, 49–66.

Phinney, J., & Rotheram, M. (Eds.) (1987). *Children's ethnic socialization: Pluralism and development*. Newbury Park, CA: SAGE Publications.

Piaget, J., & Weil, A. M. (1951). The development in children of the idea of the homeland and of relations to other countries. *International Social Science Journal*, *3*, 561–578.

Powlishta, K. K. (1995). Intergroup processes in childhood: Social categorization and sex role development. *Developmental Psychology*, *31*, 781–788.

Ruble, D. N., & Martin, C. L. (1998). Gender development. In W. Damon & N. Eisenberg (Eds.), *Handbook of child psychology, Vol. 3: Social, emotional and personality development* (5th ed., pp. 933–1016). New York: John Wiley & Sons.

Sani, F., Bennett, M., & Joyner, L. (1999). *Developmental aspects of contextual variability in the stereotype of the in-group: The case of Scottish children*. Paper presented at the Annual Conference of the Social Psychology Section of the British Psychological Society, Lancaster, UK.

Simon, B. (1992). The perception of in-group and out-group homogeneity: Reintroducing the intergroup context. *European Review of Social Psychology*, *3*, 1–30.

Simon, B., & Brown, R. J. (1987). Perceived intragroup homogeneity in minority–majority contexts. *Journal of Personality and Social Psychology, 53,* 703–711.

Simon, B., & Hamilton, D. L. (1994). Self-stereotyping and social context: The effects of relative in-group size and in-group status. *Journal of Personality and Social Psychology, 66,* 699–711.

Tajfel, H. (1978). *Differentiation between social groups: Studies in the social psychology of intergroup relations.* London: Academic Press.

Tajfel, H., Jahoda, G., Nemeth, C., Campbell, J., & Johnson, N. (1970). The development of children's preference for their own country: A cross-national study. *International Journal of Psychology, 5,* 245–253.

Tajfel, H., & Turner, J. C. (1986). The social identity theory of intergroup behaviour. In S. Worchel & W. G. Austin (Eds.), *Psychology of intergroup relations* (2nd ed., pp. 7–24). Chicago, IL: Nelson-Hall.

Turner, J. C. (1999). Some current issues in research on social identity and self-categorization theories. In N. Ellemers, R. Spears, & B. Doosje (Eds.), *Social identity* (pp. 6–34). Oxford: Blackwell.

Turner, J. C., Hogg, M. A., Oakes, P. J., Reicher, S. D., & Wetherell, M. S. (1987). *Rediscovering the social group: A self-categorization theory.* Oxford: Blackwell.

Turner, J. C., & Onorato, R. S. (1999). Social identity, personality and the self-concept: A self-categorization perspective. In T. R. Tyler, R. M. Kramer, & O. P. John (Eds.), *The psychology of the social self* (pp. 11–46). Mahwah, NJ: Lawrence Erlbaum Associates, Inc.

Verkuyten, M. (2001). National identification and intergroup evaluation in Dutch children. *British Journal of Developmental Psychology, 19,* 559–571.

Wilson, H. (1998). *The development of national identity in 5 to 11 year old English schoolchildren.* Unpublished PhD Thesis, University of Surrey.

Wilson, H., Barrett, M., & Lyons, E. (1995, July). *English children's beliefs and feelings about national groups in Europe: A pilot study.* Paper presented at the Second European Workshop on Children's Beliefs and Feelings about their Own and Other National Groups in Europe, University of Girona, Spain.

Yee, M. D., & Brown, R. J. (1992). Self evaluations and intergroup attitudes in children aged three to nine. *Child Development, 63,* 619–629.

7 Ethnic identity and social context

Maykel Verkuyten

This chapter is intended to make a case for the inclusion of social context when studying ethnic identity among minority (and majority) group children. Most writers agree that the social context plays a central role in ethnic identity development. However, few researchers have actually examined social context variables. Indeed, Coll et al. (1996) argue that existing research and developmental models are insufficiently specific for the study of racial and ethnic minority populations. An understanding of minority groups would require explicit attention to negative social circumstances, such as racism and discrimination, in relation to concrete environmental influences. They argue, for example, that very little systematic research has been done to examine how school variables promote or inhibit the well-being and social competency of minority group children. Similarly, Rotheram and Phinney (1987, p. 14) argue that:

> The importance and meaning of ethnic identity varies with the specific context and with changes in the social milieu and will be more salient in some situations than in others. Children's exposure to situations in which they are aware of their ethnicity will vary depending on their status as minority or majority group members, as well as on the degree of ethnic homogeneity or heterogeneity in their daily activities. For example, ethnicity is likely to be more salient for one white child in a class of 20 Black peers than for the same child in a predominantly white classroom.

Hence, the context is considered a central factor in understanding ethnic identity, but there are relatively few studies on, for example, experiences with discrimination and school characteristics. In this chapter I discuss our empirical research that examines contextual issues among children in late childhood (9 to 12 years old) living in the Netherlands[1].

The notion of context is variously defined across many psychological

---

1 Much of this research has been conducted together with Barbara Kinket and with Jochem Thijs.

paradigms. For example, context is taken to refer to the particular task or activity in which children are engaged, such as the comparative context in eliciting self and group evaluations or the public or private expression of these evaluations. Furthermore, the notion of context is used for historical and cultural circumstances, immigration conditions, and actual social situations, such as in schools and neighbourhoods. This chapter focuses on cultural and status differences between ethnic groups and actual local conditions. It will be argued that an understanding of ethnic minority identity requires explicit attention to cultural characteristics in addition to negative social circumstances, such as discrimination, and in relation to concrete environmental influences. Hence, both the "ethnic" and the "minority" aspect of ethnic minorities are considered. The former aspect is typically not examined by social psychologists, who focus on minority status and the related issues of prejudice and discrimination. The ethnic aspect is stressed in cross-cultural psychology and by those researchers who examine ethnicity in terms of cultural differences. Both of these aspects are likely to play a role in the development of ethnic identity, but they are typically not examined in relation to each other.

The notion of context is not only variously defined but also addressed from different theoretical perspectives. For example, in line with the symbolic interactionist perspective, some theories focus on how socialisation experiences with significant others and the wider sociocultural context influence the way children come to view themselves ethnically (see Phinney & Rotheram, 1987). In this chapter, ideas of social psychological intergroup theories will be drawn upon, particularly social identity theory (SIT; Tajfel & Turner, 1986) and its elaboration self-categorisation theory (SCT; Turner, Hogg, Oakes, Reicher, & Wetherell, 1987; Turner, Oakes, Haslam, & McGarty, 1994). I will try to show that these theories offer useful and important frameworks for studying ethnic identity among children, but that they also have limitations.

The first section gives a short historical description of psychological perspectives on the development of ethnic identity. The second section discusses the (for this chapter) most relevant ideas of SIT and SCT. The third and fourth sections present empirical results concerning perceived discrimination and cultural orientations, and their relationships with ethnic identity. In the fifth and sixth sections, the issue of the context dependency of ethnic identity will be addressed. In the final section, a key aspect of SCT is examined, namely the idea that children's perceptions and evaluations are affected by identity change or difference in self-categorisations.

FROM SOCIAL COGNITION TO SITUATION

Inquiry into the development of racial and ethnic identity has a well-established research tradition in psychology. The early research by E. L. Horowitz (1939), Clark and Clark (1947), and Goodman (1952) inspired many studies. Empirically, a great deal of effort has been directed at describing the ontogeny of children's awareness of, identification with, and preference for racial and ethnic categories (see Aboud, 1988; Fishbein, 1996, for reviews).

Theoretically, different explanations have been offered in trying to account for the appearance of racial and ethnic identity. Some major theories focus on qualitative differences in racial and ethnic self-understanding that are associated with broad stages of cognitive development. An age-related progression in the ability to perceive and interpret ethnic stimuli and inter-ethnic behaviours is assumed (e.g., Aboud, 1987; Ramsey, 1987). The focus is on processes and abilities, and the theoretical result is a sequence of steps or stages in the development of aspects of ethnic identity[2]. The emphasis is very much on the individual child and racial and ethnic identity is predominantly examined as a psychological attribute. These cognitive theories have a strong "individualistic" perspective in which there is little consistent simultaneous examination of individual and contextual variables.

However, developments in the structural complexity of children's thinking say little about the *particular* beliefs and knowledge children acquire or express. Racial and ethnic self-understandings are also determined by social beliefs that are related to historical, cultural, and sociorelational contexts. These social circumstances are important for examining and interpreting possible differences between ethnic majority and minority group children (Vaughan, 1987). Early studies conducted in America saw black children as more or less passive recipients of the existing prejudice and stigmatisation to which blacks as a group are subject. The core idea was that minority group members come to internalise society's negative view about their group and therefore show the "mark of oppression" (Kardiner & Ovesey, 1951). Studies found that black children were more ambivalent about their racial identity than were whites, sometimes also showing preference for and identification with the white out-group (see Brand, Ruiz, & Padilla, 1974; Milner, 1983, for reviews). Although these studies have been criticised on methodological and theoretical grounds (e.g., Banks, 1976; Brand ct al., 1974), research in other settings, such as Hong Kong (Morland, 1969), New Zealand (Vaughan, 1964), and Britain (Milner, 1973) has reported similar results.

These differences between minority and majority group children were typically interpreted in terms of the nature of inter-ethnic relations in society and existing social structure. Social circumstances in the wider society were also used to interpret the results of later studies conducted in America that

---

2 The cognitive development perspective has most often been used for generating theories about ethnic identity development in children. Erikson's work on identity development has also been applied to ethnic identity but mainly to account for changes beyond childhood (e.g., Phinney, 1989; Weinreich, 1986). The same is true for the work of Cross (1991), who has proposed a stage-model based on the African-American experience.

showed a change in black children's racial self-identification, from the former ambivalence to a more consistent in-group identification and preference (e.g., Hraba & Grant, 1970; Mahan, 1976)[3]. This change was interpreted in terms of the changing situation of blacks in American society, expressed in "black pride" and civil rights movements (e.g., Fine & Bowers, 1984). However, most of these studies failed to examine social context variables as such. Changes in the wider society were used to interpret empirical results, but there remained the question as to how actual experiences in concrete settings affect children's ethnic identity (Rosenberg, 1979).

Examining the role of context more systematically is in agreement with some theories of human development, and also with the growing social psychological interest in the importance of situational conditions. In developmental psychology the ecological theory of Bronfenbrenner (1979), for example, gives priority to the environment. Bronfenbrenner stresses the role of interrelated and nested environmental structures, such as family, school, and society, in affecting the content and structure of development. In genetic social psychology (e.g., Emler & Ohana, 1993) the emphasis is on the construction of knowledge as a social process, and on meanings as social products; it is argued that theories of social cognition must go beyond the individualistic doctrine of the cognitive-developmental approach. And in social psychology, groups and group membership are seen as deriving their identity from a particular context, and approaches such as self-categorisation theory try to give a systematic account of the role of situational conditions.

INTERGROUP THEORIES

Social identity theory (SIT) and self-categorisation theory (SCT) offer many possibilities for examining children's social self-definitions and understanding of existing social relationships, in addition to psychological processes such as categorisation and the need for positive self-esteem. However, developmental studies using these theories have typically focused on intergroup relations rather than social identity as such, and have not examined the actual normative context, nor the role of status and cultural differences (e.g., Bennett, Sani, Lyons, & Barrett 1998; Bigler, Jones, & Lobliner, 1997; Nesdale, 2000; Powlishta, Serbin, Doyle, & White, 1994; Rutland, 1999; Yee & Brown, 1992).

Because SIT and SCT are presented extensively in Chapter 1, I will focus only on those aspects that are most relevant to the present discussion of ethnic identity. The starting point for the theories is the distinction between

---

3 When comparing earlier (Milner, 1973) and later studies (Davey & Mullin, 1980), a similar trend can be found in Britain.

personal and social identity. Personal identity refers to those idiosyncratic characteristics and qualities that define the individual in relation to other people, particularly in-group members. Social identity refers to social category memberships. Both personal and social identity are considered equally valid and authentic conceptions of the self and refer to different levels of self-definition. People are both individuals and social group members, and self-definition at the personal level and the group level is, psychologically speaking, equally real. The relevance of the distinction between personal and social identity lies in its differential consequences for perception, evaluation, and behaviour (see Brewer & Miller, 1996; Oakes, Haslam, & Turner, 1994, for reviews).

In conceptualising social identity, SIT and SCT have somewhat different emphases. SIT stresses that social identity is connected with and derives from the membership of emotionally significant social categories or groups (Tajfel, 1978), whereas in SCT the emphasis is on self-definitions. Hence, SIT stresses more the motivational and affective aspects of social identities, whereas SCT emphasises the situational and cognitive aspects. SCT is more concerned with the contextually sensitive ways in which self-categorisations become salient and less with group identification or the degree to which group membership is psychologically central and valued. Hence, the concept of *ethnic self-categorisation* emphasises the significance and consequences of a child's ethnicity within a particular context, whereas the concept of *ethnic identification* emphasises individual differences in the degree to which ethnicity develops in a psychologically central and valued group membership.

SCT does not deny the existence of more stable individual differences in the tendency to define oneself in group terms (Turner, 1999). Some people are more inclined than others to see themselves as a group member and some value their group membership more than others (e.g., R. Brown & Williams, 1984). From a self-categorisation perspective, measures of identification are useful for assessing the centrality and emotional value attached to a group membership. Group identification is an important factor affecting a person's readiness to use a social category for self-description. Identification reflects one of the psychological resources – together with individual motives, needs, and goals – that are used to make sense of oneself and others in a particular context. The momentary salience of particular self-categorisations is argued to be determined by the individual's readiness in interaction with the "fit" between situational cues in the real world and the normative expectations about group differences.

However, SCT's emphasis on context and variation implies that the theory has relatively little concern with explaining individual differences in group identification or the affective commitments to, in our case, the ethnic group. SIT and ideas developed in cross-cultural psychology are useful here.

Tajfel (1978) addressed the social psychology of ethnic minorities. He saw the unfavourable social position of a group as the defining principle of minority groups, and as the central issue for understanding minority identity.

That is, the "minority" aspect of ethnic minorities is considered central. Tajfel distinguished between numerical and psychological minorities, and defined the latter as a group that feels bound together by common traits that are held in low regard. He focused on the status differences between the majority and the minority group and addressed the question of the psychological effects of minority membership with respect to the threat to social identity that a minority position implies. He described how, depending on the perceived legitimacy and stability of the social system, individuals can accept or reject a negative social identity, and how minority groups may alter the valuation of their group through creativity or social competition (Tajfel & Turner, 1986).

Following this conceptualisation, social and developmental psychologists have investigated children's ethnic minority identity as an example of the more general effect of status differences between groups and its concomitant disadvantages, victimisation, and stigmatisation (e.g., Corenblum & Annis, 1993; Nesdale, 2001). Being a minority group member is seen as a threat to a positive social identity. Children can respond to this threat differently: One response is cross-ethnic identification, whereby minority group children distance themselves from their ethnic group and by doing so improve their self-feelings. Another response is accentuating positively valued differences between the in-group and out-groups, and strong and more lasting ethnic group identification (Branscombe, Schmitt, & Harvey, 1999; Cross, 1991).

Authors using SIT typically see ethnic awareness, identification, and group evaluations as reactions or responses to status differences and the predicaments of negative stereotypes, discrimination, and forms of racism. However, there are also limits to using an exclusively social position perspective. Ethnic identity is not composed simply of a minority status; treating it as such greatly limits the ability to examine and understand the richness of the meanings and experiences associated with this identity (Sellers, Smith, Shelton, Rowley, & Chavous, 1998). In focusing on the "minority" aspect, ethnic minority groups are treated as any low-status or powerless group to which the same social-psychological processes are applied. As a result, the "ethnic" aspect is ignored and there is a failure to theorise ethnicity.

In the social sciences, the notion of ethnicity is conceptualised in many different ways. However, almost all link ethnicity to history and culture, although in different ways (see Cornell & Hartman, 1998). Many social scientists follow Max Weber (1968) in emphasising that ethnicity is primarily a sense of belonging to particular (assumed) ancestry and origin (e.g., Cornell & Hartman, 1998; DeVos, 1995; Roosens, 1994). An ethnic group is thought to exist whenever the belief in common descent is used to bind people together to some degree. This sense of origin is often accomplished by defining ethnicity in terms of metaphors of kinship: Ethnicity is family writ large (D. L. Horowitz, 1985). In addition to ancestry, ethnicity is most often thought of as culture that is transmitted across generations.

Culture offers an important framework for interpreting the world.

Members of different cultures sample and interpret the environment differently. Many studies emphasise various cultural characteristics that shape perception and behaviour (e.g., Hofstede, 1980; Markus, Kitayama, & Heiman, 1999; Smith & Bond, 1993). For example, the most widely examined distinction in cross-cultural studies currently is between collectivism and individualism, which is studied not only at the cultural level but also at the individual level (Singelis, 1994; Triandis, Leung, Villareal, & Clack, 1985). Collectivism can be thought of as a worldview or interpretative frame that functions to focus attention and thinking. A collectivist worldview promotes the perception of self and others in terms of ascribed group membership, such as family and ethnicity: The group is the centre of the psychological field (Oyserman, 1993; Triandis, 1994). Enculturation in a more collectivist culture implies a relatively high group consciousness and a strong predisposition to identify with one's own ethnic group.

In our research we have focused on individual and ethnic group differences in perceived discrimination and in collectivism as a cultural value orientation. Furthermore, various studies on ethnic identity (e.g., Garza & Herringer, 1987; Phinney, 1990; Sellers et al., 1998), and social identity in general (e.g., Ellemers, Kortekaas, & Ouwerkerk, 1999; Jackson & Smith, 1999; Smith, Murphy, & Coats, 1999), have shown that different aspects of identity can be distinguished. In SIT, social identity is linked to the value and evaluative significance of group membership. This theory assumes that a group member is motivated by a need for positive self-esteem *as* a group member. In this chapter the focus is on this aspect of social identity for which the term ethnic self-esteem will be used (see Ellemers et al., 1999). Finally, in our research, characteristics of school settings have been used for examining the role of local situational circumstances. In particular, the ethnic composition of schools and normative issues related to multicultural education have been examined.

PERCEIVED DISCRIMINATION[4]

In social psychology, increasing attention is being paid to the phenomenology of being a target of prejudice and discrimination (see Crocker, Major, & Steele, 1998; Swim & Stangor, 1998). There is a growing interest in the minority member's or insider's perspective (Oyserman & Swim, 2001).

---

4 Experiences with discrimination are discussed here as more enduring or pervasive features that influence ethnic identification. However, discrimination can also be more incidental and situational (L. M. Brown, 1998; Verkuyten & Thijs, 2001) and therefore may affect contextual self-categorisations. Furthermore, the direction of the relationships between discrimination and identification is not fixed: Ethnic identification may also affect the perception of discrimination (Phinney, Madden, & Santos, 1998). For example, if a child perceives discrimination, he or she may suffer from a more negative sense of ethnic identity, which, in turn, may lead to increased sensitivity to others and to behaviour that elicits discriminatory responses from others.

However, these issues are typically examined with university student and adult samples, and not with children.

In a number of studies among older children we have investigated the issue of discrimination and its relationship with ethnic self-esteem. We started our investigation by examining children's own understandings of discrimination (Verkuyten, Kinket, & Van der Wielen, 1997). Using open-ended instruments and short stories, we found shared beliefs and ideas about when a specific act is considered discriminatory among both Dutch and ethnic minority children. According to the children, the prototypical example of discrimination was a situation in which a Dutch child called a minority child names. To a lesser degree, an unequal division of valued objects among contemporaries and social exclusion from play by peers were also seen as discrimination. In short, children's understanding about discrimination was predominantly in terms of peer relations and not on the level of the wider society. This understanding may be important for ethnic self-esteem. Studies by Harter (1999) have shown that (dis)approval from peers, such as classmates, is far more predictive of self-evaluations than is (dis)approval from one's close friends. Furthermore, in general, social exclusion is more strongly related to self-evaluation than is social inclusion (Leary & Baumeister, 2000).

A second step in our research was to investigate the perception of discrimination (in terms of ethnic name-calling and social exclusion by peers) by ethnic minority and Dutch children. In different studies we found a clear difference in perceived discrimination between both groups of children (Verkuyten, 2001; Verkuyten & Thijs, 2002). Turkish, Moroccan, and Surinamese children felt more discriminated against than did Dutch children. In addition, Turkish children reported higher discrimination than the other ethnic minority groups. This is in agreement with studies showing that the Turks are the group that is least liked by Dutch adolescents and adults (Hagendoorn, 1995) and by older children (Verkuyten & Kinket, 2000). These results show that not all ethnic minority groups face the same level of derogation and social exclusion. Ethnic minority groups are distinguishable from others in terms of their relationship to the majority group.

In different studies we further found that minority and majority group children perceive a higher level of discrimination directed at their group as a whole than at themselves as individual members of that group (Verkuyten, 2002b). Taylor, Wright, Moghaddam, and Lalonde (1990) have labelled this phenomenon the personal/group discrimination discrepancy (PGD). This discrepancy is a robust finding among an array of (disadvantaged) groups and using different wordings of questions (see Taylor, Wright, & Porter, 1993). Several explanations have been offered for this phenomenon, such as the denial of personal discrimination, the exaggeration of discrimination directed at the group as a whole, and basic features of information processing. Whatever the explanation, the phenomenon seems real and our results show that it is not restricted to students and adults. Children in late childhood also make a clear distinction between the personal and group level. This has also been found by Rosenberg (1979), who established that children may agree with ethnic stereotypes about their group without believing that these characterise them personally. Thus, although we found minority group children to perceive far more discrimination both directed at their group and at themselves as members of that group, both minority and majority group children showed the discrepancy between personal and group discrimination.

Most authors argue for a close relationship between ethnic identity and the existence of prejudice and discrimination. Discrimination is considered one of the major factors affecting ethnic minority identity (e.g., Cross, 1991; Keefe, 1992). In our studies we have found a clear negative relationship between perceived discrimination (name-calling and social exclusion) and ethnic self-esteem, particularly among Turkish children (Verkuyten & Thijs, 2000, 2002b). When children experience more ethnic discrimination they evaluate their ethnic identity less positively. Furthermore, personal discrimination was found to affect ethnic identification negatively (Verkuyten, 2002b). In addition, perceived group discrimination affected ethnic self-esteem negatively, but only among children who considered their ethnic identity an important part of the self.

Thus, ethnic name-calling and exclusion from play because of one's ethnicity are more common experiences for ethnic minority group children and have a negative impact on their ethnic self-evaluation. This does not imply, however, that for these children ethnic identity is psychologically less central and more negative compared to the majority group. On the contrary, discrimination can be one of the reasons why ethnicity is a very central identity (Keefe, 1992). Numerous authors have argued that ethnic identity is crucial or at least central to the self-concept and psychological functioning of ethnic minorities (see Cross, 1991; Liebkind, 1992; Phinney, 1990). We have found in several studies that ethnic identity is more important for minority than for Dutch children, and that discrimination has a modest but significant positive correlation (around .20) with the importance that children attach to their ethnic identity (Verkuyten & Thijs, 2000).

In addition, different studies in the Netherlands have consistently found that children of ethnic minority groups evaluate their group membership more positively and feel more committed to their group than do majority group children (see Verkuyten, 1999, for a review). One possible explanation for these findings is in terms of SIT. According to SIT, children who strongly identify with their group are motivated to evaluate their own group positively in comparison to other groups. For these children, the group membership has important implications for the self-concept, and as such for the striving for a positive self. Minority status and discrimination are considered to be a threat to a positive ethnic identity and that threat can be counteracted by accentuating positive distinctiveness and stronger in-group identification.

Empirical results, also in the Netherlands, indicate that children typically demonstrate a positive bias towards their own ethnic group, and do not necessarily evaluate out-groups negatively (Cameron, Alvarez, Ruble, &

Fuligni, 2001; Verkuyten, 1999). Furthermore, among ethnic minority group children, in-group identification and positive in-group evaluation are often not accompanied by stronger intergroup differentiation. Ethnic identification is typically related to in-group preference rather than to out-group dislike (see Verkuyten, 1999).

There are some important assumptions to the SIT explanation of strong group identification and positive in-group evaluation among ethnic minority groups. One assumption is that ethnic minority children define and evaluate their identity in relation to the dominant majority group (Vaughan, 1987). In SIT, the emphasis is often on dichotomous and competitive intergroup comparisons whereby the majority group is implicitly assumed to be the only really significant other (Spielman, 2000). However, minority group children may value their ethnic identity because of supportive relationships with other in-group members and because they prefer similarities over differences (Brewer, 1999; Cameron et al., 2001; Fishbein, 1996). In addition, most ethnic minority groups have their own rich history, culture, and traditions. These are important sources for developing pride and satisfaction in one's ethnic background and a positive ethnic identity (Hutnik, 1991). Ethnic minority groups are "ethnic" from the inside and have their own social networks and sources for a positive ethnic identity. Furthermore, ethnic minority group parents are often in a position of striving to sustain cultural values and traditions that are different from the values of the society in which they live. For example, Turkish parents in the Netherlands are, in general, very concerned with transmitting their traditions, history, and cultural values to their children (e.g., De Vries, 1987; Nijsten, 1998). From birth on, the child's intimate contact is with members of his or her group. So, for example, Turkish children know from early experience that stereotypes such as Turkish people being unfriendly, dishonest, and lazy are not true. They learn to value Turkish people and Turkish culture from early on and develop an intimate knowledge of the way Turkish people are.

In a study among Turkish and Dutch participants, we found among the former, but not among the latter group, a positive correlation between children's ethnic self-esteem and parental intergroup attitudes (Verkuyten, 2002a). Furthermore, ethnic minority group children who have poor cultural knowledge tend to reject their ethnic identity (Bagley & Coard, 1975). In addition, similar to ethnic minority group differences in social status positions and experiences with discrimination, there can also be cultural differences between minority groups that may account for differences in ethnic identification. For example, Milner (1973) found stronger in-group identification among Asian than West Indian children living in Britain. He argued that "the more autonomous, self-reliant Asian communities and the traditional family-life of their members promote a more positive identity in the Asian child" (p. 293).

CULTURAL ORIENTATIONS

From the position of genetic social psychology, cognition must be seen as being embedded in historical, cultural, and sociorelational contexts. People who are members of the same culture or group will share the contents of thought in the form of shared knowledge and beliefs (Emler, 1987; Moscovici, 1984). Cognitions are not purely individual constructions, but are greatly influenced by the kinds of beliefs available in the child's surrounding environment.

Existing studies on self-identification assume that individual children differ in their psychological group membership: Children identify more or less strongly with their ethnic group. However, this assumption may not be equally adequate for minority groups with a more collectivistic culture in which the interdependence of in-group members is emphasised. In these cultures group membership may be far less negotiable and "the question of why individuals become committed to groups and identify with them is unlikely to be asked" (Markus et al., 1999, p. 900). Children may become attached to a group for interpersonal reasons, and being committed to the group can be more a self-evident matter and an issue of duty and moral obligation. This is particularly likely to happen with ethnic groups that are defined in terms of common ancestry and family-origin metaphors (Roosens, 1994). However, in studies among ethnic minority children, individual differences in ethnic identification are nonetheless found and these may be related to individual differences in cultural value orientations.

In different studies we have examined the issue of collectivism and its relationship with ethnic self-esteem. Cultural tendencies towards collectivism have different aspects including subordination of own goals to the goals of others, concern for the in-group, interdependence and sociability, and family connectedness. Collectivist cultures emphasise the interconnected nature of the self, group solidarity and sharing, stable and predetermined relationships, and family harmony and dependency (e.g., Triandis, 1994). Collectivism can be studied both at the cultural and individual level. To distinguish clearly between these levels, Triandis et al. (1985) refer to collectivism at the personal level as allocentrism. In our studies we have predominantly focused on family allocentrism, which is considered a central aspect of collectivism. Family allocentrism is probably also one of the most meaningful dimensions for children and its importance has been highlighted in cross-cultural work (Kağitçibaşi, 1990). Furthermore, in the context of acculturation processes, the family plays an important role and family allocentrism has been found to have significant implications for immigrant experiences and ethnic identity (Lay et al., 1998; Phinney & Rosenthal, 1992).

Ethnic minority groups in the Netherlands, such as Turks and Moroccans, are originally from more collectivist cultures (Hofstede, 1980). Hence, as a group Turkish and Moroccan children can be expected to endorse collectivist values more strongly than the Dutch. In several studies we have indeed found this to be the case (Verkuyten, 2001), and this is also found among young adolescents (e.g., Huiberts, Vollebergh, & Meeus, 1999; Verkuyten & Masson, 1996).

This group difference in collectivism may (partly) explain the finding that compared to the majority group, minority group children perceive more ethnic discrimination. Collectivism implies attentiveness to group members. The group operates as a cognitive schema that influences perception with a relatively high awareness and attention to information related to one's group, such as a heightened sensitivity to ethnic-relevant information. In two studies we found a significant correlation between family allocentrism and perceived discrimination (Verkuyten, 2002b). Independent of ethnic identification, higher allocentrism was associated with more perceived personal and group discrimination. This relationship was found for different ethnic groups, including the Dutch. It suggests that for children high on allocentrism, the in-group is part of the self and the group functions as a cognitive schema that influences perception. Compared to children low on allocentrism, attention is more focused on group-related information involving a greater attentiveness and sensitivity to one's ethnic group and ethnic group membership.

Using open-ended instruments, different studies among older samples have examined group differences in collectivism in relation to self-descriptions. These studies have found that collectivist groups give self-descriptions that include more social identities, including ethnic identity (e.g., Cousins, 1989; Rhee, Uleman, Lee, & Roman, 1995). However, there are only a few studies among children (e.g., Rotenberg & Cranwell, 1989): An example is Van Den Heuvel, Tellegen, and Koomen (1992), who found that Turkish and Moroccan children referred more to social group memberships compared to Dutch children, who gave more self-descriptions related to psychological characteristics. Another example is our own research, in which we found that Turkish children gave more ethnic self-descriptions than Dutch contemporaries (Kinket & Verkuyten, 1997). Hence, cultural differences between ethnic groups seem to be related to the type of ethnic self-descriptions. This is also true at the level of the individual child. Controlling for discrimination, we found among Turkish and Dutch children a positive association between family allocentrism and ethnic self-descriptions (Verkuyten, 1999).

Ethnic group differences in collectivism may further explain (in part) the differences found for ethnic self-esteem. The fact that, in general, ethnic minority group children evaluate their ethnic identity more positively may be due to their stronger collectivist worldview. This relationship can also be examined at the individual level. Because allocentric individuals are more likely to define themselves in relation to their in-group, evaluations of in-group membership is particularly important for their well-being. In different studies among ethnic minority and Dutch children we found a positive cor-relation (around .30) between family allocentrism and ethnic self-esteem (Verkuyten, 2001, 2002b). Moreover, this association was found after control-ling for perceived discrimination. Hence, higher allocentrism was related to a more positive ethnic identity. Furthermore, both discrimination and allocentrism had independent effects on ethnic self-esteem, showing the importance of taking both kinds of factors into account simultaneously.

ETHNIC SELF-ESTEEM AND CONTEXT

Identification with a group is typically conceptualised as an individual differ-ence variable representing some kind of stable self-structure or trait-like aspect that is expressed independently of the social situation (e.g., Crocker & Luhtanen, 1990). The idea is that particular group memberships will develop a central and more or less fixed place in children's self-understanding. Hence, identification is, by definition, relatively independent from context. This does not mean, however, that children will always feel the same about their ethnic group membership across situations. It only means that ethnic identity is not strongly governed by situational influences. Situational variability will exist, but gradually the child will probably also develop a more stable affective and evaluative attitude towards his or her ethnic background. This would mean that the value and emotional significance that children attach to their ethnic identity will not differ much between situations.

To my knowledge there are no studies that have examined the temporal stability of ethnic self-esteem among children, nor whether children evaluate their ethnic identity differently across relational contexts. In our research we have examined the context dependency of ethnic self-esteem by studying classroom contexts. This research was conducted within classrooms so that the class context was salient. In three studies involving more than 200 class-rooms, we investigated ethnic self-esteem using multilevel modelling. Multi-level modelling allows the simultaneous analysis of individual and group level variables without compromising the quality of the information at any level (Kenny, Kashy, & Bolger, 1998)[5]. In our research the samples consisted of school classes and children within these classes: The children are nested within their classes. Hence, ethnic self-esteem is explained by children's indi-vidual characteristics and by properties of the classroom. A significant effect found at the level of the classroom indicates that the similarity in ethnic self-esteem between children in the same classroom is greater than between children in different classes.

In three different studies we found a very similar result (Verkuyten, 2001;

---

5 Multilevel analysis is also necessary because there are statistical disadvantages to handling contextual variables at the individual level. Assigning group level variables to individuals may lead to spurious significant results because the standard errors, which are based on the higher number of disaggregated cases, are too small. Hence, originally small differences between contexts will become significant because of an increased number of observations. Further-more, groups, and in particular classes in school, are hardly ever formed randomly and chil-dren that belong to the same class will share many experiences. Therefore, the assumption of independence of observations is often violated (Kenny & Judd, 1984).

Verkuyten & Thijs, 2003). In all three, the multilevel analysis indicated that the class-level variance was significant for ethnic self-esteem. In some classes children evaluated their ethnic identity more positively than in others. However, in all three, the percentage of the variance explained by the grouping structure was low (between 6.9% and 8.2%). Hence, the within-class variance (between 93.1% and 91.8%) was much larger than the between-class variance. Therefore individual factors clearly explained more variance in ethnic self-esteem than did classroom features[6]. Thus, although ethnic self-esteem was affected by the school setting, it predominantly depended on individual characteristics. This is not to say that ethnic self-esteem is some kind of fixed or stable personality characteristic that is chronically salient across situations and expressed independently of social circumstances. It merely suggests that measures of ethnic self-esteem reflect individual differences in the affective and evaluative involvement in one's ethnic group and thereby in the child's readiness to self-categorise in ethnic terms.

ETHNIC SELF-CATEGORISATION

For SCT, the context dependency of self-categorisation is central. The theory is concerned with explaining the extent to which, in our case, one's ethnicity is psychologically salient at a *particular moment* and in a *particular situation*. Following this idea, it can be expected that children's ethnic self-definitions will strongly depend – and depend more strongly than ethnic self-esteem – on the actual social situation.

In a study among Turkish and Dutch children we investigated this idea in relation to the classroom context (Kinket & Verkuyten, 1997). Children were asked to give 10 self-descriptions. Answers referring explicitly to ethnic group membership were coded. Most of the children (65%) did not refer to their ethnicity when asked to describe themselves. However, the multilevel analysis indicated that the between-class variance was significant. As much as 44% of the variance in ethnic self-descriptions was explained by the grouping structure. Hence, independently of individual differences, children were far more likely in some classes than in others to refer to their ethnicity in their spontaneous self-descriptions. The salience of ethnicity was highly sensitive to the context of the classroom situation. Thus, compared to ethnic self-esteem, the self-definition depended more strongly on who was present and on the way the context was defined. One classroom characteristic that affected ethnic

---

6 Of the different classroom characteristics, ethnic composition, as well as educational issues, had an effect. For example, Turkish children evaluated their ethnic group membership more positively when the percentage of Turkish classmates was higher. Ethnic self-esteem was also more positive in classes where the importance of multicultural issues was stressed and teachers reacted to incidences of ethnic harassment with sanctioning of the perpetrator. A full discussion of these and other effects can be found in the articles.

self-description was the percentage of in-group pupils. The Turkish children were more likely to use ethnicity in their self-descriptions when the percentage of Turkish classmates was higher. The trend was reversed for the Dutch children: They were more likely to describe themselves in ethnic terms when the number of Dutch pupils was lower.

According to SCT, self-categorisation involves depersonalisation of self-perception leading to self-stereotyping or the perception of increased similarity between the self and typical in-group members. As argued earlier, ethnic self-esteem is a main factor determining self-categorisation. Thus, the extent to which children value their group membership and commit themselves to their group can be expected to be related to the perception of similarity and prototypicality of the self in relation to the group. Children who identify with or commit themselves strongly to their ethnic group may have a greater tendency to self-stereotype.

In a study among Dutch and Turkish children we examined this expectation (Verkuyten, 1999). Our focus was not on self-stereotyping in terms of specific group traits and attributes but on the perception of general prototypicality. Self-stereotyping was assessed in terms of one's general similarity to other children of one's ethnic group and the extent to which children consider themselves a typical group member. Principal components analysis showed that ethnic self-esteem is empirically distinguishable from self-stereotyping. Further, Turkish children exhibited a significantly higher level of self-stereotyping than the Dutch. However, among both groups there was a similar significant association between ethnic self-esteem and self-stereotyping ($r = .38$, $p < .001$). As expected, higher ethnic self-esteem was related to stronger ethnic self-stereotyping. Hence, children who identify strongly with their ethnic group had a greater tendency to self-stereotype.

In summary, compared to ethnic self-esteem, ethnic self-definition is strongly dependent on the social context. The former seems to reflect the centrality and affective meaning of one's ethnic group membership, which determines children's readiness to define themselves in ethnic terms and to see themselves as typical group members. However, whether the child in a particular situation actually self-categorises in ethnic terms depended not only on ethnic identification. Various personal needs, motives and goals are important in interaction with the normative expectations about group differences and the distribution of stimuli in the social context, such as the number of classmates from one's own ethnic group.

ETHNIC SELF-CATEGORISATION AND BEHAVIOUR

Although differences in ethnic identification are of central interest to the social identity perspective, self-categorisation is considered to constitute the psychological basis for behaviour. According to SCT, social categories influence behaviour when individuals define themselves in terms of those categories. It is argued that when a given identity is salient, children will think and act in terms of those beliefs and standards that define the salient identity. Hence, when identities change, beliefs and standards change and, therefore, perceptions and judgments will also change. This section of the chapter discusses two experimental studies that illustrate this process. In the first, the distinction between personal and ethnic identity was used; the second concerned social identities of bicultural children.

The first study set out to examine peer victimisation in relation to the distinction between personal and social identity (see Verkuyten & Thijs, 2001). Studies on peer victimisation typically do not consider ethnic discrimination (see Hawker & Boulton, 2000), whereas studies on peer group discrimination do not consider other forms of victimisation. However, in order to understand the precise role of discrimination, other forms of victimisation should be considered. A distinction between personal and ethnic victimisation may be particularly useful. Personal victimisation refers to those situations where negative peer experiences are related to individual characteristics, such as acting "strange" and stuttering. Ethnic group victimisation occurs when children's negative experiences are connected to their ethnic group membership.

This distinction between personal and group victimisation is related to the distinction between personal and social identity. Applying the personal-social distinction to feelings of self-worth, we focused on personal self-esteem and ethnic self-esteem. Differences in personal and ethnic self-esteem were expected to predict self-reported peer victimisation. In order to examine this prediction, we elicited self-reports on experiences with either personal or ethnic victimisation. Following SIT and SCT, self-reported victimisation was expected to be related to self-esteem at the same level of abstraction. Hence, it was predicted that personal self-esteem and not ethnic self-esteem would be negatively related to self-reported personal victimisation. On the other hand, ethnic self-esteem, and not personal self-esteem, was expected to be negatively related to group victimisation. These predictions were tested in an experimental questionnaire study among 106 Turkish children. As expected, it was found that personal self-esteem negatively predicted personal victimisation but not ethnic victimisation, and ethnic self-esteem tended to predict reports of ethnic victimisation but not personal victimisation.

In addition, to examine the causal effects of both personal and ethnic victimisation, we assessed momentary self-feelings directly after self-reported peer victimisation. It was expected that peer victimisation would have a negative effect on momentary self-feelings, independently of the level of personal and ethnic self-esteem. Furthermore, in order to examine the possible different effects of personal and ethnic victimisation, a between-subjects design was used with two conditions. For one group of Turkish children, experiences with personal victimisation were elicited, whereas for the other group ethnic victimisation was made salient. We explored whether personal and ethnic victimisation differ in their negative impact on momentary self-feelings. In contrast to personal victimisation, ethnic victimisation is more specific for ethnic minority children than for children of the majority group. Hence, compared to personal victimisation, ethnic victimisation may be more strongly related to negative self-feelings. The results showed that peer victimisation had a negative causal effect on momentary self-feelings independent of the level of personal and ethnic self-esteem. In addition, peer victimisation based on ethnic group membership had a somewhat stronger negative effect on self-feelings than victimisation based on personal characteristics.

The second example is a study in which we examined the effect of social identity salience on bicultural children's self-evaluations. Ethnic minority group children not only belong to their own ethnic group but are often also citizens of the country where they were born, live, and where their future is. These children have to deal with the expectations and demands of their own ethnic group as well as those of the majority group. Beliefs and standards that are valued and learnt within the ethnic in-group may differ from beliefs and standards that are stressed in society and its institutions such as schools. Children have to learn to adapt to this bicultural situation. Different models have been proposed for describing and understanding these adaptation processes, such as alternation and fusion models (see LaFromboise, Coleman, & Gerton, 1993). However, little is known about why children shift between these frameworks and what the consequences of these shifts are. One possibility is that this switching occurs in response to contextual cues that activate different social identities.

SCT argues that when a given identity is salient, beliefs and standards that define that salient identity will govern people's thinking and acting. Hence, changes in identities imply changes in beliefs and standards leading to changes in perceptions and judgments. As argued earlier, ethnic differences are predominantly understood in terms of culture. Many studies have found ethnic group differences in cultural value orientations, such as collectivism and individualism (e.g., Gaines et al., 1997; Rotenberg & Cranwell, 1989). These cultural orientations influence perceptions and judgments, including self-evaluations (see Markus et al., 1999). For example, in self-description tasks, people in individualistic cultures are more likely than those in collectivist cultures to make self-enhancing statements. However, a self-evaluation motive is not necessarily absent in collectivist cultures. Members of these cultures are more likely to evaluate their social identities favourably, whereas in individualist cultures, personal identities are more likely to be evaluated positively (Hetts, Sakuma, & Pelham, 1999; Pelham & Hetts, 1999). Furthermore, Hetts and colleagues have argued, and found among ethnic minority groups, that these tendencies are most evident for more indirect or implicit measures of self-evaluation. These measures are thought to reflect people's nonconscious feelings about the self that are related to the normative beliefs and values learnt in early socialisation. Explicit self-evaluations are more transparent and are probably more dependent on the current social and cultural context (Greenwald & Banaji, 1995). Hence at the more conscious level, ethnic minorities will probably endorse the kind of favourable conceptions of the self that are promoted in individualistic cultures, such as self-enhancement.

Following SCT and these findings on cultural differences, it can be expected that bicultural children will evaluate themselves and their group differently depending on whether their ethnic minority identity or Dutch identity is salient. In particular, when ethnic identity is salient a more positive implicit evaluation of social identity can be expected, whereas personal identity will be more positive when Dutch identity is salient. For explicit questions on self-enhancement few or no differences can be expected.

To test these predictions we conducted a study among 74 bicultural Greek-Dutch children[7] (Verkuyten & Pouliasi, 2002). Greek culture has been found to be more collectivist than the Dutch one (Hofstede, 1980). For priming ethnic and Dutch identity we used iconic cultural symbols and language. That is, similar to the work of Hong, Morris, Chiu, and Benet-Martinez (2000), we randomly presented Greek-Dutch children with either Dutch icons (e.g., national flag, windmills) or Greek icons (e.g., national flag, Acropolis) in the Dutch and Greek language respectively. The combination of icons and language was considered an effective means of activating the two different identities. For more implicit measures of personal and ethnic self-evaluation we asked the children about their feelings about the words "I" and "We" (Hetts et al., 1999). The results were in agreement with the expectations. Compared to the Dutch identity condition, in the Greek condition, the children had a significantly more positive response to "We" and a more negative response to "I". Hence, depending on the salient social identity, the more implicit evaluation of the personal and social self differed. In contrast, for the explicit measure of self-enhancement, no significant difference between the two conditions was found.[8]

---

7 Dutch children and Greek children in Greece also participated in this study, for two reasons. First, finding a difference in self-evaluations between the Greek and the Dutch identity priming conditions does not necessarily reflect cultural identity switching. One alternative interpretation for a more positive social identity evaluation in the Greek condition is that the minority position of the in-group in the Netherlands is made salient. As argued by SIT, in such a situation people can respond by emphasising their social identity and accentuating positive in-group distinctiveness. A cultural interpretation is more convincing when the result for Greek identity activation among bicultural children is similar to that for Greek children in Greece, and the result for Dutch identity activation is similar to that for Dutch children. This was found to be the case. Second, by including a sample of monocultural Dutch children and Greek children in Greece, it can be examined whether there are indeed significant cultural differences in collectivism between the children of both societies. This was also the case.

8 These results can, of course, be interpreted in different ways. One is in terms of an explicit structural model in which the personal and social self are seen as cognitively represented and stored in two distinct "baskets" (Trafimow, Triandis, & Goto, 1991). Another explanation is

CONCLUSION

This chapter has tried to make a case for the inclusion of social context when studying ethnic identity among children. Most writers agree that the social context plays a central role, but few empirical studies have addressed this issue. The present discussion has been on cultural and status differences between ethnic groups and actual local conditions. An understanding of ethnic minority identity requires explicit attention to cultural characteristics and negative social circumstances, such as discrimination, in relation to concrete environmental influences.

Theoretically, the development of ethnic identity is typically studied from a social-cognitive perspective. Although the models differ somewhat, they all describe an age-related progression in the ability to perceive and interpret ethnic differences (see Aboud, 1988; Brown, 1995; Phinney & Rotheram, 1987, for reviews). The focus is on processes and abilities and the theoretical result is a sequence of steps or stages in the development of aspects of cognition. This perspective has been fruitful for describing and explaining the development of ethnic identity, but there are also challenges. For example, it is unclear to what extent these models are applicable to children from ethnic minority groups (R. Brown, 1995; Coll et al., 1996). Furthermore, general developments in the structural complexity of children's thinking and the way children process information and acquire knowledge do not say much about the *particular* beliefs, knowledge, and attitudes children acquire or express. This depends on what is available and common in children's social environments. Cognition is embedded in historical, cultural, and sociorelational contexts (see Resnick, Levine, & Teasley, 1991; Thompson & Fine, 1999). Ethnic identity does not only depend on cognitive structures and processes but is also determined by social beliefs and context. Although there are important exceptions (e.g., Bronfenbrenner, 1979; Emler, 1987), developmental psychology has typically elaborated the internal, psychological aspects of development. The emphasis is on psychological rather than social processes. However, as I have tried to show, social information about status differences, cultural values, and situational conditions play an important role in children's ethnic self-understanding.

In social psychology, SIT and particularly SCT emphasise the importance

---

offered by Hong et al. (2000), who present a more dynamic constructivist rather than structural model for understanding what they call frame switching in bicultural individuals. They argue that culture is not internalised in the form of an integrated structure but rather as domain-specific knowledge, such as implicit theories. Furthermore, individuals would be able to acquire more than one cultural frame, but these frames will not simultaneously guide thinking. Accessibility of constructs and contextual salience are the concepts used by Hong et al. to explain how particular pieces of cultural knowledge become operative in particular situations. These ideas are quite similar to SCT and offer the possibility to connect SCT with theories developed in cross-cultural work.

of the social context. These theories are very useful for examining how children make sense of ethnic differences in particular social settings. Ethnic self-categorisation is considered to be a function of the relative size and status of the group, and the cultural and normative meanings associated with particular social categories in interaction with the child's readiness to make ethnic distinctions. This chapter has used these ideas for presenting some of the results of our studies on ethnic minority children in the Netherlands. The separate studies can be interpreted in different ways, but the findings as a whole can be understood in terms of these social-psychological theories. The research supports some of the key ideas of these theories, but also raises additional issues and questions.

For example, perceived discrimination and collectivism were examined as two central conditions for the development of ethnic identity among minority groups. Both have an effect on children's ethnic identification. This shows that not only the "minority" or structural aspect of ethnic minorities – which is stressed by SIT – but also the "ethnic" or cultural aspect needs to be considered.

There are also limitations to the way intergroup theories are typically presented and used. In many countries around the world, ethnic group situations consist of a series of groups that differ in cultural background and in which ethnicity or related characteristics such as race, language, and religion are criteria for group differences. Studies drawing upon SIT have a tendency, however, to focus exclusively on status differences between the majority and minority groups. A majority–minority dichotomy is typically used, in which there is a tendency to treat minority groups as a homogeneous category. Differences between ethnic minority groups and within-group differences are often not considered.

Obviously, there are important differences between the group of majority children and that of minority children. For example, minorities perceive, in general, more personal and group discrimination than majority group children do. Hence, minority group children seem to be well aware of their group's lower status and do not deny the existence of personal discrimination. Not all minority groups, however, are perceived in the same way. Studies in various countries have found that different minority groups experience varying degrees of social acceptability (see Hagendoorn, 1995; Owen, Eisner, & McFaul, 1981, for reviews). For example, in the Netherlands, studies on children, adolescents, and adults have found that the Turks are the least liked minority group (Hagendoorn, 1995; Verkuyten & Kinket, 2000). In agreement with this finding, Turkish children have been found to perceive more personal and group discrimination than, for example, Moroccan and Surinamese children. Furthermore, the negative relationship between discrimination and ethnic self-esteem is most evident among the Turks. In addition, there are also many visible and cultural features that shape the everyday life and life experiences of ethnic minority groups differently. Turkish children have been found, for example, to have a more collectivist value orientation compared to Surinamese children. Also, related to their Islamic background, gender differentiation is more evident on the level of beliefs and actual practices among the Turks and Moroccans than among, for example, the Surinamese. In fact, among the two Islamic groups, there is a strong association between gender and ethnicity. Turkish and Moroccan people in the Netherlands partly define their identity in terms of their cultural specific beliefs about gender roles.

Thus, for understanding the development of ethnic identity, it is not only differences between the majority group and the minorities as a group that are relevant, but also differences between ethnic minority groups. In addition, there are individual differences – such as experiences with discrimination and in collectivism – that highlight the need to examine distinctions among children in general and within the same ethnic group in particular. Attention to between-group differences should not lead to overlooking within-group heterogeneity (Celious & Oyserman, 2001). Hence, to understand the development of ethnic identity it is necessary to pay attention to within-group differences, in addition to differences between ethnic minority groups, between the majority group and ethnic minorities, and also to more basic capacities and tendencies that pervade across ethnic lines. Furthermore, there are not only ethnic distinctions but also differences associated with other important characteristics, such as gender (Celious & Oyserman, 2001; Frable, 1997). In addition, ethnic identity is a multidimensional construct. Its various components may develop differently and be related differently to self-perceptions (e.g., Garza & Herringer, 1987; Phinney, 1990).

SIT and SCT emphasise the role of social context but say little about the development of ethnic identity. These theories do not systematically address developmental issues. SIT focuses on processes of social comparison and self-evaluation, and in SCT cognitive-developmental constraints are typically not considered. For SCT, development seems to be a question of growing flexibility in categorical judgments and increasing understanding and knowledge of the social meanings associated with social categories. However, the particular cognitive and affective correlates of children's social understandings and of their proclivity to ethnic self-definitions are not addressed. The emphasis is on the processes of category use in context, and not on how self-understandings are conceptually organised and change in structure with age[9]. Cognitive-developmental theories make a contribution here because they try to account for qualitative reorganisations in children's ideas and feelings about themselves (Corenblum & Annis, 1993). Hence, cognitive theories are clearly important for understanding ethnic identity development. The same is

---

9 However, SCT presents a dynamic and functional approach to the self. The focus is on comparative, relational judgments that define people in their social context; that is, on self-conception rather than on a structured self-concept. Turner and Onorato (1999) have rejected structural models of the self for reasons of cognitive economy and for being unable to explain the formation of new categories (Turner, 1999).

true, for example, for theories that focus on social learning processes. However, as I have tried to argue, social-psychological intergroup theories offer a useful additional framework for examining ethnic identity in context. A focus on context provides an important perspective on the multifaceted question about how children learn to adapt to their ethnically diverse world, and the complex issue of ethnic self-understanding.

REFERENCES

Aboud, F. E. (1987). The development of ethnic self-identification and attitudes. In J. S. Phinney & M. J. Rotheram (Eds.), *Children's ethnic socialization: Pluralism and development* (pp. 32–55). Newbury Park, CA: SAGE Publications.

Aboud, F. (1988). *Children and prejudice*. Oxford: Blackwell.

Bagley, C., & Coard, B. (1975). Cultural knowledge and rejection of ethnic identity in West Indian children in London. In G. K. Verma & C. Bagley (Eds.), *Race and education across cultures* (pp. 321–331). London: Heinemann.

Banks, W. C. (1976). White preference in blacks: A paradigm in search of a phenomenon. *Psychological Bulletin, 83,* 1179–1186.

Bennett, M., Sani, F., Lyons, E., & Barrett, M. (1998). Children's subjective identification with the group and in-group favouritism. *Developmental Psychology, 34,* 902–909.

Bigler, R. S., Jones, L. C., & Lobliner, D. B. (1997). Social categorization and the formation of intergroup attitudes in children. *Child Development, 68,* 530–543.

Brand, E. S., Ruiz, R. A., & Padilla, A. M. (1974). Ethnic identification and preference: A review. *Psychological Bulletin, 81,* 860–890.

Branscombe, N. R., Schmitt, M. T., & Harvey, R. D. (1999). Perceiving pervasive discrimination among African Americans: Implications for group identification and well-being. *Journal of Personality and Social Psychology, 77,* 135–149.

Brewer, M. B. (1999). The psychology of prejudice: In-group love or out-group hate? *Journal of Social Issues, 55,* 429–444.

Brewer, M. B., & Miller, N. (1996). *Intergroup relations*. Buckingham, UK: Open University Press.

Bronfenbrenner, U. (1979). *The ecology of human development: Experiments by nature and design*. Cambridge, MA: Harvard University Press.

Brown, L. M. (1998). Ethnic stigma as a contextual experience: A possible selves perspective. *Personality and Social Psychology Bulletin, 24,* 163–172.

Brown, R. (1995). *Prejudice: Its social psychology*. Oxford: Blackwell.

Brown, R. (2000). Social identity theory: Past achievements, current problems and future challenges. *European Journal of Social Psychology, 30,* 745–778.

Brown, R., & Williams, J. A. (1984). Group identification: The same thing to all people. *Human Relations, 37,* 547–564.

Cameron, J. A., Alvarez, J. M., Ruble, D. N., & Fuligni, A. J. (2001). Children's lay theories about in-groups and out-groups: Reconceptualizing research on prejudice. *Personality and Social Psychology Review, 5,* 118–128.

Celious, A., & Oyserman, D. (2001). Race from the inside: An emerging heterogeneous race model. *Journal of Social Issues, 57,* 149–165.

Clark, K. B., & Clark, M. P. (1947). Racial identification and preference in Negro children. In T. M. Newcombe & E. L. Hartley (Eds.), *Readings in social psychology* (pp. 169–178). New York: Holt, Rinehart & Winston.

Coll, C. G., Lamberty, G., Jenkins, R., McAdoo, H. P., Crnic, K., Wasik, B. H., & Garcia, H. V. (1996). An integrative model for the study of developmental competencies in minority children. *Child Development, 67*, 1891–1914.

Corenblum, B., & Annis, R. C. (1993). Development of racial identity in minority and majority children: An affect discrepancy model. *Canadian Journal of Behavioral Science, 25*, 499–521.

Cornell, S., & Hartmann, D. (1998). *Ethnicity and race: Making identities in a changing world.* London: Pine Forge Press.

Cousins, S. D. (1989). Culture and self-perception in Japan and the United States. *Journal of Personality and Social Psychology, 56*, 124–131.

Crocker, J., & Luhtanen, R. (1990). Collective self-esteem and in-group bias. *Journal of Personality and Social Psychology, 58*, 60–67.

Crocker, J., Major, B., & Steele, C. (1998). Social stigma. In D. T. Gilbert, S. T. Fiske, & G. Lindzey (Eds.), *The handbook of social psychology* (4th ed., pp. 504–553). New York: McGraw-Hill.

Cross, W. E. (1991). *Shades of Black: Diversity in African-American identity.* Philadelphia, PA: Temple University Press.

Davey, A. G., & Mullin, P. N. (1980). Ethnic identification and preference of British primary school children. *Journal of Child Psychology and Psychiatry, 21*, 241–251.

DeVos, G. A. (1995). Ethnic pluralism, conflict and accommodation. In L. Romanucci-Ross & G. DeVos (Eds.), *Ethnic identity: Creation, conflict and accommodation* (pp. 15–47). Walnut Creek, CA: AltaMira.

DeVries, M. (1987). *Ogen in je rug.* Alphen aan den Rijn, The Netherlands: Samsom.

Ellemers, N., Kortekaas, P., & Ouwekerk, J. W. (1999). Self-categorisation, commitment to the group and group self-esteem as related but distinct aspects of social identity. *European Journal of Social Psychology, 29*, 371–189.

Emler, N. (1987). Socio-moral development from the perspective of social representations. *Journal for the Theory of Social Behaviour, 17*, 371–388.

Emler, N., & Ohana, J. (1993). Studying social representations in children. In G. M. Breakwell & D. V. Canter (Eds.), *Empirical approaches to social representations* (pp. 63–89). Oxford: Clarendon.

Fine, M., & Bowers, C. (1984). Racial self-identification: The effects of social history and gender. *Journal of Applied Social Psychology, 14*, 136–146.

Fishbein, H. D. (1996). *Peer prejudice and discrimination: Evolutionary, cultural, and developmental dynamics.* Boulder, CO: Westview Press.

Frable, D. E. S. (1997). Gender, racial, ethnic, sexual, and class identities. *Annual Review of Psychology, 48*, 139–162.

Gaines, S. O., Marelich, W. D., Bledsoe, K. L., Steers, W. N., Henderson, M. C., Granrose, C. S., Barájas, L., Hicks, D., Lyde, M., Takahashi, Y., Yum, N., Ríos, D. I., Garciá, B. F., Farris, K. R., & Page, M. S. (1997). Links between race/ethnicity and cultural values as mediated by racial/ethnic identity and moderated by gender. *Journal of Personality and Social Psychology, 72*, 1460–1476.

Garza, R. T., & Herringer, L. G. (1987). Social identity: A multidimensional approach. *The Journal of Social Psychology, 127*, 299–308.

Goodman, M. E. (1952). *Race awareness in young children*. New York: Macmillan.

Greenwald, A. G., & Banaji, M. R. (1995). Implicit social cognition: Attitudes, self-esteem, and stereotypes. *Psychological Review, 102*, 4–27.

Hagendoorn, L. (1995). Intergroup biases in multiple group systems: The perception of ethnic hierarchies. In W. Stroebe & M. Hewstone (Eds.), *European review of social psychology* (pp. 199–228). Chichester, UK: John Wiley & Sons.

Harter, S. (1999). *The construction of the self: A developmental perspective*. New York: Guilford Press.

Hawker, D. S. J., & Boulton, M. J. (2000). Twenty years' research on peer victimization and psychosocial maladjustment: A meta-analytic review of cross-sectional studies. *Journal of Child Psychology and Psychiatry, 41*, 441–455.

Hetts, J. J., Sakuma, M., & Pelham, B. W. (1999). Two roads to positive regard: Implicit and explicit self-evaluation and culture. *Journal of Experimental Social Psychology, 35*, 512–559.

Hofstede, G. (1980). *Culture's consequences*. Beverly Hills, CA: SAGE Publications.

Hong, Y.-Y., Morris, M. W., Chiu, C. Y., & Benet-Martinez, V. (2000). Multicultural minds: A dynamic constructivist approach to culture and cognition. *American Psychologist, 55*, 709–720.

Horowitz, D. L. (1985). *Ethnic groups in conflict*. Berkeley, CA: University of California Press.

Horowitz, E. L. (1939). Racial aspects of self-identification in nursery school children. *Journal of Psychology, 7*, 91–99.

Hraba, J., & Grant, G. (1970). Black is beautiful: A re-examination of racial preference and identification. *Journal of Personality and Social Psychology, 16*, 398–402.

Huiberts, A. M., Vollebergh, W. A. M., & Meeus, W. (1999). Individualisme en collectivisme bij Nederlandse, Turkse en Marokkaanse jongeren. *Tijdschrift voor Orthopedagogiek, 38*, 342–356.

Hutnik, N. (1991). *Ethnic minority identity*. Oxford: Clarendon.

Jackson, J. W., & Smith, E. R. (1999). Conceptualizing social identity: A new framework and evidence for the impact of different dimensions. *Personality and Social Psychology Bulletin, 25*, 120–135.

Kağitçibaşi, C. (1990). Family and socialisation in cross-cultural perspective: A model of change. In J. Berman (Ed.), *Nebraska symposium on motivation 1989: Cross-cultural perspectives*. Lincoln: University of Bebraska Press.

Kardiner, A., & Ovesey, L. (1951). *The mark of oppression*. New York: Norton.

Keefe, S. E. (1992). Ethnic identity: The domain of perceptions and attachment to ethnic groups and cultures. *Human Organization, 51*, 35–43.

Kenny, D. A., & Judd, C. M. (1984). Estimating the nonlinear and interactive effects of latent variables. *Psychological Bulletin, 96*, 201–210.

Kenny, D. A., Kashy, D. A., & Bolger, N. (1998). Data analysis in social psychology. In D. T. Gilbert, S. T. Fiske, & G. Lindzey (Eds.), *The handbook of social psychology* (4th ed., pp. 233–265). Boston, MA: McGraw-Hill.

Kinket, B., & Verkuyten, M. (1997). Levels of ethnic self-identification and social context. *Social Psychology Quarterly, 60*, 338–354.

LaFromboise, T., Coleman, H. L. K., & Gerton, J. (1993). Psychological impact of biculturalism: Evidence and theory. *Psychological Bulletin, 114*, 395–412.

Lay, C., Fairlie, P., Jackson, S., Ricci, T., Eisenberg, J., Sato, T., Teeäär, A., & Melamud, A. (1998). Domain-specific allocentrism–idiocentrism: A measure of family connectedness. *Journal of Cross-Cultural Psychology, 29*, 434–460.

Leary, M. R., & Baumeister, R. F. (2000). The nature and function of self-esteem: Sociometer theory. In M. Zanna (Ed.), *Advances in experimental social psychology, Vol. 32* (pp. 1–61). San Diego, CA: Academic Press.

Liebkind, K. (1992). Ethnic identity: Challenging the boundaries of social psychology. In G. M. Breakwell (Ed.), *Social psychology of identity and the self-concept.* London: Surrey University Press.

Mahan, J. (1976). Black and white children's racial identification and preference. *Journal of Black Psychology, 3,* 47–53.

Markus, H. R., Kitayama, S., & Heiman, R. J. (1999). Culture and "basic" psychological principles. In E. T. Higgins & A. W. Kruglanski (Eds.), *Social psychology: Handbook of basic principles* (pp. 857–913). New York: Guilford Press.

Milner, D. (1973). Racial identification and preference in "black" British children. *European Journal of Social Psychology, 3,* 281–295.

Milner, D. (1983). *Children and race: Ten years on.* London: Ward Lock Educational.

Morland, J. K. (1969). Race awareness among American and Hong Kong Chinese children. *American Journal of Sociology, 75,* 360–374.

Moscovici, S. (1984). The phenomenon of social representations. In R. Farr & S. Moscovici (Eds.), *Social representations* (pp. 3–69). Cambridge: Cambridge University Press.

Nesdale, D. (2000). Developmental changes in children's ethnic preferences and social cognitions. *Journal of Applied Developmental Psychology, 20,* 501–519.

Nesdale, D. (2001). The development of prejudice in children. In M. Augoustinos & K. J. Reynolds (Eds.), *Understanding prejudice, racism and social conflict* (pp. 57–72). London: SAGE Publications.

Nijsten, C. (1998). *Opvoeden in Turkse gezinnen in Nederland.* Assen, The Netherlands: Van Gorcum.

Oakes, P. J., Haslam, S. A., & Turner, J. C. (1994). *Stereotyping and social reality.* Oxford: Blackwell.

Owen, C., Eisner, H., & McFaul, T. (1981). A half-century of social distance research: National replication of the Bogardus studies. *Sociology and Social Research, 66,* 80–98.

Oyserman, D. (1993). The lens of personhood: Viewing the self and others in a multicultural society. *Journal of Personality and Social Psychology, 65,* 993–1009.

Oyserman, D., & Swim, J. K. (2001). Stigma: An insider's perspective. *Journal of Social Issues, 57,* 1–14.

Pelham, B. W., & Hetts, J. J. (1999). Implicit and explicit personal and social identity: Toward a more complete understanding of the social self. In T. R. Tyler, R. M. Kramer., & O. P. John (Eds.), *The psychology of the social self* (pp. 115–143). Mahwah, NJ: Lawrence Erlbaum Associates, Inc.

Phinney, J. (1989). Stages of ethnic identity in minority group adolescents. *Journal of Early Adolescents, 9,* 34–49.

Phinney, J. S. (1990). Ethnic identity in adolescents and adults: A review of research. *Psychological Bulletin, 108,* 499–514.

Phinney, J. S., Madden, T., & Santos, L. J. (1998). Psychological variables as predictors of perceived ethnic discrimination among minority and immigrant adolescents. *Journal of Applied Social Psychology, 28,* 937–953.

Phinney, J. S., & Rosenthal, D. A. (1992). Ethnic identity in adolescence: Process, context, and outcome. In G. R. Adams, T. P. Gullotta, & R. Montemayor (Eds.), *Adolescent identity formation* (pp. 145–172). New York: Academic Press.

Phinney, J. S., & Rotheram, M. J. (Eds.), *Children's ethnic socialization: Pluralism and development.* Newbury Park, CA: SAGE Publications.

Powlishta, K. K., Serbin, L. A., Doyle, A.-B., & White, D. R. (1994). Gender, ethnicity, and body type biases: The generality of prejudice in childhood. *Developmental Psychology, 30,* 526–536.

Ramsey, P. G. (1987). Young children's thinking about ethnic differences. In J. S. Phinney & M. J. Rotheram (Eds.), *Children's ethnic socialization: Pluralism and development* (pp. 56–72). Newbury Park, CA: SAGE Publications.

Resnick, L. B., Levine, J. M., & Teasley, S. D. (Eds.) (1991). *Perspectives on socially shared cognition.* Washington, DC: American Psychological Association.

Rhee, E., Uleman, J. S., Lee, H. K., & Roman, R. J. (1995). Spontaneous self-descriptions and ethnic identities in individualistic and collectivistic cultures. *Journal of Personality and Social Psychology, 69,* 142–152.

Roosens, E. (1994). The primordial nature of origins in migrant ethnicity. In H. Vermeulen & C. Govers (Eds.), *The anthropology of ethnicity: Beyond "ethnic groups and boundaries".* Amsterdam: Spinhuis.

Rosenberg, M. (1979). *Conceiving the self.* New York: Basic Books.

Rotenberg, K. J., & Cranwell, F. R. (1989). Self-concept in American Indian and White children. *Journal of Cross-Cultural Psychology, 20,* 39–53.

Rotheram, M. J., & Phinney, J. S. (1987). Introduction: Definitions and perspectives in the study of children's ethnic socialization. In J. S. Phinney & M. J. Rotheram (Eds.), *Children's ethnic socialization: Pluralism and development* (pp. 10–28). Newbury Park, CA: SAGE Publications.

Rutland, A. (1999). The development of national prejudice, in-group favouritism and self-stereotypes in British children. *British Journal of Social Psychology, 38,* 55–70.

Sellers, R. M., Smith, M. A., Shelton, J. N., Rowley, S. A. J., & Chavous, T. M. (1998). Multidimensional model of racial identity: A reconceptualization of African American racial identity. *Personality and Social Psychology Review, 2,* 18–39.

Singelis, T. M. (1994). The measurement of independent and interdependent self-construals. *Personality and Social Psychology Bulletin, 20,* 580–591.

Smith, P. B., & Bond, M. H. (1993). *Social psychology across cultures: Analysis and perspectives.* New York: Harvester Wheatsheaf.

Smith, E. R., Murphy, J., & Coats, S. (1999). Attachments to groups: Theory and measurement. *Journal of Personality and Social Psychology, 77,* 94–110.

Spielman, D. A. (2000). Young children, minimal groups, and dichotomous categorization. *Personality and Social Psychology Bulletin, 26,* 1433–1441.

Swim, J. K., & Stangor, C. (1998). *Prejudice: The target's perspective.* New York: Academic Press.

Tajfel, H. (1978). *The social psychology of minorities.* London: Minority Rights Group.

Tajfel, H., & Turner, J. C. (1986). The social identity theory of intergroup behavior. In S. Worchel & W. Austin (Eds.), *Psychology of intergroup relations* (pp. 7–24). Chicago, IL: Nelson-Hall.

Taylor, D. M., Wright, S. C., Moghaddam, F. M., & Lalonde, R. N. (1990). The personal/group discrimination discrepancy: Perceiving my group, but not myself, to be a target of discrimination. *Personality and Social Psychology Bulletin, 16,* 254–262.

Taylor, D. M., Wright, S. C., & Porter, L. E. (1993). Dimensions of perceived discrimination: The personal/group discrimination discrepancy. In M. P. Zanna &

J. M. Olson (Eds.), *The psychology of prejudice: The Ontario symposium, Vol. 7* (pp. 233–255). Hillsdale, NJ: Lawrence Erlbaum Associates, Inc.

Thompson, L., & Fine, G. A. (1999). Socially shared cognition, affect, and behavior: A review and integration. *Personality and Social Psychology Review, 3,* 278–302.

Trafimow, D., Triandis, H. C., & Goto, S. G. (1991). Some tests of the distinction between the private and the collective self. *Journal of Personality and Social Psychology, 60,* 649–655.

Triandis, H. C. (1994). Theoretical and methodological approaches to the study of collectivism and individualism. In U. Kim, H. C. Triandis, C. Kagitcibasi, S. C. Choi, & G. Yoon (Eds.), *Individualism and collectivism: Theory, method, and applications* (pp. 41–51). Thousand Oaks, CA: SAGE Publications.

Triandis, H. C., Leung, K., Villareal, M. J., & Clack, F. L. (1985). Allocentric and idiocentric tendencies: Convergent and discriminant validation. *Journal of Research in Personality, 19,* 395–415.

Turner, J. C. (1999). Some current issues in research on social identity and self-categorization theories. In N. Ellemers, R. Spears, & B. Doosje (Eds.), *Social identity: Context, commitment, content* (pp. 6–34). Oxford: Blackwell.

Turner, J. C., Hogg, M. A., Oakes, P. J., Reicher, S. D., & Wetherell, M. S. (1987). *Rediscovering the social group: A self-categorization theory.* Oxford: Blackwell.

Turner, J. C., Oakes, P. J., Haslam, S. A., & McGarty, C. (1994). Self and collective: Cognition and social context. *Personality and Social Psychology Bulletin, 20,* 454–463.

Turner, J. C., & Onorato, R. S. (1999). Social identity, personality, and the self-concept: A self-categorization perspective. In T. R. Tyler, R. M. Kramer, & O. P. John (Eds.), *The psychology of the social self.* Mahwah, NJ: Lawrence Erlbaum Associates, Inc.

Van den Heuvel, H., Tellegen, G., & Koomen, W. (1992). Cultural differences in the use of psychological and social characteristics in children's self-understanding. *European Journal of Social Psychology, 22,* 353–362.

Vaughan, G. M. (1964). The development of ethnic attitudes in New Zealand school children. *Genetic Psychology Monographs, 70,* 135–175.

Vaughan, G. M. (1987). A social psychological model of ethnic identity development. In J. S. Phinney & M. J. Rotheram (Eds.), *Children's ethnic socialization: Pluralism and development* (pp. 73–91). Newbury Park, CA: SAGE Publications.

Verkuyten, M. (1999). *Etnische identiteit: Theoretische en empirische benaderingen.* Amsterdam: Spinhuis.

Verkuyten, M. (2001). Global self-esteem, ethnic self-esteem and family integrity: Turkish and Dutch early adolescents in The Netherlands. *International Journal of Behavioural Development, 25,* 357–366.

Verkuyten, M. (2002a). Ethnic attitudes among minority and majority children: The role of ethnic identification, peer group victimisation and parents. *Social Development, 11,* 558–570.

Verkuyten, M. (2002b). Perceptions of ethnic discrimination by minority and majority early adolescents in The Netherlands. *International Journal of Psychology, 37,* 321–332.

Verkuyten, M., & Kinket, B. (2000). Social distances in a multi ethnic society: The ethnic hierarchy among Dutch preadolescents. *Social Psychology Quarterly, 63,* 75–85.

Verkuyten, M., Kinket, B., & Van der Wielen, C. (1997). Preadolescents' understanding of ethnic discrimination. *Journal of Genetic Psychology, 158,* 97–112.

Verkuyten, M., & Masson, K. (1996). Culture and gender differences in the perception of friendship by adolescents. *International Journal of Psychology, 31,* 207–217.

Verkuyten, M., & Pouliasi, K. (2002). Biculturalism among older children: Cultural frame-switching, attributions, self-identification and attitudes. *Journal of Cross-Cultural Psychology, 33,* 596–608.

Verkuyten, M., & Thijs, J. (2000). *Leren (en) waarderen: Discriminatie, zelfbeeld, relaties en leerprestaties in 'witte'en 'zwarte' basisscholen.* Amsterdam: Thela Thesis.

Verkuyten, M., & Thijs, J. (2001). Peer victimization and self-esteem of ethnic minority group children. *Journal of Community and Applied Social Psychology, 11,* 227–234.

Verkuyten, M., & Thijs, J. (2002). Racist victimization among children in the Netherlands: The effect of ethnic group and school. *Ethnic and Racial Studies, 25,* 310–331.

Verkuyten, M., & Thijs, J. (2003). Global and ethnic self-esteem in social context: Minority and majority groups in the Netherlands. *Social Indicators Research* (forthcoming).

Weber, M. (1968). *Economy and society: An outline of interpretive sociology.* New York: Bedmeister.

Weinreich, P. (1986). The operationalisation of identity theory in racial and ethnic relations. In J. Rex & D. Mason (Eds.), *Theories of race and ethnic relations* (pp. 299–344). Cambridge: Cambridge University Press.

Yee, M., & Brown, R. (1992). Self evaluations and intergroup attitudes in children aged three to nine. *Child Development, 63,* 619–629.

Part III
Applications

8   Social identity processes and children's ethnic prejudice

Drew Nesdale

Although the presence of ethnic prejudice is destructive in any sector of a community, the possibility that it may emerge in school-age children is of particular concern. During this period, children acquire social knowledge and attitudes that often endure into adulthood and which, in the case of ethnic prejudice, would foster intergroup divisions and, at worst, physical harm to members of minority groups.

In response to these long-held concerns, a considerable amount of research has addressed the development of children's ethnic prejudice (i.e., their feelings of dislike or hatred towards members of ethnic out-groups), together with related issues such as the acquisition of ethnic awareness, ethnic self-identification, and ethnic stereotyping (see reviews by Aboud, 1988; D. Nesdale, 2001a). Given the difficulties in measuring such constructs, especially in young children, researchers have used a variety of measurement techniques, including ethnic preferences, trait assignments, structured interviews, behaviour observations, questionnaires, sociograms, and projective tests, although the first two, ethnic preferences and trait assignments, have dominated the field (see D. Nesdale, 2001a, for a review).

Based largely on the ethnic preference and trait attribution techniques, a remarkably consistent set of findings has emerged, especially in relation to dominant group children. The ethnic preference studies indicate that children can differentiate among people based on racial cues (e.g., skin colour) from a very early age and certainly by around 4 years of age their racial awareness enables them to distinguish explicitly among members of different racial groups. There is also extensive evidence that from 4 years of age onwards, children from the ethnically dominant group can accurately identify their own ethnic group membership, and that they reveal increasingly strong in-group bias in their choices. Similarly, trait attribution studies have consistently revealed that dominant group children display an increase in in-group positivity/out-group negativity in their trait attributions from 3 to 4 years of age (see reviews by Aboud, 1988; D. Nesdale, 2001a). Based on her review of the literature and her own more recent findings, Aboud further concluded that this bias actually peaks at around 6 to 7 years of age, and then gradually declines during mid childhood.

However, despite the apparently high level of consistency in the findings, an agreed-upon understanding of the nature of the development of ethnic prejudice in children has yet to emerge. A major reason relates to the nature of the foregoing findings. Although some researchers argue to the contrary (e.g., Aboud, 1988; Gregor & McPherson, 1966), a common view of the preceding findings is that they simply reflect the children's *in-group preferences* rather than their feelings of *out-group dislike or hatred* (e.g., Brand, Ruiz, & Padilla, 1974; Cameron, Alvarez, Ruble, Fuligni, 2001; Katz, 1976; D. Nesdale, 2001a; Proshansky, 1966; Stephan & Rosenfield, 1979). On this basis alone, it is not surprising that there is currently little agreement on issues such as the age at which prejudice emerges in children, whether or not there are age-related phases or stages through which prejudice develops, what the psychological processes or mechanisms are which govern the acquisition of ethnic prejudice, and what impact is exerted by children's emerging linguistic and cognitive abilities upon their acquisition and retention of ethnic prejudice.

The aim of this chapter is to outline a model that is designed to provide a comprehensive account of the development of children's prejudice. The model draws heavily upon social identity theory (SIT; Tajfel & Turner, 1979) and its more recent elaboration, self-categorisation theory (SCT; Turner, Hogg, Oakes, Reicher, & Wetherell, 1987), which arguably provides the most widely endorsed current explanation of ethnic prejudice in adults. Since SIT (and SCT) was not designed to explain the development of prejudice in children, social identity development theory (SIDT) is proposed to account for the acquisition of prejudice in children, taking into account their unique circumstances of change and development as they increase in age. Central to SIDT is the assumption that social identity processes fundamentally influence the development of children's prejudice.

To provide a context for the description of SIDT, the three main explanations of children's prejudice that have been proposed to date will be briefly considered. These approaches include the view that ethnic prejudice in children is a form of emotional maladjustment; that ethnic prejudice emerges in children as a reflection of the views of significant others; and that ethnic prejudice is determined by changes in children's perceptual-cognitive acquisitions. A description of the main tenets of SIDT follows, together with the results of recent studies designed to assess the theory.

EXPLANATIONS OF CHILDREN'S PREJUDICE

The *emotional maladjustment* approach links the acquisition of prejudice in children to the development of a particular personality type, the authoritarian personality (Adorno, Frenkel-Brunswik, Levinson, & Sanford, 1950). Much of children's prejudice influenced by Freudian thinking, is considered to stem from emotional maladjustment arising from a repressive and harshly disciplined upbringing. Under these circumstances, the child's resulting frustration, anger, and hostility towards his/her parents is considered to be displaced away from the parents towards scapegoats who are weaker and lack authority and power, such as members of minority groups (D. Nesdale, 1999a).

While a positive feature of this theory is that it provides an explanation for any differences in levels of prejudice that may occur between individuals (Aboud, 1988), it does not account for the uniformity of prejudice across whole groups of people that may occur in particular places and times, nor why some groups are the recipients of prejudice but not others (Brown, 1995). In general, the approach ignores the influence on people's (including children's) intergroup attitudes and behaviour of important aspects of their social environment, including the attitudes of significant others, prevailing societal norms, and the relationships between the members of the dominant cultural group and the members of minority groups.

The *social reflection* approach takes the latter point as a fundamental premise – children's prejudice is considered to reflect the community's attitudes and values, which are typically transmitted by the child's parents. The most widely accepted version of this approach has been that children simply learn their ethnic attitudes from these sources in the same way that they learn other social behaviours (e.g., Allport, 1954; Rosenfield & Stephan, 1981). Thus, as Horowitz put it as far back as 1936, "attitudes toward Negroes, are now chiefly determined not by contact with Negroes but by contact with the prevalent attitude towards Negroes" (pp. 34–35). Presumably, such learning occurs because the children are rewarded for their imitative behaviour and/or want to please their parents.

However, although the importance accorded to parents (and, later, peers) as the primary source of children's ethnic attitudes has remained largely unchallenged over many years, research support for this approach is actually quite mixed. On the one hand, consistent with it are findings of positive correlations between the ethnic attitudes of children and their parents (e.g., Bird, Monachesi, & Burdick, 1952; Goodman, 1952; Harris, Gough, & Martin, 1950; Horowitz & Horowitz, 1938; Mosher & Scodel, 1960; Radke & Trager, 1950) and that there are distinct similarities in the statements of parents and their children concerning ethnic minority groups (e.g., Radke-Yarrow, Trager, & Miller, 1952). On the other hand, however, some studies have reported either low (e.g., Bird et al., 1952; Frenkel-Brunswik & Havel, 1953) or nonexistent correlations (e.g., Aboud & Doyle, 1996b; Pushkin, cited in Davey, 1983) between children and their parents in terms of their ethnic attitudes. Still other studies have found that when there is a similarity between parents and children in their negative statements towards ethnic minorities, the children frequently explicitly source the statements to their parents, declining to take ownership of them (e.g., Horowitz & Horowitz, 1938; Porter, 1971; Radke, Trager, & Davis, 1949). In addition, although children as young as 5 years of age incorporated trait-like terms or implied dispositions (e.g., "bad", "dirty", "ugly") in their verbal descriptions of minority group children (e.g., Horowitz & Horowitz, 1938; Porter, 1971; Radke-Yarrow et al., 1952), there was little sense that such terms had trait connotations for them and/or that they were part of a set of beliefs that were shared by their group (i.e., a stereotype). In other words, there was scant evidence that the attributes or behaviours were perceived to reflect stable characteristics of members of the particular ethnic out-group that might be revealed on other occasions (see D. Nesdale, 2001b, for a review of the relationship between parents, language, and ethnic prejudice in children).

Overall, the preceding discussion suggests that it would be incorrect to assume that children should be regarded as empty containers into which prevailing societal prejudices are poured, or as sponges that soak up dominant ethnic attitudes (R. Brown, 1995; Davey, 1983; Milner, 1996). Children may hold the same ethnic attitudes as their parents and peers, but this situation does not arise as a matter of necessity. As a considerable amount of research has made clear, children's intellectual capacities reveal dramatic development through the mid childhood years and they are active participants in seeking to understand and control both their cognitive and social worlds (e.g., Durkin, 1995).

To a certain extent, the latter view accords with recent accounts of children's prejudice that have emphasised the influence exerted on children's ethnic attitudes by perceptual-cognitive considerations (e.g., Aboud, 1988; Aboud & Doyle, 1996a, 1996b; Bigler, 1995).

Aboud and her colleagues, for example, have argued that there is no strong evidence that children's prejudice is influenced by the attitudes of parents and peers. Instead, according to Aboud's (1988) *sociocognitive theory* (ST), a child's attitude to other groups of children depends on his/her levels of development in relation to two overlapping sequences of perceptual-cognitive development. One sequence involves the *process* that dominates a child's experience at a particular time. The child is initially dominated by affective-perceptual processes associated with fear of the unknown and attachment to the familiar. Perceptual processes subsequently dominate, preference for the (similar) in-group and rejection of the (different) out-group being determined primarily by physical attributes (e.g., skin colour, language, body size). Thereafter, cognitive processes take ascendancy with the advent of the concrete operational stage of cognitive development around 7 years of age and, later, formal operational thinking (Flavell, 1963). The effect of the transition to cognitive processes is that the child is increasingly able to understand the individual rather than the group-based qualities of people. Overlapping this sequence is a second sequence of development concerned with changes in the child's *focus of attention*. Whereas very young children mostly focus on themselves and their preferences and perceptions, older children emphasize categories of people such that individuals are seen as members of these categories or groups. Still later, however, children focus on individuals, who are liked or disliked for their personal rather than group qualities.

Based on these sociocognitive developments, Aboud (1988) argued that in-group bias and out-group prejudice increase to a peak between 5 to 7 years of age, when group differences are paramount. However, with subsequent increases in the child's cognitive abilities, occasioned by the onset of concrete operational thinking around 7 years of age, Aboud claimed that there is a systematic decline in group-based biases, which is further enhanced when the child's ever-increasing cognitive abilities allow him/her to attend to the differences between individuals.

Although ST offers a theoretically consistent account of children's prejudice in terms of their perceptual-cognitive processes, it is fair to say that research support for this theory is also currently mixed (see D. Nesdale, 2001a, 2001b, for a review). On the one hand, consistent with ST are studies in which children from the ethnically dominant group displayed increasing in-group positivity/out-group negativity up to 6 to 7 years of age, followed by a systematic decline (e.g., Aboud, 1988; Bigler & Liben, 1993; Doyle & Aboud, 1995). In addition, research has revealed that children's understanding of conservation (an achievement of the concrete operational stage of cognitive development) is correlated with ethnic flexibility, the understanding that ethnically similar and different individuals can have different and similar attributes, respectively (e.g., Doyle, Beaudet, & Aboud, 1988), and ethnic constancy, the understanding that ethnicity remains the same despite superficial transformations in skin colour or clothing (e.g., Aboud, 1984; Semaj, 1980). Research has also revealed that the acquisition of concrete operational thinking coincided with a decrease in in-group prejudice, and that conservation preceded a reduction in prejudice (e.g., Doyle & Aboud, 1995; Doyle et al., 1988).

On the other hand, however, whereas ST's account might be taken to indicate that ethnic prejudice ceases to be a problem during the elementary school years, or is substantially ameliorated, as a result of children's increasing cognitive abilities, research suggests that this is not the case. For example, in studies that have reported an association between conservation and prejudice, up to 50% of the children who could conserve still displayed ethnic prejudice (e.g.., Doyle & Aboud, 1995).

Further, the actual nature of the pattern of children's responses that ST seeks to explain is not unambiguous. Although there are certainly a number of studies that have reported an unambiguous decrease in preference/ prejudice after 7 years of age, as sociocognitive theory would predict (e.g., Aboud & Mitchell, 1977; George & Hoppe, 1979; Vaughan, 1964; Williams, Best, & Boswell, 1975), other studies have reported not only that in-group preference remained at the same level from 7 to 12 years of age (e.g., Asher & Allen, 1969; Banks & Rompf, 1973; Davey, 1983; Milner, 1973; Teplin, 1976; Weiland & Coughlin, 1979) but also that in-group preference actually increased during these years (e.g., Bartel, Bartel, & Grill, 1973; Hraba & Grant, 1970; Rice, Ruiz, & Padilla, 1974; Vaughan & Thompson, 1961).

Perhaps of critical importance, however, is the claim noted above that the main body of findings that ST seeks to explain may actually consist of children's *in-group preferences* rather than their out-group *dislike or prejudice* (e.g., Brand et al., 1974; Katz, 1976; D. Nesdale, 2001a; Proshansky, 1966; Stephan & Rosenfield, 1979). The basis of this view is that the main methods commonly used to assess children's ethnic prejudice, certainly up to the 1990s, rested on children's choice of ethnically differentiated dolls, photos, or drawings, or the attribution of traits to such stimuli, and hence might only index their level of in-group preference (see review by D. Nesdale, 2001a). Consistent with this are findings indicating a lack of correspondence between children's ethnic preferences and their choice of friends and playmates (e.g., Fishbein & Imai, 1993; Jansen & Gallagher, 1966), and that children who are given the opportunity to rate minority group children on bipolar scales (i.e., like–dislike) tend to express greater liking for the in-group versus the out-group, rather than liking for the in-group and dislike for the out-group (e.g., Aboud & Mitchell, 1977; D. Nesdale, 1999b). Indeed, contrary to Aboud's position, a number of writers have argued that real ethnic prejudice, signified by, for example, racial cleavage, epithets, or tension, when it does emerge in children, does not actually appear until children are well into mid childhood, around 9 or 10 years of age (e.g., Goodman, 1952; Katz, 1976; Milner, 1996; Proshansky, 1966).

Finally, ST offers a developmental account that is largely indifferent to the social context and motivational considerations. For example, it is unlikely that the initiation of prejudice in children is governed simply by the child's affective-perceptual processes associated with fear of the unknown (and attachment to the familiar). On the contrary, some but not all physical differences are associated with prejudice in both children and adults, the physical differences to which young children respond are also those of racial significance to adults (Katz, Sohn, & Zalk, 1975), and strong prejudices (e.g., towards particular national groups, religions) can occur even in the absence of physical differences (Tajfel, Jahoda, Nemeth, Rim, & Johnson, 1972). Together, these points emphasise the fact that the differentiation of racial cues by young children is not determined solely by their perceptual distinctiveness based on unfamiliarity. Rather, the cues to which even young children respond have a distinctiveness that is socially determined, particularly by the labels and evaluative statements applied to groups by peers and adults (Katz, 1976; Vaughan, 1987).

In sum, although the preceding review is necessarily abbreviated, it is clear that markedly different theoretical constructions have been built upon the available body of research findings. Although each approach accounts for some of the findings, none provides a comprehensive explanation of the development of children's prejudice, encompassing within it the full range of findings that have been revealed to date.

However, the review has served to identify a number of central issues, which must be taken into account in any comprehensive explanation of the development of children's prejudice. First, the theory must account for the appearance of out-group dislike and hatred versus mere in-group prefer-ence. Second, the theory must account for the fact that children's attitudes are not necessarily mere reflections of those of their parents or siblings. Third, it must take into account the fact of children's developing perceptual, cognitive, and linguistic abilities. Fourth, the theory must give due recognition to social-motivational issues. Fifth, the theory must account for the fact that some children develop ethnic prejudice whereas others do not.

Social identity development theory (SIDT) has been devised as a response to these central issues. Rather than drawing upon individual differences between children, their supposed tendency to mimic significant others, or their perceptual-cognitive acquisitions, SIDT pays particular regard to children's social motivations and their growing awareness of the nature of the social world in which they live. On this basis, some of SIDT's core prop-ositions are greatly influenced by social identity theory (Tajfel & Turner, 1979).

SOCIAL IDENTITY THEORY AND ETHNIC PREJUDICE

An approach that places considerable emphasis on social-motivational con-siderations and awareness of social structure in accounting for ethnic preju-dice is provided by social identity theory (SIT; Tajfel & Turner, 1979) and its recent elaboration, self-categorisation theory (SCT; Turner et al., 1987). Briefly, according to SIT, prejudice and discrimination towards members of ethnic out-groups ultimately derives from the desire of individuals to identify with social groups that are considered to be positively distinctive or compara-tively superior to other groups, in order to enhance their own self-esteem. The consequences of group identification are that in-group members are per-ceived to be similar and to possess positive qualities and hence are subject to positive bias. In contrast, out-group members are perceived to be different and to possess less favourable qualities and hence may attract prejudice and discrimination. Numerous studies of adults and adolescents have now pro-vided broad support for SIT (see reviews by Brewer, 1979; R. Brown, 1995; Hogg & Abrams, 1988; Mullen, Brown, & Smith, 1991), especially in research using the minimal group paradigm (Tajfel, Billig, Bundy, & Flament, 1971).

However, although SIT is probably the most widely endorsed social-psychological account of ethnic prejudice in adults at the present time, the theory is virtually mute on the issue of the development of prejudice in children. Nevertheless, according to several researchers, there are good grounds for supposing that SIT might provide the basis of an explanation of ethnic prejudice in *both* children and adults (e.g., Davey 1983; Milner, 1996; D. Nesdale, 1999a, 1999b; D. Nesdale & Flesser, 2001; Vaughan, 1988). For example, consistent with the basic assumptions of the theory are anecdotal reports that children from as young as 3 years of age have a developing aware-ness of which groups in a community are better off and more highly regarded than others, and that children make comparisons between their standing as a member of one ethnic group versus other ethnic groups (e.g., Davey, 1983; Goodman, 1946; Milner, 1996; Radke & Trager, 1950; Vaughan, 1987). In addition, the findings of ethnic preference studies are consistent with SIT's assumption that people, including children, seek the positive distinctiveness conferred by membership of higher- rather than lower-status groups in order to enhance their self-esteem. Thus, whereas dominant-group children rarely misidentify their ethnic group, members of low-status minority groups (e.g., black, native, and Hispanic Americans) frequently misidentify with the dominant (e.g., white American) cultural group (e.g., Asher & Allen, 1969; Greenwald & Oppenheim, 1968; Hunsberger, 1978; Morland, 1966; Teplin, 1976).

However, while there are some grounds for concluding that the behaviour of even young children accords with the basic assumptions of SIT, the theory still has little to say concerning the unique circumstances of growing children. Issues such as the nature of the instigation of the developmental process in young children, whether or not there are age-related changes in the acquisition process, whether these changes are influenced by other cognitive and linguistic acquisitions, and so on, are not addressed by SIT.

The remainder of this chapter sketches out a model that is designed to provide a more complete account of the development of prejudice in children. The model draws upon SIT for its core assumptions, but recognises that there are changes in children's intergroup behaviour that are linked to increasing age.

SOCIAL IDENTITY DEVELOPMENT THEORY OF CHILDREN'S ETHNIC PREJUDICE

Social identity development theory (SIDT) proposes that children who display ethnic prejudice pass through four sequential development phases (undifferentiated, ethnic awareness, ethnic preference, ethnic prejudice). The phases are differentiated in terms of the behaviours that characterise them, and the events that precipitate changes from one phase to the next.

Developmental phases

Phase 1: Undifferentiated

Prior to 2–3 years of age, racial cues are typically not salient to young children – they respond to objects and people in their environment, initially in terms of what catches their attention. Increasingly, however, they become more selective and discriminating and begin to respond differentially to cues such as gender and age.

Phase 2: Ethnic awareness

Ethnic awareness begins to emerge at around 3 years of age, particularly among those children who reside in multiracial societies. A number of studies have confirmed that children can accurately identify and distinguish between skin colour hues at this age (e.g., K. B. Clark & Clark, 1939; Goodman, 1946; Stevenson & Stevenson, 1960). As Katz (1976) has emphasised, it is likely that awareness begins following an adult's identification/labelling of an out-group member (e.g., "yes, that person has black skin – he is an Aboriginal/Afro-American"). It is the perception of such differences, particularly when accompanied by a verbal label, that is likely to facilitate social categorisation based on skin colour. It is important to note, however, that young children do not appear to construct social categories on an idiosyncratic basis (e.g., "yes, that person has blue shorts/a big nose"). Children enter an environment in which the key social categories are already specified and the nature of inter-group relations is established. Accordingly, the social categories that children are likely to emphasise are not simply those that are strange and unfamiliar (cf. Aboud, 1988) – they will be those that have social significance in the community (e.g., Katz, 1976; Vaughan, 1987).

Children's awareness of these categories will be sharpened by any negative evaluations communicated by adults, verbally or nonverbally (Milner, 1983). In addition, it is possible that, in relation to the white and black social categories, the evaluative associations will be further enhanced by the positive and negative associations with the colours white and black (e.g., Renninger & Williams, 1966; Williams & Roberson, 1967) and light and dark (e.g., G. Brown & Johnson, 1971; Katz, 1973), respectively. However, while ethnic awareness may begin to emerge at around 3 years of age, the further refine-ment, elaboration, and clarification of the child's concept of a racial/ethnic group continues over many years, perhaps even up to 10 to 11 years of age, and appears to comprise a number of age-related phases (see Vaughan, 1963).

A crucially important and early achievement in this sequence concerns the child's *ethnic self-identification* – the realisation that he or she is a member of a particular group. The evidence suggests that self-identification begins to occur soon after children become aware of ethnic or racial categories. Accur-ate ethnic self-identification has been reported in dominant group children as young as 3 years of age (Marsh, 1970) and in virtually all dominant group children in multiracial communities by 6 to 7 years of age (see Aboud, 1988, for a review). It remains unclear whether awareness of a child's own ethnic identity precedes or follows his/her awareness of another person's ethnicity, although there are reasons to suppose that it is the former (see below). How-ever, the particular significance of this achievement is that it ushers in the next phase in the sequence, which overlaps the child's ongoing development of ethnic awareness.

Phase 3: Ethnic preference

Self-identification as a member of the dominant social group comprises a crucially important piece of a child's identity jigsaw – in this case, it is a central piece (together with his/her gender) of the child's developing social (as compared with personal) identity (Turner et al., 1987). The child learns that he or she belongs to, or is a member of, a particular ethnic group.

The major effect of this new understanding is an early focusing on the in-group rather than the out-group, on similarity rather than difference, on relative superiority rather than inferiority. That is, consistent with SIT (Tajfel & Turner, 1979), and ST (Turner et al., 1987), the effect of being categorised into a group is that children begin an ongoing focus on, and preference for, their in-group(s). Indeed, research by Katz and her colleagues (e.g., Katz, 1973; Katz & Seavey, 1973; Katz et al., 1975) has revealed that white children as young as 3 years of age more readily distinguished faces of their own versus another ethnic group. That is, the effect of ethnic self-identification and the application of group labels was that out-group faces were actually made less differentiable and/or accessible.

However, the critically important point to be emphasised here is that SIDT differs from both ST (Aboud, 1988) and SIT (Tajfel & Turner, 1979) in terms of the impact of ethnic self-categorisation on the child. Whereas both ST and SIT assume that ethnic self-caregorisation is sufficient to instigate both in-group favouring *and* out-group prejudice responses (Rubin & Hewstone, 1998), SIDT argues that ethnic self-categorisation mainly activates a focus on, and accompanying preference for, the *in-group*.

With the passage of time, children are exposed to and extract information that is consistent with, and enhances the positive distinctiveness of, their group. Inevitably, at the same time as children acquire positively discriminating information about the in-group, they begin to hear and acquire information that is (typically) less positive/more negative about comparison ethnic out-groups. Note that while this information may be retained and may form the basis of an eventual out-group stereotype, it does not appear to be the focal concern of children at this age. As noted earlier, ethnic stereotypes do not appear to consolidate until 8 or 9 years of age. Nevertheless, negative out-group information may still contribute to their sense of relative in-group superiority and self-esteem (Milner, 1996).

In short, rather than instigating out-group prejudice (cf. Aboud, 1988; Tajfel & Turner, 1979), the effect of ethnic self-identification is to instigate an in-group focus and bias. Consistent with this view is the array of findings that have emerged in ethnic preference studies (see Nesdale, 2001a, for a review). For example, when given a forced or restricted choice between in-group and out-group stimulus figures (e.g., dolls, pictures, drawings), dominant group children almost invariably indicate a preference for the in-group figure. Similarly, if required to make a choice between assigning positive versus negative attributes to in-group versus out-group figures, the in-group figure will be awarded the more positive attributes. While there is an obvious ambiguity in this data, the present position is that these findings reveal children's *preference for the in-group* rather than dislike or rejection for the out-group.

In addition, research indicates that friendship and playmate preferences are unrelated to ethnic preferences or out-group stereotype responses (e.g., Fishbein & Imai, 1993; Hraba & Grant, 1970), that there is no correlation between out-group stereotypes and out-group bullying (e.g., Boulton, 1995), that the negativity of the out-group stereotype drops when the response is open-ended versus forced choice (e.g., Lerner & Buehrig, 1975; Lerner & Schroeder, 1971), and that young children rarely give rejection of the out-group stimulus figure as a reason for their choice of the in-group stimulus figure (e.g., Zinser, Rich, & Bailey, 1981).

Further, as noted previously, in the few studies in which young children have given independent responses to in-group and out-group stimulus figures, and the responses have been on a like–dislike bipolar scale, the children have almost invariably used only the liking half of the scale. That is, the out-group stimulus figure has been rated as relatively less likeable than the in-group stimulus figure, not as disliked (e.g., Aboud & Mitchell, 1977; Genesee, Tucker, & Lambert, 1978; D. Nesdale, 1999b). Also of importance is the evidence that ethnicity is typically not an especially salient social category to young children, and is certainly not as salient as the gender category – friendship and playmate preferences are typically determined by gender, at least up to 10 or 11 years of age (e.g., Fishbein & Imai, 1993; Helgerson, 1943). Interestingly, in contrast to ethnicity, research has revealed that children as young as 4 or 5 years of age are quite prepared to reveal a strong dislike towards opposite versus same gender stimulus persons – here, the stimulus figures are unambiguously rated in the "disliked" half of a bipolar scale (e.g., Yee & Brown, 1994).

In sum, according to the present analysis, ethnic self-identification is a process that tends to occur in all children, sooner or later. It facilitates and reflects a growing understanding of the social structure in the community, the standing of the different groups, and their interrelationships, and the language used to describe other group members. For dominant group children it prompts a focus on, and preference for, the ethnic in-group. (In contrast, minority group children often reject their in-group in favour of the culturally dominant out-group.) However, if ethnic preference is merely that (i.e., preference not prejudice), the question remains as to how ethnic preference turns into a negative attitude or prejudice.

Phase 4: Ethnic prejudice

Contrary to Aboud's (1988) claim that ethnic prejudice diminishes in children from 7 years of age onwards as a result of cognitive acquisitions, SIDT contends that it is precisely in this period that prejudice actually crystallises and emerges *in those children who come to hold such attitudes*. That is, according to SIDT, prejudice does not emerge in all children as a matter of course (cf. Aboud, 1988).

In essence, according to SIDT, prejudice entails an active process of change from a state of mere ethnic preference. It requires shifts in focus in each of the child's perceptual, affective, cognitive, and behavioural domains. Rather than being focused on the in-group and its positive differentiation from the out-group, prejudice implies at least an equal focus on in-group and out-group, if not an obsessive focusing on the out-group. Instead of liking an out-group member less than an in-group member, prejudice means that out-group members are disliked or hated. Rather than knowing and being able to reproduce (negative) "facts" about ethnic minorities, a prejudiced person holds them as his/her own. Finally, instead of engaging in interethnic play and friendship, prejudice means derogating and discriminating against minority group members whenever the occasion arises.

Clearly, the transition from having a preference for the in-group to feeling prejudice towards an ethnic minority group is not inconsiderable. According to SIDT, the transition from ethnic preference to prejudice depends on several elements.

Acquisition of ethnic constancy

An essential prerequisite of ethnic prejudice appears to be the acquisition of the concept of ethnic constancy – the understanding that ethnic group membership is immutable and, like gender, does not change with age (Katz, 1976; Semaj, 1980). As part of children's developing and elaborating concept of ethnic group noted earlier, they learn the significant ethnic cues that differentiate groups and they can correctly label positive and negative instances. Moreover, children learn that ethnic cues, unlike size, are resilient to changes in age (e.g., Katz, 1976).

Given that ethnic constancy concerns the ability to appreciate the immutability of a quality or construct despite contextual changes, it follows that ethnic constancy is likely to relate to the acquisition of concrete operational thinking that occurs in most children at around 7 years of age (e.g., Flavell, 1963). Consistent with this expectation, Semaj (1980) has reported, in a study with 4- to 11-year-old black children, that conservation of mass and weight preceded ethnic constancy, which increased with age. The importance of ethnic constancy is that when it is acquired, the perceptual and cognitive components of ethnic attitudes are now bought into functional inter-relationship – minority out-groups (as well as the in-group) now have a substance and longevity to which negative (or positive) attitudes may be attached (e.g., Semaj, 1980).

Acquisition of social-cognitive skills

Other things being equal, whether or not children who have ethnic constancy develop and express prejudice towards minority group members is likely to be influenced by whether they acquire several important social-cognitive abilities. These include the ability to decentre and take the perspective of a minority group child, the ability to empathise and experience the feelings of such children, and the ability to engage in higher-level moral reasoning (Feffer & Gourevitch, 1960; Kohlberg, 1976; Selman & Byrne, 1974).

There are good grounds for supposing that these abilities would impact upon whether children develop ethnic prejudice. For example, it might be anticipated that dominant group children who are able to decentre and perceive the social environment from the perspective of a minority group child, and to share the feelings of the latter, would be less likely to develop prejudice towards members of that out-group. Similarly, it might be supposed that children whose moral judgments go beyond the external consequences of actions and the individual's need satisfactions to focus on right as defined by social authority or universal principles, would also be less likely to develop ethnic prejudice. However, although there is some indirect evidence consistent with these speculations (e.g., A. Clark, Hocevar, & Dembo, 1980; Madge, 1976), the impact of children's developing social-cognitive abilities on their ethnic prejudice remains to be assessed directly.

Social identity processes

While the acquisition of sociocognitive abilities such as decentration, empathy, and moral reasoning are certainly contrary to the development of prejudice, SIDT proposes that the principal determinant of children's prejudice is a social process. That is, instead of merely preferring the in-group, dominant group children change to disliking minority out-groups when they adopt the negative ethnic attitudes that prevail in their social group.

As noted earlier, however, children do not simply ape the ethnic attitudes and behaviours of those around them. Rather, they begin actively disliking ethnic minorities when they adopt, *as their own*, the negative out-group attitudes that prevail among those people whom they value and with whom they identify, in their social environment. That is, children adopt a particular attitude because it fits with their view of themselves as belonging to a social group with a particular set of attitudes, beliefs, and behaviours, and they derive positive distinctiveness from that group membership (Milner, 1996).

It is important to note that the change from preference to prejudice is unlikely to be immediate and would typically represent the culmination of a period of exposure to the dislike or hatred felt by significant others towards minority group members, the negative "facts" (i.e., stereotypic beliefs) that are espoused in relation to minority group members, and the observation of discriminatory behaviours directed at them. According to a number of writers, children are capable of reproducing these "second-hand" learnings during the ethnic preference phase but, at that stage, they are not the children's own and typically do not impact upon their play and friendship preferences – at this age, children "do not walk the talk" (e.g., Chyatte, Schaefer, & Spiaggia, 1951; Goodman, 1946; D. Nesdale, 2001b; Proshansky, 1966; Radke et al., 1949).

SIDT proposes that three factors facilitate the change from ethnic preference to prejudice. First, the probability of children adopting an ethnic prejudice as their own will increase to the extent that children identify with a (dominant) group in which prejudice is widely shared by the group members. As consensus increases, prejudice will become increasingly normative, with concomitant expectations that it will be adopted by all in-group members.

Second, the tendency for children to develop ethnic prejudice will increase as tension and threat increases between members of the dominant and ethnic minority group(s) (Brown, 1995). Under these circumstances, in-group identification and bias will increase, giving rise to an increasing tendency towards out-group rejection and dislike.

Third, the tendency towards ethnic prejudice in children will be greatest when there is a state of conflict between members of the two groups.

Although evidence consistent with the preceding three predictions has been reported in relation to adults (e.g., Branscombe & Wann, 1994; Hamm, 1993; Levin & McDevitts, 1993; Long, Spears, & Manstead, 1994; Quillian, 1995; Stephan, Ybarra, Martinez, Schwarzwald, & Tur-Kaspa, 1998), the impact of these factors on children's ethnic prejudice remains to be assessed.

Implications of SIDT

Several implications follow from SIDT. For example, whereas positive correlations between the ethnic attitudes of children and their parents might normally be expected, this need not necessarily be so. Indeed, Pushkin (in Davey, 1983) found a closer relationship between children's attitudes and those of people in the neighbourhood, than between the children's attitudes and those of their parents. Further, several studies have reported that the children of black activist parents displayed greater pro-white preference than the children of less active parents (Branch & Newcombe, 1980; Floyd, in Williams & Morland, 1976). This pattern of findings is clearly supportive of the view that the particular ethnic attitudes adopted by children reflect their own interests and perceptions rather than those who might either be expected to or seek to influence them.

A further implication is that the factors described above, which are proposed to enhance children's social identification processes, are likely to overwhelm the sociocognitive acquisitions of role-taking and moral reasoning, at least in relation to particular disliked ethnic out-groups. Consistent with this are several studies reporting that 7-year-old children were accurate at taking the role of another ethnic person, provided that the out-group person was a member of a liked group. If that person was disliked, then the role-taking was inaccurate (Aboud & Mitchell, 1977; Middleton, Tajfel & Johnson, 1970). According to Aboud and Mitchell, such findings reflect the impact of negative attitudes on the utilisation of perceptual cues, whereas Middleton et al. considered that a negative attitude prevents a child from circumventing his egocentric tendencies. Either way, the findings endorse the greater influence exerted by social and motivational factors over social-cognitive factors.

Another implication is that since SIDT is primarily founded upon social-motivational rather than perceptual-cognitive considerations, it would not predict that the appearance of ethnic prejudice in children would be linked to specific ages (cf. Aboud, 1988). According to SIDT, although prejudice is unlikely to occur in children younger than 6 or 7 years of age because their cognitive abilities would not have achieved the requisite level of development, its emergence thereafter would be dependent on their unique social situation. At any time, children's attitudes towards members of ethnic out-groups might increase, decrease, or remain the same, depending on their prevailing social group identification.

A final implication of the present model is that children (and adults) may never display ethnic prejudice because they choose not to identify with a social group that has a negative attitude towards an ethnic minority group(s). Interestingly, this does not necessarily imply that such children would not continue to prefer their in-group(s) over other out-groups for, at one level, identification means preference, not prejudice (see also R. Brown, 1995).

Recent research support for SIDT

Although SIDT provides a good account of the results of the extant ethnic preference and trait attribution studies, it needs to be remembered that these paradigms have distinct limitations, if not outright flaws. In particular, as noted above, these paradigms typically necessitate a choice being made between photos or dolls representing members of different ethnic groups. In addition, the transparency of the intent of these procedures enhances the likelihood of children giving socially desirable responses, even in the more contemporary versions of the technique (e.g., Black-Gutman & Hickson, 1996: Boulton, 1995; Doyle et al., 1988), particularly as children increase in age. On this basis, more recent research has typically utilised the minimal group paradigm in which the participants are randomly assigned membership in one of several groups (Tajfel et al., 1971). The advantage of this technique in terms of research on children's intergroup attitudes is that their responses can be examined in relation to the members of their in-group, as well as to members of out-groups, rather than simply to an individual.

Of particular importance to the present discussion is the fact that recent research using this paradigm has focused on identifying when children reveal in-group identification, what factors promote it, if and when children are responsive to status differences between groups, what effect group membership has on children, and what factors contribute to children changing from mere ethnic preference to out-group prejudice.

For example, consistent with SIDT, Bigler and her colleagues revealed that the random assignment of 6- to 11-year-old children to groups (e.g., "red" group, "green" group) in a minimal group paradigm prompted in-group favouritism in the children in both groups, regardless of age and gender. Compared with control group children, those assigned to colour groups did not want to change groups, rated their own group as most likely to win a series of three contests, and chose more members of the in-group versus the out-group to participate in a field trip (Bigler, 1995; Bigler, Jones, & Lobliner, 1997). Bigler et al. also reported that children with higher levels of self-esteem showed higher levels of intergroup stereotyping.

Further, while these researchers explicitly sought to de-emphasise social comparisons and competitiveness between the groups, other research has indicated that when the latter are emphasised, in-group favouritism increases (Vaughan, Tajfel, & Williams, 1981; Yee & Brown, 1992). For example, Vaughan et al. emphasised intergroup comparison in another minimal group study with 7- and 11-year-old children who had also been randomly assigned to groups. They found that the children allocated rewards to in-group and out-group participants so as to maximise the difference between the groups, in favour of the in-group.

Importantly, in their study D. Nesdale and Flesser (2001) sought to examine the effect of status differences that exist between members of dominant and minority groups. They randomly assigned 5- and 8-year-old children to teams that supposedly varied in drawing ability (i.e., high versus low), in order to manipulate social status. Their results indicated that even the 5-year-old children were sensitive to the status of their social group, that they liked their group more, and that they saw themselves as being more similar to the in-group members, when their group had high versus low status. In addition, low- versus high-status group members sought to change their group membership and, like adults, their liking and similarity ratings of in-group and out-group members were influenced by whether they could change groups.

However, although the preceding findings are clearly consistent with SIDT's predictions, it is important to recognise that these studies focused on children's responses to contrived or invented groups rather than to particular ethnic out-groups. Accordingly, to provide a further test of SIDT, D. Nesdale, Durkin, Maass, and Griffiths (2001b) examined 5-, 7-, and 9-year-old children's attitudes to members of particular ethnic groups that differed in status. Intergroup status was manipulated as in the research by D. Nesdale and Flesser (2001), and each Anglo-Australian participant was allocated to a same-sex plus same-ethnicity (i.e., Anglo-Australian) team whereas the out-group competitor team was revealed (via photographs) to be comprised of Anglo-Australian children or Pacific Islander children. Again, consistent with SIDT, the results confirmed that children as young as 5 years of age are sensitive to status differences between groups and that they wish to be members of the high- versus low-status group. In addition, the findings also confirmed the importance of self-categorisation – that children liked the members of their in-group more than out-group members. Most importantly, the findings revealed that this effect was enhanced when the out-group was comprised of members who shared a different ethnic background. The ethnicity difference apparently sharpens and accentuates the category differ-ence, with the effect that different-ethnicity out-group members are liked less than same-ethnicity out-group members. At the same time, it is important to note that the children did not actually reveal *dislike* towards the different-ethnicity out-group members. Instead, the latter group was attributed *less liking* than the same-ethnicity out-group. That is, the children's ratings of the out-group, regardless of its ethnicity, were never lower than the midpoint of the bipolar scale. According to SIDT, these findings would confirm that the children were actually in the *ethnic preference* phase, with their major focus being the interests of the in-group, not directing prejudice towards an ethnic out-group.

A more recent study by D. Nesdale, Durkin, Griffiths, and Maass (2001a) has further extended these findings. Drawing upon SIDT, the reasoning behind this study was that if it is the case that children are primarily con-cerned with their in-group, they will not tend to respond to out-group eth-nicity unless it happens to be coincident with the boundary between the two groups (i.e., the in-group's ethnicity differs from that of the out-group). Under the latter circumstances, differential ethnic preference would be expected to be displayed as a result of the category difference. The implica-tion here is that, whereas children in the ethnic preference phase will like a different ethnicity out-group less than a same ethnicity out-group, a different ethnicity in-group (i.e., one that contains members of different ethnicity to the target child) will be liked no less than a same ethnicity in-group.

To test this reasoning, 5-,7-, and 9-year-old Anglo-Australian children par-ticipated in a minimal group study in which they were assigned to a high-status in-group that included other Anglo-Australian or Pacific Islander children. As in the previous study, the children also expected to compete with an out-group that contained Anglo-Australian or Pacific Islander children.

Consistent with SIDT, and with D. Nesdale et al. (2001b), children in a same-ethnicity (i.e., Anglo-Australian) in-group indicated greater liking for the in-group over the out-group, but more so when the latter was comprised of members of the same (i.e., Anglo-Australian) versus a different ethnicity (i.e., Pacific Islander) out-group. However, the inclusion of a different-ethnicity (i.e. Pacific Islander) in-group yielded a critically important and dif-ferent pattern of findings. First, as predicted, having in-group members whose ethnicity differed from one's own had no impact on the children's liking for the in-group. That is, the children rated the same and different in-groups as being equally likeable, and more likeable than the out-group. Clearly, these findings indicate that, depending on the context, ethnicity sim-ply does not matter to children, at least up to 9 years of age: If different ethnicity children happen to be members of the in-group, then the in-group is liked no less than one that is made up of same-ethnicity members. As specified by SIDT (and with SIT, Tajfel & Turner, 1979), it is the categorisation that matters, not the ethnicity per se.

Second, and compared with the same-ethnicity in-group results, the analysis revealed that when the in-group was made up of different ethnicity members, the children liked the same-ethnicity out-group *less* than the different-ethnicity out-group. In short, the children's standard of comparison appeared to have changed. Rather than seeing different-ethnicity out-group members as markedly different, as occurred when the in-group was comprised of same-ethnicity members, in the case of a different-ethnicity in-group, the members of a different-ethnicity out-group were perceived as less different than a same-ethnicity out-group. Again, consistent with SIDT, this finding emphasises that in the absence of threat and conflict, young children up to 9 years of age are simply not repositories of ethnic dislike and prejudice (cf. Aboud, 1988).

Although the results of the preceding studies have emphasised the impact of ethnic self-categorisation and intergroup status differences on children, even those as young as 5 years of age, and provides considerable support for SIDT, additional light is shed on these processes by two further studies. Contrary to the preceding research, the latter studies have not employed the minimal group paradigm. Instead, these studies sought to examine the effect of different sorts of information on children's attitudes towards particular members of their own and other ethnic groups, using a paradigm that minimised the transparency of the goal of the research by reducing the salience of ethnicity and the focus on prejudice. This technique (e.g., A.R. Nesdale & McLaughlin, 1987) involves children reading (or being read) a short story involving two characters, one being of the same, and the other of different, ethnicity to the subject. The story is thematic (e.g., "a day at the zoo") and each character reveals a particular set of traits and behaviours as the story unfolds. Thus, the salience of ethnicity, as well as the focus on prejudice, are both de-emphasised and the task is made more familiar and realistic because of the array of information presented, as well as the other issues that are addressed (e.g., what did the characters wear, what did they do, etc.), in addition to how much the children liked the story characters.

The first study (Nesdale, 1999b) was designed to examine the interplay between children's cognitive abilities and social motivations, as the children increased in age from 8 to 10 to 12 years. The Anglo-Australian children listened to a story about an in-group Anglo-Australian boy and an out-group Vietnamese boy, each of whom displayed equal numbers of the relevant ethnic stereotype-consistent and stereotype-inconsistent traits. Each story character also displayed a positive and a negative behaviour. The results indicated that although the children's responses changed with increasing age, reflecting their increasing cognitive abilities, their responses were not merely dependent on their expanding abilities to differentiate individuals. Instead, consistent with SIDT, the children's attention was not shared equally between the in-group and out-group characters. Of particular significance to the children as they increased in age was the stereotype inconsistency of the in-group story character.

Thus, the results revealed that, as they increased in age, the children remembered more of the in-group versus the out-group story character's stereotype-inconsistent traits and that they increasingly disliked the in-group story character. In addition, the in-group and out-group story characters' negative behaviours were attributed to internal and external causes, respectively, whereas their positive behaviours were attributed to external and internal causes, respectively. In short, rather than diminishing their interest in, and preference for, their in-group as they increased in age, the children's responses were increasingly motivated by their concerns regarding the in-group character's worthiness to be a member of their in-group.

What is also noteworthy, however, is that this in-group orientation did not necessarily lead them to reject, dislike, or express prejudice towards the out-group member as a matter of course. Indeed, the older children actually expressed more liking for the out-group than the in-group story character. This response is certainly consistent with the ethnic preference phase specified by SIDT and has been reported as the "black sheep" effect in adults (e.g., Marques, Robalo, & Rocha, 1992; Marques, Yzerbyt, & Leyens, 1988).

The second study (D. Nesdale & Brown, 2001) utilised the same paradigm to develop this line of research further. Since previous research has shown that children's in-group versus out-group stereotypes are almost invariably positive (A. R. Nesdale, 1987), one possibility was that converting half the in-group's stereotypic traits to counterstereotypic traits in the D. Nesdale (1999b) study might have given rise to an in-group character who was especially unattractive, particularly in comparison with the out-group character. Accordingly, in this study, 6-, 9-, and 12-year-old Anglo-Australian children listened to a story about an Anglo-Australian and a Chinese boy, each of whom displayed two positive and two negative traits that pilot research had revealed were matched in positivity and negativity, respectively.

In addition, in order to assess whether SIDT's distinction between ethnic preference and ethnic prejudice could be demonstrated empirically, the study also sought to manipulate the relationship between the two story characters. Thus, for half the children, the story characters were revealed to be the best of friends who shared lots of activities. In contrast, for the remaining children, the story characters were described as being bad friends whose relationship had been characterised by lots of disputes. Consistent with D. Nesdale (1999b), it was assumed that ethnic preference would be instigated when the story characters had a positive relationship, but that this might turn to dislike/prejudice when the relationship between the out-group character and favoured in-group character was one of enmity (i.e., due to their shared group membership, the children would join with the in-group character in disliking the out-group character).

However, the results revealed that, regardless of the story characters' relationship, the children gave ethnic preference responses. As they increased in age, the children remembered more of the in-group character's negative versus positive traits, saw themselves as increasingly dissimilar to him, and they liked him less. In contrast, with increasing age, the children remembered more of the out-group character's positive versus negative traits, saw themselves as increasingly similar to him, and liked him more.

Although the preceding findings are consistent with those predicted by SIDT for children in the ethnic preference phase, the negative relationship manipulation apparently did not instigate ethnic prejudice. That is, it did not enhance the children's identification with the in-group character and result in them, in consort with the in-group story character, feeling threatened by the enmity from the out-group story character. Rather, the story characters' relationship was simply not seen as being greatly relevant to the children's primary focus on, and preference for, the in-group. Clearly, the implication from these findings is that a different and stronger manipulation will be required in order to test SIDT's proposals concerning the transition of children from ethnic preference to prejudice.

CONCLUSIONS

To date, three main accounts of children's ethnic prejudice have been proposed. These accounts include the view that ethnic prejudice in children is a form of emotional maladjustment arising from a faulty parent–child relationship; that ethnic prejudice emerges in children as a reflection of the views of significant others; and that ethnic prejudice is determined by changes in children's perceptual-cognitive abilities. Although each approach accounts for some of the extant findings, the present review suggests that none provides a comprehensive explanation of the development of children's ethnic prejudice.

In particular, the present analysis argues that the critical issues upon which the preceding approaches fall short concern the need to differentiate in-group preference from out-group prejudice, the fact that children simply do not as a matter of course adopt as their own the ethnic attitudes and behaviours of their parents and peers, the fact that changes in perceptual and cognitive abilities do not straightforwardly determine ethnic attitudes, and the importance of children's need to be members of valued social groups.

In contrast to the extant approaches, social identity development theory (SIDT) has been designed to take these issues into account. Importantly, SIDT emphasises the critical significance of social identity processes in the development of children's ethnic attitudes and, in so doing, facilitates a long-overdue shift away from the prevailing emphasis in much social-developmental research on the predominance of cognitive processes.

As the discussion has revealed, the case for SIDT is compelling. The theory provides a good fit for the findings that have been revealed via ethnic preference and trait attribution studies, as well as the results obtained using other paradigms. In addition, support for the theory has been strengthened by the results from newer paradigms that have enabled the intensity of children's intergroup attitudes to be assessed. The results of the latter studies have supported many of the main tenets of SIDT.

In particular, the results have confirmed that children as young as 5 years of age are sensitive to status differences between groups and that they wish to be members of high- versus low-status groups. The findings have also confirmed the impact of self-categorisation on children. The evidence indicates that self-categorisation gives rise to a considerable positive orientation to the in-group. The effect is that children feel themselves to be similar to and they like the members of their in-group. Indeed, children like different-ethnicity in-group members as much as same-ethnicity in-group members, and both are liked more than out-group members. Further, their positive orientation to the in-group is such that if in-group members are perceived to behave in a manner inappropriate to the group, they will be seen as "black sheep" and liked less than an equally negative out-group member.

In contrast to their attitudes towards the in-group, the findings have revealed that the children's liking for out-group members may be influenced by the ethnicity of the out-group. If the in-group and out-group are differentiated by ethnicity, then the ethnicity difference apparently sharpens and accentuates the category difference, with the effect that different-ethnicity out-group members are liked less than same-ethnicity out-group members. However, consistent with SIDT, it is important to note that children reveal *less liking* rather than *dislike or hatred* towards out-group members, even those of differing ethnicity, in the absence of intergroup threat or conflict.

Although the preceding findings provide good support for SIDT, there are several important issues that still require resolution. For example, of central interest is the issue of how young children's status preferences relate to their ethnic attitudes. The results of several studies (e.g., D. Nesdale & Flesser, 2001; Yee & Brown, 1992) indicate that children do wish to be members of high-status groups. However, in the two studies in which status was manipulated, and group membership was realistically displayed via photographs (i.e., Yee & Brown, 1992; D. Nesdale et al., 2001b), status had no impact on liking. Indeed, even in the study in which group status was revealed to have an effect on in-group liking (i.e., D. Nesdale & Flesser, 2001), status had no effect on out-group liking, as might be predicted by SIDT. That is, children in the low-status in-group did not evidence an equal or greater liking for the high-status out-group; instead, they still preferred their in-group. Although these findings suggest that children are attracted by group status, but that their liking is determined by group membership, this issue requires more research attention.

Another important issue concerns the nature of the transition process between the ethnic preference and ethnic prejudice phases, as proposed by

SIDT. To date, most of the research has focused on children in the ethnic preference phase. The questions that are now of focal concern relate to the specification of the factors that instigate the transition, as well as the nature of the changes in children as they move from a state of ethnic preference to ethnic prejudice. At present, little research has addressed these issues. The final assessment of the viability of SIDT as an account of the development of children's prejudice waits upon the outcome of this research.

REFERENCES

Aboud, F. E. (1984). Social and cognitive bases of ethnic identity constancy. *Journal of Genetic Psychology, 184,* 217–230.

Aboud, F. (1988). *Children and prejudice.* Oxford: Blackwell.

Aboud, F., & Doyle, A. (1996a). Does talk of race foster prejudice or tolerance in children? *Canadian Journal of Behavioural Science, 28,* 161–170.

Aboud, F., & Doyle, A. (1996b). Parental and peer influences on children's racial attitudes. *International Journal of Intercultural Relations, 20,* 371–383.

Aboud, F. E., & Mitchell, F. G. (1977). Ethnic role taking: The effects of preference and self-identification. *International Journal of Psychology, 12,* 1–17.

Adorno, T. W., Frenkel-Brunswik, E., Levinson, D. J., & Sanford, R. N. (1950). *The authoritarian pesonality.* New York: Harper & Row.

Allport, G. W. (1954). *The nature of prejudice.* Cambridge, MA: Addison-Wesley.

Asher, S. R., & Allen, V. L. (1969). Racial preference and social comparison processes. *Journal of Social Issues, 25,* 157–167.

Banks, W. C., & Rompf, W. J. (1973). Evaluative bias and preference behaviour in black and white children. *Child Development, 44,* 776–783.

Bartel, H. W., Bartel, N. R., & Grill, J. J. (1973). A sociometric view of some integrated open classrooms. *Journal of Social Issues, 29,* 159–173.

Bigler, R. S. (1995). The role of classification skill in moderating environmental influences on children's gender stereotyping: A study of the functional use of gender in the classroom. *Child Development, 66,* 1072–1087.

Bigler, R. S., Jones, L. C., & Lobliner, D. B. (1997). Social categorisation and the formation of intergroup attitudes in children. *Child Development, 68,* 530–543.

Bigler, R. S., & Liben, L. S. (1993). A cognitive-developmental approach to racial stereotyping and constructive memory in Euro-American children. *Child Development, 64,* 1507–1518.

Bird, C., Monachesi, E. D., & Burdick, H. (1952). Infiltration and the attitudes of white and Negro parents and children. *Journal of Abnormal Social Psychology, 47,* 688–689.

Black-Gutman, D., & Hickson, F. (1996). The relationship between racial attitudes and social-cognitive development in children: An Australian study. *Developmental Psychology, 32,* 448–456.

Boulton, M. (1995). Patterns of bully/victim problems in mixed race groups of children. *Social Development, 4,* 277–293.

Branch, C. W., & Newcombe, N. (1980). Racial attitude development among young black children as a function of parental attitudes: A longitudinal and cross-section study. *Child Development, 57,* 712–21.

Brand, E. S., Ruiz, R. A., & Padilla, A. M. (1974). Ethnic identification and preference: A review. *Psychological Bulletin, 81*, 860–890.

Branscombe, N. R., & Wann, D. L. (1994). Collective self-esteem consequences of outgroup derogation when a valued social identity is on trial. *European Journal of Social Psychology, 24*, 641–657.

Brewer, M. B. (1979). Ingroup bias in the minimal intergroup situation: A cognitive motivational analysis. *Psychological Bulletin, 86*, 307–324.

Brown, G., & Johnson, S. P. (1971). The attribution of behavioural connotations to shaded and white figures by Caucasian children. *British Journal of Social and Clinical Psychology, 10*, 306–312.

Brown, R. (1995). *Prejudice: Its social psychology*. Oxford: Basil Blackwell.

Cameron, J. A., Alvarez, J. M., Ruble, D. N., & Fuligni, A. J. (2001). Children's lay theories about ingroups and outgroup: Reconceptualizing research on prejudice. *Personality and Social Psychology Review, 5*, 118–128.

Chyatte, C., Schaefer, D. F., & Spiaggia, M. (1951). Prejudice verbalisation among children. *Journal of Educational Psychology, 42*, 421–431.

Clark, A., Hocevar, D., & Dembo, M. H. (1980). The role of cognitive development in childen's explanations and preferences for skin colour. *Developmental Psychology, 16*, 332–339.

Clark, K. B., & Clark, M. K. (1939). Segregation as a factor in the racial identification of Negro pre-school children: A preliminary report. *Journal of Experimental Psychology, 8*, 161–163.

Davey, A. (1983). *Learning to be prejudiced*. London: Edward Arnold.

Doyle, A. B., & Aboud, F. E. (1995). A longitudinal study of white children's racial prejudice as a social-cognitive development. *Merrill-Palmer Quarterly, 41*, 209–228.

Doyle, A. B., Beaudet, J., & Aboud, F. E. (1988). Developmental patterns in the flexibility of children's ethnic attitudes. *Journal of Cross-Cultural Psychology, 19*, 3–18.

Durkin, K. (1995). *Developmental social psychology: From infancy to old age*. Oxford: Blackwell.

Feffer, M., & Gourevitch, V. (1960). Cognitive aspects of role-taking in children. *Journal of Personality, 28*, 383–396.

Fishbein, H. D., & Imai, S. (1993). Preschoolers select playmates on the basis of gender and race. *Journal of Applied Developmental Psychology, 14*, 303–316.

Flavell, J. H. (1963). *The developmental psychology of Jean Piaget*. New York: Litton Educational Publishing.

Frenkel-Brunswik, E., & Havel, J. (1953). Prejudice in the interviews of children: Attitudes toward minority groups. *Journal of Genetic Psychology, 82*, 91–136.

Genessee, F., Tucker, G. R., & Lambert, W. E. (1978). The development of ethnic identity and ethnic role-taking skills in children from different school settings. *International Journal of Psychology, 13*, 39–57.

George, D. M., & Hoppe, R. A. (1979). Racial identification, preference, and self-concept. *Journal of Cross-Cultural Psychology, 10*, 85–100.

Goodman, M. (1946). Evidence concerning the genesis of interracial attitudes. *American Anthropologist, 48*, 624–630.

Goodman, M. (1952). *Race awareness in young children*. Cambridge, MA: Addison-Wesley.

Greenwald, H. J., & Oppenheim, D. B. (1968). Reported magnitude of self-misidentification among negro children – artifact? *Journal of Personality and Social Psychology, 8,* 49–52.

Gregor, A. J., & McPherson, D. A. (1966). Racial attitudes among White and Negro children in a deep-south standard metropolitan area. *Journal of Social Psychology, 68,* 95–106.

Hamm, M. S. (1993). *American skinheads: The criminology and control of hate crime.* Westport, CT: Praeger.

Harris, D., Gough, H., & Martin, W. E. (1950). Children's ethnic attitudes. II: Relationships to parental beliefs concerning child training. *Child Development, 21,* 169–181.

Helgerson, E. (1943). The relative significance of race, sex, and facial expression in choice of playmate by the preschool child. *Journal of Negro Education, 12,* 617–622.

Hogg, M. A., & Abrams, D. (1988). *Social identifications: A social psychology of intergroup relations and group processes.* London: Routledge.

Horowitz, E. L. (1936). The development of attitude toward the Negro. *Archives of Psychology, 194,* 2–48.

Horowitz, E. L., & Horowitz, R. E. (1938). Development of social attitudes in children. *Sociometry, 1,* 301–338.

Hraba, J., & Grant, G. (1970). Black is beautiful: A reexamination of racial preference and identification. *Journal of Personality and Social Psychology, 16,* 398–402.

Hunsberger, B. (1978). Racial awareness and preference of White and Indian Canadian children. *Canadian Journal of Behavioural Science, 10,* 176–179.

Jansen, V. G., & Gallagher, J. J. (1966). The social choices of students in racially integrated classes for the culturally disadvantaged talented. *Exceptional Children, 33,* 221–226.

Katz, P. A. (1973). Perception of racial cues in preschool children: A new look. *Developmental Psychology, 8,* 295–299.

Katz, P. A. (1976). The acquisition of racial attitudes in children. In P. A. Katz (Ed.), *Towards the elimination of racism* (pp. 125–154). New York: Pergamon Press.

Katz, P. A., & Seavey, C. (1973). Labels and children's perception of faces. *Child Development, 44,* 770–775.

Katz, P. A., Sohn, M., & Zalk, S. R. (1975). Perceptual concomitants of racial attitudes in urban grade-school children. *Developmental Psychology, 11,* 135–144.

Kohlberg, L. (1976). Moral stages and moralisation: The cognitive-developmental approach. In T. Lickona (Ed.), *Moral development and behaviour.* New York: Holt, Rinehart & Winston.

Lerner, R. M., & Buehrig, C. J. (1975). The development of racial attitudes in young Black and White children. *Journal of Genetic Psychology, 127,* 45–54.

Lerner, R. M., & Schroeder, C. (1971). Kindergarten children's active vocabulary about body build. *Developmental Psychology, 5,* 179.

Levin, J., & McDevitts, J. (1993). *Hate crimes: The rising tide of bigotry and bloodshed.* New York: Plenum Press.

Livesley, W. J., & Bromley, D. B. (1973). *Person perception in childhood and adolescence.* New York: John Wiley & Sons.

Long, K. M., Spears, R., & Manstead, A. S. R. (1994). The influence of personal and collective self-esteem on strategies of social differentiation. *British Journal of Social Psychology, 33,* 313–319.

Madge, N. J. H. (1976). Context and the expressed ethnic preferences of infant school children. *Journal of Child Psychology and Psychiatry, 17,* 337–344.

Marques, J. M., Robalo, E. M., & Rocha, S. A. (1992). Ingroup bias and the "black sheep" effect: Assessing the impact of social identification and perceived variability on group judgments. *European Journal of Social Psychology*, *22*, 331–352.

Marques, J. M., Yzerbyt, V. Y., & Leyens, J. P. (1988). The "black sheep effect": Extremity of judgments towards in-group members as a function of group identification. *European Journal of Social Psychology*, *18*, 1–16.

Marsh, A. (1970). Awareness of racial differences in West African and British children. *Race*, *11*, 289–302.

Middleton, M. R., Tajfel, H., & Johnson, N. B. (1970). Cognitive and affective aspects of children's national attitudes. *British Journal of Social and Clinical Psychology*, *9*, 122–134.

Milner, D. (1973). Racial identification and preference in "black" British children. *European Journal of Social Psychology*, *3*, 281–295.

Milner, D. (1983). *Children and race: Ten years on*. London: Ward Lock Educational.

Milner, D. (1996). Children and racism: Beyond the value of the dolls . . . In W. Peter Robinson (Ed.), *Social groups and identities: Developing the legacy of Henri Tajfel*. Oxford: Butterworth-Heinemann.

Morland, J. K. (1966). A comparison of race awareness in Northern and Southern children. *American Journal of Orthopsychiatry*, *36*, 22–31.

Mosher, D. L., & Scodel, A. (1960). Relationships between ethnocentrism in children and the ethnocentrism and authoritarian rearing practices of their mothers. *Child Development*, *31*, 369–376.

Mullen, B., Brown, R., & Smith, C. (1991). Ingroup bias as a function of salience, relevance and status: An integration. *European Journal of Social Psychology*, *22*, 103–122.

Nesdale, A. R. (1987). Ethnic stereotypes and children. *Multicultural Australia Papers*, Whole No. 57.

Nesdale, A. R., & McLaughlin, K. (1987). Effects of sex stereotypes on young children's memories, predictions and liking. *British Journal of Developmental Psychology*, *5*, 231–241.

Nesdale, D. (1999a). Social identity and ethnic prejudice in children. In P. Martin & W. Noble (Eds.), *Psychology and society* (pp. 92–110). Brisbane: Australian Academic Press.

Nesdale, D. (1999b). Developmental changes in children's ethnic preferences and social cognitions. *Journal of Applied Developmental Psychology*, *20*, 501–519.

Nesdale, D. (2001a). Development of prejudice in children. In M. Augoustinos & K. Reynolds (Eds.). *Understanding prejudice, racism, and social conflict*. London: SAGE Publications.

Nesdale, D. (2001b). Language and the development of children's ethnic prejudice. *Journal of Language and Social Psychology*, *20*, 90–110.

Nesdale, D., & Brown, K. (2001). *Development of children's ethnic attitudes*. Unpublished manuscript, Griffith University.

Nesdale, D., & Flesser, D. (2001). Social identity and the development of children's group attitudes. *Child Development*, *72*, 506–517.

Nesdale, D., Durkin, K., Griffiths, J., & Maass, A. (2001a). *Effects of ingroup and outgroup ethnicity on children's attitudes towards the ingroup and outgroup*. Unpublished manuscript, Griffith University.

Nesdale, D., Durkin, K., Maass, A., & Griffiths, J. (2001b). *Social identity processes and children's ethnic attitude*. Unpublished manuscript, Griffith University.

Peevers, B. H., & Secord, P. F. (1973). Developmental changes in attribution of descriptive concepts to persons. *Journal of Personality and Social Psychology*, *27*, 120–128.

Porter, J. D. R. (1971). *Black child, white child: The development of racial attitudes*. Cambridge, MA: Harvard University Press.

Proshansky, H. M. (1966). The development of intergroup attitudes. In L. W. Hoffman & M. L. Hoffman (Eds.), *Review of child development research* (pp. 311–371). New York: Russell Sage.

Quillian, L. (1995). Prejudice as a response to perceived group threat: Population composition and anti-immigrant and racial prejudice in Europe. *American Sociological Review*, *60*, 586–611.

Radke, M. J., & Trager, H. G. (1950). Children's perceptions of the social roles of Negroes and whites. *Journal of Psychology*, *29*, 3–33.

Radke, M. J., Trager, H. G., & Davis, H. (1949). Social perceptions and attitudes of children. *Genetical Psychology Monographs*, *40*, 327–447.

Radke-Yarrow, M., Trager, H., & Miller, J. (1952). The role of parents in the development of children's ethnic attitudes. *Child Development*, *23*, 13–53.

Renninger, C. A., & Williams, J. E. (1966). Black–white colour connotations and race awareness in pre-school children. *Perceptual and Motor Skills*, *22*, 771–785.

Rice, A. S., Ruiz, R. A., & Padilla, A. M. (1974). Person perception, self-identify, and ethnic group preference in Anglo, Black and Chicano preschool and third grade children. *Journal of Cross-Cultural Psychology*, *5*, 100–108.

Rosenfield, D., & Stephan, W. G. (1981). Intergroup relations among children. In S. S. Brehm, S. M. Kassin, & F. X. Gibbons (Eds.), *Developmental social psychology* (pp. 271–297). New York: Oxford University Press.

Rubin, M., & Hewstone, M. (1998). Social identity theory's self-esteem hypothesis: A review and some suggestions for clarification. *Personality and Social Psychology Bulletin*, *2*, 40–62.

Selman, R. L., & Byrne, D. F. (1974). A structural-developmental analysis of levels of role-taking in middle childhood. *Child Development*, *45*, 803–806.

Semaj, L. (1980). The development of racial evaluation and preference: A cognitive approach. *Journal of Black Psychology*, *6*, 59–79.

Stephan, W. G., & Rosenfield, D. (1979). Black self-rejection: Another look. *Journal of Educational Psychology*, *71*, 708–716.

Stephan, W. G., Ybarra, O., Martinez, C. M., Schwarzwald, J., & Tur-Kaspa, M. (1998). Prejudice toward immigrants to Spain and Israel. *Journal of Cross-Cultural Psychology*, *29*, 559–576.

Stevenson, H. W., & Stevenson, N. G. (1960). Social interaction in an interracial nursery school. *Genetic Psychology Monographs*, *61*, 37–75.

Tajfel, H., Billig, M. G., Bundy, R. P., & Flament, C. (1971). Social categorisation and intergroup behaviour. *European Journal of Social Psychology*, *1*, 149–178.

Tajfel, H., Jahoda, G., Nemeth, C., Rim, Y., & Johnson, N. B. (1972). The devaluation by children of their own national and ethnic group: Two case studies. *British Journal of Social and Clinical Psychology*, *11*, 235–243.

Tajfel, H., & Turner, J. (1979). An integrative theory of intergroup conflict. In W. G. Austin & S. Worchel (Eds.), *The social psychology of intergroup relations*. Monterey, CA: Brooks/Cole.

Teplin, L. A. (1976). A comparison of racial/ethnic preferences among Anglo, Black and Latino children. *American Journal of Orthopsychiatry*, *46*, 702–709.

Turner, J. C., Hogg, M. A., Oakes, P. J., Reicher, S. D., & Wetherell, M. S. (1987). *Rediscovering the social group: A self-categorisation theory.* Oxford: Basil Blackwell.

Vaughan, G. M. (1963). Concept formation and the development of ethnic awareness. *Journal of Genetic Psychology, 103*, 93–103.

Vaughan, G. M. (1964). The development of ethnic attitudes in New Zealand school children. *Genetic Psychology Monographs, 70*, 135–175.

Vaughan, G. M. (1987). A social psychological model of ethnic identity development. In J. S. Phinney & M. J. Rotheram (Eds.), *Children's ethnic socialisation.* London: SAGE Publishers.

Vaughan, G. M. (1988). The psychology of intergroup discrimination. *New Zealand Journal of Psychology, 17*, 1–14.

Vaughan, G., Tajfel, H., & Williams, J. A. (1981). Bias in reward allocation in an intergroup and an interpersonal context. *Social Psychology Quarterly, 44*, 37–42.

Vaughan, G. M., & Thompson, R. H. T. (1961). New Zealand children's attitudes toward Maoris. *Journal of Abnormal Social Psychology, 62*, 701–704.

Weiland, A., & Coughlin, R. (1979). Self-identification and preferences: A comparison of white and Mexican-American first and third graders. *Journal of Cross-Cultural Psychology, 10*, 356–365.

Williams, J. E., Best, D. L., & Boswell, D. A. (1975). The measurement of children's racial attitudes in the early school years. *Child Development, 46*, 494–500.

Williams, J. E., & Morland, J. K. (1976). *Race, colour and the young child.* Chapel Hill, NC: University of North Carolina Press.

Williams, J. E., & Roberson, J. K. (1967). A method for assessing racial attitudes in preschool children. *Educational and Psychological Measurement, 27*, 671–689.

Yee, M. D., & Brown, R. (1992). Self-evaluations and intergroup attitudes in children aged three to nine. *Child Development, 63*, 619–629.

Yee, M. D., & Brown, R. (1994). The development of gender differentiation in young children. *British Journal of Social Psychology, 33*, 183–196.

Zinser, O., Rich, M. C., & Bailey, R. C. (1981). Sharing behaviour and racial preference in children. *Motivation and Emotion, 5*, 179–187.

9 The development and self-regulation of intergroup attitudes in children

Adam Rutland

From the age of five, children are exposed to the problems. Not mixing with people from the other side of the community becomes the norm. It's just not the thing to do. It's been like that for so many years that it's normal now.

A Protestant from Belfast, Northern Ireland
(*The Guardian*, 4th January, 2002)

The above quotation suggests that at a surprisingly early age children may form "self" and "other" representations in reference to social category membership. It also suggests that when forming these intergroup attitudes, children may be fully aware of the social norms of the prevailing context. The aim of this chapter is to demonstrate that a comprehensive account of children's intergroup attitudes requires an understanding that children can self-regulate their expression of intergroup bias in line with internalised normative beliefs. Moreover, it will be argued that they do this strategically, to present a positive image of themselves to valued members of their in-group.

The chapter starts with a short overview of the literature on children's developing intergroup attitudes and cognitive-developmental theory (CDT). Research into national prejudice development will be presented to highlight both empirical and conceptual problems with CDT. Next, social identity theory (SIT) will be briefly discussed as an alternative account of prejudice development. Finally some recent experiments will be outlined that demonstrate how self-regulation plays an important role in the development of intergroup attitudes.

CHILDREN'S INTERGROUP ATTITUDES AND COGNITIVE-DEVELOPMENTAL THEORY

There is an abundance of psychological research suggesting that children even as young as 3 years of age identify with social categories and express clear affective preference for one rather than the other. For example, research on ethnicity has shown that by the age of 3 or 4 years, children typically express more positive attitudes towards their own ethnic group than towards others (see reviews by Aboud, 1988; Aboud & Amato, 2001; Brown, 1995; Cameron, Alvarez, Ruble, & Fuligni, 2001; Katz, 1976; Nesdale, 2001). Negative intergroup attitudes with respect to gender are typically found between 4 and 5 years of age (Bigler, 1995; Bigler & Liben, 1992; Powlishta, 1995a, 1995b; Powlishta, Serbin, Doyle, & White, 1994; Yee & Brown, 1994). Studies have even shown intergroup bias in minimal or transitory groups at around 5 and 6 years of age (e.g., Abrams, Rutland, Cameron, & Marques, 2003; Bigler, 1995; Bigler, Brown, & Markell, 2001; Bigler, Jones, & Lobliner, 1997; Durkin & Judge, 2001; Nesdale & Flesser, 2001; Spielman, 2000; Vaughan, Tajfel, & Williams, 1981).

A common finding in the literature has been a "peaking" of childhood prejudice around 5 to 7 years of age and then a decline in subsequent years. Discovery of this developmental sequence was key to the formation of the dominant theoretical account of children's developing intergroup attitudes. Cognitive-developmental theory (CDT) is probably the most well-known account of how children's intergroup attitudes develop (Aboud, 1988; Katz, 1976; Lambert & Klineberg, 1967). CDT argues that prejudice is caused by information-processing errors due to young children's poor cognitive ability to perceive people of different racial groups in individualised terms (e.g., friendly, hardworking). This theory argues that cognitively immature young children are prone to prejudice because they cannot process multiple classifications and attend simultaneously to two or more different perspectives (i.e., decentre). Young children see the world only in bipolar terms and cannot simultaneously process the internal and group-related qualities of an individual. Thus they cannot see the similarities between individuals in different groups and the differences between people within groups. Only with cognitive development do children shift from social categorical to individuated thinking and begin to make judgments in terms of unique interpersonal rather than intergroup qualities.

CDT would predict that 5-year-old children should show high levels of intergroup bias and that prejudice should "peak" at around 7 years of age and then, with the acquisition of concrete operational thought, begin to decline. There is a large body of evidence indicating that prejudice, especially in the domain of ethnicity, is high among young children and then decreases with age (see reviews, Aboud, 1988; Aboud & Amato, 2001). However, some research suggests that this developmental sequence is not always evident. There are various examples of research indicating that children in mid childhood and early adolescence still show intergroup bias (e.g., Abrams, 1985, 1989; Augoustinos & Rosewarne, 2001; Bennett, Lyons, Sani, & Barrett, 1998; Durkin & Houghton, 2000; Hoover & Fishbein, 1999; Rutland, 1999; Tajfel, Nemeth, Jahoda, Campbell, & Johnson, 1970; Verkuyten, 2001). CDT has difficulty accounting for prejudice development across all domains, especially gender and nationality. For example, problematically for CDT, there is evidence that girls are more likely than boys to maintain own-gender bias attitudes irrespective of their age (Brown, 1995; Maccoby, 1988; Powlishta et al., 1994; Yee & Brown, 1994). Furthermore, there are problems using CDT to understand the intergroup attitudes of children from minority or subordinate groups. Evidence suggests that children from dominant groups almost always show strong in-group bias, whereas minority group children show a much more varied pattern of responses, ranging from out-group favouritism, through "fairness", to in-group bias (Brown, 1995).

The findings of research into children's national attitudes also raise questions about the generality of CDT. For example, Tajfel et al. (1970) conducted a large-scale cross-national study of children's preference for their own country. They found strong and significant evidence of intergroup bias among 9- to 12-year-olds in England, Belgium, and Austria, though the overall tendency to assign better-liked photographs to the national in-group decreased with age. Interestingly, there were two exceptions to this general pattern. In Louvain, regarding both the Belgian and Flemish assignments, national intergroup bias showed a marked increase in age. However, in Glasgow the children of all ages showed little, if any, tendency to prefer their own national group (i.e., "Scottish"). Tajfel, Jahoda, Nemeth, Rim, and Johnson (1972) presented evidence suggesting that the lack of simple, unique, and overtly salient national labels in the sociopolitical context of Belgium and Scotland may explain the failure to find intergroup bias in young children. They also contended that the "effects of social context on the attitudes of children" (p. 239) was evidenced in the increase with age of national preference among the Flemish but not the Scottish. Tajfel and colleagues argued that self-denigrating stereotypes found among Scottish adults in the 1970s (see Cheyne, 1970) might have affected children's national attitudes. Indeed, Tajfel and colleagues believed that they "provided evidence of the very high sensitivity of young children to the more primitive aspects of the value systems of their societies" (p. 243).

RECENT RESEARCH ON CHILDREN'S NATIONAL INTERGROUP ATTITUDES

In 1995 I began a longitudinal research project to investigate the value of CDT as an account of children's intergroup attitudes. This project primarily investigated changes in children's national in-group bias and national prejudice over a 3-year period between 1995 and 1997 inclusive (see Rutland, 1999, for the findings from data collection during 1995). Almost all the children (aged 6 to 16 years) studied in 1995 were again interviewed in 1996 and also in 1997. Each year national in-group bias and prejudice was measured using the same photograph evaluation task. This task involved the children evaluating 10 passport-style photographs showing people's heads in two conditions: with or without the national category label applied. The national labels were British, American, German, Australian, and Russian.

The longitudinal data showed clearly that national in-group bias varied over the 3 years of the project. The data from 1995 showed no evidence of national in-group bias among the 6- and 8-year-olds. Bias was found only in children over 10 years of age. However, there was a significant increase in terms of national in-group bias across the two subsequent years of the project. In 1996 and 1997 there was evidence of significant national in-group bias in every age group. The children's responses to informal questioning suggest that these differences may be accounted for by children's level of national self-category salience. This is both the child's awareness that they belong to the national category and the degree to which they identify with the nation. Regardless of age, levels of national self-category salience appeared higher in 1996 and 1997. This was especially true among the young children, and may have reflected nationally significant events, such as the European Football Championships (Euro '96), held in the UK. These findings are in line with previous research drawing upon SIT, which has shown that self-category salience influences children's intergroup attitudes (Bigler et al., 1997; Tajfel et al., 1972) and, more specifically, that national identification affects national in-group bias (Kinket & Verkuyten, 1999; Verkuyten, 2001). Evidence of temporal variability in children's national in-group bias poses an important challenge to CDT. This theory would expect a stable age pattern in the development children's in-group bias across each year of the project, because according to the theory, intergroup attitudes are primarily determined by the child's cognitive capacities. The data also clearly shows that national in-group bias does not "peak" at 7 years of age and then decline, as predicted by CDT. Indeed, it was evident that children maintained their levels of national in-group bias well into adolescence.

Moreover, Rutland (1999) found in 1995 that children showed national prejudice only towards the German out-group. No evidence of prejudice towards the Americans, Australians, or Russians was found. Prejudice towards Germans showed signs of appearing at 12 years of age and was clearly evident among 14 and 16-year-olds. Again, in 1996 national prejudice was only shown towards the Germans among the children above 13 years of age. These findings too are incompatible with the predictions of CDT.

Importantly, the project also found evidence of temporal variability in national prejudice towards the Germans. In 1997 the data showed no clear sign of out-group derogation of the Germans. The most parsimonious explanation of this finding is the lack of any significant event in 1997 to highlight a contrast between the in-group and Germany. During 1997 there was no significant event like the VE Day (Victory in Europe, i.e., the ending of World War II in Europe) 50th anniversary in 1995 or Euro '96, to focus attention on Germany as a salient and distinctive out-group. This temporal shift in prejudice towards Germans raises doubts about the explanatory power of CDT and suggests that contextual factors may play an important part in the onset of prejudicial beliefs among children.

A recent study by Fyfe and Rutland (2000), like Tajfel et al., (1970), found cross-national differences in children's national intergroup attitudes. The nations used within this study were chosen because they varied in terms of group status. Contrary to CDT, social identity theory (SIT) would predict that children from high-status groups should show greater intergroup bias than those from low-status groups because their group membership should allow for greater enhancement of self-esteem (Bigler et al., 2001; Brown, 1984; Doosje, Ellemers, & Spears, 1999; Nesdale & Flesser, 2001; Yee & Brown, 1994). Seventy-two Maltese children (i.e., from a "low"-status country) and the same number of Scottish children (i.e., from a relatively "high"-status country) were included in the study. These children were aged between 6 and 16 years. A picture preference task was used to assess attitudes towards the in-group and the English, Germans, French, and Italians. The Maltese showed no evidence of national in-group bias or out-group derogation. In contrast, the Scottish children showed significant national in-group bias, some evidence of negativity towards French and Maltese at 6 to 8 years of age, and signs of negativity towards the English and Germans at 14 to 16 years of age. Like the early work by Tajfel and colleagues, this study suggests children's national intergroup attitudes are very sensitive to contextual factors.

The findings of the studies described above raise doubts about the generality of CDT. The "dip" predicted by CDT in children's negative intergroup attitudes was not evident in these studies of national intergroup attitudes. Rather, the children's attitudes towards countries showed both contextual and temporal variability. There was evidence of national in-group bias among young children in both England and Scotland, while it was absent among Maltese children. National prejudice did manifest itself among English and Scottish children, though this was often particular to a salient out-group and showed temporal flexibility. In contrast, no evidence of national prejudice was found among Maltese children.

SOCIAL IDENTITY THEORY

The limitations associated with CDT have encouraged some researchers to turn to social identity theory (SIT: Tajfel & Turner, 1979, 1986) as an alternative account of prejudice development (Nesdale, 2001). SIT has been described in sufficient detail elsewhere not to require a further full exposition here (see Chapter 1 by Bennett & Sani, and Chapter 8 by Nesdale; also Brown, 2000; Capozza & Brown, 2000; Ellemers, Spears, & Doosje, 1999).

Despite its prominence within the social-psychological literature, SIT says nothing about age trends in children's intergroup attitudes and consequently is unable to account for age effects in this field when they are found. Children clearly undergo significant age-linked changes in their cognitive, linguistic, and social abilities and these changes are likely to have a significant bearing on their intergroup attitudes. SIT, with its emphasis on motivational concerns and the social context, is silent on how these changes may be associated with particular age trends in children's intergroup attitudes. There is no mechanism or psychological process within SIT to explain why children's attitudes can change as they become older. Specifically, these theories have a problem explaining the common finding that ethnic intergroup bias is strong among young children and then decreases with age (Aboud, 1988; Doyle & Aboud, 1995).

SELF-REGULATION AND CHILDREN'S INTERGROUP ATTITUDES

No one theory to date has offered a comprehensive explanation of children's developing intergroup attitudes. CDT has provided a clear account of the developmental trends commonly found in the domain of ethnic prejudice – namely the well-documented "peaking" of prejudice at around 5 to 7 years of age and then the gradual decline into late childhood (see Aboud, 1988; Brown, 1995; Katz, 1976). However, CDT faces problems when attempting to explain children's intergroup attitudes in other domains (e.g., nationality and gender). This nevertheless does not negate the fact that clear developmental patterns, especially in ethnic prejudice, are often found in the literature on children's intergroup attitudes, and these need explanation. SIT is not a developmental theory and therefore make no specific predictions regarding developmental trends in children's intergroup attitudes.

The findings of previous research on national and ethnic prejudice may become compatible if it is accepted that the developmental path of prejudice may be dependent on children's ability to self-regulate their expression of prejudice in accordance with normative beliefs. Children may gradually learn with age to associate particular labels (e.g., nasty, friendly) with certain types of social categories (e.g., blacks, whites, Germans, French). However the degree to which they demonstrate explicit prejudice towards these categories may well be moderated by their ability to critically evaluate the legitimacy and acceptability of these implicit associations. This process of critical evaluation could be influenced to a large degree by internalised normative beliefs about the expression of particular views. The expression of negative attitudes, then, may vary as a function of both age and domain. Thus, given the recognition that children can regulate their expression of prejudice, it is empirically conceivable that sometimes children above 7 to 9 years of age will show low prejudice (i.e., with regard to ethnic groups) and also high prejudice (i.e., with regard to national groups).

This alternative account of development trends in children's intergroup attitudes was hinted at when Brown (1995) stated, "one might add, too, though this is not much emphasized in Aboud's account, that as children mature they become more sensitive to norms of adult society and hence more aware of the social undesirability of expressing certain kinds of prejudice too overtly" (p. 155). It has been argued before that the internalisation of normative beliefs regarding legitimate and admissible forms of prejudice and stereotyping might help explain differences in the expression of stereotypical thoughts (e.g., Macrae, Bodenhausen, & Milne, 1997). Rutland (1999) explained the contradiction between his results on national prejudice development and previous research on ethnic prejudice in terms of the divergent norms in our society regarding the legitimacy of expressing national and ethnic prejudice. It is fair to say that in most societies, prejudice is viewed negatively, as irrational and uninformed thought. Among most people ethnic prejudice is certainly seen as unreasonable, but with national prejudice this is not always the case. Sometimes it is seen as a tolerable form of expression among the majority (Billig, 1991). It seems reasonable, then, to suggest that older children and adolescents may show reduced ethnic prejudice due to the influence of social norms regarding the illegitimacy of ethnic prejudice. In contrast, social norms surrounding national prejudice might actually encourage more prejudice. Indeed, research involving adults has clearly shown that manipulation of in-group social norms can increase levels of intergroup discrimination (e.g., Jetten, Spears, & Manstead, 1996, 1997; Long & Manstead, 1997; Rutland & Brown, 2001).

There is evidence that children can actively engage in self-presentation and present normative intergroup behaviour to win positive evaluations from their in-group. Jahoda, Thomson, and Bhatt (1972) investigated ethnic identity and preferences among 6- to 10-year-old Asian children in Glasgow. In their first study they found that the children's host community powerfully influenced Asian children as they showed preferences towards the white outgroup. However, in their second study the ethnicity of the experimenter was changed as they used an Asian psychologist to test the children. This had a significant effect on the Asian children's responses. They no longer showed out-group favouritism; rather, their preferences moved in the direction of Asian cultural values and they showed significant in-group bias. Jahoda and colleagues concluded that it is difficult to ascertain the "real" values of these children: they "may be in a state of somewhat precarious balance, fraught with potential conflict; they can only avoid this by expressing the values that appear to them situationally appropriate" (p. 31). A more recent study also showed experimenter effects on children's intergroup attitudes. Pedersen, Walker, and Glass (1999) found in-group preferences were higher in 5- to 12-year-old Aboriginal-Australian children using an in-group Aboriginal compared to an out-group white experimenter.

Recently, some social identity theorists researching with adults have argued that conscious, strategic self-management may override automatic responses in certain contexts and drive intergroup attitudes, especially when the audience or social context requires the avoidance of negative, and the promotion of positive, identities (Abrams, 1990, 1994; Abrams & Brown, 1989; Barreto & Ellemers, 2000; Noel, Wann, & Branscombe, 1995; Postmes, Branscombe, Spears, & Young, 1999; Reicher, Spears, & Postmes, 1995;

Spears, 2001). This research suggests that the exclusive use of explicit measures when investigating intergroup attitudes allows participants to strategically claim positive and valued identities (e.g., a fair-minded person), while downplaying negative identities (e.g., an irrational bigot).

Research in developmental psychology indicates that even children as young as 4 years of age can actively engage in self-presentational efforts to win positive identities and evaluations from the in-group when they are highly motivated to make good impressions. Banerjee and Lintern (2000) found that 4- to 6-year-old boys produced more gender-stereotypical self-descriptions when in front of a group of same-sex peers than when alone. There was no evidence of a peer audience effect on the self-descriptions of 4- to 8-year-old girls. This finding was not unexpected, given that research has shown that girls demonstrate less gender-typing than boys (e.g., Huston, 1985; Serbin, Conner, Burchardt, & Citron, 1979). However, as Banerjee and Lintern suggest, it implies that peer groups of males produce more conformity to in-group norms than do females. The fact that peer group effects were strongest for young boys, who showed high levels of gender-typing in the baseline condition, suggests males are concerned about social evaluation because they wish to appear consistent with the norms of the peer group. These results and those from other studies (e.g., Banerjee & Yuill, 1999a, 1999b; Bennett & Yeeles, 1990) indicate that school-age children have the capacity to understand self-presentational motives and, by approximately 8 years of age, they can provide spontaneous explanations for complex self-presentational behaviour.

IMPLICIT MEASURES OF CHILDREN'S INTERGROUP ATTITUDES

One way to examine whether children regulate the expression of prejudice is to use methods that limit the possibility of their giving socially desirable responses. Researchers have begun to countenance the possibility that reductions of prejudice with age may reflect "greater sensitivity to the social appropriateness of responses" (Powlishta et al., 1994, p. 533). Indeed, Powlishta and her colleagues suggest that to reduce the potential impact of social desirability responding, future studies should adopt more subtle measures of prejudice that are less dependent on conscious awareness. Nesdale (2001) made a similar point when he reviewed the existing measures typically used in research on childhood prejudice. He stated that the "shared weakness of each of the preceding measurement techniques concerns their transparency of intent, even to young children, with the resulting problem that each invites children to construct responses which they consider to be more socially acceptable" (p. 62). Researchers are beginning to realise that new methodologies are required to minimise social desirability effects in children. Indeed, Nesdale suggests the transparency problems can be handled by using psychologically relevant measures of which children are unaware, namely implicit rather than explicit measures of bias. Though such measures are becoming more common in social psychology (see Devine, 2001; Greenwald & Banaji, 1995; Maass, Castelli, & Arcuri, 2000), they have rarely been used with children.

Most research on childhood prejudice has used direct measures of attitudes, which by implication make the assumption that attitudes operate in a conscious mode and are exemplified by traditional self-report measures. However, recent work within social psychology has established that attitudes can be activated automatically and outside of conscious attention (e.g., Bargh, Chaiken, Govender, & Pratto, 1992). This can result in judgments occurring without awareness of the causation. Greenwald and Banaji (1995) defined implicit attitudes as "introspectively unidentified (or inaccurately identified) traces of past experience that mediate favorable or unfavorable feeling, thought, or action toward social objects" (p. 8). Intuitively one might expect implicit prejudice, as assessed in response latency paradigms, and explicit self-reported prejudice, to be based on the same experiences and socialisation. Thus they should be directly related, but research typically does not support this expectation; on the contrary: Dissociations are common (Banaji & Greenwald, 1995; Dovidio, Kawakami, Johnson, Johnson, & Howard, 1997). Differences between implicit and explicit measures are especially likely to be observed for socially sensitive issues and particularly for racial attitudes (Greenwald, McGee, & Schwartz, 1998). Conceivably, differences between response latency and self-report measures may reflect the distinction between activation and application. The presence of an attitude object may automatically activate an association evaluation from memory, which *may* be applied in subsequent judgments (Dovidio et al., 1997).

DISSOCIATION BETWEEN IMPLICIT AND EXPLICIT MEASURES

Evidence of a dissociation between response latency measures of implicit bias and self-reported explicit measures of bias would suggest that children are engaging in self-regulation when expressing their explicit attitudes. Children should gradually become aware of particular implicit associations surrounding social categories, but whether these associations are endorsed and applied will depend on children's self-regulation of explicit prejudice in line with normative beliefs. Therefore, when social norms prohibit the articulation of explicit bias we should find a weak relationship between measures of implicit and explicit prejudice. Rutland, Morrison, and Arnold-Dorman (2001) examined the relationship between implicit and explicit measures in two studies of young females' body image bias. Among young females there is evidence of a decrease in explicit body image bias, with age. Powlishta et al. (1994) found females showed less bias against overweight body images with increasing age.

This finding suggests that, with age, females become increasingly aware of the unacceptability of expressing blatant body image bias, even though they may still, at some level, subscribe to an image of beauty that does not involve an overweight body image (e.g., Balaam & Haslam, 1998; Muth & Cash, 1997). Given these findings, it seems reasonable to expect dissociation between measures of implicit and explicit body image bias.

The first study examined 60 females aged between 8 and 21 years. They were presented with an explicit and an implicit task. The explicit measure was a trait attribution task similar to the one utilised by Powlishta et al. (1994). The participants had to indicate which of two female silhouettes, one slim and one overweight, was more likely to be characterised by each of a list of 12 positive and 8 negative traits. The implicit measure was the Stroop colour-naming task, a task that has previously been used to measure adults' processing of weight- and shape-related words (e.g., Cooper & Fairburn, 1992). Each participant was presented with three computer screens of words that constituted three conditions (neutral, colour, and weight). These screens contained five word columns with the same five words in each column. The columns contained either neutral words (sit, dare, object, tower, wool), colour words (orange, red, blue, green, brown), or weight/body shape words (fat, diet, thighs, cakes, hips). The words were written in different colour ink and the participants were asked to name the colour of all the words on each screen. The ordering of the ink colour and the words on each screen were randomised. Response times for correct completion of each screen were recorded. It was predicted that participants would be slower responding to the weight word screen than the neutral word screen. This finding would indicate selective processing of information relating to weight words among our female participants.

The findings showed a noticeable drop in the females' explicit bias with age. There was a significant decrease with age in the number of positive attributes assigned to the slim silhouette, whereas the number of positive attributions to the overweight silhouette increased with age. Negative trait attributions to the slim silhouette increased with age, while the overweight silhouette received significant fewer negative attributions with age. Post hoc analysis revealed across all attributions that body image bias decreased significantly between 8–9 years and 14–15 years of age.

In contrast, the implicit measure showed the Stroop effect in all age groups. The females' response times at all ages were significantly faster for the neutral words compared to the weight-salient and colour words. There was no evidence of an equivalent decrease in this implicit measure with age, and these findings were replicated in the second study. Together these results suggest the females had a significant subconscious disturbance or interference regarding weight. Though this indicates that the females had an implicit difficulty with weight issues it does not necessarily suggest that they were implicitly biased against overweight people. Indeed, the Stroop naming task has been traditionally used within clinical psychology more as a measure of implicit self-body image disturbance rather than implicit bias towards body shape (e.g., Cooper & Fairburn, 1992; Cooper, Anastasiades, & Fairburn, 1992).

THE IMPLICIT ASSOCIATION TEST

The second study, therefore, also included an implicit method known to measure implicit attitudinal bias directly. This was the Implicit Association Test (IAT) developed by Greenwald et al. (1998). The IAT was devised to measure automatic concept-attribute associations and an underlying assumption of the test is that strongly associated (compatible) attribute-concept pairs should be easier to classify together than weakly associated or opposed (incompatible) attribute-concept pairs. The IAT measures implicit bias in the participants by presenting them with a series of words on a computer screen. They have to categorise these words (as compatible or incompatible) as quickly as possible by pressing a left or right key on a keyboard.

The IAT consisted of a sequence of five blocks, which together assessed the association between a target concept and an attribute dimension. The procedure started with an introduction to the target concept block. In this block the participants were required to categorise words that were recognisable as either coming from one of two concepts: slim (e.g., slender or toned) or overweight (obese or fat). The second block involved the introduction of the attribute dimension. The children were presented with either positive or negative adjectives and asked to categorise these words as pleasant versus unpleasant in meaning. After this introduction to the target concepts and to the attribute dimension, the two were superimposed in the third block. The stimuli for target and attribute discriminations appeared on alternate trials. This was the intuitive block, as the target slim words were paired with positive words and the target overweight words were paired with the negative words. In the fourth block, the participants learnt a reversal of response assignments for the target concepts: They were presented with the same stimulus as in the first block except they responded to slim and overweight words using the opposite keys (i.e., left or right) to those used in the first block. Then in the fifth and final counterintuitive block, the target concepts were reversed and combined with the same attribute discriminations as in third block. This meant that the target slim words were now paired with negative words and the target overweight words were paired with the positive words.

It was found that the target concepts ("slim" and overweight) were differentially associated with the positive and negative attributes. The participants in all age groups recorded quicker response times in the intuitive block compared to the counterintuitive block (i.e., an IAT effect). The concept "slim" was seen as more compatible with positive adjectives than the concept "overweight"; and vice versa for negative adjectives. Unlike explicit body image bias, the IAT effect did not decrease with age. In addition, there was not a significant correlation between the explicit and implicit measures. These two studies show that implicit and explicit measures of body image bias follow different developmental paths. Dissociation between these two types of measure suggests that the participants were sensitive to social desirability and normative concerns. This is evidenced by the fact that with increasing age they were unwilling to express explicit or blatant body image bias, even though they still showed signs of implicit bias regarding an overweight body image.

PUBLIC SELF-FOCUS AND CHILDREN'S ETHNIC INTERGROUP ATTITUDES

The argument that children's intergroup attitudes are dependent on their ability to engage in self-presentation and regulate their expression of prejudice in accordance with normative beliefs can also be investigated through studies that manipulate public self-focus. Public self-focus involves attention to one's self-portrayal (Scheier & Carver, 1981), namely, to how significant others may perceive the self in a specific context. Abrams (1990) suggests that when people focus on the public self they take up general standards of socially legitimate behaviour (e.g., equity norms) and show intragroup compliance. This means that when attention is directed towards managing an appropriate public impression, behaviour may follow the specific norms of the audience or, if these are unclear, general social norms (e.g., to please the experimenter).

A recent study by Rutland, Cameron, Milne, and McGeorge (2002) investigated directly whether heightened public self-focus in children will typically reduce explicit ethnic bias in compliance with internalised normative beliefs. Evidence of self-presentation would be apparent if the children showed significantly lower explicit ethnic bias when public self-focus is high rather than low. However, this effect was predicted only among young children, since research (e.g., Bennett & Yeeles, 1990) indicates that children above approximately 8 years of age *spontaneously* understand and engage in self-presentational behaviour when they are highly motivated to make good impressions or claim a positive identity. This study also examined the developmental paths of explicit and implicit ethnic bias through the inclusion of the modified pictorial version of the IAT (Greenwald et al., 1998) as an implicit measure of intergroup attitude. No equivalent drop in implicit ethnic bias was expected with the public self-focus manipulation since implicit attitudes should be automatically activated outside conscious self-control (Greenwald & Banaji, 1995).

The study involved 162 white children with equal numbers in three age groups: 6–8, 10–12, and 14–16 years. Initially, a preliminary study determined the prevailing normative context in a similar cohort of 118 children. These 14- to 16-year-olds were asked to rate on a 9-point scale (the higher the score the more inappropriate) how appropriate they thought it was in their society to judge someone on the basis of their social group. Thirty-five social groups were used (e.g., blacks, Asians, criminals, French, Germans, and whites). The mean score for all ethnic groups combined was 7.23, significantly higher than the composite score for all national groups ($M = 6.75$; $p < .01$) and criminals ($M = 4.38$; $p < .001$). These findings suggest that the children thought it was extremely inappropriate to judge someone on the basis of their ethnic group.

Following this, our sample was presented with two social exclusion vignettes. One was used with boys and involved two black boys being excluded by white boys from a five-a-side soccer game because of their ethnicity. The other vignette was presented to girls and showed two black girls being excluded by white girls from eating their school lunch during a break, again because of their ethnicity. These vignettes were used to evaluate whether children had internalised the norm that ethnic bias was inappropriate. After the vignettes the children were asked how bad they thought the white children were. They had to answer on a 4-point scale (1= *OK*, 2 = *bad*, 3 = *very bad*, and 4 = *very very bad*). Overall only 3% of the children answered "OK" and 65% said "very very bad". There were significant age differences in their answers to the question. The 14–16 ($M = 3.66$) and 10–12 ($M = 3.57$) age groups gave more negative answers compared to the 6–8 age group ($M = 3.27$). Nevertheless these means indicate that children in all age groups had to a certain degree internalised the norm surrounding ethnic prejudice, although the internalisation process had clearly progressed further in the older children.

The explicit measure in the main study was a trait attribution task similar to the one utilised by Powlishta et al. (1994). The participants had to indicate which of two social groups (blacks or whites) was more likely to display a list of 10 positive and 10 negative traits. A positive attribution bias score was computed by subtracting the number of positive traits assigned to blacks from the number given to whites: The higher the score, the more in-group bias. A negative attribution bias score was obtained by subtracting the number of negative traits assigned to whites from the number given to blacks: The higher the score, the more negative out-group bias. Public self-focus was manipulated using a video camera (see Macrae et al., 1997; Wicklund & Duval, 1971). In the high public self-focus condition the children completed the explicit and implicit measures when the video camera was turned "on". The children were told that a video recording was being taken to keep a record of the testing session and that it may be shown to other adults. The video camera was turned "off" in the low public self-focus condition.

In the low public self-focus condition there was the usual decline in ethnic positive bias with age. The 6- to 8 year-olds showed significantly more positive bias than the 10- to 12 and 14- to 16-year-olds. However, there was no significant decline in ethnic positive bias with age in the high public self-focus condition. The age groups showed similar low levels of positive bias. The positive bias scores of the 6- to 8-year-olds were significantly above the midpoint in the low public self-focus condition but not in the high public self-focus condition. In relation to the ethnic negative bias score there was a significant age × public self-focus interaction. Again there was the expected decline in negative bias with age in the low public self-focus condition. The 6- to 8-year-olds showed significantly more negative bias than the 10- to 12 and 14- to 16-year-olds. In contrast, when public self-focus was high, each age group showed similar levels of ethnic negative bias. The 6- to 8-year-old children's negative bias scores in the low public self-focus condition could be seen as ethnic prejudice since they were significantly above the midpoint of the scale.

The IAT scores showed significant implicit ethnic bias amongst all children. All age groups produced faster reaction times in the intuitive block compared to the counterintuitive block. That is, children were quicker to pair positive attributes with white faces and negative attributes with black faces than visa versa. The public self-focus manipulation had no effect on the IAT scores and correlations between the explicit measures and the IAT scores were nonsignificant.

These findings were in line with our expectations. The 6- to 8-year-old children showed more positive ethnic intergroup attitudes when public self-focus was high rather than low. The usual decline in explicit ethnic bias was only found when public self-focus was low. These results suggest that the young children were inhibiting their explicit ethnic bias according to normative beliefs surrounding ethnic prejudice expression when public self-focus was high. That is, they were engaging in self-presentation. The older children's ethnic intergroup attitudes were unaffected by the public self-focus manipulation. The simplest explanation for this finding is that the older children were spontaneously enacting self-presentation and bias regulation even in the low public self-focus condition, whereas the young children required high public self-focus in order to prompt a self-presentational strategy. The differences between the age groups on the vignette tasks measuring the internalisation of normative beliefs suggests that the older children had a firmer grasp of the normative context. Nevertheless, the vast majority of the younger children still considered the behaviour of the white children in the social exclusion stories to be "very very bad". This implies that age differences in responses to the public self-focus manipulation may have little to do with whether norms were internalised. Rather these differences may be better explained by young children's inability to engage in spontaneous self-presentation in this domain of ethnic intergroup attitudes.

CONCLUSION

At present no one theory can fully explain the development of intergroup attitudes in children. Each theory has its limitations. Cognitive-developmental theory has particular problems explaining variations in prejudice development over different domains (e.g., gender and nationality) and why it is that prejudice is sometimes still strongly evident in mid childhood and adolescence. In contrast, SIT makes no attempt to provide an account of clear developmental trends in ethnic attitudes throughout childhood. This theory specifies no mechanisms or psychological processes that can explain why, for example, young children show strong ethnic prejudice that then declines in mid childhood and into adolescence. The research reviewed at the end of this chapter suggests a resolution to many of the anomalies in the literature on childhood prejudice. This requires a recognition that children can self-regulate their expression of explicit prejudice in accordance with internalised normative beliefs. Arguably, then, children can be seen as social tacticians who strategically express their intergroup attitudes through a process of effortful on-line construction in context. Their aim may well be to present a positive image to valued others within their collectives and so to win a positive self-identity. Indeed, the strategic dimension of the child's expression of prejudice may be relational to the ideological and normative significance of the particular social category. More research is undoubtedly needed to further validate this claim.

REFERENCES

Aboud, F. E. (1988). *Children and prejudice*. Oxford: Blackwell.

Aboud, F. E., & Amato, M. (2001). Developmental and socialization influences on intergroup bias. In R. Brown & S. L. Gaertner (Eds.), *Blackwell handbook of social psychology: Intergroup processes* (pp. 65–85). Oxford: Blackwell.

Abrams, D. (1985). Focus of attention in minimal intergroup discrimination. *British Journal of Social Psychology*, *24*, 65–74.

Abrams, D. (1989). Differential association: Social developments in gender identification during adolescence. In S. Skevington & D. Baker (Eds.), *The social identity of women* (pp. 59–83). London: SAGE Publications.

Abrams, D. (1990). The self regulation of group behaviour: An integration of self awareness and social identity theory. In D. Abrams & M. A. Hogg (Eds.), *Social identity theory: Constructive and critical advances* (pp. 89–112). London: Harvester Wheatsheaf.

Abrams, D. (1994). Social self-regulation. *Personality and Social Psychology Bulletin*, *20*, 473–484.

Abrams, D., & Brown, R. J. (1989). Self-consciousness and social identity: Self-regulation as a group member. *Social Psychology Quarterly*, *52*, 311–318.

Abrams, D., Rutland, A., Cameron, L., & Marques, J. (2003). The development of subjective group dynamics: When in-group bios gets specific. *British Journal of Developmental Psychology*, *21*, 155–176.

Augoustinos, M., & Rosewarne, D. L. (2001). Stereotype knowledge and prejudice in children. *British Journal of Developmental Psychology*, *19*, 143–156.

Balaam, B. J., & Haslam, A. S. (1998). A closer look at the role of social influence in the development of attitudes to eating. *Journal of Community and Applied Social Psychology*, *8*, 195–212.

Banaji, M. R., & Greenwald, A. G. (1995). Implicit gender stereotyping in judgments of fame. *Journal of Personality and Social Psychology, 68*, 181–198.

Banerjee, R., & Lintern, V. (2000). Boys will be boys: The effect of social evaluation concerns on gender typing. *Social Development, 9*, 397–408.

Banerjee, R., & Yuill, N. (1999a). Children's explanations of self-presentational behaviour. *European Journal of Social Psychology, 29*, 105–111.

Banerjee, R., & Yuill, N. (1999b). Children's understanding of self-presentational display rules: Associations with mental-state understanding. *British Journal of Developmental Psychology, 17*, 111–124.

Bargh, J. A., Chaiken, S., Govender, R., & Pratto, F. (1992). The generality of the automatic activation effect. *Journal of Personality and Social Pyschology, 62*, 893–912.

Barreto, M., & Ellemers, N. (2000). You can't always do what you want: Social identity and self-presentational determinants of the choice to work for a low status group. *Personality and Social Psychology Bulletin, 26*, 891–906.

Bennett, M., Lyons, E., Sani, F., & Barrett, M. (1998). Children's subjective identification with the group and in-group favoritism. *Developmental Psychology, 34*, 902–909.

Bennett, M., & Yeeles, C. (1990). Children's understanding of the self-presentational strategies of ingratiation and self-promotion. *European Journal of Social Psychology, 20*, 455–461.

Bigler, R. S. (1995). The role of classification skill in moderating environmental influences on children's gender stereotyping: A study of the functional use of gender in the classroom. *Child Development, 66*, 1072–1087.

Bigler, R. S., Brown, C. S., & Markell, M. (2001). When groups are not created equal: Effects of group status on the formation of intergroup attitudes in children. *Child Development, 72*, 1151–1162.

Bigler, R. S., Jones, L. C., & Lobliner, D. B. (1997). Social categorization and the formation of intergroup attitudes in children. *Child Development, 68*, 530–543.

Bigler, R. S., & Liben, L. S. (1992). Cognitive mechanisms in children's gender stereotyping: Theoretical and educational implications of a cognitive-based intervention. *Child Development, 63*, 1351–1363.

Billig, M. (1991). *Ideology and opinions: Studies in rhetorical psychology*. London: SAGE Publications.

Brown, R. J. (1984). The effects of intergroup similarity and cooperative versus competitive orientation on intergroup discrimination. *British Journal of Social Psychology, 23*, 21–33.

Brown, R. J. (1995). *Prejudice: Its social psychology*. Oxford: Blackwell.

Brown, R. J. (2000). Social identity theory: Past achievements, current problems and future challenges. *European Journal of Social Psychology, 30*, 745–778.

Cameron, J. A., Alvarez, J. M., Ruble, D., & Fuligni, A. J. (2001). Children's lay theories about in-groups and out-groups: Reconceptualizing research on prejudice. *Personality and Social Psychology Review, 5*, 118–128.

Capozza, D., & Brown, R. (Eds.) (2000). *Social identity processes: Trends in theory and research*. London: SAGE Publications.

Cheyne, W. N. (1970). Stereotyped reactions to speakers with Scottish and English regional accents. *British Journal of Social and Clinical Psychology, 9*, 77–79.

Cooper, M. J., Anastasiades, P., & Fairburn, C. G. (1992). Selective processing of eating, shape and weight-related words in persons with bulimia nervosa. *Journal of Abnormal Psychology*, *101*, 352–355.

Cooper, M. J., & Fairburn, C. G. (1992). Selective processing of eating, weight and shape related words in patients with eating disorders and dieters. *British Journal of Clinical Psychology*, *31*, 363–365.

Devine, P. G. (2001). Implicit prejudice and stereotyping: How automatic are they? Introduction to the special section. *Journal of Personality and Social Psychology*, *81*, 757–759.

Doosje, B., Ellemers, N., & Spears, R. (1999). Commitment and intergroup behaviour. In N. Ellemers, R. Spears, & B. Doosje (Eds.), *Social identity, context, commitment and content* (pp. 84–106). Oxford: Blackwell.

Dovidio, J. F., Kawakami, K., Johnson, C., Johnson, B., & Howard, A. (1997). On the nature of prejudice: Automatic and controlled processes. *Journal of Experimental Social Psychology*, *33*, 510–540.

Doyle, A., & Aboud, F. (1995). A longitudinal study of white children's racial prejudice as a social-cognitive development. *Merrill-Palmer Quarterly*, *41*, 209–228.

Durkin, K., & Houghton, S. (2000). Children's and adolescents' stereotypes of tattooed people as delinquent. *Legal and Criminological Psychology*, *5*, 153–164.

Durkin, K., & Judge, J. (2001). Effects of language and social behaviour on children's reactions to foreign people in television. *British Journal of Developmental Psychology*, *19*, 597–612.

Ellemers, N., Spears, R., & Doosje, B. (Eds.) (1999). *Social identity, context, commitment and content*. Oxford: Blackwell.

Fyfe, C., & Rutland, A. (2000, September). *A comparative study of national prejudice and in-group bias in Scottish and Maltese children.* Paper presented at the British Psychological Society (BPS) Social Psychology Section Annual Conference, Nottingham Trent University.

Greenwald, A. D., & Banaji, M. R. (1995). Implicit social cognition: Attitudes, self-esteem, and stereotypes. *Psychological Review*, *102*, 4–27.

Greenwald, A. D., McGee, D. E., & J. L. K. Schwartz (1998). Measuring individual differences in implicit cognition: The implicit association test. *Journal of Personality and Social Psychology*, *74*, 1464–1480.

Hoover, R., & Fishbein, H. D. (1999). The development of prejudice and sex role stereotyping in white young adolescents and white young adults. *Journal of Applied Developmental Psychology*, *20*, 431–448.

Huston, A. C. (1985). The development of sex typing: Themes from recent research. *Developmental Review*, *5*, 1–17.

Jahoda, G., Thomson, S. S., & Bhatt, S. (1972). Ethnic identity and preferences among Asian immigrant children in Glasgow: A replicated study. *European Journal of Social Psychology*, *2*, 19–32.

Jetten, J., Spears, R., & Manstead, A. S. R. (1996). Intergroup norms and intergroup discrimination: Distinctive self-categorization and social identity effects. *Journal of Personality and Social Psychology*, *71*, 1222–1223.

Jetten, J., Spears, R. & Manstead, A. S. R. (1997). Strength of identification and intergroup differentiation: The influence of group norms. *European Journal of Social Psychology*, *27*, 603–609.

Katz, P. A. (1976). The acquisition of racial attitudes in children. In P. A. Katz (Ed.), *Towards the elimination of racism* (pp. 125–154). New York: Pergamon.

Kinket, B., & Verkuyten, M. (1999). Intergroup evaluations and social context: A multilevel approach. *European Journal of Social Psychology, 29*, 219–237.

Lambert, W. E., & Klineberg, O. (1967). *Children's views of foreign peoples: A cross-national study.* New York: Appleton-Century-Crofts.

Long, K. M., & Manstead, A. S. R. (1997). Group immersion and intergroup differentiation: Contextual shifts in categorization. *British Journal of Social Psychology, 36*, 291–303.

Maass, A., Castelli, L., & Arcuri, L. (2000). Measuring prejudice: Implicit versus explicit techniques. In D. Capozza & R. Brown (Eds.), *Social identity processes: Trends in theory and research.* London: SAGE Publications.

Maccoby, E. (1988). Gender as a social category. *Developmental Psychology, 24*, 755–765.

Macrae, C. N., Bodenhausen, G. V., & Milne, A. B. (1997). Saying no to unwanted thoughts: Self-focus and the regulation of mental life. *Journal of Personality and Social Psychology, 74*, 578–589.

Muth, J. L., & Cash, T. F. (1997). Body-image attitudes: What differences does gender make? *Journal of Applied Social Psychology, 27*, 1436–1452.

Nesdale, D. (2001). Development of prejudice in children. In M. Augoustinos & K. J. Reynolds (Eds.), *Understanding prejudice, racism and social conflict* (pp. 57–72). London: SAGE Publications.

Nesdale, D., & Flesser, D. (2001). Social identity and the development of children's group attitudes. *Child Development, 72*, 506–517.

Noel, J. G., Wann, D. L., & Branscombe, N. R. (1995). Peripheral in-group membership status and public negativity toward out-groups. *Journal of Personality and Social Psychology, 68*, 127–137.

Pedersen, A., Walker, I., & Glass, C. (1999). Experimenter effects on in-group preference and self-concept of urban Aboriginal children. *Australian Journal of Psychology, 51*, 82–89.

Postmes, T., Branscombe, N., Spears, R., & Young, H. (1999). Comparative processes in personal and group judgments: Resolving the discrepancy. *Journal of Personality and Social Psychology, 76*, 320–338.

Powlishta, K. (1995a). Intergroup processes in childhood: Social categorization and sex role development. *Developmental Psychology, 31*, 781–788.

Powlishta, K. (1995b). Gender bias in children's perceptions of personality traits. *Sex Roles, 32*, 17–28.

Powlishta, K., Serbin, L. A., Doyle, A., & White, D. R. (1994). Gender, ethnic, and body type biases: The generality of prejudice in childhood. *Developmental Psychology, 30*, 526–536.

Reicher, S. D., Spears, R., & Postmes, T. (1995). A social identity model of de-individuation phenomena. *European Review of Social Psychology, 6*, 161–198.

Rutland, A. (1999). The development of national prejudice, in-group favoritism and self stereotypes in British children. *British Journal of Social Psychology, 38*, 55–70.

Rutland, A., & Brown, R. (2001). Stereotypes as justifications for prior intergroup discrimination: Studies of Scottish national stereotyping. *European Journal of Social Psychology, 31*, 127–141.

Rutland, A., Cameron, L., Milne, A., & McGeorge, P. (2002, June). *The development and regulation of children's implicit and explicit intergroup attitudes.* Paper presented at the 13th General Meeting of the European Association of Experimental Social Psychology (EAESP), San Sebastián, Spain.

Rutland, A., Morrison, E., & Arnold-Dorman, C. (2001). *The development of implicit and explicit weight bias in girls and young females.* Unpublished manuscript, University of Kent, Canterbury, UK.

Scheier, M. F., & Carver, C. S. (1981). Private and public aspects of self. In L. Wheeler (Ed.), *Review of personality and social psychology, Vol. 2.* London: SAGE Publications.

Serbin, L. A., Conner, J. M., Burchardt, C. J., & Citron, C. C. (1979). Effects of peer presence on sex-typing of children's play behaviour. *Journal of Experimental Child Psychology, 27*, 303–309.

Spears, R. (2001). The interaction between the individual and the collective self: Self-categorization in context. In C. Sedikides & M. B. Brewer (Eds.), *Individual self, relational self, and collective self: Partners, opponents or strangers?* Philadelphia, PA: Psychology Press.

Spielman, D. A. (2000). Young children, minimal groups, and dichotomous categorization. *Personality and Social Psychology Bulletin, 26*, 1433–1441.

Tajfel, H., Jahoda, G., Nemeth, C., Rim, Y., & Johnson, N. (1972). The devaluation by children of their own national and ethnic group: Two case studies. *British Journal of Social and Clinical Psychology, 11*, 235–243.

Tajfel, H., Nemeth, C., Jahoda, G., Campbell, J. D., & Johnson, N. (1970). The development of children's preference for their own country: A cross-national study. *International Journal of Psychology, 5*, 245–253.

Tajfel, H., & Turner, J. (1979). An integrative theory of intergroup conflict. In W. G. Austin & S. Worchel (Eds.), *The social psychology of intergroup relations.* Monterey, CA: Brooks/Cole.

Tajfel, H., & Turner, J. C. (1986). The social identity theory of intergroup behavior. In S. Worchel & W. G. Austin (Eds.), *The psychology of intergroup relations* (pp. 7–24). Chicago, IL: Nelson-Hall.

Vaughan, G., Tajfel, H., & Williams, J. A. (1981). Bias in reward allocation in an intergroup and an interpersonal context. *Social Psychology Quarterly, 44*, 37–42.

Verkuyten, M. (2001). National identification and intergroup evaluations in Dutch children. *British Journal of Developmental Psychology, 19*, 559–571.

Wicklund, R. A., & Duval, S. (1971). Opinion change and performance facilitation as a result of objective self-awareness. *Journal of Experimental Social Psychology, 7*, 319–342.

Yee, M., & Brown, R. J. (1994). The development of gender differentiation in young children. *Child Development, 33*, 183–196.

10 Reducing stepfamily conflict: The importance of inclusive social identity

Brenda S. Banker, Samuel L. Gaertner, John F. Dovidio, Missy Houlette, Kelly M. Johnson, and Blake M. Riek

> He drew a circle that shut me out –
> Heretic, rebel, a thing to flout.
> But love and I had the wit to win –
> We drew a circle that took him in.
> Edwin Markham

This chapter explores what happens when members of stepfamilies are asked, as in Markham's poem, to draw their circle of social inclusion wider. Does love and harmony characterise the relations among those who are included? We examine the consequences of this metaphor within a domain of group life that provides a new, fundamental social identity for many people, the step-family. Developing a stepfamily identity implicitly requires the expansion of a person's most basic and intimate social boundary, the biological family unit, to include others, who arrive with their own sense of family identity. The present chapter examines the role of group identity in establishing harmony in stepfamilies and considers the factors that may inhibit or promote a more inclusive family identity.

The stepfamily research we feature in this chapter was undertaken primarily to explore the utility of the common in-group identity model (Gaertner & Dovidio, 2000; Gaertner, Dovidio, Anastasio, Bachman, & Rust, 1993) for increasing harmony between social groups. This model, derived from the social categorisation approach (Allport, 1954; Tajfel, 1969), proposes that factors that induce members of two groups to conceive of themselves as members of a common, more inclusive in-group reduce intergroup conflict by enabling cognitive and motivational processes that contribute to pro-in-group favouring biases to be redirected to include former out-group members (Gaertner, Mann, Murrell, & Dovidio, 1989). Before presenting the details of our own stepfamily research, we first present our rationale for viewing the stepfamily as an intergroup context and then we review the theoretical and empirical evidence of the role of social categorisation in initiating intergroup bias and its potential for producing intergroup harmony.

The logic of viewing the stepfamily as an intergroup context is derived primarily from Allport (1954), who stated that the "biological family ordinarily constitutes the smallest and firmest of one's in-groups" (p. 41) and that "every society on earth" regards the child "as a member of his parents' groups" (p. 30). Members of first-married families generally share family memories, ancestral histories and traditions, daily rituals, and a common name, all of which contribute to a strong sense of family group identity (e.g., see Settles, 1993). When divorce or death separates the first-married couple, and remarriage to a new partner occurs, the biologically related parents and their children who come together as a result of that remarriage do so as two separate "in-groups", with little or no common ground to bind them. For many stepfamilies the unfortunate reality is that they remain fragments of two separate families living together in conflict (Anthony, 1974).

Combining two groups into a single structure is complex and potentially discordant. Whereas the initial development of each participating group normally involved the interaction and socialisation of *individuals* who arrived separately, stepfamily unions primarily represent a collision between *groups*. Such mergers (see Gaertner, Bachman, Dovidio, & Banker, 2001), therefore, are primarily an intergroup phenomenon. Moreover, families are particularly influential groups in their members' lives. They are fundamentally linked to one's social, economic, and psychological well-being and to personal and collective identity.

Although interpersonal relations are not always smooth and harmonious, intergroup relations are usually even more conflictual. Group members who are interdependent with other groups are more distrusting and less likely to be concerned with maximising joint outcomes compared to individuals who share interdependence (Insko et al., 2001). As a consequence, the potential for conflict and failure in stepfamilies is likely to be higher than in the formation of each original family (Haunschild, Moreland, & Murrell, 1994). In addition, conflict between groups in stepfamilies is generally more intractable than conflict between individuals because disputants arrive with a network of social support for their respective positions. Ironically, in an atmosphere of distrust and propensity for conflict, members of stepfamilies are expected to identify with the new entity and to become committed to its well-being – with the hopes of possibly living together "happily ever after".

Unfortunately, stepfamily marriages have an extraordinarily high failure rate. For second marriages the divorce rate is estimated at 60% (Norton & Miller, 1992; White & Booth, 1985). This rate is even higher when children are involved (Furstenberg & Spanier, 1984). Apparently, something very frequently goes awry that threatens the success and longevity of the stepfamily. Given the substantial emotional consequences that result from such failures, it is important to understand some of the fundamental causes of these intergroup catastrophes as well as factors that are related to successful marriages between formerly separate family units. Indeed, there are reasons to believe that the intergroup nature of these relationships, in part, places the success of the stepfamily in jeopardy and it is the purpose of this chapter to examine the stepfamily entity from the perspective of intergroup theory and research. In particular we focus on the implications of the common in-group identity model (Gaertner & Dovidio, 2000; Gaertner et al., 1993), a theoretical framework we developed to conceptualise factors that are instrumental to the creation and reduction of intergroup bias and conflict.

THE ROLE OF SOCIAL CATEGORISATION AND INTERGROUP RELATIONS

Social categorisation has critical implications for one's attitudes towards others. Attraction and prejudice are fundamentally related to social categorisation and to the perception of intergroup boundaries – boundaries that define who is included in one's own group (a "we") and who is excluded (a "they"). Upon social categorisation, people favour in-group members in terms of evaluations, attributions, material resources, helping, and social support. Thus, changing the nature of ingroup inclusion and exclusion can have important consequences for interpersonal and intergroup relations.

Social identity theory (SIT; Tajfel & Turner, 1979) and, more recently, self-categorisation theory (SCT; Turner, 1985; see also Onorato & Turner, 2001) consider the crucial role of social categorisation and identity in social relations. With respect to one's sense of identity, SIT and SCT view the distinction between personal identity and social identity as a critical one (see Spears, 2001). When personal identity is salient, a person's individual needs, standards, beliefs, and motives primarily determine behaviour. In contrast, when social identity is salient, "people come to perceive themselves as more interchangeable exemplars of a social category than as unique personalities defined by their individual differences from others" (Turner, Hogg, Oakes, Reicher, & Wetherell, 1987, p. 50). Under these conditions, collective needs, goals, and standards are primary. Moreover, Tajfel and Turner proposed that a person's need for positive self-identity partially may be satisfied by membership in prestigious social groups. Thus, this need motivates social comparisons that favourably differentiate in-group from out-group members.

From a social categorisation perspective, when people or objects are categorised into groups, actual differences between members of the same category tend to be perceptually minimised (Tajfel, 1969) and often ignored in making decisions or forming impressions. Members of the same category seem to be more similar than they actually are, and more similar than they were before they were categorised together. In addition, between-group differences tend to become exaggerated and overgeneralised, emphasising social difference and group distinctiveness. The magnitude of these biases is a function of the salience of social categorisation (Abrams, 1985; Turner, 1985). Moreover, these within- and between-group perceptual distortions have a tendency to generalise to additional dimensions (e.g., character traits) beyond those that originally differentiated the categories (Allport, 1954).

Whether people perceive others as a member of their group or of another group impacts the emotional significance of group differences, and thus leads to further perceptual distortion and to evaluative biases that reflect favourably on the in-group and consequently on the self (Tajfel & Turner, 1979). Upon social categorisation of individuals into in-groups and out-groups, people spontaneously experience more positive affect towards other members of the in-group (Otten & Moskowitz, 2000), particularly towards those who are most prototypical of the group (Hogg & Hains, 1996). They also favour in-group members directly in terms of evaluations and resource allocations (Mullen, Brown, & Smith, 1992). In terms of cognitive processing, people retain more information in a more detailed fashion for in-group members than for out-group members (Park & Rothbart, 1982), have better memory for information about ways in which in-group members are similar to and out-group members are dissimilar to the self (Wilder, 1981), and remember less positive information about out-group members (Howard & Rothbart, 1980). Perhaps due to the greater self–other overlap in representations for people defined as in-group members (Smith & Henry, 1996), people process information about and make attributions to in-group members more on the basis of self-congruency than they do for out-group members (Gramzow, L. Gaertner, & Sedikides, 2001).

Social categorisation also plays an important role in interpersonal and intergroup attributions. People are more generous and forgiving in their explanations for the behaviours of in-group relative to out-group members. Positive behaviours and successful outcomes are more likely to be attributed to internal, stable characteristics (the personality) of in-group than out-group members, whereas negative outcomes are more likely to be ascribed to the personalities of out-group members than of in-group members (Hewstone, 1990; Pettigrew, 1979). As a consequence, negative behaviours of out-group members are less affected by mitigating evidence than are those of in-group members (Beal, Ruscher, & Schnake, 2001). Relatedly, observed behaviours of in-group and out-group members are encoded in memory at different levels of abstraction (Maass, Salvi, Arcuri, & Semin, 1989). Undesirable actions of out-group members are encoded at more abstract levels that presume intentionality and dispositional origin (e.g., she is hostile) than are identical behaviours of in-group members (e.g., she slapped the girl). Desirable actions of out-group members, however, are encoded at more concrete levels (e.g., she walked across the street holding the old man's hand) relative to the same behaviours of in-group members (e.g., she is helpful).

These cognitive biases help to perpetuate social biases and stereotypes even in the face of countervailing evidence. For example, because positive behaviours of out-group members are encoded at relatively concrete levels, it becomes less likely that counterstereotypic positive behaviours would generalise across situations or other out-group members (see also Karpinski & Von Hippel, 1996). People do not remember that an out-group member was "helpful", but only the very concrete descriptive actions. Thus, out-group stereotypes containing information pertaining to traits, dispositions, or intentions are not likely to be influenced by observing counterstereotypic out-group behaviours.

Language plays another role in intergroup bias through associations with collective pronouns. Collective pronouns such as "we" or "they", which are used to define people's in-group or out-group status, are frequently paired with stimuli having strong affective connotations. As a consequence, these pronouns may acquire powerful evaluative properties of their own. These words (we, they) can potentially increase the availability of positive or negative associations and thereby influence beliefs about, evaluations of, and behaviours towards other people, often automatically and unconsciously (Perdue, Dovidio, Gurtman, & Tyler, 1990).

The process of social categorisation, however, is not completely unalterable. Categories are hierarchically organised, with higher-level categories (e.g., nations) being more inclusive of lower-level ones (e.g., cities or towns). By modifying a perceiver's goals, motives, perceptions of past experiences, and expectations, as well as factors within the perceptual field and the situational context more broadly, there is an opportunity to alter the level of category inclusiveness that will be primary or most influential in a given situation. This malleability of the level at which impressions are formed is important because of its implications for altering the way people think about members of in-groups and out-groups, and consequently about the nature of intergroup relations. Because categorisation is a basic process that is fundamental to intergroup bias, social psychologists have targeted this process as a starting point to begin to improve intergroup relations. In the next section we explore how the forces of categorisation can be harnessed and redirected towards the reduction, if not the elimination, of intergroup bias.

REDUCING INTERGROUP BIAS AND CONFLICT

For almost 60 years, the contact hypothesis (Allport, 1954; see also Pettigrew, 1998) has represented the primary strategy for reducing intergroup bias and facilitating harmony between groups. This hypothesis proposes that for contact between groups to reduce bias successfully, certain prerequisite features must be present. These characteristics of contact include equal status between the groups, cooperative (rather than competitive) intergroup interaction, opportunities for personal acquaintance between the members, especially with those whose personal characteristics do not support negative stereotypic expectations, and supportive norms by authorities within and outside of the contact situation (Pettigrew, 1998). Research in laboratory and field settings generally supports the efficacy of this list of prerequisite conditions for achieving improved intergroup relations (see Pettigrew & Tropp, 2000). In the stepfamily literature, as well, research indicates that cooperation in the stepfamily, as well as positive interaction between the steprelatives, are associated with better overall stepfamily functioning and happiness (e.g., see Anderson & White, 1986; Crosbie-Burnett, 1984; James & Johnson, 1987).

Recent research, however, has moved beyond specifying what conditions moderate the reduction of bias to understanding what underlying processes, such as those involving social categorisation, may be involved (see Pettigrew, 1998). From the social categorisation perspective, the issue to be addressed is how intergroup contact can be structured to alter inclusive–exclusive collective representations of others. Two of the approaches that have been proposed involve decategorisation and recategorisation. Decategorisation refers to influencing whether people identify themselves primarily as group members or as distinct individuals on the continuum proposed by Tajfel and Turner (1979; see also Brewer, 1988; Brewer & Miller, 1984; Fiske, Lin, & Neuberg, 1999). Recategorisation, in contrast, is not designed to reduce or eliminate categorisation, but rather to structure a definition of group categorisation at a higher level of category inclusiveness in ways that reduce intergroup bias and conflict (Allport, 1954, p. 43; see Dovidio, Gaertner, & Kafati, 2000; Gaertner & Dovidio, 2000).

In each case, reducing the salience of the original inclusive–exclusive group boundaries is expected to decrease intergroup bias. With decategorisation, group boundaries are degraded, inducing members of different groups to conceive of themselves and others as separate individuals (Wilder, 1981) and encouraging more personalised interactions. When personalised interactions occur, people "attend to information that replaces category identity as the most useful basis for classifying each other" (Brewer & Miller, 1984, p. 288), and thus category-based biases are reduced.

With recategorisation as proposed by the common in-group identity model (Gaertner & Dovidio, 2000; Gaertner et al., 1993), inducing members of different groups to conceive of themselves as a single, more inclusive superordinate group rather than as two completely separate groups produces attitudes towards former out-group members that become more positive through processes involving pro-in-group bias. That is, the processes that lead to favouritism towards in-group members would now be directed towards former out-group members as they become redefined from exclusive to inclusive categories.

The decategorisation and recategorisation strategies and their respective means of reducing bias were directly examined in a laboratory study (Gaertner et al., 1989). In this experiment, members of two separate laboratory-formed groups were induced through various structural interventions (e.g., seating arrangement) either to decategorise themselves (i.e., conceive of themselves as separate individuals) or to recategorise themselves as one superordinate group. Supporting the proposed value of altering the level of category inclusiveness, these changes in the perceptions of intergroup boundaries reduced intergroup bias. Furthermore, as expected, these strategies reduced bias in different ways. Decategorising members of the two groups reduced bias by decreasing the attractiveness of former in-group members. In contrast, recategorising in-group and out-group members as members of a more inclusive group reduced bias by increasing the attractiveness of the former out-group members. Consistent with SCT, "the attractiveness of an individual is not constant, but varies with the ingroup membership" (Turner, 1985, p. 60).

In the next section, we present support for the common in-group identity model and the effects of recategorisation. In addition, we discuss the value of a "dual identity" in which original group identities are maintained but within the context of a superordinate identity.

The common in-group identity model

In the common in-group identity model, we outline specific potential antecedents and outcomes of direct or symbolic intergroup contact, as well as identify possible mediating social categorisation processes. In particular, we hypothesise that the different types of intergroup interdependence and cognitive, perceptual, linguistic, affective, and environmental factors can either independently or in concert alter individuals' cognitive representations of the aggregate. These resulting cognitive representations (i.e., one group, two subgroups with one group, two groups, or separate individuals) are then proposed to produce specific cognitive, affective, and overt behavioural consequences. Thus, the causal factors (which include features specified by the contact hypothesis) are proposed to influence members' cognitive representations of the memberships that in turn mediate the relationship, at least in part, between the causal factors and the cognitive, affective, and behavioural consequences. In addition, we propose that common in-group identity can be achieved by increasing the salience of existing common superordinate memberships (e.g., a school, a company, a nation) or by introducing factors (e.g., common goals or shared fate) that are perceived to be shared between the original groups.

Once out-group members are perceived as in-group members, it is proposed that they would be accorded the benefits of in-group status. There would probably be more positive thoughts, feelings, and behaviours towards these former out-group members by virtue of their recategorisation as in-group members. These more favourable impressions of out-group members are not likely to be finely differentiated, at least initially (see Mullen & Hu, 1989). Rather, we propose that these more elaborated, personalised impressions can soon develop within the context of a common identity because the newly formed positivity bias is likely to encourage more open communication and greater self-disclosing interaction between former out-group members. Thus, as proposed by Pettigrew (1998; see also Hewstone, 1996), the nature of intergroup contact can influence group representations in different ways sequentially across time. We suggest that, over time, a common identity can lead to decategorisation and encourage personalisation of out-group members and thereby initiate a second route to achieving reduced bias. That is, *when viewed over time*, decategorisation, recategorisation, and mutual inter-group differentiation that preserves group identities are strategies for reducing intergroup bias that are not competitors. Rather they can each con-tribute to the reduction of intergroup bias and they can also reciprocally facilitate each other (see also Hewstone, 1996). Thus, recategorisation can lead to more interpersonally friendly, self-revealing interactions (e.g., see Dovidio, Gaertner, Validzic, Matoka, Johnson, & Frazier 1997) and, as Hew-stone speculated, a "common ingroup identity can affect decategorisation (and possibly, over time differentiation, too)" (p. 354).

Within this model, we also acknowledge that the development of a com-mon in-group identity does not necessarily require each group to forsake its less inclusive group identity completely. As Brewer (2000) noted, individuals belong simultaneously to several groups and possess multiple potential iden-tities. As depicted by the "sub-groups within one group" (i.e., a dual identity) representation, we believe that it is possible for members to conceive of two groups (for example, parents and children) as distinct units within the context of a superordinate (i.e., family) identity. This aspect of the common in-group identity model is compatible with, although not identical to, other models that propose that maintaining the salience of intergroup distinctions can be important for producing generalised and longer-term reductions in inter-group bias (Hewstone & Brown, 1986). In the next section, we examine some empirical tests of the common in-group identity model.

Among the antecedent factors proposed by the common in-group identity model are the features of contact situations (Allport, 1954) that are necessary for intergroup contact to be successful (e.g., interdependence between groups, equal status, egalitarian norms). From our perspective, cooperative inter-action may enhance positive evaluations of out-group members and reduce intergroup bias, at least in part, by transforming interactants' representations of the memberships from two groups to one group.

In one test of this hypothesis, we conducted an experiment that brought two three-person laboratory groups together under conditions designed to vary independently (1) the members' representations of the aggregate as one group or two groups through manipulation of the contact situation, and (2) the presence or absence of intergroup cooperative interaction (Gaertner, Mann, Dovidio, Murrell, & Pomare, 1990). The interventions designed to emphasise common group membership through structural changes in the contact situation (e.g., integrated vs. segregated seating; a new group name for all six participants vs. the original group names; the same or different colored tee shirts for both groups) and to encourage cooperative interaction (joint evaluation and reward vs. independent outcomes) both reduced inter-group bias. Moreover, they did so through the same mechanism. Contextual features emphasising common "groupness" and joint outcomes each increased one-group representations (and reduced separate-group representa-tions), which in turn related to more favourable attitudes towards original out-group members and lower levels of bias. Consistent with the common in-group identity model, more inclusive, one-group representations *mediated* the relationship between the interventions and the reduction of bias.

The advantage of this experimental design is that interdependence preceded changes in participants' representations of the aggregate from two groups to one group and also changes in intergroup bias. In addition, because the representations of the aggregate were manipulated in the absence of interdependence, the development of a one-group representation preceded changes in intergroup bias. Thus, we can be confident about the directions of causality in this study. In other experiments we have manipulated structural aspects of intergroup contact situations, such as segregated or integrated seating, and found that these manipulations directly influenced group representations and, ultimately, intergroup bias (see Gaertner & Dovidio, 2000). These studies provide convergent evidence for a clear sequence of events and identification of causal relations.

An additional laboratory study (Houlette & Gaertner, 1999) explored the effects of varying the degree of inclusiveness of a superordinate identity on intergroup bias between three-person groups of liberals and conservatives. The recategorisation manipulation emphasised members' common affiliation with their ad hoc six-person laboratory work group, their identity as University of Delaware students, or their common national citizenship (i.e., America). Intergroup bias decreased directly with greater inclusiveness of their common superordinate entity (i.e., from the six-person work group to national citizenship). Because participants' identification with these superordinate entities was also stronger with increasing levels of inclusiveness, we cannot be certain whether reduced bias was driven by increased group identification or by the greater inclusiveness of the superordinate entity per se. In either case, however, these findings provide additional experimental evidence of the effectiveness of interventions designed to emphasise common group membership for reducing intergroup bias.

In a subsequent series of studies we utilised survey techniques under more naturalistic circumstances to examine the impact of common group identity for a range of types of intergroup bias. These studies offer converging support for the hypothesis that the features specified by the contact hypothesis reduce intergroup bias, in part, because they transform members' representations of the memberships from separate groups to one more inclusive group. Participants in these studies included students attending a multi-ethnic high school (Gaertner, Rust, Dovidio, Bachman, & Anastasio, 1996), and banking executives who had experienced a corporate merger involving a wide variety of banks across America (Bachman, 1993).

To provide a conceptual replication of the laboratory study of cooperation, the surveys included items (specifically designed for each context) to measure participants' perceptions of the conditions of contact (i.e., equal status, self-revealing interaction, cooperation, and egalitarian norms), their representations of the aggregate (i.e., one group, two subgroups within one group, two separate groups, and separate individuals), and a measure of intergroup bias (see Gaertner, Dovidio, Nier, Ward, & Banker, 1999). For the high school study, the main outcome measure was a bias in affective reactions, such as feeling good and respectful towards in-group as compared to out-group members. For the corporate merger study, the main measure of bias was the extent to which the corporate executives perceived members of the different organisations to have varying levels of positive work-related trait characteristics (i.e., intelligent, hardworking, organised, skilled, and creative).

Consistent with the role of an inclusive group representation that is hypothesised in the common in-group identity model, across these studies (1) conditions of intergroup contact that were perceived as more favourable predicted lower levels of intergroup bias, (2) more favourable conditions of contact predicted more inclusive (one group) and less exclusive (different groups) representations, and (3) more inclusive representations of mediated lower levels of intergroup bias and conflict (see Gaertner et al., 1999).

While supportive of the basic framework of our model, these cross-sectional survey studies in natural group settings do not establish the direction of causality among conditions of contact, group representations, and reductions in bias. Longitudinal methods that investigate the relationships among these variables over time provide more direct insight into the direction of causality. In the next section, in two studies that we present in greater detail, we examine these hypothesised relationships in the context of step-families. One of these studies, using cross-sectional data as in our earlier survey studies, employs causal modelling to test the predicted effects. The other study extends this line of research, and further tests for the proposed causal sequence between the constructs in the model by using a longitudinal survey methodology.

STEPFAMILY MARRIAGES

As we noted at the beginning of this chapter, families involve a primary form of group membership. Beyond genetic relatedness, there is a profound social connection among family members. Biological, or first-married families generally share memories, ancestral histories, traditions, daily rituals, and a common family name that contribute to a strong sense of family group identity (see Settles, 1993).

Given the importance of family group identity, stepfamilies represent an interesting domain in which to examine the utility of the common in-group identity model. When the first-married family is fragmented by divorce or death and remarriage to a new partner occurs, the biological parents and children from the two families come together under new circumstances. Through remarriage, members of two separate "in-groups", with no common memories, histories, daily rituals, or even family name find themselves in an intensive intergroup context.

Relative to biologically related, first-married families, stepfamilies have generally been described as more stressful and less cohesive. Stepfathers, for example, not only report being less satisfied with their own lives than do first-married fathers, they also indicate that the lives of their stepchildren are less than satisfactory as well (Fine, McKenry, Donnelly, & Voydanoff, 1992). Bray and Berger (1993) found that, in couples remarried for 5 to 7 years, there were less positive wife-to-husband and biological parent–child interactions in stepfamilies than in their first-married counterparts. And several studies have found that stepparent–stepchild relationships are more conflict-ridden than are those between biological parents and children in first-married families (Anderson & White, 1986; Furstenberg, 1987; Sauer & Fine, 1988).

One reason why stepfamilies may experience greater conflict is less than satisfactory contact among the stepfamily members. James and Johnson (1987) reported that competitiveness in stepfamilies is related to marital dissatisfaction and psychological pathology in both husbands and wives. Cooperativeness, however, relates to marital satisfaction for both partners, and to the husbands' positive psychological adjustment. Furthermore, the failure of stepchildren to respond in kind to their stepparents' positive behaviours towards them has been found to be associated with stepfamily dysfunction (Anderson & White, 1986; Brown, Green, & Druckman, 1990). A more positive relationship between the stepparent and stepchild, in contrast, is associated with more positive stepfamily functioning (Anderson & White, 1986) and happiness (Crosbie-Burnett, 1984).

Stepfamily relations

In our first study with stepfamilies (Banker & Gaertner, 1998), using a cross-sectional, rather than a longitudinal, design, our goals were (a) to investigate the validity of our vision of stepfamilies as an intergroup entity and (b) to empirically support the utility of the common in-group identity model in this intergroup context. Consistent with these goals, we hypothesised that (1) stepfamily members would see their stepfamilies as being more like two separate families and less like one family than first-married families, (2) there would be a significant relationship between positive conditions of contact in the stepfamily household and increased stepfamily harmony, and (3) the relationship between positive conditions of contact and increased harmony would be mediated by a one-family representation of the stepfamily such that the greater the one-family representation, the greater the harmony.

To test these hypotheses, we surveyed university students who identified themselves as either living at home in a "complex" stepfamily (i.e., the remarried parents each have at least one child from their previous marriage so as to create an "intergroup" household) or in a first-married family. There were 86 stepfamily participants and 65 participants from first-married families. In 46 stepfamily households, the stepsibling(s) lived in the same household as the participant full-time. In 40 households there was a visitation arrangement;

the average visitation was 4 days/month. All of the participants from first-married families had at least one biologically related sibling at home.

The participants completed identical surveys containing items designed to tap their perceptions of the conditions of contact in the household using 1–7 scales. This measure included items representing perceptions of cooperation (e.g., "There is generally a spirit of competition rather than cooperation in the house" [reverse scored], or "It feels like my stepsiblings are always competing with my siblings and/or me" [reverse scored]), equality (e.g., "I feel that I have as much private space at home as do the other people living in the house" or "There are different household rules for me and my siblings than there are for my stepsiblings" [reverse scored]), and opportunities for personalisation (e.g., "Holiday outings or vacations are usually planned so that everyone in the household is included"). Participants also, using 1–7 ratings, completed measures of the cognitive representation of the family (e.g., one family: "Living in my house it feels like one family") and family harmony (e.g., "I would characterise the environment at my house as 'harmonious' ").

A comparison of the responses from these two family types reveals that stepfamilies felt more like two separate families ($M = 2.24$) than did first-married families ($M = 1.53$) and less like one family ($M = 5.18$) than first-married families ($M = 5.97$). These results provide initial empirical support for our assumption that stepfamilies may commonly represent a naturalistic intergroup entity. In addition, the correlations among the variables were consistent with the hypotheses derived from the common in-group identity model. As expected, more favourable conditions of contact in the stepfamily related to higher levels of stepfamily harmony ($r = .54$). More favourable conditions of contact also related to stronger perceptions of the stepfamily as one family ($r = .75$) and to weaker perceptions of the stepfamily as two separate families ($r = -.73$).

Taken together, these results satisfy preliminary requirements of mediation analysis[1] (Baron & Kenny, 1986). That is, the independent variable (condi-

---

1 According to Baron and Kenny (1986), the idea of mediation originated with Woodworth's (1928, cited in Baron & Kenny, p. 1176) S-O-R model, which proposes that some psychological transformation within the *organism* intervenes between a *stimulus* and a *response*. This intervening variable represents the mechanism or process by which the stimulus (the independent variable) is hypothesised to influence the response (the dependent variable). For example, in an experiment discussed earlier in this chapter (Gaertner et al., 1990), we hypothesised that cooperative intergroup interaction reduces intergroup bias *because* cooperation changes members' cognitive representations of the aggregate from two groups to one group. In that study, the independent variable that we manipulated (the stimulus) involved whether the contact between the two groups that we arranged represented cooperative or independent activities. The dependent variable that we measured (the response) was intergroup bias. The proposed mediating variable (or the intervening organismic variable in the S-O-R model) was members' perceptions of the aggregate as one group. Statistically, Baron and Kenny outline a procedure involving a series of multiple regression analyses to demonstrate mediation. The first regression tests whether the independent variable predicts the dependent variable. Mediation can

tions of contact) predicted the dependent variable (stepfamily harmony) and the proposed mediating variable, more inclusive cognitive representations (e.g., one-family representation of the stepfamily). Next, using AMOS hardware (Arbuckle, 1997), we directly tested the critical mediation hypothesis. Providing evidence of at least partial mediation, the path from conditions of contact to stepfamily harmony was weaker (*Beta* = .37) when cognitive representations were considered simultaneously as predictors in the regression equation. Moreover, the indirect path from the conditions of contact through one family to stepfamily harmony was significant (*Beta* = .19). Thus, following the proposed sequence, the more positive were the conditions of contact, the more the stepfamily felt like one family and the greater was the stepfamily harmony.

The results of this study (Banker & Gaertner, 1998) provide strong initial support for the utility of our intergroup relations perspective in modelling the reduction of stepfamily conflict. Because these data are cross-sectional, as we noted earlier, the results are correlational: We cannot be certain about the direction of causality of the variables. That is, while the results suggest that a strong one-group cognitive representation of the stepfamily leads to lower stepfamily conflict, it may very well be that lower stepfamily conflict makes the stepfamily feel more like one family. Our next study, presented in the following section, addresses this issue by using a longitudinal design.

Stepfamily relations over time

A primary focus of our longitudinal study was to examine more directly the hypothesised direction of causality of the variables specified by the contact hypothesis (Allport, 1954; Cook, 1985) and the common in-group identity model (Gaertner & Dovidio, 2000) in stepfamilies. Over time, positive conditions of contact were expected to reduce stepfamily conflict by making the stepfamily feel more like one family than two. Again, we hypothesised that the stronger the one-family representation, the less conflict there would be in the stepfamily household.

For this study, we recruited members of complex stepfamilies through appeals to classes, through newspaper advertisements, and through contacts made with the Stepfamily Association of America. In the first phase of the study (Time 1), there were 148 stepchild participants (53 male and 95 female). In the second wave (Time 2), conducted 9 months later, there were 66

only be statistically demonstrated if the independent variable (the stimulus) is first shown to influence the dependent variable (the response) significantly. Next, to show mediation, the second regression must reveal that the independent variable significantly predicts the proposed mediating variable. Then, in a third regression equation in which the independent variable and the mediating variable are considered simultaneously as predictors of the dependent variable, for mediation to occur the mediating variable should emerge as a significant predictor while the effect of the independent variable should be significantly weaker than in the first regression equation, and with complete mediation, nonsignificant.

participants (44.6% of Phase 1; 30 male and 36 female). The average age of the participants at Time 1 was 18.3 years; at Time 2, it was 18.7 years. At Time 1, there were 60 households in which the stepsibling(s) lived full-time and 88 households in which they visited. The average yearly visitation was 3.7 months. At Time 2, there were 26 households in which the stepsibling(s) lived full-time and 40 households in which they visited. The average yearly visitation was 4.0 months.

The surveys used in the two phases of this research were similar to those used in our previous stepfamily study. These surveys included an 11-item measure of conditions of contact (Cronbach alphas = .91 at each time), cognitive representations of the stepfamily (one family: "Living in my house, it feels like one family"; two separate families: "Living in my house, it feels like two separate families."), and a 4-item measure of stepfamily harmony/conflict (e.g., "There is conflict between individuals from Family A and B in the household"; Cronbach alphas = .77 and .82 at Time 1 and Time 2).

Consistent with the results of our earlier stepfamily study, more favourable conditions of contact were related to higher ratings of one family ($r = .68$) and to lower ratings of two separate families ($r = -.58$). More favourable conditions of contact were also significantly correlated with less conflict (i.e., more harmony) in the household ($r = -.69$). Similar relations were obtained among these measures at Time 2: $rs = .67, -.52$, and $-.67$.

On the basis of the data from the 66 participants who were studied across the 9-month period, we tested the hypothesised causal relationships (using AMOS software; Arbuckle & Wothke, 1999). Specifically, we examined the stepchildren's longitudinal panel data in a series of cross-lagged structural equation models to assess the degree of empirical support there is for our primary hypotheses. We expected that, over time, positive conditions of contact at Time 1 would lead to a decrease in stepfamily conflict measured at Time 2, and to a stronger one-family representation of the stepfamily at Time 2. This would be more supportive of our model than if conflict at Time 1 strongly predicted the conditions of contact at Time 2, although we recognise that these relationships are probably bidirectional. Finally, we hypothesised that a one-family representation of the stepfamily at Time 1 would lead to a reduction in perceived stepfamily conflict at Time 2. These analyses controlled for demographic variables, such as the respondent's age[2].

---

2 The structural components of the cross-lagged models include the covariance between the Time 1 variables and four paths: two autoregressive paths from each Time 1 variable to its Time 2 counterpart (e.g., Contact 1 to Contact 2), and the two cross-lagged paths from each Time 1 variable to the other variable at Time 2 (e.g., Contact 1 to Conflict 2, and Conflict 1 to Contact 2). Because several demographic variables (e.g., child's age) were found to significantly relate to the variables of interest, each was tested as a covariate. These demographic variables were entered into the structural equation model as covariates when appropriate. Each of these cross-lagged models fit our data very well in terms of the chi-square and goodness of fit indices (i.e., GFI, AGFI, CFI, and RMSEA).

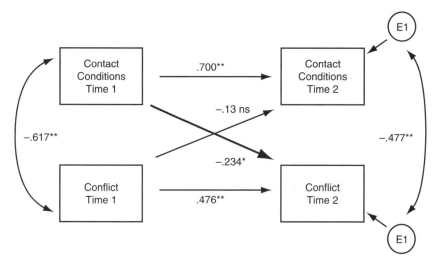

χ^2 (6) = 3.51, *p* = .743, *N* = 64; GFI = .985; AGFI = .929; CFI = 1.00; RMSEA = .000.
**p < .025 (1-tail); *p < .05 (1-tail).

Figure 10.1 Longitudinal analysis: Contact and conflict

As hypothesized, the results (see Figure 10.1) reveal that positive conditions of contact at Time 1 significantly predict a decrease in conflict (*Beta* = –.234) at Time 2, controlling for initial levels of conflict in the household at Time 1. Also, in terms of the direction of causality being reversed from what we expected, conflict at Time 1 did not significantly predict conditions of contact at Time 2 (*Beta* = –.13). Also, in support of the direction of causality specified by the common in-group identity model, we hypothesised that positive conditions of contact at Time 1 would lead to increased perceptions of the stepfamily as one family at Time 2. The results of the cross-lagged path analysis (see Figure 10.2) reveal that, as hypothesised, positive conditions of contact at Time 1 reliably related to an increase in the one-family representation of the stepfamily at Time 2 (*Beta* = .254), controlling for the level of the one-family representation at Time 1. Also, the nonpredicted path from one-family representation at Time 1 to conditions of contact at Time 2 was not significant.

The idea that is central to the common in-group identity model is the expectation that, when two groups interact, the relationship between the contact conditions and intergroup conflict is *mediated* by the cognitive representation of the groups: The more the groups feel like "one group", the less the intergroup conflict. To test this mediation hypothesis longitudinally, we predicted that a one-family representation of the stepfamily at Time 1 would significantly relate to decreased conflict at Time 2. The results of the cross-lagged structural equation analysis (see Figure 10.3) reveals a significant path indicating, as predicted, that the more the stepfamily feels like one family at

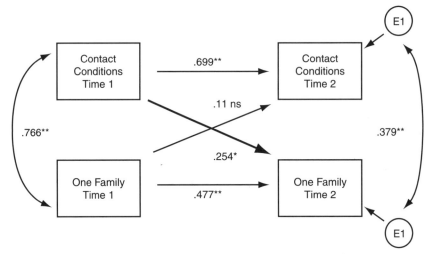

χ^2 (6) = 4.44, p = .617, N = 61; GFI = .980; AGFI = .906; CFI = 1.00; RMSEA = .000.
**p < .025 (1-tail); *p < .05 (1-tail).

Figure 10.2 Longitudinal analysis: Contact and one family

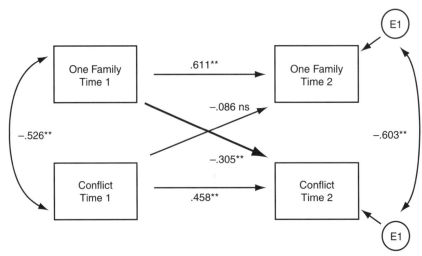

χ^2 (6) = 5.09, p = .532, N = 60; GFI = .977; AGFI = .890; CFI = 1.000; RMSEA = .000.
**p < .025 (1-tail); *p < .05 (1-tail).

Figure 10.3 Longitudinal analysis: One family and conflict

Time 1, the less conflict there is at Time 2 (*Beta* = –.305), controlling for the level of conflict at Time 1. Furthermore, the nonpredicted path from conflict at Time 1 to one family at Time 2 was not significant, and additional analyses strongly suggested that the path from one family at Time 1 to conflict at Time 2 was unidirectional. Therefore, extrapolating from the causal paths described in the above analyses (see Figures 10.1, 10.2, and 10.3), there is general support for the idea proposed by the common in-group identity model that over time, the conditions of contact lead to changes in the cognitive representation of the stepfamily as one family, and that the representation of the stepfamily as one family leads to a reduction in stepfamily conflict.

CONCLUSIONS

In our research with stepfamilies, we utilise the perspective of the common in-group identity model (Gaertner & Dovidio, 2000) to investigate and model the pursuit of stepfamily harmony. Our results (Banker & Gaertner, 1998) indicate that stepfamilies feel more like two separate families and less like one family than do first-married families, and that this is problematic for stepfamily members. These earlier findings reveal, for example, that positive conditions of contact in the stepfamily household relate to feeling more like one family, which in turn relates to greater harmony in the stepfamily household. Together, the results of Banker and Gaertner and our recent longitudinal research suggest that viewing one's stepfamily as "one family" may be an important causal link in the attainment of stepfamily harmony and the reduction of stepfamily conflict. Indeed, results of our longitudinal study indicate that having a one-family representation of the stepfamily at Time 1 significantly relates to a reduction in stepfamily conflict at Time 2.

The results of our longitudinal study support the proposed direction of causality of the variables specified by the common in-group identity model (Gaertner & Dovidio, 2000) in the naturally occurring intergroup context of the stepfamily. Specifically, positive conditions of contact in the stepfamily household at Time 1 lead to less conflict at Time 2 and a one-family representation of the stepfamily at Time 2. Also, having a one-family representation of the stepfamily at Time 1 leads to less stepfamily conflict at Time 2.

There remains, however, a possibility that for these stepchildren the causal systems under investigation actually involve reciprocal feedback over time, for example, between conditions of contact and stepfamily conflict. That is, in reality, favourable conditions of contact reduce stepfamily conflict, and the decrease in conflict may, in turn, strengthen the favourableness of the conditions of contact. The potential of such feedback systems is quite plausible within or outside of the consideration of our model. In future studies, three waves of data collection may be necessary to verify or negate these suppositions. Nevertheless, with two waves of data available, Finkel (1995) suggests that "when a causal system is one of continuous reciprocal feedback" . . . "the cross-lagged model 'tends not to be misleading about the *direction* of causal influence' " (p. 25). In any event, the results of our longitudinal analyses suggest that helping stepfamily members to see their stepfamily as one family, or as one common in-group, can only help in the stepfamily's pursuit of harmony. Apparently, factors that promote stepfamily harmony, or decrease stepfamily conflict, in part cast wider circles of inclusion.

The results of our research offer support for the common in-group identity model and its utility for studying stepfamily marriages. Moreover, the findings support and extend previous work in family research and suggest ways that stepfamily harmony can be achieved. Indeed, the mediation by the one-family representation of the stepfamily of the relationships between the conditions of contact and harmony in the stepfamily, and between the conditions of contact and stepfamily conflict, suggest that the process of *recategorisation* from two separate groups to one, single, inclusive family is central to harmonious stepfamily relations. Supportive of the model, the more the stepfamily feels like one family, the less the conflict and the greater the harmony in the stepfamily.

These results also offer an explanation for how the lack of cooperative interaction among stepfamily members (James & Johnson, 1987) may become associated with stepfamily dysfunction or disharmony. In the future, other stepfamily issues (e.g., family economics) may also be identified as possibly influencing stepfamily members' perceptions of the stepfamily unit and harmony. For example, it was suggested by Fishman (1983) that stepfamilies who pool their financial resources for the stepfamily's general use regardless of biological ties (i.e., the "common pot economy") are more unified than are those who maintain separate bank accounts (i.e., the "two pot economy") that are used for one's own and one's biological relatives' needs (p. 359). From the perspective of the common in-group identity model, Fishman's common pot economy would be expected to contribute to the perception of the stepfamily as one family and to yield greater stepfamily harmony. The identification of activities and relationships that contribute to the perception of the stepfamily as one family also might one day aid in the clinical evaluation of stepfamily functioning, as well as form the basis for new therapeutic tools with which to understand and treat problems encountered by stepfamily members. Likewise, the identification of factors that contribute to the perception of the stepfamily as one family may also inform theories of intergroup relations and provide new tools with which to understand and heal intergroup problems across a variety of settings.

In conclusion, bringing families together to create a successful stepfamily is a complex task with a substantial risk of failure. Because families are primary groups closely connected to one's social identity, successful stepfamily outcomes require managing intergroup as well as interpersonal processes in constructive and productive ways. Our research indicates that the development of a common in-group identity – that is, changing the stepfamily members' perceptions of the stepfamily unit from "us" and "them" to a more inclusive "we" – plays a central role in reducing stepfamily conflict and in facilitating harmonious stepfamily relations.

Acknowledgements

Preparation of this chapter was supported by NIMH Grant MH 48721.

REFERENCES

Abrams, D. (1985). Focus of attention in minimal intergroup discrimination. *British Journal of Social Psychology, 24*, 65–74.

Allport, G. W. (1954). *The nature of prejudice*. Cambridge, MA: Addison-Wesley.

Anderson, J. Z., & White, G. D. (1986). An empirical investigation of interaction and relationship patterns in functional and dysfunctional nuclear families and stepfamilies. *Family Process, 25*, 407–422.

Anthony, E. J. (1974). Children at risk from divorce: A review. In E. J. Anthony & C. Koupernik (Eds.), *The child in his family, Vol. 3*. New York: John Wiley & Sons.

Arbuckle, J. L. (1997). *AMOS users' guide: Version 3.6*. Chicago: SPSS.

Arbuckle, J. L., & Wothke, W. (1999). *AMOS users' guide. Version 4.0*. Chicago: SPSS.

Bachman, B. A. (1993). *An intergroup model of organizational mergers*. Unpublished PhD dissertation, University of Delaware, Newark, DE.

Banker, B. S., & Gaertner, S. L. (1998). Achieving stepfamily harmony: An intergroup-relations approach. *Journal of Family Psychology, 12*, 310–325.

Baron, R. M., & Kenny, D. A. (1986). The moderator-mediator variable distinction in social psychological research: Conceptual, strategic, and statistical considerations. *Journal of Personality and Social Psychology, 51*, 1173–1182.

Beal, D. J., Ruscher, J. B., & Schnake, S. B. (2001). No benefit of the doubt: Intergroup bias in understanding causal explanation. *British Journal of Social Psychology, 40*, 531–543.

Bray, J. H., & Berger, S. H. (1993). Developmental issues in stepfamilies research project: Family relationships and parent–child interactions. *Journal of Family Psychology, 7*, 76–90.

Brewer, M. B. (1988). A dual process model of impression formation. In T. K. Srull & R. S. Wyer, Jr. (Eds.), *Advances in social cognition* (Vol. 1, pp. 1–36). Hillsdale, NJ: Lawrence Erlbaum Associates, Inc.

Brewer, M. B. (2000). Reducing prejudice through cross-categorization: The effects of multiple social identities. In S. Oskamp (Ed.), *Reducing prejudice and discrimination* (pp. 165–183). Mahwah, NJ: Lawrence Erlbaum Associates, Inc.

Brewer, M. B., & Miller, N. (1984). Beyond the contact hypothesis: Theoretical perspectives on desegregation. In N. Miller & M. B. Brewer (Eds.), *Groups in contact: The psychology of desegregation* (pp. 281–302). Orlando, FL: Academic Press.

Brown, A. C., Green, R. J., & Druckman, J. (1990). A comparison of stepfamilies with and without child-focused problems. *American Orthopsychiatric Association, 60*, 556–566.

Cook, S. W. (1985). Experimenting on social issues: The case of school desegregation. *American Psychologist, 40*, 452–460.

Crosbie-Burnett, M. (1984). The centrality of the step-relationship: A challenge to family theory and practice. *Family Relations, 33*, 459–463.

Dovidio, J. F., Gaertner, S. L., & Kafati, G. (2000). Group identity and intergroup relations: The common in-group identity model. In S. R. Thye, E. J. Lawler, M. W. Macy, & H. A. Walker (Eds.), *Advances in group processes, Vol. 17* (pp. 1–34). Stamford, CT: JAI Press.

Dovidio, J. F., Gaertner, S. L., Validzic, A., Matoka, K., Johnson, B., & Frazier, S. (1997). Extending the benefits of re-categorization: Evaluations, self-disclosure and helping. *Journal of Experimental Social Psychology, 33*, 401–420.

Fine, M. A., McKenry, P. C., Donnelly, B. W., & Voydanoff, P. (1992). Perceived adjustment of parents and children: Variations by family structure, race, and gender. *Journal of Marriage and the Family, 54*, 118–127.

Finkel, S. E. (1995). *Causal analysis with panel data.* Thousand Oaks, CA: SAGE Publications.

Fishman, B. (1983). The economic behavior of stepfamilies. *Family Relations, 32*, 359–366.

Fiske, S. T., Lin, M., & Neuberg, S. L. (1999). The continuum model: Ten years later. In S. Chaiken & Y. Trope (Eds.), *Dual process theories in social psychology* (pp. 231–254). New York: Guilford Press.

Furstenberg, F. F. Jr. (1987). The new extended family: The experience of parents and children after remarriage. In K. Pasley & M. Ihinger-Tallman (Eds.), *Remarriage and stepparenting: Current research and theory* (pp. 42–61). New York: Guilford Press.

Furstenberg, F. F. Jr., & Spanier, G. B. (1984). *Recycling the family: Remarriage after divorce.* Beverly Hills, CA: SAGE Publications..

Gaertner, S. L., & Dovidio, J. F. (2000). *Reducing intergroup bias: The common ingroup identity model.* Philadelphia, PA: Psychology Press.

Gaertner, S. L., Bachman, B. A., Dovidio, J. D., & Banker, B. S. (2001). Corporate mergers and stepfamily marriages: Identity, harmony, and commitment. In M. A. Hogg & D. Terry (Eds.), *Social identity processes in organization contexts* (pp. 265–282). Philadelphia, PA: Psychology Press.

Gaertner, S. L., Dovidio, J. F., Anastasio, P. A., Bachman, B. A., & Rust, M. C. (1993). The common ingroup identity model: Recategorization and the reduction of intergroup bias. In W. Stroebe & M. Hewstone (Eds.), *European review of social psychology, Vol. 4* (pp. 1–26). New York: John Wiley & Sons.

Gaertner, S. L., Dovidio, J. F., Nier, J., Ward, C., & Banker, B. (1999). Across cultural divides: The value of a superordinate identity. In D. A. Prentice & D. T. Miller (Eds.), *Cultural divides: Understanding and overcoming group conflict* (pp. 173–212). New York: Russell Sage Foundation.

Gaertner, S. L., Mann, J. A., Dovidio, J. F., Murrell, A. J., & Pomare, M. (1990). How does cooperation reduce intergroup bias? *Journal of Personality and Social Psychology, 59*, 692–704.

Gaertner, S. L., Mann, J. A., Murrell, A. J., & Dovidio, J. F. (1989). Reduction of intergroup bias: The benefits of recategorization. *Journal of Personality and Social Psychology, 57*, 239–249.

Gaertner, S. L., Rust, M. C., Dovidio, J. F., Bachman, B. A., & Anastasio, P. A. (1996). The contact hypothesis: The role of a common ingroup identity on reducing intergroup bias among majority and minority group members. In J. L. Nye & A. M. Brower (Eds.), *What's social about social cognition?* (pp. 230–360). Newbury Park, CA: SAGE Publications.

Gramzow, R. H., Gaertner, L., & Sedikides, C. (2001). Memory for in-group and out-group information in a minimal group context: The self as an informational base. *Journal of Personality and Social Psychology, 80,* 188–205.

Haunschild, P. R. , Moreland, R. L., & Murrell, A. J. (1994). Sources of resistance to mergers between groups. *Journal of Applied Social Psychology, 24,* 1150–1178.

Hewstone, M. (1996). Contact and categorization: Social psychological interventions to change intergroup relations. In N. Macrae, M. Hewstone, & C. Stangor (Eds.), *Foundations of stereotypes and stereotyping* (pp. 323–368). New York: Guilford Press.

Hewstone, M., & Brown, R. J. (1986). Contact is not enough: An intergroup perspective on the contact hypothesis. In M. Hewstone & R. Brown (Eds.), *Contact and conflict in intergroup encounters* (pp. 1–44). Oxford: Basil Blackwell.

Hogg, M. A., & Hains, S. C. (1996). Intergroup relations and group solidarity: Effects of group identification and social beliefs on depersonalized attraction. *Journal of Personality and Social Psychology, 70,* 295–309.

Houlette, M., & Gaertner, S. L. (1999). *The common ingroup identity model: Effects of inclusiveness of common ingroup identity and subgroup salience on ingroup bias.* Unpublished data, Department of Psychology, University of Delaware, Newark, DE.

Howard, J. M., & Rothbart, M. (1980). Social categorization for in-group and out-group behavior. *Journal of Personality and Social Psychology, 38,* 301–310.

Insko, C. A., Schopler, J., Gaertner, L., Wildschut, T., Kozar, R., Pinter, B., Finkel, E. J., Brazil, D. M., Cecil, C. L., & Montoya, M. R. (2001). Interindividual–intergroup discontinuity reduction through the anticipation of future interaction. *Journal of Personality and Social Psychology, 80,* 95–111.

James, S. D., & Johnson, D. W. (1987). Social interdependence, psychological adjustment, and marital satisfaction in second marriages. *Journal of Social Psychology, 128,* 287–303.

Karpinski, A., & Von Hippel, W. (1996). The role of linguistic intergroup bias in expectancy maintenance. *Social Cognition, 4,* 141–163.

Kessler, T., & Mummendey, A. (2001). Is there any scapegoat around? Determinants of intergroup conflicts at different categorization levels. *Journal of Personality and Social Psychology, 81,* 1102–1118.

Maass, A., Salvi, D., Arcuri, L., & Semin, G. R. (1989). Language use in intergroup contexts: The linguistic intergroup bias. *Journal of Personality and Social Psychology, 57,* 981–993.

Mullen, B., Brown, R. J., & Smith, C. (1992). Ingroup bias as a function of salience, relevance, and status: An integration. *European Journal of Social Psychology, 22,* 103–122.

Mullen, B., & Hu, L. T. (1989). Perceptions of ingroup and outgroup variability: A meta-analytic integration. *Basic and Applied Social Psychology, 10,* 233–252.

Norton, A. J., & Miller, L. F. (1992). *Marriage, divorce and remarriage in the 1990s* (US Bureau of the Census, Current Population Reports. Series P-23, No. 180.) Washington, DC: US Government Printing Office.

Onorato, R. S., & Turner, J. C. (2001). The "I", "me", and the "us": The psychological group and self-concept maintenance and change. In C. Sedikides & M. B. Brewer

(Eds.), *Individual self, relational self, collective self* (pp. 147–170). Philadelphia, PA: Psychology Press.

Otten, S., & Moskowitz, G. B. (2000). Evidence for implicit evaluative in-group bias: Affect-based spontaneous trait inference in a minimal group paradigm. *Journal of Experimental Social Psychology*, *36*, 77–89.

Park, B., & Rothbart, M. (1982). Perception of out-group homogeneity and levels of social categorization: Memory for the subordinate attributes of in-group and out-group members. *Journal of Personality and Social Psychology*, *42*, 1051–1068.

Perdue, C. W., Dovidio, J. F., Gurtman, M. B., & Tyler, R. B. (1990). "Us" and "them": Social categorization and the process of intergroup bias, *Journal of Personality and Social Psychology*, *59*, 475–486.

Pettigrew, T. F. (1979). The ultimate attribution error: Extending Allport's cognitive analysis of prejudice. *Personality and Social Psychology Bulletin*, *55*, 461–476.

Pettigrew, T. F. (1998). Intergroup contact theory. *Annual Review of Psychology*, *49*, 65–85.

Pettigrew, T. F., & Tropp, L. R. (2000). Does intergroup contact reduce prejudice? Recent meta-analytic findings. In S. Oskamp (Ed.), *Reducing prejudice and discrimination* (pp. 93–114). Hillsdale, NJ: Lawrence Erlbaum Associates, Inc.

Rugosa, D. (1988). Myths about longitudinal research. In K. W. Schaie, R. T. Campbell, W. Meredith, & S. C. Rawlings (Eds.), *Methodological issues in aging research* (pp. 171–209). New York: Springer.

Sauer, L. E., & Fine, M. A. (1988). Parent–child relationships in stepparent families. *Journal of Family Psychology*, *1*, 434–451.

Settles, B. H. (1993). The illusion of stability in family life: The reality of change and mobility. *Marriage and Family Review*, *19*, 5–29.

Smith, E. R., & Henry, S. (1996). An in-group becomes part of the self: Response time evidence. *Personality and Social Psychology Bulletin*, *22*, 635–642.

Spears, R. (2001). The interaction between the individual and the collective self: Self-categorization in context. In C. Sedikides & M. B. Brewer (Eds.), *Individual self, relational self, collective self* (pp. 171–198). Philadelphia, PA: Psychology Press.

Tajfel, H. (1969). Cognitive aspects of prejudice. *Journal of Social Issues*, *25*, 79–97.

Tajfel, H., & Turner, J. C. (1979). An integrative theory of intergroup conflict. In W. G. Austin & S. Worchel (Eds.), *The social psychology of intergroup relations* (pp. 33–48). Monterey, CA: Brooks/Cole.

Turner, J. C. (1985). Social categorization and the self-concept: A social cognitive theory of group behavior. In E. J. Lawler (Ed.), *Advances ingroup processes*, *Vol. 2* (pp. 77–122). Greenwich, CT: JAI Press.

Turner, J. C., Hogg, M. A., Oakes, P. J., Reicher, S. D., & Wetherell, M. S. (1987). *Rediscovering the social group: A self-categorization theory*. Oxford: Basil Blackwell.

White, L. K., & Booth, A. (1985). The quality and stability of remarriages: The role of stepchildren. *American Sociological Review*, 689–698.

Wilder, D. A. (1981). Perceiving persons as a group: Categorization and intergroup relations. In D. L. Hamilton (Ed.), *Cognitive processes in stereotyping and intergroup behavior* (pp. 213–257). Hillsdale, NJ: Lawrence Erlbaum Associates, Inc.

Part IV
Epilogue

11 The development of social identity: What develops?

Dominic Abrams

The chapters in this book bring together an impressive body of research to make an exciting and scholarly contribution to our understanding of the development of social identity. They provide a clear signpost for questions to be tackled in future research. As a whole, the book is an extremely valuable resource for anyone wishing to research social identity as a developmental phenomenon. Various themes emerge strongly, and some others find voice but with less certainty and stridency. My aims in this commentary are to pose three broad questions at the outset, consider each chapter in turn (devoting most space to a discussion of Ruble et al., simply because they raise many of the issues common to several chapters), then conclude by reflecting on how effectively the broader questions have been explored.

The majority of chapters in the book focus on the cognitive and motivational elements of self-categorisation and social identity. First perhaps, these should not be the only, or the most important, aspects of children's group membership that we need to consider. Are we asking the *right* questions about children's relationship to social groups and categories?

Second, the orientation to social identity development offered by chapters in this book seems to focus more strongly either on social context or on cognitive development. There might be other elements in the developmental equation that are being neglected. Are we analysing social identity *comprehensively* as a developmental phenomenon?

Third, there are controversies in the adult literature surrounding various assumptions made by social identity theory and self-categorisation theory. How far does the developmental research reflect these controversies?

THE CHAPTERS

Ruble et al.

Ruble, Alvarez, Bachman, Cameron, Fuligni, Garcia Coll, and Rhee provide an excellent resource for anyone interested in social categorisation in childhood, offering a careful analysis of the different ways in which self-conception and intergroup behaviour are connected. (Nonetheless, there are several interesting points that could be added or developed further – see below.) After referring to a variety of approaches to the social self, Ruble et al. propose that it is collective identity that is of most interest in connection with the development of categorisation in the cognitive-development literature. They state that, "the nature of such categorisation and comparison processes are likely to change dramatically between the early and mid elementary school years".

It is an empirical question as to quite how dramatic the changes might be, but there is also the question of why these changes might happen. For example, a self-categorisation theory (SCT) line might be that the *content* and *focus* of categorisation might change, and this might provide opportunities for different social comparisons. However, once children are able to categorise things, the fundamental cognitive *process* should not change (see also David et al., Chapter 5). If this is true, perhaps the changes observed in the *application* of categories to people might result from a variety of different cognitive or social processes or a particular combination of them.

We know that older children are more sophisticated than younger children in their judgments of people, including themselves. However, I believe we should be careful not to attribute these changes entirely to cognitive development. Presumably a portion of this developmental change may result from a lengthy period of exposure to a developmentally ordered social environment (Bronfenbrenner, 1999). For example, Ruble et al. refer to the "deeper meanings" taken on by gender and race in mid childhood. There must be, surely, a relationship between the meanings that are conveyed within a child's environment and those that the child makes use of. The behaviour of other children and of adults, the content of mass media directed towards children, and even the physical accessibility of objects in the world (determined by strength, height, freedom to roam, etc.) must all impinge on the meanings available to a child. It seems there is a risk that this point is taken for granted rather than analysed directly by social identity researchers.

Ruble et al. focus on the ages 7–10 years as " key period" for studying the incorporation of social category memberships into the emerging self-concept. This does seem to fit the evidence, but perhaps a similar argument could be made for other age periods? For example, for identical twins perhaps the ages of 1–3 years would be critical in the formation of a "we" unit (cf. Nicole & Del Miglio, 1995). Equally, adolescence is arguably a period in which peer-group affiliations become more established and in which the question "what sort of person am I?" may be central to which social norms are relevant for the self-concept. Perhaps "key periods" can be identified at many age boundaries because the social milieu changes externally depending on one's age. Imagine yourself as a 2-, 5-, 8-, 12-, 16-, 20-, or 25-year-old today. Each of these ages is likely to be found inhabiting a distinct social environment (see Alfieri, Ruble, & Higgins, 1996, for an example of an environment-based age-related change). It might be argued, perhaps in evolutionary terms, or perhaps on the basis of cognitive and physical capacity, that these environments are somehow tailored to meet the particular needs of each age group. However, historical changes in age-related social environments (and indeed in the self, see Baumeister, 1999) suggest that is likely to be only part of the story. For example, it is less than 50 years ago that children in Britain might have left school at 14 to work in the mills, the mines, or on the farm. At the start of the 21st century the majority remain in the education system until well past 18 years of age. These rapid changes in societal arrangements might imply that the mission of capturing critical moments in the development of social identity is likely to falter because those moments involve combinations of both cognitive and social factors, and either or both may be absent or present at various times. The slipperiness of critical developmental stages in social identity development is also illustrated throughout the book in the evidence presented by Bennett and Sani, Verkuyten, Barrett et al., and Rutland.

Ruble et al. and Powlishta note that gender awareness emerges by the age of 2–3 years, whereas racial and ethnic awareness emerge later. This lag may point to a difference in the functional value of these categories rather than just a cognitive advantage for gender. Ruble's question as to whether, between 3 and 5 years of age, ethnic self-labelling "means anything more than empty labels", invites a further set of questions. Presumably, group labels acquire meaning if they signify a difference or similarity in relation to some other object or person. We have to ask: Why are such labels used? A likely reason is that they are a meaningful concept in communication with others (Lyons & Kashima, 2001; Stangor, Sechrist, & Jost, 2001). With use, experience, and relevance, that meaning is likely to increase in richness. For example, group differences in ethnic constancy should encourage us to examine the role of the social environment. Why would racial constancy lag behind for African-American and Asian-American children? Ruble et al. propose that African-American children need to be more flexible about race as they face the challenge of identifying with both their own racial and ethnic group and the larger European-American society, or that African-American children disidentify. An alternative possibility is that precisely the opposite happens. African-American children may live in a more racially homogeneous environment than their European-American counterparts. Therefore it may be less meaningful to refer to race and ethnicity because it is a homogeneous background to their social world. In certain circumstances, being non-white may not be remarkable (W. J. McGuire & McGuire, 1988; W. J. McGuire, McGuire, Child, & Fujioka, 1978). In contrast, European-Americans may experience other races as salient and distinctive, and therefore it may be more meaningful to note the differences.

How closely might we expect social categorisation and self-categorisation to reflect one another? Again, the role of the social environment seems critical. As Ruble et al. note, "there are wide individual and group variations in how salient various social categories are to the self-concept. ... Future research must examine the moderating influence of context". Of course, the context can be defined either broadly (culture, historical period) or specific-ally (as in the comparative context). Distinctions between the implications of these different aspects of context may be something to which we need to pay more attention.

Ruble et al. also invoke the notion of centrality, perhaps the chronic sali-ence, of identity. From a self-categorisation perspective these two are related simply because the more often an identity is salient the more accessible it will be and (presumably) the better it will fit a regularly encountered environment. The finding by Alvarez, Ruble, and Bolger (2001) that the son/daughter identity was more central than other social identities illustrates this point. On the other hand, the Alvarez et al. study does not seem to illuminate whether, in a different context (e.g., the playground), other social identities might dom-inate (Strough & Marie-Covatto, 2002). Some further theoretical work is probably required regarding the extent to which centrality may describe a structural feature in *the* self-concept or whether it involves contextual centrality in the process of self-conception (see also David et al., Chapter 5).

Ruble et al. place weight on the role of evaluation in the development of social identity. The motivational assumptions of social identity theory have been interpreted by many researchers as a drive to sustain self-esteem. There are various mechanisms and processes that appear to operate in adults that result in a relatively automatic bias towards self (cf. Otten & Wentura, 1999), and these seem to operate outside conscious awareness (Perdue, Dovidio, Gurtman, & Tyler, 1990). However, the preoccupation in North American research with the potential low self-esteem of minority group members should not be taken as a paradigm for analysing the social identity of mem-bers of all social categories (cf. Emler 2001; Heine, Lehman, Markus, & Kitayama, 1999). Motivation for self-esteem could have numerous con-sequences, only *one* of which is in-group favouritism or bias (Abrams, 1992; Abrams & Hogg, 1988, 2001). Moreover, it is not at all clear that in-group favouritism is always motivated by need for self-esteem, even if it results in changes in self-esteem (Abrams & Hogg, 1988; Stangor & Thompson, 2002). Many forms of social differentiation do not involve bias or prejudice. For example, in a school, children and adults know quite clearly that the "staff room" is for adults. It seems unlikely that observance of this rule affects the self-esteem of either group. Similarly, girls and boys may be assigned different washrooms. Use of the designated room is unlikely to have self-esteem impli-cations (although entering the wrong room may well cause embarrassment). Instead of the self-esteem principle, Michael Hogg and I (Abrams, 1992; Abrams & Hogg, 1988, 2001; Hogg, 2001; Hogg & Abrams, 1993) proposed that a motivational priority is to establish meaning – to make sense of one's location in a social environment. This is a prerequisite for engagement in actions that are socially appropriate and effective and that can be under-stood by others. It also reduces subjective uncertainty, which may be a psychologically satisfying state (see also Kruglanski & Webster, 1996).

A further problem arises in the operationalisation of self-esteem.

Researchers have a tendency to interpret and measure self-esteem in personal rather than collective terms. However, in SIT the person–group distinction is just as relevant to self-esteem as it is to identity (Tajfel, 1974) and behaviour (cf. Runciman, 1966). It is explicit that groups and individuals may be judged differently on different dimensions, and that there may even be a dynamic relationship among these evaluations. Assessments of the in-group bias–self-esteem link too often used global measures of self-esteem (e.g., feeling positive about the self overall, or the group as a whole, or possibly all groups to which one belongs) rather than focusing on a specific social identification and dimensions of comparison (e.g., feeling good about the specific group's academic status, team performance, cultural vitality). For SIT it may be that the act of evaluating an in-group more highly than an out-group on a specific dimension *is* the enhancement of social identity (see Abrams & Hogg, 1988; Rubin & Hewstone, 1998).

Despite these cautionary notes, there are reasons to study personal self-esteem in intergroup situations. Indeed, Gaertner, Sedikides, Vevea, and Iuzzini (2002) propose that the individual self has motivational primacy over the collective and contextual self. Given the evidence that personality appears to comprise a considerable element of genetically determined stability (e.g., Hur, McGue, & Iacono, 1998; McGue, Bacon, & Lykken, 1993; S. McGuire, Neiderhiser, Reiss, Hetherington, & Plomin, 1996), it is not surprising that there is also self-generated stability in self-esteem. Along with this stability there is also reliable variation between individuals that can be attributed to different types of environment (e.g., Caspi, Taylor, Moffitt, & Plomin, 2000). Indeed, self-concept stability may be partly associated with environmental stability but over time provides a gradually "moving baseline" against which there are situational fluctuations (Demo, 1992; cf. Ardelt, 2000). Irrespective of the weight of evidence surrounding the person-situation and environment-gene debates, what seems clear is that all of these variables contribute to personality and a host of other socially expressed attributes. There is also a strong case that a psychological self-structure develops that is relatively stable, at least in terms of its motivational components (cf. Higgins, 1989). It is therefore not surprising to find evidence in the adult literature that global personal self-esteem is related to in-group bias (Aberson, Healy, & Romero, 2000). Similarly, the evidence described by Powlishta shows that children's personal self-evaluation rises in line with gender in-group favouritism. Moreover, the fact that the self-esteem–bias relationship is stronger among girls than boys suggests that variables other than social identification may underpin this male–female difference.

Sani and Bennett

Sani and Bennett propose that children's knowledge of group identities moves through age-related stages, such that they only begin to focus on beliefs and attitudes related to identity quite late on. It is encouraging that children aged 12 years or so are sensitive to sociopolitical issues that might underpin perceptions of shared beliefs. This is also reflected in the inclusion of these issues as part of the school curriculum for older children, but not younger children. More intriguing is that older children have developed a framework or vocabulary for describing the impact of values and beliefs on behaviour even when they encounter new intergroup contexts. Children as young as 5 years of age appear to be able to make a clear connection between psychological attributes and category memberships, but only older children have more extensive notions of the principles and ideas underlying commitment to an identity. As Sani and Bennett point out, the understanding of belief-based differences is more central to some category memberships than others, and there may be important questions of domain-relevant expertise that need to be understood. Although Sani and Bennett point to the fact that social identities differ (following Deaux, Reid, Mizrahi, & Cotting, 1999), perhaps an equally relevant point is that social identification can involve different types of content depending on a *variety* of factors. Some of these are cognitive, but an important set may be found in the social context, the nature of particular relationships, the relative power and status of different social groups, and the child's active engagement as a self-directed agent in their social world (Abrams, 1992).

Sani and Bennett, and David et al., are enthusiastic about the idea that social identity (and stereotyping and group preference) is flexible. Sani and Bennett suggest that since contextual variability in stereotyping emerges at 7 years of age, "once applied to the in-group, stereotype variability is conceptually equivalent to social identity variability". Although this proposition is attractive theoretically, perhaps we need to be cautious in predicting the cognitive and motivational connections between group evaluations, group stereotypes, and the self-concept.

In their Study 5, Sani and Bennett asked children to make comparative judgments between age and gender categories (not to rate stereotypes per se), and found that children were sensitive to relevant dimensions for category differentiation. This may demonstrate stereotype flexibility, as Sani and Bennett conclude. However, an additional possibility might be that children are skilled in highlighting the most *relevant* features within a context. Their apparent flexibility in selecting these features may demonstrate that they possess reasonably well-developed, and quite stable, representation of a variety of different stereotypes (see Devine, 1989; Monteith, Ashburn-Nardo, Voils, & Czopp, 2002, for distinctions between stereotype activation and application). Moreover, the finding that boys and girls appear to differ in their levels of differentiation suggests that the processes at work are in part social, and not entirely cognitive or developmental. The existence of cultural differences in the scope and variability of self-descriptions across situations also supports this point (see also Kanagawa, Cross, & Markus, 2001).

Social identity theory proposes that people are motivated to evaluate their social identity positively. The link between group membership and social identity is made through the *evaluation* of the in-group. One way to do this is to create a stereotypical advantage for the in-group, but there are numerous other ways that do not rely on existing stereotypes (e.g., the use of social creativity strategies, or simple in-group favouritism).

Turning from stereotypes to identity, evidence on the linkage between evaluation and identity in adults does not always suggest a very "flexible" set of phenomena. As mentioned earlier, among adults, Gaertner et al.'s (2002) meta-analytic evidence shows that in response to certain threats and opportunities for enhancement the individual self has motivational primacy over the collective self and the contextual self. Moreover, work by Deaux and others (see Abrams, 1992; Deaux, 1992) indicates that the self-concept has considerable stability because people develop a psychological commitment to a particular view of themselves. Thus, it may be important not to assume that a process that allows the self to be defined flexibly requires that the self structure is entirely a function of social context (Abrams, 1996, 1999). For example, in Sani and Bennett's Study 7 there are some curious results. Consistent with an SCT prediction, male children's self-descriptions became *more* stereotypical in the intergroup than in the self-only condition. However, there was not a qualitative alteration in their self-descriptions. In addition, female children did not reveal so much difference as a function of condition, suggesting some imperviousness to intergroup (gender) context.

The idea that "it is not until around 7 years of age at the earliest that children internalise particular social identities" is also worthy of further research. This conclusion may be apt for situations in which there is no obvious conflict between groups. However, just as evidence from the adult literature shows that increased conflict and other factors can make social identity more salient and impactful, it seems likely that under some circumstances children may internalise social identifications at a younger age. For example, perhaps young Israeli and Palestinian children have (at least) a rudimentary sense of their identity within the intergroup context (Zecharia, 1990). In other words, it seems likely to me, and on the basis of previous evidence on gender and ethnicity, that there is an interaction between the strength and meaningfulness of social categories in the organisation of daily life, and the extent to which children internalise group memberships early or late.

Another potentially useful direction for research is implied in the final paragraph of Sani and Bennett's chapter, i.e., that it is "fruitful to conceive of the origins of social identities in terms of co-construction (i.e., between novice and elder), rather than in terms of purely individual cognitive construction". I agree with this, and would amplify it. Co-construction may happen within a peer group, or between elder and novice, or family members, or within a church, or between school and child. The social-psychological task is to make sense of a social context or situation in order to engage with it. This requires a system of social consensus (cf. Berger & Luckman, 1971; Moscovici, 1976; Stangor et al., 2001). Once children are able to share in a social consensus they can move beyond egocentrism (cf. Mead, 1934).

Gender

Powlishta

Powlishta provides an excellent review of the evidence for male/female relations in childhood, and proposes that generic intergroup processes are at work. Powlishta wonders why gender stereotypes persist in the face of the apparent absence of objective differences (Maccoby, 1998). Maybe this is not such a puzzle, though. First, even when distributions are highly overlapping, persistent differences are likely to become highly apparent across multiple comparisons (e.g., the height of North American and British adults is apparent to most people even though the distributions are highly overlapping). More centrally, some of the evidence cited by Powlishta relates to reactions to transgressions against behavioural norms rather than against stereotypes. There is little question that many of the behavioural norms applying to males and females remain distinct (e.g., dress codes, etiquette, child-bearing; see Glick & Fiske, 2001, Glick et al., 2000).

The distinction between norms and stereotypes is likely to be helpful because it may be that children focus more closely on how boys and girls *should behave* than on complexities of the underlying traits. Indeed, the same trait (e.g., friendliness) could be manifested quite differently depending on prevailing social norms. That is, both boys and girls might consider themselves to be stereotypically friendly, but at certain ages friendliness might involve befriending only own-gender children. As Powlishta, Sen, Serbin, Poulin-Dubois, and Eichstedt (2001) observe, there is not merely a linkage between attributes and gender categories but an evaluative response to each association. It seems likely that social norms are highly relevant in defining how stereotypes are to be applied. This might imply that investigation of the development of social identity could benefit as much from studying children's sensitivity to social norms as from researching their stereotypes (Abrams, Rutland, Cameron, & Marques, in press).

Powlishta proposes that males may start with a status advantage in the early years (cf. Glick & Hilt, 2000) and that girls' negative reactions to boys may reflect their resentment over lower status. However, other evidence (e.g., see Abrams, 1988; Abrams, Sparkes, & Hogg, 1985; David et al., Chapter 5; Eccles, 1985) shows that girls have the advantage in terms of competency and performance in school. This suggests an alternative interpretation in terms of girls' awareness and evaluations, reflecting that they have higher status within the classroom (cf. Mullen, Brown, & Smith, 1992). Other questions posed by Powlishta, such as why boys show more gender segregation, are also important. One possibility is that girls, as the more powerful group, actually show greater control over and variability in their behaviour (cf. Guinote, Judd, & Brauer, 2002). Thus boys may be denied the opportunity to behave in flexible (and less masculine) ways, whereas girls are not. The intriguing question is how this power differential reverses itself in adulthood.

Powlishta also suggests that, "attention to gender also may become less important as gender-role expertise is developed". While it may well be true that children become less concerned with simple intergroup differentiation with age, surely children become *more* sensitised to gender and, in particular, concerned with the nature of the potentially romantic and sexualised relationships between males and females (Montgomery & Sorell, 1998), a trend that can have negative academic consequences for girls (Brendgen, Vitaro, Doyle, Markiewicz, & Bukowski, 2002; Neeman, Hubbard, & Masten, 1996). Children are likely to become increasingly interested in media images that depict men and women as romantic and sexual partners (Livingstone & Bovill, 2001). This implies that they might differentiate more strongly with age, but that the biases they show become more subtle, specific, and, in some senses, complementary (see Abrams, 1989, for a detailed review).

At the end of the chapter Powlishta wonders about the advantages of using techniques that might inhibit the use of gender-based categories or redirect children's attention to other bases of categorisation. While this seems laudable in some respects, and reminiscent of Bem's (1981) call for people to become "gender aschematic", it could be problematic in other respects. Gender pervades most social situations, and is particularly relevant to the social norms within many. It seems likely that children, and people generally, learn quickly when and whether to apply gender-based judgments to their own and others' actions. Most of the action in the application (and nonapplication) of gender norms seems likely to reflect social norms rather cognitive constraints (see Abrams & Masser, 1998; cf. Monteith et al., 2002).

David et al.

David, Grace, and Ryan's fundamental assumption is that "since social contexts are potentially infinite in number, so are the selves that will be determined by them". I do not share their confidence that this working assumption can be easily sustained. Aside from previous debates on this point in relation to adult's social environments (see Abrams, 1992, 1996, 1999), children's social environments are by no means infinitely flexible. They are externally restricted and are limited in number, essentially revolving around the home/caring and educational contexts. There is a high degree of adult control over which environment the child moves into, how, and when. Along with the lack of environmental flexibility, there does not seem to be evidence that children's self-concept wavers greatly (Eder, 1990). Children aged 18 months seem to show constancy in self-recognition (Campbell, Shirley, Heywood, & Crook, 2000). So, is social identity infinitely malleable or it is not? If self-categorisations are "a direct consequence of the genuine economic, political, and social circumstances of our lives" (David et al., Chapter 5), surely they will have the same degree of stability, inertia, and interdependency as those circumstances provide. As a result, infinite flexibility may be a theoretical but not empirical possibility (cf. James & Prout, 1990; Jenks, 2002).

It may be useful to draw a distinction between comparative variation and flexibility in the self-concept. Ryan and David's (2002) study shows that whether people define themselves as connected or independent may vary according to the comparison group. The David (2000) study shows that, when given a task by an adult in which age is made relevant, children sort on the basis of age first and gender second. When only gender is made relevant they sort by gender. David et al. interpret these results as showing that, "very clearly . . . the self is not a fixed construct". However, another way to look at the findings is that people relate their relatively stable self-concept to the comparative context in a meaningful way (cf. Canter & Ageton, 1984). It is perfectly reasonable to describe oneself as introverted compared to a clown but extraverted compared to a monk, as wise compared to one's children, but inexperienced compared to one's parents. This does not mean one has no stable sense of one's level of introversion, wisdom, or experience. The task is even simpler for objective characteristics. A child may know that he or she is taller than a sibling, shorter than most adults, and is 1 metre tall. I am suggesting that comparative variation in self-description does not necessarily imply an equally flexible self-concept.

David et al. suggest that, "none of the dominant theories provide a rationale for the virulence of the primary school separatist 'war', and that self-categorisation theory provides a compelling account of this". They propose that, "when gender identity is salient . . . children will tend to perceive all boys as the same, all girls as the same, and boys and girls as fundamentally different from each other. Girls see the difference as favouring them, while boys see it as favouring them". It would be useful to develop these ideas more precisely because the qualifying words, "tend to" may imply either that some children may not perceive things in this way, or that all children do but not to a full extent. David et al. claim that males' and females' struggle for positive distinctiveness explains the "hostility" of primary school gender interactions. Yet it is not clear that boys and girls see positive distinctiveness as an important goal, nor that they are particularly hostile to one another (see Hartup & Abecassis, 2002; Hymel, Vaillancourt, McDougall, & Renshaw, 2002; also Nesdale, Chapter 8). For example, it seems more likely that instances of direct hostility will occur within than between groups (Abecassis, Hartup, Haselager, Scholte, & Van Lieshout, 2002). It is important to explain why, once gender is made "salient", boys and girls *do not* apply gender stereotypes completely and unambiguously. Why are girls more likely to show in-group favouritism than boys at one age, but the reverse pattern occurs at another (e.g., Strough & Marie-Covatto, 2002)?

David et al. suggest that, with puberty, "gender loses its appearance of 'chronic' salience, it becomes less important to 'maximise the difference', and gender stereotypes become less prescriptive". This idea seems at odds with the possibility that puberty may heighten the salience of gender (and sex), and increase the prescriptiveness of gender-related norms (Abrams, 1989; Abrams, Marques, Bown, & Henson, 2000; Brendgen et al., 2002; Glick & Hilt, 2000; Montgomery & Sorell, 1998; Strough & Marie-Covatto, 2002).

David et al. characterise adolescent girls as "internalising the social reality of sexual inequality and becoming disempowered young women". It seems likely, however, that this state may apply to some females but not to all, or even most. As Condor (1986) and Abrams (1989) pointed out, and as is clear from pervasive attitudinal variation in forms of sexism (Glick & Fiske, 1996), people do not necessarily accept traditional sex role ideology or sex stereo- types. For example, some women identify more than others with other women, or more precisely with particular types of women. Women may endorse either traditional or progressive sex role ideologies. The same is true for men (see Glick & Fiske, 1999). Arguably, then, David et al.'s analysis would benefit from an acknowledgement that people tend to reflect on the meaning of their gender identity, and play an active role in how it develops.

Finally, somewhat in line with Powlishta's thinking, David et al. conclude that gender is not a special case, but merely an instance of intergroup rela- tions. This strikes me as doubtful, because it is difficult to think of any other intergroup relationship that involves pervasive, almost ubiquitous, and strongly prescribed, intimate relationships between members of the different groups, nor one in which interdependency between the "groups" is an essen- tial feature of human survival (see also Katz, 1986). There are some very specific social practices that allow this to happen, such as arranged marriages, the informal age gap in heterosexual romantic involvement (which starts with differential onset of puberty and persists into adulthood), and society's heavy reliance on women to bear and raise children. I wholly endorse the idea that gender must be analysed as a form of intergroup relationship, but I think it should also be acknowledged that, for various reasons, gender *is* different from the general case (Abrams, 1989).

Ethnicity, race, nationality, and the family

Verkuyten

The theme of a normative context for intergroup relations is stressed by Verkuyten. The interesting point, made very clearly by his research, is that there are ethno-cultural differences in the way children evaluate their own and other ethnic groups. This takes us away from the idea of a single devel- opmental pathway, driven strongly by cognitive processes, and towards the idea of social pathways that depend on cultural and social practices (Spencer, 1995). As Verkuyten points out, "minority group children may value their ethnic identity because of supportive relationships with other in-group mem- bers and because they prefer similarities over differences". That is to say, the enduring and meaningful relationships that children have with others within their own groups shapes the way they understand their ethnicity and ethnic identity. In contrast to David et al., Verkuyten treats social identity as "a stable self-structure or trait-like aspect that is expressed independently of a social situation". Verykuten's evidence that differences in ethnic identification were greater within than between classrooms does not necessarily imply that contextual effects are unimportant (classroom may not be a relevant contextual variable). The within-classroom ethnic composition did affect the salience of ethnic self-description. However, the correlation between self-categorisation and self-stereotyping was low ($r = .38$), which reminds us that much of the variance in social identity might not be accounted for simply by self-categorisation. There is more going on, and much of it seems attributable to culture. This invites further exploration of *how* cultural values and norms become embodied in the social identity of children.

Barrett et al.

Much of the research evidence cited in this book presses towards adoption of an SIT/SCT perspective. Barrett, Lyons, and del Valle's chapter rings loud warning bells. They describe what must have been a somewhat frustrating quest of testing how predictions from SCT and SIT apply to national identity. Across a wide spectrum of national groups they conclude that the evidence is very inconsistent (Barrett et al., 1997). Children in all countries tended to show in-group preference in liking, but varied in terms of evaluations based on positive and negative attributes. There was little evidence that national in-group preference and evaluations were related to in-group identification (aside from among Spanish children, who appear to have a special "social identity" switch!). In the Barrett, Wilson, and Lyons (1999) study there was no effect of comparative context on attribution of characteristics to national groups (see also Sani, Bennett, & Joyner, 1999), no evidence of a relationship between identification and stereotyping, and no evidence that minority group children would identify more strongly. Most telling, and in line with Abrams and Hogg (1988), some children who did not identify strongly with their national group still showed in-group favouritism. Barrett et al.'s evidence is also notable for the absence of a consistent developmental pattern. As in Verkuyten's chapter, this suggests again the importance of social processes in the way children (of varying ages) respond to issues of national identity. Taken together, the evidence seems consistent with the idea that there may be strong norms at work that may facilitate or inhibit the expression of nationalistic judgments over and above effects of self-categorisation and social identity, and possibly age. Barrett et al. note that Turner (1999) has recently accepted that core social identity processes may interact with numerous other factors, meaning that it might be inappropriate to look for correlations between pairs of variables. Perhaps the myriad of different developmental and national patterns in Barrett et al.'s data reflect the moderating effects of several of these factors. In this case, it could be argued that the way forward is to develop a more complex, multifaceted, and multivariate approach to research national identity. However, this risks creating unmanageably large and complex research designs, particularly for use with children. In the light of all their evidence it is tempting to accept Barrett et al.'s conclusion that SIT/SCT are potentially impervious to empirical evaluation because all findings can be explained post hoc. The protective layers around the key ideas do sometimes seem to render SCT and SIT invulnerable to refutation (see also Abrams, 1992). However, it would be premature to give up the expedition just because some of the trails are impassable or circular! Perhaps we need to concentrate on specifying when SIT will and will not be likely to provide a useful explanation of children's intergroup attitudes and behaviour.

Nesdale

Nesdale highlights a distinction made by some other contributors between in-group preference and out-group rejection. He offers *social identity development theory* as a way of accommodating this distinction. Nesdale's theory offers a clear developmental framework within which social identity processes may emerge, at least for ethnicity. He outlines several tasks for such a theory, including accounting for the discrepancy between children's attitudes and those of their family members, recognising the developmental changes in perceptual, cognitive, and linguistic abilities, the operation of social motivations, and the fact that some children seem not to develop ethnic prejudices. Along with Rutland, Nesdale notes that SIT and SCT have nothing particular to say about cognitive abilities.

The first important distinction is that children respond to ethnic self-categorisation by focusing only on the in-group. The emergence of prejudice, or active dislike for an out-group, occurs later and depends on children adopting as their own the prejudices of members of an in-group with which they identify. Prejudice is thus more likely if the group as a whole is prejudiced or is in conflict with or threatened by the out-group.

A particularly valuable contribution of Nesdale's analysis is that it specifies conditions under which we would not expect children to express prejudice. As he notes, "young children up to 9 years of age are simply not repositories of ethnic dislike and prejudice" (see also Hartup & Abecassis, 2002). Only when the context and motivation are pressing towards prejudice is it likely to appear. Similar points can be made in relation to a range of social categorisations, including age, gender, and nationality.

Nesdale shows how a developmental approach can be combined with SCT and SIT. This approach adopts a stage-based analysis, which implies cognitive and/or social limits on what children might do in relation to social categories at different ages. It would be nice to see this framework extended. The competence/performance distinction is certainly relevant here, as are a host of interesting questions. What are the developmental steps in children's ability to judge the relationships between social attributes and social categories that do and do not include themselves? Do the same categorisation processes (e.g., metacontrast) operate as in adulthood, and can we simply draw the regression line back from adulthood to childhood? At what age does the metacontrast process emerge? What precedes it? When does depersonalisation start to happen? What precedes it? What are the initial motivations that accompany self-categorisation? Is there an automatic desire for positive distinctiveness or is this a culturally determined motive (Heine et al., 1999)? During childhood, are the changes in social identification and intergroup behaviour reflective of qualitative changes (in process) or merely a gradual quantitative change that culminates in adult-like behaviour? How does the development of other social competencies combine with the development of categorisation processes? Can the development of social identity tell us something new about the processes that might operate in adults? Why do some children who apparently share the same social environment display different intergroup attitudes and behaviour? Are these differences attributable to cognitive differences or are there powerful social factors beyond the immediate context that must be better understood? By pointing to the fact that children's ethnic identity does not conform to the stereotypical intergroup template, Nesdale reminds us that the incorporation of SIT and SCT in a developmental framework requires additional theorising about both development and social identity processes.

Rutland

Given my interest in self-regulation in children (Abrams, 1984, 1985) and normative processes generally (Abrams & Hogg, 1990), I welcome Rutland's exploration of the way children self-regulate their intergroup attitudes. Indeed, the issue of self-presentation is surely relevant for children in most experimental studies, within which they are implicitly or explicitly accountable to an adult for their behaviour. Introducing the use of implicit attitude measurement to the area of children's social identity, Rutland reports evidence that explicit biases may decrease with age but implicit ones may not. Children's moderation of public expressions of prejudice is an important phenomenon. It indicates that they understand prevailing norms regarding the expression of intergroup attitudes. It also implies that they may be more motivated to accommodate to those norms than to serve their social identity. The more general point is that the social environment within which children learn ethnic, gender, and national attitudes may contain powerfully internalised norms that affect their expression of prejudice. In turn, against a politically liberal background this may restrict the levels of prejudice that actually exist (see Nesdale's theory, and also Stangor et al., 2001).

Just as norms may vary, so will the impact of norms on prejudice and behaviour. Presumably the children of Hutus and Tutsis in Rwanda developed profound intergroup hatred from a very early age, reinforced by extremely strong social norms. The point is that we need to build an understanding of how children learn and embrace such norms into our theorising about the development of social identity and patterns of prejudice. Given the current interest in social self-regulation of prejudice in adults (Abrams, 1990, 1994; Abrams & Masser, 1998; Monteith et al., 2002; Plant & Devine, 1998), it seems that this area is well-worth pursuing in the analysis of children's prejudice.

Banker et al.

Banker, Gaertner, Dovidio, Houlette, Johnson, and Riek expand the context of childhood into the realm of families. This chapter is less concerned with the cognitive-developmental processes within individuals than with the way families may be characterised by different intergroup relations. Banker et al. find that the perception of the stepfamily as part of a common group does much to reduce conflict and facilitate positive relationships.

The idea of viewing stepfamilies in group terms raises interesting possibilities for promoting harmony within families in general. In particular, there may be several ways that families could be partitioned into different groups (e.g., generational groups, geographical groups). How would different models of intergroup contact propose that family relationships could be sustained most positively? Pettigrew's (1998) reformulated contact model proposes that positive intergroup attitudes are most likely to develop if initial contact is depersonalised, intergroup differences are subsequently attended to, and finally a superordinate identity is recognised. Perhaps this sort of sequence is a natural aspect of widening one's family (e.g., the addition of in-laws). Other approaches (e.g., Hewstone & Brown, 1986; Hornsey & Hogg, 2000) suggest that a dual identity strategy is likely to succeed, in which people are able to sustain positive intergroup distinctiveness at the same time as sharing a common identity.

The application of the *common in-group identity model* at the level of families also raises interesting questions about the way children might develop or inhibit different aspects of social identity. For example, how can a child who sees his or her parents and self as a unit also differentiate strongly between men and women or boys and girls? Is the family unit the primary group for most children? If so, why has the study of children's intergroup perceptions ignored this unit in preference to other group memberships? Given that family is often a central group for collectivist cultures (cf. Trafimow, Triandis, & Goto, 1991), perhaps there is more to be learnt here.

CONCLUSIONS

My aim in this chapter has been to highlight some of the ideas and findings in this book that will provide a spur for debate and further research. Although I have focused on issues that are debatable, my overall sense is that the book portrays a relatively coherent and consensual view of what research can tell us about the development of social identity. Clearly the social identity approach offers plenty of interesting research questions for developmentalists, and vice versa.

At the outset of this chapter I asked whether the cognitive-motivational elements of self-categorisation and social identity should be the only, or the most important, aspect of children's group membership that should attract our interest. Are we asking the right questions about children's relationship to social groups and categories? I think future research would benefit by devoting further attention to the social (e.g., cultural, intragroup, and interpersonal) processes by which intergroup relationships are defined, sustained, and given continued meaning for children.

Second, the different chapters in this book reveal a certain tension between social-contextual and cognitive-developmental accounts of social identity in children. I asked what other elements in the developmental equation may have been neglected. As Bennett and Sani note in their introduction, there are good reasons to think that social identity involves developmental processes across the lifespan as well as between situations, contexts, and intergroup relationships. Perhaps equally important is to be aware that social identity is not all in the head. It is something that must acquire *shared* meaning, and that necessarily involves social interaction between people and in relatively stable social environments. Rather little of the work described in this book examines directly how those interactions may be involved in the way social identity is constructed, and this could be a very productive avenue for future research.

Third, there is controversy in the adult literature surrounding various assumptions made by social identity theory and self-categorisation theory. How far does developmental research reflect these controversies? There has been some progress, and a host of interesting questions invite further exploration. For example, these include the way children regulate their behaviour as group members, the developmental impact of different motivational elements such as uncertainty reduction, need for cognition, terror management, impression management, optimal distinctiveness, and self-verification, and the link between communication and social identity.

To conclude, the important point to emerge from all of the fascinating work and ideas in this book is that social identity phenomena invite an analysis that goes beyond a cognitive-developmental approach and beyond a social-cognitive approach. We do need to specify the distinctive effects of cognitive development and of self-categorisation and social identification. But to predict how these will be manifested as children grow older almost certainly requires a more extensive analysis of the way culture, cultural rules and traditions, and specific group norms are maintained within groups, as well as an account of the historical context of intergroup relations. The chapters in this book reflect very substantial progress in clearing the ground theoretically and methodologically. The book as a whole provides a stimulus for many interesting and important questions for future research.

REFERENCES

Abecassis, M., Hartup, W. W., Haselager, G. J. T., Scholte, R. H. J., & Van Lieshout, C. F. M. (2002). Mutual antipathies and their significance in middle childhood and adolescence. *Child Development, 73*, 1543–1556.

Aberson, C. L., Healy, M., & Romero, V. (2000). In-group bias and self-esteem: A meta-analysis. *Personality and Social Psychology Review, 4*, 157–173.

Abrams, D. (1984). *Social identity, self-awareness and intergroup behaviour.* PhD thesis, University of Kent, Canterbury, UK.

Abrams, D. (1985). Focus of attention in minimal intergroup discrimination. *British Journal of Social Psychology, 24*, 65–74.

Abrams, D. (1988). Sex-role ideology, siblings and educational attainment: Social and psychological factors. *ESRC 16–19 Initiative Working Paper.* Swindon: Economic and Social Research Council.

Abrams, D. (1989). Differential association: Social developments in gender identity and intergroup relations during adolescence. In S. Skevington & D. Baker (Eds.), *The social identity of women* (pp. 59–83). London: SAGE Publications.

Abrams, D. (1990). The self-regulation of group behaviour: An integration of self-awareness and social identity theory. In D. Abrams & M. Hogg (Eds.), *Social Identity theory: Constructive and critical advances* (pp. 89–112). Hemel Hempstead: Harvester Wheatsheaf.

Abrams, D. (1992). Processes of social identification. In G. Breakwell (Ed.), *The social psychology of the self-concept* (pp 57-100). London: Academic Press/Surrey University Press.

Abrams, D. (1996). Social identity, self as structure and self as process. In W. P. Robinson (Ed.), *Social groups and identities: Developing the legacy of Henri Tajfel* (pp. 143–168). London: Butterworth Heinemann.

Abrams, D. (1999). Social identity, social cognition and the self: The flexibility and stability of self-categorization. In D. Abrams & M. A. Hogg (Eds.), *Social identity and social cognition* (pp. 197–229). Oxford: Blackwell.

Abrams, D., & Hogg, M. A. (1988). Comments on the motivational status of self-esteem in social identity and intergroup discrimination. *European Journal of Social Psychology, 18*, 317–334.

Abrams, D., & Hogg, M. A. (1990). Social identification, self-categorisation and social influence. In M. Hewstone & W. Stroebe (Eds.), *Review of European social psychology, Vol. 1* (pp. 195–228). Chichester, UK: John Wiley & Sons.

Abrams, D., & Hogg, M. A. (2001). Collective identity: Group membership and self-conception. In M. A. Hogg & S. Tindale (Eds.), *Blackwell handbook of social psychology, Vol. 3: Group processes* (pp. 425–461). Oxford: Blackwell.

Abrams, D., Marques, J. M., Bown, N. J., & Henson, M. (2000). Pro-norm and anti-norm deviance within in-groups and out-groups. *Journal of Personality and Social Psychology, 78*, 906–912.

Abrams, D., & Masser, B. (1998). Context and the social self-regulation of stereotyping: Perception, judgment and behavior. In R. S. Wyer (Ed.), *Advances in social cognition, Vol. 11* (pp. 53–67). Hillsdale, NJ: Lawrence Erlbaum Associates, Inc.

Abrams, D., Rutland, A., Cameron, L., & Marques, J. M. (in press). The development of subjective group dynamics: When in-group bias gets specific. *British Journal of Developmental Psychology.*

Abrams, D., Sparkes, K., & Hogg, M. A. (1985). Gender salience and social identity: The impact of sex of siblings on educational and occupational aspirations. *British Journal of Educational Psychology, 55*, 224–232.

Alfieri, T., Ruble, D. N., & Higgins, E. T. (1996). Gender stereotypes during adolescence: Developmental changes and the transition to junior high school. *Developmental Psychology, 32*, 1129–1137.

Alvarez, J. M., Ruble, D. N., & Bolger, N. (2001). The role of evaluation in the development of person perception. *Child Development, 72*, 1409–1425.

Ardelt, M. (2000). Still stable after all these years? Personality stability theory revisited. *Social Psychology Quarterly, 63*, 392–405.

Barrett, M., Lyons, E., Bennett, M., Vila, I., Gimenez, A., Arcuii, L., & de Rosa, A. S. (1997). *Children's beliefs and feelings about their own and other national groups in Europe.* Final Report to the Commission of the European Communities, Directorate-General Xii for Science, Research and Development, Human Capital and Mobility (HCM) Programme, Research Network No. CHRX-CT94–0687.

Barrett, M., Wilson, H., & Lyons, E. (1999, April). *Self-categorization theory and the development of national identity in English children.* Poster presented at Biennial Meeting of SRCD, Alberquerque, USA.

Baumeister, R. F. (Ed.) (1999). *The self in social psychology.* Philadelphia, PA: Psychology Press.

Bem, S. L. (1981). Gender schema theory: A cognitive account of sex-typing. *Psychological Review, 88*, 354–364.

Berger, P. L., & Luckman, T. (1971). *The social construction of reality.* Harmondsworth, UK: Penguin.

Brendgen, M., Vitaro, F., Doyle, A. B., Markiewicz, D., & Bukowski, W. M. (2002). Same-sex peer relations and romantic relationships during early adolescence: Interactive links to emotional, behavioral and academic adjustment. *Merill Palmer Quarterly, 48*, 77–103.

Bronfenbrenner, U. (1999). Environments in developmental perspective: Theoretical and operational models. In S. L. Friedman & T. D. Wachs (Eds.), *Measuring environment across the lifespan: Emerging methods and concepts* (pp. 3–28). Washington, DC: American Psychological Association.

Campbell, A., Shirley, L., Heywood, C., & Crook, C. (2000). Infants' visual preference for sex-congruent babies, children, toys and activities: A longitudinal study. *British Journal of Developmental Psychology, 18*, 479–498.

Canter, R. J., & Ageton, S. S. (1984). The epidemiology of adolescent sex-role attitudes. *Sex Roles, 11*, 657–676.

Caspi, A., Taylor, A., Moffitt, T. E., & Plomin, R. (2000). Neighborhood deprivation affects children's mental health: Environmental risks identified in a genetic design. *Psychological Science, 11*, 338–342.

Condor, S. G. (1986). Sex role beliefs and "traditional" women: Feminist and inter-group perspectives. In S. Wilkinson (Ed.), *Feminist social psychology* (pp. 97–118). Milton Keynes, UK: Open University Press.

Deaux, K. (1992). Personalizing identity and socializing self. In G. Breakwell (Ed.), *Social psychology of identity and the self-concept* (pp. 9–34). London: Academic Press.

Deaux, K., Reid, A., Mizrahi, K., & Cotting, D. (1999). Connecting the person to the social: The functions of social identification. In T. R. Tyler, R. M. Kramer, & O. P.

John (Eds.), *The psychology of the social self: Applied social research* (pp. 91–113). Mahwah, NJ: Lawrence Erlbaum Associates, Inc.

Demo, D. H. (1992). The self-concept over time: Research issues and directions. *Annual Review of Sociology, 18,* 303–326.

Devine, P. G. (1989). Stereotypes and prejudice: Their automatic and controlled components. *Journal of Personality and Social Psychology, 56,* 5–18.

Eccles, J. (1985). Sex differences in achievement patterns. In R. A. Dienstbier & T. B. Sonderegger (Eds.), *Nebraska Symposium on Motivation, 1984* (pp. 97–132). Lincoln, NE: University of Nebraska Press.

Eder, R. A. (1990). Uncovering young children's psychological selves: Individual and developmental differences. *Child Development, 61,* 849–863.

Emler, N. P. (2001). *Self-esteem: The costs and causes of low self-worth.* York, UK: Joseph Rowntree Foundation/York Publishing Services.

Gaertner, L., Sedikides, C., Vevea, J. L., & Iuzzini, J. (2002). The "I", the "we" and the "when". A meta-analysis of motivational primacy in self-definition. *Journal of Personality and Social Psychology, 83,* 574–591.

Glick, P., & Fiske, S. T. (1996). The ambivalent sexism inventory: Differentiating hostile and benevolent sexism. *Journal of Personality and Social Psychology, 70,* 491–512.

Glick, P., & Fiske, S. T. (1999). The ambivalence toward men inventory: Differentiating hostile and benevolent beliefs about men. *Psychology of Women Quarterly, 23,* 519–536.

Glick, P., & Fiske, S. T. (2001). Ambivalent sexism. In M. P. Zanna (Ed.), *Advances in experimental social psychology, Vol. 33* (pp. 115–188). San Diego, CA: Academic Press.

Glick, P., Fiske, S. T., Mladinic, A., Saiz, J. L., Abrams, D., Masser, B., Adetoun, B., Osagie, J. E., Akande, A., Alao, A., Anneteje, B., Willmsen, T. M., Chipeta, K., Dardenne, B., Dijsterhuis, A., Wigboldus, B., Eckes, T., Six-Materna, I., Exposito, F., Moyal, M., Foddy, M., Kim, H. J., Lameiras, M., Sotelo, M. J., Micchi-Faina, A., Romani, M., Sakalli, N., Udegbe, B., Yamamoto, M., Ui, M., Ferreira, M. C., & Lopez, W. L. (2000). Beyond prejudice as simple antipathy: Hostile and benevolent sexism across cultures. *Journal of Personality and Social Psychology, 79,* 763–775.

Glick, P., & Hilt, L. (2000). Combative children to ambivalent adults: The development of gender prejudice. In T. Eckes & H. Traunter (Eds.), *The developmental social psychology of gender* (pp. 243–272). Mahwah, NJ: Lawrence Erlbaum Associates, Inc.

Guinote, A., Judd, C. M., & Brauer, M. (2002). Effects of power on perceived and objective group variability: Evidence that more powerful groups are more variable. *Journal of Personality and Social Psychology, 82,* 708–721.

Hartup, W. W., & Abecassis, M. (2002). Friends and enemies. In P. K. Smith & C. H. Hart (Eds.), *Blackwell handbook of childhood social development* (pp. 285–306). Oxford: Blackwell.

Heine, S. H., Lehman, D. R., Markus, H. R., & Kitayama, S. (1999). Is there a universal need for positive self-regard? *Psychological Review, 106,* 766–794.

Hewstone, M., & Brown, R. J. (1986). Contact is not enough: An intergroup perspective on the "contact hypothesis". In M. Hewstone & R. J. Brown (Eds.), *Contact and conflict in intergroup encounters: Social psychology and society* (pp. 1–44). Oxford: Blackwell.

Higgins, E. T. (1989). Self-discrepancy theory: What patterns of self-beliefs cause people to suffer? In L. Berkowitz (Ed.), *Advances in experimental social psychology, Vol. 22* (pp. 93–136). San Diego, CA: Academic Press.

Hogg, M. A. (2001). Self-categorization and subjective uncertainty resolution: Cognitive and motivational facets of social identity and group membership. In J. P. Forgas, K. D. Williams, & L. Wheeler (Eds.), *The social mind: Cognitive and motivational aspects of interpersonal behavior* (pp. 323–349). New York: Cambridge University Press.

Hogg, M. A., & Abrams, D. (1993). An uncertainty reduction model of group motivation. In M. A. Hogg & D. Abrams (Eds.), *Group motivation: Social psychological perspectives* (pp. 173–190) London: Harvester Wheatsheaf.

Hornsey, M. J., & Hogg, M. A. (2000). Subgroup relations: A comparison of mutual intergroup differentiation and common ingroup identity models of prejudice reduction. *Personality and Social Psychology Bulletin, 26*, 242–256.

Hur, Y.-M., McGue, M., & Iacono, W. G. (1998). The structure of self-concept in female preadolescent twins: A behavioral genetic approach. *Journal of Personality and Social Psychology, 74*, 1069–1077.

Hymel, S., Vaillancourt, T., McDougall, P., & Renshaw, P. D. (2002). Peer acceptance and rejection in childhood. In P. K. Smith & C. H. Hart (Eds.), *Blackwell handbook of childhood social development* (pp. 265–284). Oxford: Blackwell Publishing.

James, A., & Prout, A. (1990). *Constructing and reconstructing childhood*. Basingstoke, UK: Falmer.

Jenks, C. (2002). A sociological approach to childhood development. In P. K. Smith & C. H. Hart (Eds.), *Blackwell handbook of childhood social development* (pp. 79–96). Oxford: Blackwell.

Kanagawa, C., Cross, S. E., & Markus, H. R. (2001). "Who am I?" The cultural psychology of the conceptual self. *Personality and Social Psychology Bulletin, 27*, 90–103.

Katz, P. A. (1986). Gender identity: Development and consequences. In R. D. Ashmore & F. K. Del Boca (Eds.), *The social psychology of female–male relations: A critical analysis of central concepts* (pp. 21–68). New York: Academic Press.

Kruglanski, A. W., & Webster, D. M. (1996). Motivated closing of the mind: "Seizing" and "freezing". *Psychological Review, 103*, 263–283.

Livingstone, S., & Bovill, M. (Eds.) (2001). *Children and their changing media environment: A European comparative study*. Mahwah, NJ: Lawrence Erlbaum Associates, Inc.

Lyons, A., & Kashima, Y. (2001). The reproduction of culture: Communication processes tend to maintain cultural stereotypes. *Social Cognition, 19*, 372–394.

Maccoby, E. E. (1998). *The two sexes: Growing up apart, coming together*. Cambridge, MA: Harvard University Press.

McGue, M., Bacon, S., & Lykken, D. T. (1993). Personality stability and change in early adulthood: A behavioral genetic analysis. *Developmental Psycholoy, 29*, 96–109.

McGuire, S., Neiderhiser, J. M., Reiss, D., Hetherington, E. M., & Plomin, R. (1996). "Genetic and environmental influences on perceptions of self-worth and competence in adolescence: A study of twins, full siblings and step-siblings:" Erratum. *Child Development, 67*, 3417.

McGuire, W. J., & McGuire, C. V. (1988). Content and process in the experience of the self. In L. Berkowitz (Ed.), *Advances in experimental social psychology, Vol. 21. Social psychological studies of the self: Perspectives and programs* (pp. 97–144). San Diego, CA: Academic Press.

McGuire, W. J., McGuire, C. V., Child, P., & Fujioka, T. (1978). Salience of ethnicity in the spontaneous self-concept as a function of one's ethnic distinctiveness in the social environment. *Journal of Personality and Social Psychology, 36*, 511–520.

Mead, G. H. (1934). *Mind, self and society*. Chicago, IL: University of Chicago Press.

Monteith, M. J., Ashburn-Nardo, L., Voils, C. I., & Czopp, A. M. (2002). Putting the brakes on prejudice: On the development and operation of cues for control. *Journal of Personality and Social Psychology, 83*, 1029–1050.

Montgomery, M. J., & Sorell, G. T. (1998). Love and dating experience in early and middle adolescence: Grade and gender comparisons. *Journal of Adolescence, 21*, 677–689.

Moscovici, S. (1976). *Social influence and social* change. London: Academic Press.

Mullen, B., Brown, R.J., & Smith, C. (1992). Ingroup bias as function of salience, relevance and status: An integration. *European Journal of Social Psychology, 22*, 103–122.

Neeman, J., Hubbard, J., & Masten, A. S. (1996). The changing importance of romantic relationship involvement to competence from late childhood to late adolescence. *Development and Psychopathology, 7*, 727–750.

Nicole, S., & Del Miglio, C. (1995). Self-awareness in monozygotic twins: A relational study. *Acta Geneticae Medicae et Gemellologiae: Twin Research, 44*, 107–115.

Otten, S., & Wentura, D. (1999). About the impact of automaticity in the Minimal Group Paradigm: Evidence from affective priming tasks. *European Journal of Social Psychology, 29*, 1049–1071

Perdue, C. W., Dovidio, J. F., Gurtman, M. B., & Tyler, R. B. (1990). Us and them: Social categorization and the process of intergroup bias. *Journal of Personality and Social Psychology, 59*, 475–486.

Pettigrew, T. F. (1998). Intergroup contact theory. *Annual Review of Psychology, 49*, 65–85.

Plant, E. A., & Devine, P. G. (1998). Internal and external motivation to respond without prejudice. *Journal of Personality and Social Psychology, 75*, 811–832.

Powlishta, K. K., Sen, M. G., Serbin, L. A., Poulin-Dubois, D., & Eichstedt, J. A. (2001). From infancy through middle childhood: The role of cognitive and social factors in becoming gendered. In R. K. Unger (Ed.), *Handbook of the psychology of women and gender* (pp. 116–132). New York: John Wiley & Sons.

Rubin, M., & Hewstone, M. (1998). Social identity theory's self-esteem hypothesis. A review and some suggestions for clarification. *Personality and Social Psychology Review, 2*, 40–62.

Runciman, W. G. (1966). *Relative deprivation and social justice*. London: Routledge & Kegan Paul.

Ryan, M., & David, B. (2002). *A gendered self or a gendered context: A self-categorization approach to independence and interdependence*. Manuscript submitted for publication.

Sani, F., Bennett, M., & Joyner, L. (1999). *Developmental aspects of contextual variability in the stereotype of the ingroup: The case of Scottish children*. Paper presented at the Annual Conference of the Social Psychology Section of the British Psychological Society, Lancaster, UK.

Spencer, M. B. (1995). Cultural cognition and social cognition as identity correlates of black children's personal-social development. In M. B. Spencer, G. K. Brookins, & W. R. Allen (Eds.), *Beginnings: The social and affective development of black children: Child psychology* (pp. 215–230). Hillsdale, NJ: Lawrence Erlbaum Associates, Inc.

Stangor, C., Sechrist, G. B., & Jost, J. T. (2001). Changing racial beliefs by providing consensus information. *Personality and Social Psychology Bulletin, 27*, 486–496.

Stangor, C., & Thompson, E. P. (2002). Needs for cognitive economy and self-enhancement as unique predictors of intergroup attitudes. *European Journal of Social Psychology, 32*, 563–575.

Strough, J., & Marie-Covatto, A. (2002). Context and age differences in same- and other-gender peer preferences. *Social Development, 11*, 346–361.

Tajfel, H. (1974). Social identity and intergroup behaviour. *Social Science Information, 13*, 65–93.

Trafimow, D., Triandis, H. C., & Goto, S. (1991). Some tests of the distinction between the private self and the collective self. *Journal of Personality and Social Psychology, 60*, 649–655.

Turner, J. C. (1999). Some current issues in research on social identity and self-categorization theories. In N. Ellemers, R. Spears, & B. Boosje (Eds.), *Social identity* (pp. 6–34). Oxford: Blackwell.

Zecharia, D. S. (1990). Development of an ethnic self-definition: The ethnic self-concept "Jew" among Israeli children. *International Journal of Behavioral Development, 13*, 317–332.

12 Towards a developmental social psychology of the social self

Kevin Durkin

Children begin life as members of a social group, or they die. For the human infant, it is essential to be linked to another person or persons in order to obtain nutrition, accommodation, basic physical care, and a range of sensory stimulation matched to innate potentialities. Group membership is a raw necessity, and nature and cultures have evolved together to ensure that it is underwritten, universally, by the enduring collectives that we call families.

Children continue their progress into society by joining and identifying with more groups. At least one of these is of universal significance, highly salient in all known societies: gender. Others are almost as common and sometimes imbued with still greater phenomenological consequence: class/caste, ethnicity, nationality, territory, religion, language group, school. Yet others are more parochial, though not necessarily less vital to the people involved in them: friendship groups, sports teams, local child/youth organisations, gangs, fashions in appearance/music.

With starting points like these, it is not surprising that social affiliations are important to human beings. It is not surprising that group identities have motivational, affective, and informational significance. What is surprising is that developmental psychologists have tended to neglect group identity and social psychologists have tended to ignore the origins of groups. The many provocative theoretical and empirical contributions of this volume provide an overdue correction and demonstrate that exciting research prospects come into view if we dare to cast off our subdisciplinary blinkers.

I have been asked to comment from a developmental perspective and will concentrate on issues that relate to how developmental changes come about – though it will be clear that this entails acknowledging the many ways in which developmental psychologists can profit from the perspectives of our social colleagues. I will not reiterate the contents: The editorial introduction provides an excellent summary and the chapters themselves are impressively clear. Instead, I will attempt to highlight a number of themes that seem to me to be interwoven through the chapters, sometimes very explicitly, sometimes implicitly or tangentially, and perhaps occasionally notable largely because of their absence. The reader who has followed the text this far will need no further persuasion that the authors have provided us with many insights and valuable new findings. Hence, I will focus primarily upon issues for future research on the premise that, for all the advances that it records, the still greater outlook for this volume is that it will prove to be a catalyst.

Readers will doubtless detect many themes and questions (see also Abrams, Chapter 11), and the comments below are offered in a catalytic spirit, that they may contribute to the plentiful reactions the authors have initiated. For this reader, they lead to the following: (1) the family as the first group, (2) developmental changes and continuities, (3) language and the development of social selves, (4) competition between developmental and social processes, (5) age as a social identity, (6) promoting better social selves, and (7) social selves through the lifespan. These will be discussed in turn.

THE FAMILY AS THE FIRST GROUP

To the developmentalist, it seems obvious that the family is important. As indicated above, the family is crucial to survival and is the gateway to virtually everything else that children encounter in their early social activities. The family is the first group (the first "we") a person joins and it is usually the longest lasting. To the developmentalist, group processes begin here and social psychologists appear to be overlooking something fundamental by disregarding the family or by treating it as just one group among many. On the other hand, developmentalists tend to pay little attention to the fact that families stand in some kind of relationship to each other – that is, that there are in-groups ("my family") and out-groups ("your family", "that family") – as well as to other levels of community and society. It takes a social-psychological perspective to begin to see why this could be important.

Several chapters agree that in-group bias associated with social categories is operating in normally developing children by around 5 or 6 years of age (Barrett et al., Nesdale, Ruble et al., Rutland, Sani & Bennett). The evidence is extensive, but perhaps not comprehensive. We have not yet identified the starting point or the early developmental course of in-group bias. If it is reasonable to suppose that precursors can be traced to the emotional embrace of the first group then a more comprehensive account will entail asking how the powerful processes of attachment and the sustained obligatory location within a social structure (the secure base: Bowlby, 1988), relate to the feelings and cognitions that children (and older individuals) develop about other groups.

Family relations appear to be central, in Ruble et al.'s sense of the term, to many children's representations of their social selves. In Ruble et al.'s studies of self-definition, family relations rank alongside gender and ethnicity in a elicitation task, and ahead of them in a forced-choice task. The family is the initial context within which children develop the two social identities that have been most prominent in this volume, namely gender and ethnicity. It becomes clear in Verkuyten's chapter that ethnic minority, immigrant families transmit traditions and values that bear on their children's subsequent intergroup experiences and attitudes. Furthermore, the family may provide a protective buffer or alternative source of self-esteem in the face of awareness of negative social categorisation of one's ethnic status (Ruble et al., Verkuyten).

It is striking that the editors introduce Banker et al.'s chapter on stepfamily conflict by noting, quite accurately, that it is a "relatively unusual application of the social identity approach". It is unusual, but perhaps it tells us as much about what is usual in that it seems on first sight quite radical to traverse the territory between the minimal groups' laboratory and the realities of intergroup mergers in the modern family. Yet, as Banker et al. demonstrate, the conceptual apparatus fits very well and helps explain processes that can go awry as well as guide interventions designed to promote family cohesion and well-being.

Verkuyten quotes the perceptive remark of Horowitz that "ethnicity is family writ large". We might go on to venture that there is a sense in which the family is writ large in all of our social selves. This is more than a truism and less than an explanation: Some aspects of family processes may be reflected in our orientations to other social categories (emotional affiliation, in-group bias, deriving self-esteem from membership), and some may be more indirectly related or even contradictory. Children's social selves are likely to become more complex as they are exposed to a new social environment outside the family but it is plausible, as implied by Ruble et al., that the family remains a reference/comparison point for a long time.

Both SIT and SCT maintain that categorisation and internalisation of a social identity precede the motivational consequences. Turner, Hogg, Oakes, Reicher, & Wetherell et al. (1987) see group formation as "an adaptive social psychological process that makes social cohesion, cooperation and influence possible" (p. 40; and see Bennett & Sani, Chapter 3). Yet social cohesion, cooperation, and influence are not merely possible but indispensable at the beginnings of life: We start out with motivations (to survive, to attach, to explore, to understand) and, for better or worse, our first group is waiting for us.

DEVELOPMENTAL CHANGES AND CONTINUITIES

Among the fundamental yet most difficult questions facing the broad enquiry represented here are identifying what the developmental changes are and specifying when and how they occur. As Bennett and Sani note at the outset, developmentalists interested in the self have tended to focus on age-related changes over time, as developmentalists are wont to do. But as we proceed through the careful and multifaceted investigations in this book, we find repeatedly that a clear developmental framework is elusive. If at any point we seem to be getting closer, then context rears its polysemous head.

In the course of collaborative research, it is often a disappointment to nondevelopmental colleagues to learn that developmentalists no longer feel confident in offering "hard" stage models, delineating exactly what children can and cannot do at particular age points. This book demonstrates why we cannot. Certainly, broad cognitive changes can be sketched out. Ruble et al. highlight the shift from awareness of physical characteristics to the incorporation of psychological attributes; Sani and Bennett show a development from awareness of actions and dispositions to understanding of identity-related beliefs; Nesdale charts development from an undifferentiated phase (with respect to ethnic categorisation), through ethnic awareness, to ethnic preference and then, for some, ethnic prejudice. These illuminate important reference points for future developmental work in this area and they are persuasive that mid to late childhood is a major period for the comprehension and internalisation of many social identities. But, as becomes very clear through the various discussions, social identities are diverse; development of any one is multidetermined and intersects with many other powerful social processes.

Barrett et al., for example, articulate a very clear strategy for how we might examine SIT/SCT predictions in developmental terms with specific reference to national identity and they test them against findings from an impressive multisite research programme. First, they propose we should ask: Do the full set of specified processes occur at a given age? If they do, then this would be good news for the generality of the theory. If they do not, this does not necessarily refute the theory but it leads to interesting further questions: Are the processes not yet operative or are they there in some nascent form but overridden by other processes? Barrett et al. note that more complex outcomes are possible, such as that some of the predicted processes occur and some do not in children of a particular age. Just to complicate matters a little further, the authors would doubtless agree that "age" is a rough proxy for developmental status – so it is possible that children of a given age may be responding in different ways because of individual differences in the pace of development.

But if these a priori speculations seem elaborate, the data themselves reveal a still more complex story. In brief, Barrett et al.'s findings show that different processes do and do not occur in different age groups in different ways in different societies, and different patterns are reflected with different measurements. Imagine, worse still, that Barrett et al. were able to report test–retest data, or to examine longitudinal progress (cf. Rutland, who reports different within-participant patterns at different times), or to tease out cohort effects, or to assess international variation in parent–child correspondence across the several measures employed.

It will be hard for SIT/SCT theorists to ignore the inconvenient data that Barrett et al. summarise, and those likely to be accumulated as this kind of work proceeds, on the grounds that the participants are "only children". Are social psychological theories to be middle range *and* age specific? Indeed, in light of Barrett et al.'s findings, we have no reason to suppose that things become miraculously uniform upon adulthood. On the other hand, it is salutary to reflect that, had these authors' purpose been to test a developmental theory in this domain, such an account would now be facing equally serious challenges. First, it would not even have generated several of these hypotheses. Second, those that it would generate (for example, concerning presumed-universal developmental changes) would be refuted just as firmly.

Perhaps the question becomes not "when do children start behaving, thinking, and feeling in terms of a collective self" (Sani & Bennett) but "given that children behave, think, and feel in terms of collective selves from the outset, how do their behaviours, thoughts, and feelings change as they become increasingly skilled in adapting to the behaviours, thoughts, and feelings of increasingly diverse others"?

COMPETITION BETWEEN DEVELOPMENTAL AND SOCIAL PROCESSES

A closely related and particularly intriguing theme that arises is the possibility of competition among developmental and social processes. Note that this would scarcely come into view if developmental and social psychologists remained strictly in their own territories. The contributors here show that very fertile ground is exposed once we straddle the borders. On the one hand, we have seen that there are cognitive-developmental changes in children's abilities to process social information and respond to contextual cues (Powlishta, Ruble et al., Sani & Bennett). Developmental changes can modify some primitive social stances, such as absolutist intergroup attitudes (David et al., Ruble et al.), as well as allowing the possibility of moderating the expression of biases (Rutland). During mid childhood children can begin to appreciate that an out-group (such as the opposite gender, a different ethnic group) is not homogenous, that external characteristics (such as skin colour) are superficial, and that people are motivated by different beliefs (Powlishta, Ruble et al., Sani & Bennett).

On the other hand, social factors such as intergroup competition can overwhelm developmental capacities, resulting in the establishment of crude prejudices. Some developmental aspects of social identity may be relatively predictable on at least a rough age basis but others, such as whether or not a child develops ethnic prejudices, may depend on motivational factors (Nesdale), or on "encounters" (Ruble et al.) with the political brutalities of a given society that are relatively independent of developmental status, or may even be affected by the scheduling of international events (see Rutland on the consequences of Euro '96).

We noted above that developmentalists have a natural tendency to conceive of capacities and skills improving. As Ruble et al. suggest, change over time may not invariably be irreversible or unidirectional, and it is possible that people may experience regressions. These themselves may be instigated or accentuated by interpersonal and intergroup processes. This collection provides not only examples but also means of investigating them and, ultimately, of explaining the intersecting developmental and social phenomena. Nesdale, for example, illustrates how a theory can be developmental while nonetheless accommodating to the realities of variability in social context. Rutland describes another approach, by focusing on children's ability to adjust to normative beliefs and practices concerning the expression of social prejudices.

There are points where developmental and social accounts appear to offer directly competing predictions. A striking example is David et al.'s proposal, from the perspective of SCT, that during adolescence "gender loses its prepotency". On first sight, this is difficult to reconcile with developmental evidence (1) that gender roles, especially for girls, become more stringently curtailed during adolescence (Archer, 1984), (2) that adolescents can be more traditional and more punitive in judging gender-role transgressions than are primary school age children (Stoddart & Turiel, 1985), and the fact (3) that sexual attraction and the dictates of entry to the sexual marketplace have great potency in encouraging adolescents of both genders to align their appearance and behaviour with contemporary stereotypes of attractiveness (Basow & Rubin, 1999; Furman, 2002). For many developmentalists, it follows that adolescence would be a period of intensifying gender-role development (Crouter, Manke, & McHale, 1995; Galambos, Almeida, & Peterson, 1990; Huston & Alvarez, 1990).

However, it is true that the cognitive advances of adolescence can, in principle, facilitate the capacity to entertain alternative perspectives. And it is true that, as David et al. note, the social contexts of adolescents' lives are broadening. For the SCT theorist, it follows that the fluidity and context variability of gender categories should increase during this period.

These are apparently competing accounts – and yet they could both be correct. To offer a simplistic resolution (cautiously, in light of the many demonstrations in this book that simplistic explanations do not suffice in accounting for the development of the social self), one possibility is that increasing cognitive flexibility and context sensitivity at the level of categorisation processes jars with increasing community pressure at the level of self-presentational, interpersonal, and role demands. Part of the developmental tasks of adolescence, then, is the challenge of "fitting in" (including monitoring of matters of what SCT theorists call normative and comparative fit) while adjusting simultaneously to the expanded awareness of diversity and opportunity in the adult world. The competing developmental and social processes here could lead to intra- and interpersonal conflicts that may not make gender-role development in adolescence a wholly benign experience; there is some evidence that gender intensification may be associated with depression in adolescent females (Wichstrom, 1999).

LANGUAGE

Language is the primary social medium through which we transmit information and values about the social categories shared within our communities. Mainstream social psychology's resilient indifference to language is one of the continuing mysteries of science, but the assemblage here of several developmental perspectives brings it repeatedly to our attention. Although none of the present contributors is primarily concerned with the roles of language in the development of the social self, many of them touch on interesting aspects and together the collection suggests that this will be a rewarding focus for future research.

From a cognitive or cognitive-developmental point of view, the first step towards a self-concept is the categorisation process – discovering that one is a member of a particular group (see Sani & Bennett). However, language both precedes and subserves this process. As Sani and Bennett observe, the maintenance of the "we" is not an individual conceptual activity. Through language, the categories are already there: One does not create the self label "Italian" (or "girl" or "black"), one seizes the opportunities to share something that the culture has already crystallised, identified as important, and transmitted. Through language, social categories are connected to conceptual structures (e.g., hierarchies of categories, associations, antonyms) and to evaluative connotations: One does not decide alone that being Italian is a good thing; one participates in collective discourse with many others already convinced of the fact.

The relevance of language to the social self is highlighted here in numerous ways. One of the fundamental questions is: When is verbal labelling of social categories possible (Ruble et al.)? How and when do children use verbal self-labelling? Ruble et al. point to research showing that this is not a straightforward age-related phenomenon: Substantially different proportions of Euro-American and African-American children of the same age (3 years) self-labelled based on race. Children aged 2½ years rated a person more negatively when labelled as Arab rather than Israeli. Children acquire social category labels quite early but simultaneously they attune to the values of their community.

Recognition of the verbal label for a social identity is an important "first step" (Sani & Bennett), but it is also a formative one with enduring consequences, possibly (as Sani & Bennett note, and see also David et al., Ruble et al.) directing attention and providing an anchor. Language may influence what becomes central and salient (Ruble et al.) and guide the child to the early stages of social category awareness (Nesdale). The development of language is intricately related to the development of knowledge (Ruble et al.). It is also possible for a label to be used prior to "full" understanding of its denotation. For example, Barrett et al. report that children sometimes express strong affective responses to out-group labels well in advance of accumulating basic factual information about the groups to whom the labels apply. Is this "mere" reference to public criteria (Sani & Bennett), or a developmental social process that should repay more extensive investigation? It could be that a framework for categorising and evaluating part of the world is shared and that subjective identification (Sani & Bennett) emerges as the full meaning is constructed subsequently through interaction, lexical organisation, and guided observation.

Several contributors draw attention to the fact that labels for individuals who transgress stereotypical social category boundaries can be pejorative and severe. David et al., Powlishta, and Ruble et al. remind us that name-calling and related verbal derogation are a ubiquitous feature of the practice of children's gender segregation. Verkuyten reports that name-calling where the target is a member of an ethnic minority group is seen by children as the prototypical instantiation of prejudice and is commonplace in everyday interaction in some communities. Importantly, Verkuyten shows that this is not just unpleasant banter but is predictive of the self-esteem of the targets; it is reasonable to infer that this leads in turn to other social psychological and affective consequences. Verkuyten's work also suggests that the language in which a bicultural or immigrant child is tested can affect orientations towards personal and social identities.

Through their language, other people convey information about their categorisation and stereotypes of us. For example, adults modify their speech style according to the age, gender, or ethnicity of the child, thereby communicating where they see the individual as slotting into the social fabric and what capacities and characteristics they assume she or he has (or lacks). Children, in their turn, are able early on to place someone in a social category on the basis of the language they speak (Ruble et al.) and are sensitive to the status of different languages or to language conflicts in their society (Barrett et al.; Nesdale, 2001). Other people convey, by something as seemingly minor as personal pronoun choice, whether they see us as part of the "we" or decidedly aligned with "them" (Banker et al., Ruble et al., Sani & Bennett).

Language is the foremost means through which we get under each other's skin. At present, we lack a comprehensive account of how language relates to the ontogenesis of social categories and the social self. What these various contributions make clear is that language is integral and one way in which developmental perspectives can enrich social psychological work in this area will be by insisting on closer attention to the medium through which social identities are encapsulated and shared.

AGE AS A SOCIAL IDENTITY

Ruble et al. make the interesting point that "age" stands out as a likely salient social identity for children yet has received scant research attention. It seems again that developmental psychologists, by neglecting social identity, have overlooked an important feature of children's social and cognitive worlds, while social psychologists, by studying only one age group, have missed a social category that may actually be invoked and highly pertinent in many social contexts. Modern societies are highly age-stratified. Childhood and adolescence account for about a quarter of the lifespan and within these phases there are numerous finer gradations, including school levels and more informal age classifications. Age is very relevant to the social self and is somewhat unique, in that advances are socially celebrated once a year (and reviewed every time you meet your relatives): This social category is imbued with "value and emotional significance" (Tajfel, 1981; see Bennett & Sani).

Although this was not their principal focus, Sani and Bennett's work supports the inference that age is integral to the developing social self: Children describe themselves in a different way when primed with the concept of an adult. Similarly, David et al. report lower gender stereotyping when the contrast is with "grown-ups" rather than gender. Closely correlated with this is the fact that age status is very important to the people with whom children interact: As Powlishta points out, adults make stereotypical inferences about children *as children.*

SCT in particular seems to offer an explanation of the seeming paradox that young children betray strongly negative social stereotypes about elderly people (Davidson, Cameron, & Jergovic, 1995; Goldman & Goldman, 1981) yet demonstrate great affection (positive in-group bias) when asked about their grandparents and great-grandparents (Kaiser, 1996). Although age may be an important social category it seems that it, too, is not a fixed construct but is context-sensitive.

SOCIAL IDENTITIES ARE DIVERSE – AND MAY DEVELOP DIFFERENTLY

Another reason why this book cannot offer a global template for developmental stages in the emergence of the social self is the accumulating evidence it provides that "social identities differ" (Sani & Bennett) and hence are acquired differently. Social identities differ in content and complexity (e.g., external appearance vs. belief system), in terms of personal salience (Ruble et al.), and in terms of how they fit into the broader society (e.g., virtually everyone acquires a gender identity of some sort, but not everyone has a religious identity, and though most people have an ethnic identity it is likely to have different salience according to whether or not one is in a minority group and, after Verkuyten, which minority group it is).

Ruble et al. report valuable new findings on the parallel progression in the development of gender and ethnic understanding. As they argue, this supports the assertion of a central role for cognition, though we cannot entirely rule out a contributory role for comparable task demands. Nevertheless, the authors stress that social context can affect the developmental processes and sometimes may offer better accounts of the data. They describe differences among children of different ethnic backgrounds on developmental tasks that are both poignant and theoretically attention-grabbing.

Rutland makes a convincing case that different forms of prejudice are subject to different levels of societal tolerance. Ethnic prejudice is at least controversial and often, if not invariably, condemned, whereas national prejudice is at least ambivalent: In most countries, it is acceptable to subscribe to the view that "our nation is the finest on Earth" and to express hostile views to at least some outsiders. Gender prejudice is different again: it is normative in some cultures, implicit in others, confronted by contemporary ideology in some, and perhaps occasionally acceptable in polite company when couched in antitraditional terms (e.g., directed at males).

The greater in-group gender bias among girls, noted in several chapters (David et al., Ruble et al., Powlishta, Rutland), is a further empirical reason to avoid the assumption that the development of social identities is uniform. Even in the same domain, it appears that different groups develop differently. It could be that the differential in-group bias is simply factually underwritten: Maybe boys are more troublesome, making it relatively easy for girls to derive self-esteem from in-group identification. It could be that it is socially transmitted: Parents and teachers are prone to *say* that boys are more troublesome. It could be that it is motivated by girls' sensitivity to social inequities (David et al., Powlishta). It could be that both genders are sensitive to prevailing norms and are operating as "social tacticians" (Rutland); for example, the norms of traditional paternalism and political correctness leave it less acceptable to criticise females but tolerable to denigrate males. Whatever the explanation, it does appear that children are sensitive to the value systems of their societies (Tajfel, 1981) and that this sensitivity bears on the development of social selves, resulting in different experiences and, arguably, different routes.

CAN WE CREATE BETTER SOCIAL SELVES?

The nature of the subject matter means that every chapter in this book deals with real-world phenomena of pervasive significance. Social identities matter: They are directly related to social status, to equity, to opportunity, to self-esteem, and to well-being. A natural consequence, not far from the surface in most chapters and addressed directly in some, is the question of whether developmental- and social-psychological research can be applied to promote more favourable outcomes in terms of how developing people adapt to the realities of social categories and how they treat members of out-groups.

The heartening news may be that the "process of social categorisation . . . is not completely unalterable" (Banker et al.). If the potentially volatile arena of stepfamily relations over time is less conflict-ridden when the merged initial families come to think of themselves as one group, then the scope for decategorising and recategorising (Banker et al.) becomes of wide interest.

In a similar vein, Nesdale's work also suggests grounds for optimism. In his studies, children certainly show in-group bias but this is not necessarily identical with in-group ethnic bias. If different ethnicity peers are included in the in-group, they are liked no less than same-ethnicity peers.

Modifying social categories and social identities is not a simple task and none of the contributors underestimates the magnitude, complexity, and perhaps dangers of such intervention. While there may be grounds for optimism, there are also good reasons for caution. After all, social categories didn't get where they are today by being ephemeral. There is an edge to all the suggestions and demonstrations of intervention: The risk is ever-present that the underlying processes that set the groups apart in the first place could be re-invoked suddenly and powerfully, exacerbated by a strong infusion of reactance. As the present authors remind us repeatedly, much depends on the context.

Rutland's research shows that the expression of intergroup prejudice may be ameliorated by (developmental changes in) processes of normative behaviour. His clever use of a dissociation paradigm highlights an important qualification and a challenge to future work, namely that children may become adept in achieving socially desirable self-presentations without necessarily relinquishing automatic biases. As Rutland points out, it is good to know what not to do – but this still presupposes knowledge of what could be done.

Powlishta ventures the bold proposal that better gender relations can be fostered by encouraging children to self-categorise on a dimension other than gender. David et al. disagree, arguing that self-categorisations are "not a matter of choice but a direct consequence of the genuine economic, political, and social circumstances of our lives". Powlishta might reasonably respond that someone chooses the political and social circumstances, and choices are open to review. Each perspective captures important dimensions and together they remind us that social change is inherently dialectical. Psychologists interested in these issues may have to decide whether or not it is their responsibility to subscribe to that overarching social category, the status quo.

SOCIAL SELVES THROUGH THE LIFESPAN

I will be brief here because this is very much an area that this book designates for future research rather than tackles directly. With the exception of Banker et al., the contributions have been concerned with *child* development. There is plenty to say about child development and the contributors have said much; we can rely on our colleagues in social psychology to say at least as much about the social identities and self-categorisations of 18- to 21-year-olds. Together, these provide a fitting starting point for lifespan research, and most of that lies ahead – in studies of the next three quarters of life.

We know relatively little of how people's orientations towards social identities and their processes of self-categorisation change as they progress through life. The overwhelming expectation we can derive from this book is that we will need to draw on both developmental and social-psychological perspectives if we are to investigate adequately the longer-term construction and maintenance of social selves.

The contributions and issues arising in this volume do suggest many tantalising avenues for inquiry. Several contributors note that the phenomena they are investigating are by no means unique to childhood. Ethnic prejudice obviously does not necessarily wane with chronological maturity (Nesdale). National identity is of increasing interest during childhood and adolescence (Barrett et al., Sani & Bennett), and is likely to remain prominent henceforth for many, though its centrality and salience may well be affected by both developmental/chronological attainments (such as being granted adult citizenship rights, falling within the conscription age-span) and the social impact of life events (such as war and terrorism).

Again, families are often the longest-lasting groups of people's lives, though the ways in which people relate to them – represent them as part of the social self – are likely to vary with lifestage and responsibilities. Recall the implication of Verkuyten's evidence that, among the people most disadvantaged by prejudice, a person's developmental status may well influence how she or he responds to it (e.g., parents may try to bolster their children). Banker et al. study stepfamily conflict largely at the level of the unit, but implicit in their account is the important fact that individuals have different roles and expectations as a function of developmental status. Similarly, an important part of the social self for most people is their occupational role: This changes through the lifespan. Occupational identities are not constant (indeed, at some point they cease) and they interact with other aspects of the social self that also vary with age and lifestage, not least gender identity (see David et al., Powlishta, for discussions of the persistence of gender prejudice into adulthood). It would be strange indeed if social selves did not develop through adulthood; stranger still if we ignored the fact.

CONCLUSIONS

I greatly enjoyed reading this collection, as, I imagine, will many readers. I also imagine that readers will find it difficult, as I did. The difficulty lies not in any of the individual chapters, each of which is lucid, well-structured, and well-documented, even though they do tackle very complex issues. It lies in the ambition of the collective venture: the integration of developmental and social psychological perspectives on the social self. Developmental and social psychologists, as the editors eloquently summarised in the opening chapter, may be closely related but they rarely speak the same language. They are differentiated by whole bodies of assumptions, vocabularies, methods, perspectives, and even explanatory goals. It is very difficult to reconcile them but the bilingual skills represented in this volume demonstrate that it is very worth while to attempt to do so.

The book raises many new questions and promises to inspire a vast array of new research. But it does not just set puzzles: It assembles a large amount of creatively won, thoughtfully interpreted empirical evidence and it establishes some important guidelines for future work. In particular, it has made major headway in casting the (already, as the editors comment, colossal) framework of social identity theory and self-categorisation theory into sharp developmental relief. It will also compel developmentalists to reconsider their conception of stereotypes not as a fixed body of knowledge but as "inherently comparative, flexible, and variable" phenomena (Sani & Bennett). It may persuade social psychologists to come to terms with the developmental phenomena that are integral to their participants' social being. Above all, it confirms that developmental science becomes richer when it merges the laboratory with the real world.

REFERENCES

Archer, J. (1984). Gender roles as developmental pathways. *British Journal of Social Psychology, 23*, 245–256.

Basow, S. A., & Rubin, L. R. (1999). Gender influences on adolescent development. In N. G. Johnson, M. C. Roberts, & J. Worrell (Eds.), *Beyond appearance: A new look at adolescent girls* (pp. 25–52). Washington, DC: American Psychological Association.

Battistelli, P., & Farneti, A. (1991). Grandchildren's images of their grandparents: A psychodynamic perspective. In P. K. Smith, (Ed.), *The psychology of grandparenthood: An international perspective* (pp. 143–156). London: Routledge.

Bowlby, J. (1988). *A secure base: Parent–child attachment and healthy human development*. New York: Basic Books.

Crouter, A. C., Manke, B. A., & McHale, S. M. (1995). The family context of gender intensification in early adolescence. *Child Development, 66*, 317–329.

Davidson, D., Cameron, P., & Jergovic, D. (1995). The effect of children's stereotypes on their memory for elderly individuals. *Merrill-Palmer Quarterly, 41*, 70–90.

Furman, W. (2002). The emerging field of adolescent romantic relationships. *Current Directions in Psychological Science, 11*, 177–180.

Galambos, N. L., Almeida, D. M., & Petersen, A. C. (1990). Masculinity, femininity, and sex role attitudes in early adolescence: Exploring gender intensification. *Child Development, 61*, 1905–1914.

Goldman, R. J., & Goldman, J. D. G. (1981). How children view old people and ageing: A developmental study of children in four countries. *Australian Journal of Psychology, 3*, 405–418.

Huston, A. C., & Alvarez, M. M. (1990). The socialization context of gender role development in early adolescence. In R. Montemayor, G. R. Adams, & T. P. Gullotta (Eds.), *From childhood to adolescence: A transitional period? Advances in adolescent development: An annual book series, Vol. 2* (pp. 156–179). Beverly Hills, CA: SAGE Publications.

Kaiser, P. (1996). Relationships in the extended family and diverse family forms. In E. E. Auhagen, & M. von Salisch (Eds.), *The diversity of human relationships* (pp. 141–170). Cambridge: Cambridge University Press.

Nesdale, D. (2001). Language and the development of children's ethnic prejudice. *Journal of Language and Social Psychology, 20*, 90–110.

Stoddart, T., & Turiel, E. (1985). Children's concepts of cross-gender activities. *Child Development, 56*, 1241–1252.

Tajfel, H. (1981). *Human groups and social categories: Studies in social psychology.* Cambridge: Cambridge University Press.

Turner, J. C., Hogg, M. A., Oakes, P. J., Reicher, S. D., & Wetherell, M. S. (1987). *Rediscovering the social group: A self-categorization theory.* Oxford: Blackwell Publishing.

Wichstrom, L. (1999). The emergence of gender difference in depressed mood during adolescence: The role of intensified gender socialization. *Developmental Psychology, 35*, 232–245.

Author index

Abecassis, M. 300, 303
Abell, J. 86, 114, 164, 177
Aberson, C.L. 117, 295
Aboud, F.E. 20, 29, 33, 35–37, 38, 44, 47, 52, 54, 56, 61, 159, 191, 207, 219, 220, 221, 222, 223, 224, 227, 228, 229, 230, 233, 248, 252
Abrams, D. 2–3, 6, 21, 51, 53, 60, 91, 225, 248, 253, 258, 269, 294, 295, 296, 297, 298, 299, 301, 302, 304, 305, 306, 314
Adorno, T.W. 220
Ageton, S.S. 300
Agostini, L. 43, 79, 80, 108, 121
Akiba, D. 34, 45, 47, 59
Alarcon O. 47, 54
Albert, A.A. 52, 110
Alejandro-Wright, M.N. 39
Alfieri, T. 292
Allen, V.L. 51, 223, 226
Allen, W.R. 49
Allport, G.W. 4, 106, 221, 267, 268, 269, 271, 272, 274, 279
Almeida, D.M. 318
Alvarez, J.M. 2, 17, 29, 33, 44, 46, 47, 52, 56, 63, 91–92, 192, 197–198, 220, 248, 291, 294, 314–318, 320–322
Alvarez, M.M. 318
Amato, M. 35, 52, 248
Anastasiades, P. 257
Anastasio, P.A. 267, 268, 272, 275
Anderson, D.R. 56
Anderson, J.Z. 272, 277
Andrews, G. 94
Annis, R.C. 52, 194, 209
Anthony, E.J. 268

Arbuckle, J.L. 279, 280
Archer, J. 318
Arcuri, L. 255, 270
Ardelt, M. 295
Arnold-Dorman, C. 255
Aronson, J. 59
Ashburn-Nardo, L. 296
Asher, S.R. 223, 226
Aube, J. 55,
Aubry, S. 56, 58
Augoustinos, M. 248
Averhart, C. 49
Ashmore, R.D. 30, 46

Bachman, M. 2, 17, 91–92, 267, 268, 269, 272, 275, 314–318, 320–322
Bacon, S. 295
Bacue, A. 138
Bagley, C. 198
Bahrick, L.E. 135
Bailey, R.C. 229
Balaam, B.J. 256
Baldwin, J.M. 1–2
Banaji, M.R. 135, 206, 255, 258
Bandura, A. 46, 58, 138–142
Banerjee, R. 90, 92–93, 96, 254
Banker, B. 21, 268, 276, 279, 283, 305, 315, 320, 322–324
Banks, W.C. 53, 191, 223
Barájas, L. 205
Bargh, J.A. 255
Baron, R.M. 278
Barreto, M. 253
Barrett, M. 19, 62, 78, 86–87, 90, 124, 159, 160, 161, 165, 166, 168, 175, 176, 177, 178, 180, 181, 192, 248, 293, 302–303, 314, 316–317, 319–320, 324
Bar-Tal, D. 62, 77
Bartel, H.W. 223

Bartel, N.R. 223
Bartsch, K. 78
Basow, S.A. 318
Bauer, P.J. 107, 109–110
Baumeister, R.F. 53, 196, 293
Beal, D.J. 270
Beaudet, J. 223, 233
Beeghly-Smithy, J. 33
Beere, C.A. 110
Bem, S. 39, 43, 116, 140, 146, 299
Benet-Martinez, V. 206–207
Bennett, M. 17–18, 41, 43–44, 62, 79, 80, 87–88, 92–93, 96, 108, 110, 115, 121, 124, 160, 165, 175, 177, 181, 192, 248, 251, 254, 258, 293, 295–297, 302, 306, 314–317, 319–321, 324–325
Berger, P. 297
Berglas, S. 4
Bernal, M.E. 36, 37, 159
Berndt, T.J. 110
Berger, S.H. 277
Best, D.L. 86, 110, 137, 223
Bhatt, S. 253
Biernat, M. 60, 110
Bigler, R.S. 3, 31, 38, 43, 44, 49, 50, 62, 104–106, 114–115, 117–118, 122, 126, 137, 162, 182, 192, 222, 223, 234, 248, 250, 251
Billig, M. 7–8, 104, 147, 225, 253
Bird, C. 221
Bittinger, K. 107
Black-Gutman, D. 233
Blaine, B. 50–51,
Blakemore, J.E.O. 138
Blaske, D.M. 109
Bodenhausen, G.V. 253, 259
Bolduc, D. 137

Bolger, N. 33, 46, 201, 294
Bond, M.C. 195
Booth, A. 268
Boswell, D.A. 223
Boulton, M.J. 204, 229, 233
Bourchier, A. 161,
Bourhis, R.Y. 162
Bovill, M. 299
Bowers, C. 192
Bowlby, J. 29, 314
Bown, N. 60, 301
Bradbard, M. 56
Brand, E.S. 35, 61, 191, 220, 224
Branch, C.W. 232
Brandstadter, J. 4
Brannon, L. 140, 145
Branscombe, N.R. 51, 54, 92, 114, 116, 162, 164, 180, 194, 232, 253
Brauer, M. 298
Bray, J.H. 277
Brazil, D.M. 268
Brehm, S.S. 4
Breinlinger, S. 149
Brendgen, M. 299, 299
Bretherton, B. 33,
Brewer, M.B. 3, 29, 31, 51, 61–62, 108, 193, 198, 225, 272, 274
Broadnax, S. 50–51,
Bromley, D. 29, 33, 45, 106
Bronfenbrenner, U. 192, 207, 292
Brookes, J 135
Brookes-Gunn, J. 3
Brooklins, G.K. 49
Brotherton, C.J. 114
Brown, A.C. 277
Brown, B.B. 136, 162,
Brown, G. 227
Brown, K. 237
Brown, L.M. 195
Brown, R.J. 31, 43–44, 50–51, 61, 104–107, 112, 118–119, 121, 162, 164, 192, 193, 207, 221, 222, 225, 229, 232, 233, 234, 239, 248, 249, 251, 252, 270, 274, 298, 305
Brucken, L. 109
Bruner, J.S. 13
Bryant, W.T. 112, 118, 122
Buehrig, C.J. 229
Bukowski, W.M. 299
Bundy, R.F. 7–8, 104, 147, 225
Burchardt, C.J. 254
Burdick, H. 221
Buriel, R. 39, 42

Buss, A.A. 3
Bussey, K. 46, 58, 135, 138–142
Byrne, D.F. 231

Cable, I. 164
Cairns, E. 81
Caldera, Y.M. 137
Cameron, L. 298
Cameron, J.A. 2–3, 17, 33, 45, 52, 61–62, 91–92, 197–198, 220, 248, 291, 314–318, 320–322
Cameron J.E. 42, 57
Cameron, L. 258
Cameron, P. 321
Campbell, A. 299
Campbell, J. 160, 248, 249
Cann, A. 110
Canter, R.J. 300
Cantor, N. 3
Capozza, D. 251
Carter, D.B. 43, 109, 116
Carver, C.S. 258
Case, R. 3
Cash, T.F. 256
Caspi, A. 295
Castelli, L. 255
Catalyst 138
Cecil, C.L. 268
Celious, A. 209
Chaiken, S. 255
Chan, S.Q. 39
Charlesworth, W.T. 118
Charters, W.W. 114
Chen, L.49, 55
Cheyne, W.N. 249
Chavira, V. 32,
Chavous, T.M. 42, 46, 49, 50–51, 53, 194, 195
Chi, M.T.H. 85
Chiu, C.Y. 206–207
Child, P. 44, 293
Chodorow, N. 139
Chyatte, C. 232
Citron, C.C. 254
Clack, F.L. 195, 199
Clark, A. 231
Clark, K.B. 53, 190, 227
Clark, M.P. 53, 190, 227
Clemens, L.P. 35, 107, 109
Cloud, M.J. 86
Coard, B. 198
Coats, S. 195
Coker, D.R. 44, 58
Colburne, K.A. 109, 113, 120
Coleman, H.L.K. 205
Coleman, J. 51,
Coll, C.G. 2, 17, 91–92, 189, 207

Collman, P. 109
Collins, P.A. 56
Condor, S. 301
Condry, J. 136
Condry, S. 136
Conner, J.M. 254
Connolly, P. 34, 96–97
Cook, K.V. 137, 279
Cooke, T. 94
Cooley, C.H. 1–2, 29
Cooper, J. 59
Cooper, M.J. 256, 257
Cordua, G.D. 111
Corenblum, B. 52, 194, 209
Cornell, S. 194
Cossette, L. 137
Cota, M.K 37
Cotting, D. 3, 85, 296
Coughlin, R. 223
Cousins, S.D. 200
Cowan, G. 110
Coyne, M.J. 109
Craig, J. 55
Cranwell, F.R. 200, 205
Crnic, K. 189, 207
Crocker, J. 42, 45, 49–51, 53–54, 195, 201
Crook, C. 299
Crosbie-Burnett, M. 272, 277
Cross, S.E. 143, 296
Cross, W.E. 31–2, 39, 53, 59, 191, 194, 196
Crouter, A.C. 318
Czopp, A.M. 296

Damon, W. 3, 29, 45, 78, 111
Davey, A. 43, 44, 61, 86, 192, 221, 222, 223, 225, 226, 232
David, B. 18, 20, 91, 118, 120, 138, 140, 143, 145, 292, 294, 296, 298, 299–301, 302, 318–324
Davidson, D. 321
Davis, H. 221,
Davis, S.W. 114
Day, J. 177
Deaux, K. 3, 53, 85, 114, 296, 297
Delk, J.L. 137
Del Miglio, C. 292
del Valle, A. 19, 90, 293, 302–303, 314, 316–317, 319–320, 324
Dembo, M.H. 231
Demetriou, A. 4
Demo, D.H. 295
Denmark, F. 114, 123
Deschamps, J.C. 112, 114–115, 120
Devine, P.60, 255, 296, 305

DeVos, G.A. 194
De Vries, M. 198
Diaz, I. 135
DiMartino, L. 45, 47, 59
DiMiceli, A.J. 114, 123
Dinella, L.M. 57
Dion, K.L. 120
Dobliner, D.B. 192
Doise, W. 6, 9, 105, 112, 114–115, 120
Donnelly, B.W. 277
Doosje, B. 92, 114, 144, 164, 180, 251
Dovidio, J. 21, 51, 255, 267, 268, 269, 271, 272, 273, 275, 276, 278, 279, 283, 294, 305, 315, 320, 322–324
Doyle, A.B. 52, 112, 118, 121–122, 136–137, 192, 221, 222, 223, 233, 248, 249, 252, 254, 256, 259, 299
Drabman, R.S. 111
Druickman, J. 277
Duncan, B.L. 51,
Durkin, K. 4–5, 21–22, 29, 222, 234, 235, 248
Dustin, D.S. 114
Duval, S. 259
Dweck, C. 33, 59

Eagly, A.H. 50, 61, 149
Eckes, T. 4, 6, 159
Eckles, J. 57, 298
Edelbrock, C. 109
Eder, R.A. 33, 78, 299
Edwards, C.P. 86
Egan, S.K. 55, 118, 122
Ehrhardt, A. 135
Eichstedt, J.A. 109, 110, 113, 118, 122, 124, 298
Eisenbud, L. 108
Eisenberg, J. 199
Eiser, J.R. 9
Eisner, H. 208
Ellemers, N. 144, 164, 180, 195, 251, 253
Elman, M. 118
Elmian, M. 136, 137
Elms, A.C. 6
Emler, N. 192, 199, 207, 294
Endsley, R. 56
Epperson, S.E. 148
Erikson, E. 31
Erkut, S. 47, 54
Etaugh, C. 110
Etcoff, N.L. 43
Ethier, K.A. 53
Ethridge, R. 35
Ethridge, T. 107, 109
Evans, S.M. 58

Fabes, R.A 48, 58, 125
Fagan, J.F. 107
Fagot, B.I. 35, 56, 107, 109, 135–137
Fairburn, C.G. 256, 257
Fairlie, P. 199
Farris, K.R. 205
Farroni, T. 161
Feagin, J.R. 49
Feffer, M. 231
Fein, S. 51, 54
Feinman, S. 137
Fenigstein, A. 3
Ferguson, C.K. 7, 79–80
Ferrier, G. 93
Fhagen-Smith, P. 32
Fields, J.P. 54
Fine, G.A. 207
Fine, M. 192, 277
Finkel, E.J. 268, 283
Fischer, K.W. 3
Fishbein, H.D. 191, 198, 224, 229, 248
Fishman, B. 284
Fiske, S. 43, 85, 135, 272, 298
Flament, C. 7–8, 104, 147, 225
Flavell, J.H. 4, 222, 230
Flesser, D. 49, 105, 162, 182, 225, 234, 239, 248, 251
Flett, G.L. 86
Ford, L. 3
Fordham, C. 59
Fowles, J. 86
Frable, D.E.S. 209
Frazier, S. 274
Frenkel-Brunswik, E. 220, 221
Freud, S. 139
Frey, K. 87, 31, 33, 56, 59
Fujioka, T. 44, 293
Fuligni, A. 2, 17, 33, 45, 52–53, 91–92, 197–198, 220, 248, 291
Furman, W. 318
Furstenberg, F.F.Jr. 268, 277
Fyffe, C. 250

Gaertner, S. 21, 267, 268, 269, 270, 272, 274, 275, 276, 278, 279, 283, 295, 297, 305, 315, 320, 322–24
Gaines, S.O. 205
Galambos, N.L. 318
Gallagher, J.J. 224
Garciá, B.F. 205
Garcia Coll, C. 34, 45, 47, 49, 54–55, 59, 291
Garcia, H.V 189, 207

Gardner, W. 29
Garfinkle, G.S. 45
Garza, C.A. 37, 195, 209
Gelman, S.A. 31, 109, 111, 118
Genesee, F. 229
George, D.M. 223
Gergen, K.J. 6
Gerton, J. 205
Gibbons, F.X. 4
Gibson, W.J. 92
Giles, H. 86, 122
Glass, C. 253
Glick, P. 112, 118, 122–124, 298, 301
Gochberg, B. 55
Goldberg, P. 123
Goldman, J.D.J. 321
Goldman, R.J. 321
Good, C. 59
Goodman, M.E. 190, 221, 224, 226, 227, 232
Goodnow, J. 33
Goto, S.G. 206, 305
Gough, H. 221
Gourevitch, V. 231
Govender, R. 255
Grace, D. 18, 20, 91, 118, 120, 140, 292, 299–301, 318–324
Gracely, E. 35, 107, 109
Gralinski, H. 36
Gramzow, R.H. 270
Granrose, C.S. 205
Grant, G. 192, 223, 229
Grant, P.R. 162
Green, R.J. 277
Greenwald, A.G. 206, 255, 257, 258
Greenwald, H.J. 226
Gregor, A.J.220,
Greulich, F. 55, 87
Grifiths, J. 234, 235
Grill, J.J. 223
Guinote, A. 298
Gulko, J. 58, 106, 109–110, 112–113, 119–120, 122
Gurtman, M.B. 51, 271, 294
Gutek, B.A. 138

Haaf, R.A. 109
Hafan, R. 137
Hagendoorn, L. 196, 208
Hains, S.C. 270
Hall, S.K. 55,
Halpern, D.F. 148
Halverson, C.F. 43, 56, 84, 106, 111, 116, 121
Hamilton, D.L. 85, 164
Hamm, M.S. 232
Harris, A.M. 50

Harris, D. 221
Harris, J.R. 135, 142
Harris, P. 94
Harrison, A.O. 39,
Hart, D. 3, 29, 45, 78
Hartman, D. 194
Harter, S. 2–4, 29, 33, 87, 117, 142, 196
Hartup, W.W. 300, 303
Harvey, R.D. 54, 194
Haslager, G.J.T. 300
Haslam, S.A. 4, 10–15, 17, 86–87, 91, 93, 114, 162, 163, 164, 177, 190, 193, 256
Haugh, S.S. 110
Haunschild, P.R. 268
Havel, J. 221
Hawker, D.S.J. 2004
Hayden-Thomson, L. 112
Hayes, B.K. 86–87, 164, 177
Healy, M. 117, 295
Heiman, R.J. 195, 199, 205
Heine, S.H. 294, 304
Helbing, N. 109
Helgerson, E. 229
Heller, K.A. 110
Helmreich, R. 55
Helwig, A.A. 109
Henderson, M.C. 205
Henson, N. 60, 301
Henry, S. 270
Heppen, J. 30
Herringer, L.G. 195, 209
Hetherington, E.M. 295
Hetts, J.J. 205–206
Hewstone, M. 31, 51, 54, 60, 228, 270, 273, 274, 295, 305
Heyman, G.D. 118, 119
Heywood, C.299
Hicks, D. 205
Hickson, F. 233
Higgins, E.T. 3, 29, 34, 292, 295
Hilt, L. 112, 118, 122–124, 298, 301
Hinkle, S. 162
Hirschfield, L.A. 41, 135
Ho, H. 108
Hocevar, D. 231
Hoffman, C.D. 110
Hofstede, G. 195, 199, 206
Hogg, M.A. 2, 6, 11, 13–14, 16, 31, 51, 53, 60, 79, 91, 113–114, 123, 163, 190, 220, 225, 228, 269, 270, 294, 295, 298, 302, 304, 305, 315
Holmes, R.M. 40, 44

Hong, Y.Y. 206–207
Hoover, R. 248
Hopkins, N. 43, 86, 108, 114, 121, 164, 177
Hoppe, R.A. 223
Hornsey, M.J. 305
Hort, B.E. 109
Horwitz, M. 7
Horowitz, E.L. 190, 221, 222,
Horowitz, D.L. 194, 221, 222
Houghton, S. 248
Houlette, M. 21, 275, 315, 320, 322–324
Howard, A. 255
Howard, J.M. 270
Hraba, J. 192, 223, 229
Hu, L.T. 273
Hubbard, J. 299
Hughes, D. 49, 55
Huiberts, A.M. 200
Hunsberger, B. 226
Hur, Y.M. 295
Hurtig, M.C. 119, 149
Huston, A.C. 137, 254, 318
Hutnik, N. 198
Hutton, D. 94
Hwang, C.H. 52
Hymel, S. 112, 300

Iacono, W.G. 295
Imai, S. 224, 229
Insko, C.A. 268
Intons-Peterson, M.J. 49
Iuzzini, J. 295, 297

Jacklin, C.N. 103, 112, 136–137
Jackson, D.W. 137, 195
Jackson, S. 199
Jahoda, G. 160, 161, 224, 248, 249, 250, 253
James, A. 300
James, S.D. 272, 277, 284
James, W. 1–2
Jansen, V.G. 224
Janssens, L. 114
Jaspars, J.M.F. 6, 160, 161, 165
Jenkins, R. 97, 189, 207
Jenks, C. 300
Jergovic, D. 321
Jetten, J. 253
John, O.P. 91
Johnson, B. 255, 274, 277, 284
Johnson, D.W. 272
Johnson, K. 21, 94, 315, 320, 322–324
Johnson, N. 160, 161, 165, 224, 233, 248, 249, 250

Johnson, S.P. 227
Johnston, E. 107
Jones, E.E. 3–4
Jones, J.M. 29, 44, 53, 56
Jones, L.C. 31, 50, 105–106, 114, 117, 162, 182, 192, 234, 248, 250
Jopling, D. 142
Jost, J.T. 293, 297, 304
Joyner, L. 87–88, 177, 302
Judd, C.M. 201, 298
Judge, J. 248
Jussim, L. 30

Kafati, G. 272
Kağitçibaşi, C. 199
Kail, R.V.Jr. 108
Kaiser, P. 321
Kanagawa, C. 296
Kardiner, A. 191
Karpinski, A. 270
Kashima, Y. 293
Kashy, D.A. 201
Kassin, S.M. 4
Katz, P.A. 35–36, 38–39, 49, 107, 109, 111–112, 114, 118, 122, 136, 220, 224, 227, 228, 230, 248, 252, 301
Kawakami, K. 255
Kazi, S. 4
Kee, D.W. 108, 118–119
Keefe, S.E. 197
Keller, A. 3
Kelley, H.H. 7
Kelly, C. 149, 162
Kenny, D.A. 201, 278
Khun, D. 109
Kiesler, S.B. 123
Kihlstrom, J.F. 3
Kinket, B. 196, 200, 202, 208, 250
Kitayama, S. 142, 195, 199, 205, 294, 304
Kite, M.E. 149
Klein, S. 118
Klineberg, O. 78, 86, 160, 161, 248
Klink, A. 162
Knight, G.P. 36–37, 159
Knonsberg, S. 137
Koestner, R. 55
Kofkin, J.A. 35–36, 39, 49
Kohlberg, L. 29, 30, 37–38, 56, 58, 139, 147, 231
Koomen, W. 114, 200
Kopp, C. 36,
Kortekaas, P. 164, 195
Kozar, R. 268
Kramer, R.M. 91

Kruglanski, A. 294
Ksansnak, K.R. 136

LaFreniere, P. 118
LaFromboise, T. 205
Lalonde, R.N. 42, 196
Lambert, W.E. 78, 86, 160, 161, 229, 248
Lamberty, G. 189, 207
Lamborn, S.D. 136
Larue, A.A. 138
Larwood, L. 138
Lay, C. 199
Leary, M.R. 53, 196
Lee, J. 108
Lee, H.K. 200
Lehman, D.R. 294, 304,
Leinbach, M.D. 35, 107, 109, 135–137
Lemmon, K. 4
Lerner, R.M. 4, 229
Letourneau, K.J. 56
Leung, K. 195, 199
Levin, J. 232
Levine, J.M. 207
Levine, R.V. 108
Levinson, D.J. 220
Levy, G.D. 43, 107,109, 111, 116, 118
Lewis, M. 3, 29, 135–137
Leyens, J.P. 237
Liben, L. 43, 62, 118, 126, 137, 223, 248
Liebl, M. 110
Liebkind, K. 197
Lin, M. 272
Lintern, V. 90, 253
Linville, P.W. 3
Little, J.K. 109, 110
Liss, M.B. 35, 39, 52,
Livesley, W. 29, 33, 45, 106
Livingston, M. 137
Livingstone, S. 299
Lobliner, D.B. 3, 31, 50, 62, 104–106, 114, 117, 162, 182, 234, 248, 250
Lockheed, M.E. 50, 118
Lohaus, A. 109
Long, K.M. 232, 253
Luckmann, T. 297
Luebke, J. 114, 123
Luecke-Aleksa, D. 56,
Luhtanen, R. 42, 45, 49–51, 201
Luria, Z 137
Lutz, S.E. 31, 46, 58, 61
Lyde, M. 205
Lykken, D.T. 295
Lyons, A. 293
Lyons, E. 19, 62, 78, 87, 90,

124, 160, 161, 165, 175, 176, 181, 192, 248, 293, 302–303, 314, 316–317, 319–320, 324

Maass, A. 234, 235, 255, 270
Maccoby, E. 48, 52, 103, 109–110, 112–113, 118, 120, 122, 123–124, 136–137, 141, 249, 298
Mackie, D.M. 104–106
MacPherson, J. 88
Macrae, C.N 253, 259
Madden, R.B. 137
Madden, T. 195
Madge, N.J.H. 231
Madole, K.L. 107
Madson, L. 143
Magnusson, D. 34, 45
Mahan, J. 192
Major, B. 53, 54, 114, 195
Malcuit, G. 137
Malucchi, L. 43, 79–80, 108, 121
Manke, B.A. 318
Mann, J.A. 267, 274, 278
Manstead, A.S.R. 92, 232, 253
Marcia, J. 31
Marelich, W.D. 205
Marie-Covatto, A. 294, 300, 301
Markell, M. 62, 162, 248, 251
Markham, E. 267
Markiewicz, D. 299
Markman, E.M. 31
Markstrom-Adams, C. 52
Markus, H. 3–4, 57, 142, 143, 195, 199, 205, 294, 296, 304
Marques, J.M. 3, 60, 237, 248, 298, 301
Marsh, A. 227
Martin, C.L. 29, 33, 35–37, 40, 43, 48–49, 84, 50–51, 55–60, 106, 108–112, 116, 118, 121, 125, 159
Martin W.E. 221,
Martinez, C.M. 232
Martinez-Taboada, C. 60
Masser, B. 299, 305
Masson, K. 200
Masten, A.S. 299
Masters, J.C. 4
Matoka, K. 274
McAdoo, H.P. 54, 189, 207
McDevitts, J. 232
McDougall, P. 300
McFaul, T. 208
McGarty, C. 4, 12, 14–15, 86–87, 91, 164, 177, 190

McGee, D.E. 255, 257, 258
McGeorge, P. 258
McGlynn, E.A. 52, 63
McGraw, K.O. 111
McGue, M. 295
McGuire, C.V. 44, 293
McGuire, S. 295
McGuire, W.J. 6, 44, 293
McHale, S.M. 318
McKillip, J. 114, 123
McKenry, P.C. 277
McLaughlin K. 236
McNew, S. 33
McPherson, D.A. 220
Meacham, J. 3
Mead, G.H. 1–2, 29, 297
Meeus, W. 200
Melamud, A. 199
Messick, D.M. 104–106
Meyer, G. 114
Meyers, B. 107, 109
Middleton, M. 160, 161, 165, 233
Miller, L.F. 268
Miller, N. 193, 272
Miller, R.E. 96, 107–108
Mills, C.J. 119
Milne, A.B. 253, 258, 259
Milner, D. 191, 192, 198, 222, 223, 224, 225, 226, 227, 228, 231
Mischel, W. 139
Mitchell, F.G. 223, 224, 229, 233
Mizrahi, K. 3, 85, 296
Mladinic, A. 50, 61
Moffit, T.E. 295
Moghaddam, F. 104, 196
Moller, L.C. 113, 120
Monachesi, E.D. 221
Money, J. 135
Monteith, M.J. 296, 299, 305
Montemayor, R. 57
Montgomery, M.J. 299, 301
Montoya, M.R. 268
Moore, C. 4
Moreland, R.L. 269
Morland, J.K. 52, 191, 226, 232
Morris, E. 177
Morris, M.W. 206–207
Morrison, E. 255
Moscovici, S. 6, 199, 297
Mosher, D.L. 221,
Moskowitz, G.B. 270
Mounts, N. 136
Mull, E. 52, 63
Mullally, S. 88
Mullen, B. 225, 270, 273, 298
Mullin, P.N. 192

Mummendey, A. 162
Murdoch, N. 86
Murphy, J. 195
Murrell, A.J. 267, 268, 274, 278
Muth, J.L. 256
Myers, B. 35
Myers, L.C. 43

Nadleman, L. 109
Nash, S. 109
Neeman, J. 299
Neiderhiser, J.M. 295
Neisser, U. 142
Nemceff, W.P. 50
Nemeth, C. 160, 224, 248, 249, 250
Nesdale, A.R. 236, 237, 239, 236, 237
Nesdale, D. 49, 135, 162, 182, 219, 220, 221, 222, 223, 224, 225, 228, 229, 234, 235, 236, 237, 248, 251, 254, 300, 303–304, 320, 314, 316–320, 323–324
Nesdale, L.S. 20, 105, 192, 194
Neuberg, S.L. 85, 272
Newcomb, T.M. 114
Newcombe, N. 232
Newman, L.S. 5, 33, 45, 52, 59
Newman, M.A. 35, 39
Nicole, S. 292
Nielson Media Research 138
Nier, J. 276
Nijsten, C. 198
Noel, J.G. 51, 253
Norcliffe, H. 55
Norton, A.J. 268
Nurious, P. 57
Nuttin, J.R. 114

Oaker, G. 51
Oakes, P.J. 11–16, 79, 86–87, 91, 93, 113–114, 144, 163, 164, 177, 190, 193, 220, 225, 228, 269, 315
O'Brien, M. 137
Ocampo, J.A. 37
Ogbu, J. 59
Ogilvie, D.M. 46
Ohana, J. 192
Oljenik, A.B. 138
Onorato, R.S. 17, 19, 90, 113–115, 135, 141, 143, 147, 183, 209, 269
Oppenheim, D.B. 226
Otten, S. 270, 294

Otto, S. 50
Ou, Y. 54
Ouwerkerk, J. 164, 195
Ovesey, L. 191
Owen, C. 208
Oyserman, D. 195, 208

Pachter, L.49, 55
Padilla, A.M. 35, 191, 220, 223, 224
Paez, D. 60
Page, M.S. 205
Palmer 110
Parish 112, 118, 122
Park, B. 111, 270
Parke, R.D. 42
Parsons, J.E. 34
Patterson, C.J. 109
Pederson, A. 253
Pelham, B.W. 205–206
Perdue, C.W. 51, 271, 294
Perez, S.M. 108, 118, 119
Perreault, S. 162,
Perry, D.G. 55, 118, 122, 142
Peterson, A.C. 318
Pettigrew, T.F. 270, 271, 272, 273, 305
Pheterson, G.I. 123
Phinney, J. 32, 42, 46, 53, 159, 189, 190, 191, 195, 197, 199, 207, 209
Piaget, J. 146, 160, 161, 165
Pichevin, M.F. 119, 149
Pine, C.J. 39
Pinter, B. 268
Plant, E.A. 305
Plomin, R. 295
Pomare, M. 274, 278
Pomerantz, E.M. 5, 55, 87
Pomerleau, A. 137
Porter, L.E. 196
Porter, J.D.R. 221, 222
Porter, J.R. 52, 110
Postmes, T. 253
Pouliasi, K. 206
Poulin-Dubois, D. 109–110, 113, 118, 122, 124, 298
Powlishta, K. 18–19, 58, 90, 106, 108–122, 124, 136, 141, 147, 149, 162, 192, 248, 249, 254, 256, 259, 293, 295, 298–299, 317, 320–324
Pratto, F. 255
Prawat, R.S. 122
Prentice, D.A. 135
Proshansky, H.M. 220, 224, 232
Prout, A. 300
Provenanzo, F.J. 137

Quattrone, G.A. 105
Quillian, L. 232
Quintana, S.M. 40–1,184

Rabbie, J.M. 7, 114
Radke, M.J. 221, 226, 232
Radke-Yarrow, M. 221, 222
Raglioni, S.S. 135
Ramsey, P.G. 36, 43, 45, 191
Read, S.J. 4
Reavis, R. 149
Rees, E.T. 85
Regan, M. 86, 114, 164, 177
Reicher, S.D. 3, 11, 13–14, 16, 60, 79, 113, 163, 190, 220, 225, 253, 269, 315
Reid, A. 3, 85, 296
Reingold, H.L. 137
Reis, H.T. 110
Reiss, D. 295
Renninger, C.A. 227
Renshaw, P.D. 300
Resnick, L.B. 207
Reynolds, K.J. 9–10
Rhee, E. 2, 17, 29, 36, 38, 44, 52, 56, 59, 63, 91–92, 200, 291
Rholes, W.S. 33
Ricci, T. 199
Rice, A.S. 223
Rich, M.C. 229
Riek, B.M. 315, 320, 322–324
Riley, S. 110
Rim, Y. 224, 249, 250
Ring, K. 6
Ríos, D.I. 205
Robalo, E.M. 237
Roberson, J.K. 227
Robertson, L.S. 86
Rocha, S.A. 237
Rochat, P. 3
Rodriquez, S. 45, 47, 59
Roman, R.J. 200
Romero, V. 117, 295
Rompf, W.J. 223
Romney, A.K. 47
Roosens, E. 194, 199
Rose, H. 108
Rosenberg, M. 192, 197
Rosenthal, D.A. 199
Ross, L. 4
Rosch, E. 12
Rosenfield, D. 220, 221, 224
Rosewarne, D.L. 248
Rotenberg, K.J. 200, 205
Rothbart, M. 111, 270
Rotheram, M. 159, 189, 190, 197
Rowley, S.A.J. 42, 45–46, 49–51, 53, 194, 195

Ruderman, A.J. 43
Rubin, J.Z. 137
Rubin, L.R. 318
Rubin, M. 31, 54, 112, 228, 295
Ruble, D.N. 2, 17, 29, 31, 33–40, 43–46, 49–52, 55–56, 58–59, 61–63, 87, 91–92, 109–111, 118, 140, 159, 197–198, 220, 248, 291, 292, 293, 294, 314–318, 320–322
Ruble, T.L. 55
Ruiz, R.A. 35, 191, 220, 223, 224
Runciman, W.G. 295
Ruscher, J.B. 270
Rust, M.C. 267, 269, 272, 275
Rutland, A. 3, 20–21, 62, 106, 192, 248, 249, 250, 253, 255, 258, 298, 303, 304–305, 314, 316–317, 322–323
Ryan, M.K. 18, 20, 91, 118, 120, 143, 292, 299–301, 318–324
Ryan, T.T. 137

Sadker, D. 148
Sadker, M. 148
Sahm, W.B. 109
Sakuma, M. 205–206
Salvi, D. 270
Sanford, R.N. 220
Sani, F. 17, 18, 41, 43, 44, 62, 78–80, 86, 88, 108, 115, 121, 160, 165, 175, 177, 192, 248, 251, 293, 295–297, 302, 306, 314–317, 319–321, 324–325
Santos, L.J. 195
Sato, T. 199
Sauer, L.E. 277
Schaefer, D.F. 232
Scheier, M.F. 3, 258
Schlenker, B. 4
Schlopler, J. 268
Schmidt, C.R. 136
Schmitt, K.L. 56
Schmitt, M.T. 54, 114, 116, 194
Schnake, S.B. 270
Schofield, J.W. 136
Scholte, R.H.J. 300
Schroeder, C. 229
Schwartz, J.L.K. 255, 257, 258
Schwarzwald, J. 232
Scodel, A. 221
Sears, D.O. 5
Seavey, C. 114, 228

Sechrist, G.B. 293, 297, 304
Sedikides, C. 270, 295, 297
Seidman, E. 34,
Sellers, R.M. 42, 45–46, 49, 50, 53, 194, 195
Selman, R.L. 231
Semaj, L.T. 37, 40, 46, 52, 223, 230
Semin, G.R. 270
Sen, M.G. 107, 109–110, 113, 118, 122, 124, 298
Serbin, L.A. 44, 58, 86, 106–107, 109–110, 112–113, 118–122, 124, 126, 136–137, 192, 248, 249, 254, 256, 259, 298
Settles, B.H. 268, 276
Shaller, M. 85
Shelton, J.N. 42, 45–46, 49, 50–51, 194, 195
Shepherd, P.A. 107
Sherif, M. 7
Sherman, F. 35, 39, 52
Shirley, L. 299
Short, J. 86, 161, 177
Signorella, M.L. 43, 109, 118, 137
Signorielli, N. 138
Silvern, L.E. 112–113, 118
Silvia, P.J. 114, 116
Silverman, L. 56, 58,
Simon, B. 164, 180
Sinclair, A. 105, 114
Singelis, T.M. 195
Singer, L.T. 107
Skerry, S.A. 29, 38, 47
Skinner, M. 114
Slaby, R.G. 56
Smetana, J.G. 56
Smith., C. 225, 270, 298
Smith, E.R. 195, 270
Smith, P.B. 195
Smith, M.A. 42, 45–46, 49–51, 53, 107, 194, 195
Snyder, M. 4, 109
Sockloff, A. 35, 107, 109
Sohn, M. 224, 228
Sorrell, G.T. 299, 301
Spanier, G.G. 268
Sparks, K. 298
Spears, R. 92, 114, 164, 180, 232, 251, 253, 269
Spears-Brown, C. 62
Spence, J.T. 55
Spencer, M.B. 40, 49, 52, 301
Spencer, S. 51, 54, 59
Spender, D. 149
Spiaggia, M. 232
Spielman, D.A. 198, 248

Sprafkin, C. 44, 86, 107, 112, 118, 121, 136–137
Stangor, C. 29, 37, 43, 44, 56, 85, 111, 140, 195, 293, 294, 297, 304
Starer, R. 114, 123
Steele, C.M. 3, 53, 54, 57, 59, 195
Steers, W.N. 205
Steinberg, L. 136
Stennes, L. 110
Stephan, W.G. 220, 221, 224, 232
Stephenson, G.M. 114
Sternglanz, S.H. 126
Stevenson, H.W. 135, 227
Stevenson, N.G. 135, 227
Stipek, D. 36
Stoddart, T. 318
Stringer, P. 104
Stroebe, W. 9
Strough, J. 294, 300, 301
Sugawara, A.I. 109
Suitor, J.J. 149
Swann, W.B. 4
Swim, J.K. 195
Szalacha, L.A. 54
Szkrybalo, J. 36–37, 56, 58

Takahashi, Y. 205
Tajfel, H. 1–2, 6–10, 30–31, 42, 51–52, 56, 60, 79, 104, 117, 144, 147–148, 160, 161, 162, 165, 225, 190, 193, 194, 220, 224, 228, 233, 234, 236, 248, 249, 250, 251, 267, 269, 270, 272, 295, 321, 322
Tavris, C. 139
Taylor, A. 295
Taylor, D.M. 196
Taylor, M.G. 118
Taylor, S. 43, 111, 113
Teasley, S.D. 207
Teeäär, A. 199
Tein, J.Y. 137
Tellegen, G. 200
Teplin, L.A. 223, 226
Tesser, A. 4
Thijs, J. 195–197, 202, 204
Thoits, P.A. 30–31,
Thompson, E.P. 294
Thompson, L. 207
Thomson, S. 86, 92–93, 96, 253
Thompson, S.K. 35, 107, 109, 136
Thompson, R.H.T. 223
Thorne, B. 103, 114, 136, 137, 141

Todor, N.L. 114, 123
Tonick, I.J. 126
Trafimov, D. 206, 305
Trager, H.G. 221, 222, 226
Trautner, H.M. 4, 6, 109, 159
Triandis, H.C. 195, 199, 206, 305
Trolier, T.K. 85
Tropp, L.R. 271
Tucker, G.R. 229
Tur-Kaspa, M. 232
Turiel, E. 318
Turner, J.C. 1–2, 7, 9–17, 19, 31, 42, 51–52, 60, 79, 86–87, 90–91, 93, 104, 113–115, 117, 123, 135, 139, 141, 143–144, 147–148, 162, 163, 164, 177, 183, 190, 193, 194, 209, 220, 225, 228, 236, 251, 269, 270, 272, 273, 302, 315
Tyler, R.B. 51, 271, 294
Tyler, T.R. 91
Tyrrell, D.J. 119

Uleman, J.S. 200

Vaillancourt, T. 300
Validzic, A. 274
Van Ausdale, D.V. 49
Van de Geer, J.P. 160, 161, 165
Van den Heuvel, H. 200
Van de Wielen, C. 196
Van Knippenberg, A.F.M. 118, 164
Van Lieshout, C.F.M. 300
Vartanian, L.R. 112, 117, 122
Vaughan, G. 36, 104, 191,

198, 223, 224, 225, 227, 234, 248
Vener, A.M. 109
Verkuyten, M. 19–20, 39, 44, 135, 162, 195–204, 206, 208, 248, 250, 293, 301–302, 315, 320–321, 324
Vevea, J.L. 295
Villareal, M.J. 195, 199
Virshup, L.K. 30–31
Vitaro, F. 299
Voils, C.I. 296
Vollebergh, W.A. 200
Von Hippel, W. 270
Voydanoff, P. 277

Walker, I. 253
Walker-Andrews, A.S. 135
Wann, D.L. 51, 162, 232, 253
Ward, C. 276
Wasik, B.H 189, 207
Weber, M. 194
Webster, D.M. 294
Weil, A.M. 160, 161, 165
Weiland, A. 223
Weinraub, M. 35, 107, 109
Weinreich, P. 191
Welch-Ross, M.K. 136
Wellman, H.M. 33, 78
Wentura, D. 294
Wetherell, M.S. 11, 13–14, 16, 60, 79, 104, 113, 163, 190, 220, 225, 228, 269, 315
White, D.C. 112, 118, 121–122
White, D.R. 192, 248, 249, 254, 256, 259
White, G.D. 272, 277
White, L.K. 268
Wichstrom, L. 318

Wicklund, R.A. 259
Wigfield, A. 57
Wilder, D. 30, 51, 105, 114, 270, 272
Wildschut, T. 268
Wilke, H. 164
Wilkens, G. 7, 114
Wilkes, A.L. 9, 144
Willer, S.C. 47
Williams, J.A. 193, 234, 248
Williams, J.E. 86, 104, 110, 122, 137, 223, 227, 232
Willis, H. 31
Wills, T.A. 3
Wilson, H. 87, 160, 176
Wilson, M.N. 39
Wong, D.L. 148
Wood, C.H. 110
Wootton-Millward, L. 164
Wothke, W. 280
Wright, S. 110, 196
Wurf, E. 142
Wyman, H. 58

Yarkin-Levin, K. 4
Ybarra, O. 232
Yee, M.D. 43, 44, 50–51, 105, 107, 112, 118–119, 121, 162, 192, 229, 234, 239, 248, 249, 251
Yeeles, C. 254, 258
Yip, T. 53
Young, H. 253
Yuill, N. 92–93, 96, 254
Yum, N. 205
Yzerbyt, V.Y. 237

Zalk, S.R. 112, 118, 122, 224, 228
Zecharia, D. 297
Zinser, O. 229

Subject index

Aboud's socio-cognitive theory 222, 223, 224, 247, 248, 249, 250, 251, 252, 260
Accentuation effect 15
Accentuation of intergroup differences 18, 86, 89, 103, 105, 106, 108–111, 125, 144, 147, 150, 162, 235, 239
Accentuation of self-stereotypical characteristics 92, 93–94
Accentuation of withingroup similarities 103, 105, 106, 108–111, 125, 144, 147,162, 203, 206, 269
Accessibility 13, 45, 115, 144, 146, 151, 207, 294
Affective distinctiveness 170
Allocentrism 199, 200
Anti-individualistic social psychology 6, 192
Attraction 16, 123, 125, 269, 273, 317
Authoritarian personality 220
Automatic processing 108

Black sheep effect 60, 237, 239
Body image bias 255–256, 257, 258

Categorisation – see Social categorisation.
Child as social tactician 21, 261
Children's sense of "we" – see Identification with social groups
Co-construction of identities 97, 297
Cognitive development 3, 6, 20, 21, 29, 30, 37, 38, 79, 84, 85, 90, 96, 124, 125, 146, 147, 150, 151, 191, 207, 209, 222, 223, 230, 231, 233, 236, 248, 251, 291, 292, 293, 296, 303, 306, 316, 317, 318, 319
Collective identity – see Social identity
Collectivism 195, 199, 200, 205, 206, 208, 209, 305
Common ingroup identity model 21, 267, 269, 272, 276, 277, 278, 279, 281, 283, 284, 305
Comparative context 77, 85–91, 95, 141, 163, 164, 176, 190, 209, 294, 300, 302
Competence/performance distinction 303
Confounding of ingroup favouritism and outgroup prejudice 61, 113, 220, 303

Conservation 37, 38, 223, 231
Constancy 35, 37, 38, 39, 40, 44, 48, 52, 56, 57, 58, 96, 139, 140, 151, 223, 230, 293
Contact hypothesis 271, 272, 273, 275, 279
Contextual variability of stereotypes 77, 85–91, 296
Cooperativeness 277, 278
Cross-ethnic identification 53, 194, 226
Cultural characteristics 190, 195
Cultural knowledge 198

Decategorisation 272, 273, 274, 322
Depersonalisation 15, 16, 163, 178, 203, 304, 305
Depression 55, 318
Discrimination 19, 48, 54, 253
Domain-related expertise 85, 296
Dual identity 273

Ecological theory 192
Ego identity formation 31
Essentialism 41
Eriksonian theory 31, 191
Ethnic awareness 35–36, 226, 227, 293, 316
Ethnic identity 19, 31–32, 34, 36–38, 40, 42, 45, 46, 47, 48, 56, 63, 84, 189–210, 229, 253, 304, 321
Ethnic norms 59
Ethic preference 53, 226, 228
Ethnocentrism 7, 8, 16
Ethnographic research 34, 97
Expertise – see Domain-related expertise

False self 142
Families 34, 54, 62, 96, 192, 199, 267–285, 297, 303, 305, 313, 314, 315, 322, 324
Fit 13, 151, 163, 193
    comparative 14, 96, 144, 146, 149, 318
    normative 14, 144, 146, 149, 318
Forced-choice methods 233

Gender differences 55, 58, 89, 110, 111, 117, 120, 125, 135–152, 248–249, 254, 322

Gender identity 18,34, 36–38, 42, 44, 45, 46,
  56, 57, 58, 63, 77, 84, 87–90, 135–152,
  209, 300, 301, 321
Gender norms 59, 61, 137, 301
Gender role development 106, 107, 209
  theories of 139–140
Gender role knowledge 58, 109, 119, 121, 123,
  145
Gender schematic processing theory 84, 116,
  140, 141
Gender segregation 112, 124, 125, 135, 136,
  147, 298, 320
Genetic social psychology 192
Group distinctiveness 269

Identification with social groups 17, 18, 29, 32,
  33–37, 53, 77, 91–95, 139, 146, 147, 161,
  162, 164, 168, 175, 176, 178, 182, 183,
  184, 191, 192, 193, 195, 198, 200, 201,
  208, 233, 250, 275, 292, 297, 302, 315,
  316, 320
Identity-related beliefs 78–85, 316
Individual mobility 10
Immigrant children 45, 46, 47, 48, 50, 52, 54,
  59, 189–210, 253, 315, 320
Implicit association test 257–258
Implicit measures 206, 254–258
Impression management – *see* Self-
  presentation
Individualism 195, 205
Infants 35, 36, 107, 109, 135, 136, 137,
  151
Information-seeking 56–57, 228
Ingroup bias 7–10, 18, 19, 20, 50, 51–52, 55,
  60, 61, 103, 104, 105, 106, 112–113, 114,
  115, 117, 118, 119, 120, 122, 123, 124,
  125, 147, 148 161, 163, 164, 175, 197,
  219, 223, 228, 247, 249, 250, 251, 253,
  259, 267, 272, 274, 275, 276, 294, 295,
  303, 314, 322, 323
Ingroup denigration 168
Ingroup deviants 60, 237, 239
Ingroup favouritism 31, 51, 55, 61, 103, 104,
  105, 106, 112–113, 114, 115, 117, 118,
  119, 120, 122, 123, 124, 125, 147, 148,
  160, 161, 162, 163, 165, 166, 168, 175,
  192, 194, 198, 220, 222, 224, 225, 228,
  229, 234, 239, 248, 269, 270, 294, 295,
  297, 300, 302
Ingroup homogeneity 163, 164, 176, 177,
  178–180, 181–182
Ingroup identification – *see* Identification with
  social groups
Ingroup norms 60
Intergroup comparisons 79, 87
Intergroup competition 7
Intergroup conflict 7, 60, 135, 232, 236, 268,
  272, 279, 281, 300
  children's explanations for 79–81
Intergroup contact – *see* Contact hypothesis

Intergroup differentiation 52
Intergroup discrimination 8, 9
Interaction with peers 34, 96, 196, 204, 292,
  297
Internalisation of social identity – *see*
  Identification with social groups
Intragroup comparisons 176

Kohlberg's theory 139–140, 147

Legitimate/illegitimate differential status
  10–11, 148–9, 194

Mediation analysis 278–279
Metacontrast principle 14, 96, 144, 163,
  304
Minimal group paradigm 8, 10, 11, 31, 104,
  105, 106, 120, 124, 147, 225, 233, 234,
  235, 236, 248, 315
Moral reasoning 231, 232
Multicultural education 195
Multilevel modeling 201, 202
Mutual intergroup differentiation 274

Name-calling 196, 197, 224, 320
National identity 19, 78, 79, 90, 106, 149,
  159–184, 302, 316, 324
Negotiating identities 34, 96
Normative features of group members, *see
  also* Social identity, children's
  conceptions of 78, 79
Norms 16, 221, 247, 252, 253, 254, 255, 258,
  259, 275, 298, 299, 302, 304

Outgroup derogation – *see* Prejudice
Outgroup favouritism 10, 249, 253
Outgroup homogeneity 103, 105, 106, 111,
  116, 118, 125

Peer group 96, 292, 297
Perceiver readiness 13
Permeable/impermeable group boundaries 10,
  96, 105, 148, 149, 151, 230
Personal/group discrimination discrepancy
  196, 197
Personal identity 1, 2, 12, 18, 63, 96, 113, 142,
  143, 150, 193, 204, 206, 228, 269, 295,
  297, 320
Piagetian theory 3, 38, 146, 147
Positive distinctiveness 8, 148, 149,151,
  162, 163, 168, 170, 172, 177, 197, 226,
  304
Prejudice 1, 20, 54, 60, 61–63, 122, 136, 141,
  161, 162, 190, 191, 194, 195–198, 200,
  204, 207, 208, 209, 219–240, 247, 248,
  249, 251, 252, 253, 255, 260, 261, 269,
  303, 304, 305, 316, 317, 320, 322, 323,
  324
  insider's perspective 195

Prototype 14
Prototypicality 14, 16, 203, 270
Psychoanalytic theory 139
Public self-focus 258–260

Racial identity – *see* Ethnic identity
Racism, *see also* Prejudice 62, 189, 194
Recategorisation 272, 273, 274, 275, 284, 322
Referent informational influence 16
Relational self 142
Remembered self 142

Scaffolding of identities 84
Schools 189, 192, 195, 201, 202, 294, 296, 297, 298
Self-affirmation 53
Self as process 18–19, 135, 141–145, 150, 209
Self as structure 140, 141, 201, 206, 209, 302
Self-categorisation 9, 94, 190, 193, 195, 202–206, 208, 235, 236, 239, 291, 294, 302, 303, 304, 306, 316, 323, 324
Self-categorisation theory 18, 19, 20, 60, 78, 86, 88, 96, 113, 115, 125, 141–146, 159, 161, 163–164, 176, 178, 182–185, 190, 192, 202, 204, 205, 207, 209, 220, 225, 228, 252, 261, 269, 273, 292, 297, 302, 303, 304, 306, 315, 318, 321, 325
Self-concept 1–4, 9, 12, 17, 20, 29, 30, 33, 34, 42, 45, 46, 51, 63, 87, 142–145, 192, 197, 199, 205, 209, 291, 292, 293, 294, 295, 296, 297, 300
Self-descriptions 33, 91, 200, 202, 205, 254, 297, 302
Self-efficacy 53, 55
Self-esteem 2, 9, 17, 29, 51, 52–55, 57, 104, 105, 110, 117, 125, 149, 162, 175, 192, 195, 225, 226, 228, 234, 251, 294, 315, 320, 322
    collective 49, 148, 151, 196, 197, 198, 199, 200, 201–2, 203, 204, 208, 295
    personal 49, 50, 204, 295
Self-presentation 45, 253, 254, 258, 260, 304, 306, 318, 323
Self-recognition 299
Self-regulatory processes 46, 252–261, 304, 306, 317
Self-representations 2–3, 4
Self-schemas 2, 140
Sex differences – *see* Gender differences
Social categories 29, 30
    awareness of 35–36, 319
    centrality of in self-conception 34, 45–49, 193, 203, 204, 205, 206, 294
    evaluation of 49– 51
    identification with – *see* Identification with social groups
    knowledge of 37–38, 48–49, 295
    salience of in self definition 43– 45, 103, 144, 149, 176, 204, 229, 250, 269, 273, 294

Social categories as constitutive of self 1, 33
Social categorisation 6–17, 61, 62, 104, 105, 107, 192, 227, 267, 271, 272, 273
Social change beliefs 10
Social comparison 1, 9, 31, 52, 54, 59, 61, 62, 79, 87, 162, 209, 226, 234, 292, 295
Social competition 11, 194, 234
Social context 1,5, 6, 7, 15, 39, 44, 46, 62, 63, 103, 113–115, 125, 126, 144, 147, 148, 149, 150, 161, 189–210, 224, 235, 249, 251, 253, 274, 291, 293, 294, 296, 297, 299, 301, 303, 306, 314, 315, 317, 318, 321, 323
Social creativity 10, 194, 297
Social exclusion 196, 259, 260
Social identity
    across the lifespan 4, 22, 323–324
    as a multidimensional construct 17, 30, 42, 62, 63, 209
    and engagement in school 53, 59
    children's conceptions of 17, 18, 30, 33, 35, 37–38, 40–41, 78–85, 316
    consequences of developmental change in 51– 63
    motivational consequences and 55–63, 147
Social identity development theory 20, 220, 225, 226–240, 303,
Social identity theory 1, 2, 6–17, 19, 20, 31, 42, 51, 55, 56, 58, 60, 78, 104, 105, 113, 117, 124–125, 159, 162–163, 175,176, 182–185, 190, 192, 197, 198, 204, 207, 208, 209, 220, 225–226, 228, 247, 251–252, 261, 269, 295, 296, 302, 303, 304, 306, 315, 316, 325
Social learning theory 46, 139, 140, 141, 142, 145, 146, 147, 151
Social mobility beliefs 10
Social representations 14
Social status 22, 39, 40, 48, 49, 53, 62, 105, 118, 162, 182, 183, 190, 192, 194, 198, 207, 208, 226, 232, 234, 235, 236, 239, 251, 268, 271, 275, 296, 298, 322
Socialisation 46, 49, 54, 62, 84, 89, 125, 135, 140, 152, 190, 198, 199, 221, 255
Stepfamily conflict 267–285, 324
Stereotypes 49, 56, 58, 59, 63, 85–91, 105, 109, 110, 111, 114, 121, 123, 136, 137–138, 140, 143, 145, 151, 152, 161, 164, 194, 197, 198, 228, 229, 237, 270, 271, 297, 298, 300, 301, 317, 320, 325
    cognitive structural conception 77, 85, 86, 90
    contextual variability in 71, 85–91, 296
    SCT conception 86, 90–91
Stereotyping 43, 60,62, 103, 122, 162, 219, 302, 321
    ingroup 177–178
    self 93–94, 114, 152, 178, 302
Stigmatization 53, 191,194
Stroop effect 256

Structural equation analysis 277–283
Subjective identification with social groups –
     see Identification with social groups
Symbolic interactionism 190

Theory of mind 84, 94

Uncertainty reduction 31, 294, 306

Victimization 194, 204, 205, 219, 229
Vygotskian theory 97, 297

Working self 142